C000179159

ON THE NATURE OF POETRY

By the same author

AWARENESS BEYOND MIND

BREATHING WITH THE MIND

THE SPACIOUS MIRROR

THE UNSEEN REFLECTION

SONNETS

ON THE NATURE OF POETRY

AN APPRAISAL AND INVESTIGATION OF THE ART WHICH FOR 4,000 YEARS HAS DISTILLED THE SPOKEN THOUGHTS OF MANKIND

KENNETH VERITY

Kenneth Verity

SHEPHEARD-WALWYN (PUBLISHERS) LTD

First published in 2007 by
Shepheard-Walwyn (Publishers) Ltd
15 Alder Road
London SW14 8ER

British Library Cataloguing in Publication Data
A catalogue record of this book
is available from the British Library

ISBN-13: 978-0-85683-246-8
ISBN-10: 0-85683-246-4

Typeset by Alacrity,
Winscombe, Somerset
Printed through Print Solutions, Wallington, Surrey

Dedicated to
My Critics, Confidantes,
and Counsellors

Contents

Acknowledgements

IN THIS VOLUME, directed principally towards undergraduate educational use, a general map of a large territory is presented. In the sections dealing with ten master poets, biographical notes and a comprehensive list of works (with dates) is given. The 235 poets cited, covering a span of 4,000 years, are indexed separately. Critical and comparative analysis is offered throughout.

The authorship of all fragments and extracts of poetry, however brief, is acknowledged at the point of inclusion in the text, and in the Index of Poets. Furthermore, sources in published works consulted (even where now out of print) are listed in the Bibliography.

I am indebted to the following advisers, some for their careful reading of sections of the manuscript, and for their helpful suggestions:

Kingsley Amis
Richard T. Blurton
John Bodley
Alan H. Bray
Cheng Yan
Anthony Colwell
Arthur D. Farndell
Dr A. Khare
Vasant C. Kothari
Dr John R. Marr
John Mercer
Haruyo Morita
Dr Sun Myint
Qu Lei-Lei
Sheikh Reshui
Dr Francis C. Roles
Ajahn Sumedho
Takahashi Sumie
Teik Tin San
Seung Sahn
Dr Stephen Thompson
Wang Jianan
Staff of The Society of Authors

Author's Preface

THE INTENTION in this book is to examine and analyse the essential nature of the phenomenon we call *poetry*; to seek an understanding of the power this art form exerts over mind and heart; to comprehend its potency; and to explain its perennial ability to command the respect of mankind. This examination will not attempt to explain away the inhering mystery nor allow aesthetic quality to be diminished by the process of literary analysis. I believe that sensitive observation may render the veils of poetry transparent without assailing its eternal supremacy in the Arts. The poetic Muse was, is, and will remain, foremost among the nine.

The sheer scale of the subject necessitates a certain compression in presentation. Since all major extant poetry is freely accessible, and to alleviate constraints of space I have used as examples representative extracts rather than complete poems. In quoting fragments of poetry, often tantalizingly brief, the expectation is that their power cumulatively, will convey an impression of poetry as a whole.

Gestalt, the German word meaning 'form', 'pattern', 'configuration', connotes the integration of a series of detailed perceptions into a complete experience or meaningful wholeness – an entity which is more than the sum of its parts. This book arose out of the certain knowledge that such a *gestalt* must exist as an emanation from poetry itself and that answers to questions *about* poetry lie *within* poetry. In these pages poets speak for themselves: poetry is its own voice. Where deductions are made or inferences drawn, they often stem from the poetry itself or from the actions and statements of poets.

The principal ideas constituting the foundation and coherence of art, music, and literature are also found in poetry. But poetry, more often than other forms of art, has been a vehicle for inspiration, in the sense that it surpasses old ways of seeing, hearing, thinking, and reacting. Poetry continues to be pre-eminent in evaluating and articulating the riches of the human spirit.

Just as in painting and sculpture, there is fine and gross, successful and unsuccessful, so it is with poetry. Since appreciation of any form of art arises in the mind and breast of the beholder, general taste and preference are subject to change. Nevertheless, the works of master poets have enjoyed a consistently high evaluation and have transcended cultural boundaries. If we examine the structure and development of poetry, its mysterious essential 'quality', though difficult to define, gradually declares itself. The flow and turn of the lines draw the perceptive reader unerringly towards the essential meaning behind the spoken word, to the silence beyond sound. The best verse exemplifies the principle, 'Less is more'. Where there is understatement or omission, it is the more significant for having occurred in the context of poetry. Poetry formulates truth without recourse to religion or philosophy. To say it 'awakens the soul' is another description of its power to remind us that our innate knowledge is more trustworthy than any imposed external dogma or received morality. Poetry 'works' because it acknowledges the universality of human psychology; it unites emotion with reason and tempers imagination with understanding. In the work of the master poets, individuality is usually presented in the context of universality. For expressing spiritual freedom, beauty and love, poetry is the perfect vehicle. As an art form it is of its time but timeless: it is now, but it expresses eternity.

The work of certain writers reveals competence of such a high order that during the qualitative survey in this volume, ten poets seem naturally to have merited the description master poet. The master poet is a gentle guide who leads us by an extension of our own understanding; who by his 'absence of ego' reveals the manifest presence of the 'universal Self'. In his hands poetry is a direct pointing to reality. Shakespeare wrote:

And, since you know you cannot see yourself
So well as by reflection, I, your glass,
Will modestly discover to yourself
That of yourself which you yet know not of.

Julius Caesar, Act I, Scene ii

The essential self is manifested at the expense of the personality and, as though to demonstrate this, Shakespeare seems almost transparent. As the subjective shadow cast by individuality diminishes, the objective reality is accorded more of its own radiance. Master poets cast no shadow; they do not stand in the light.

Introduction

Maturing as a poet means maturing as the whole man.

W.B. Yeats

THE FINEST POETRY is consonant with wisdom, and by means of this universal language the poet speaks for the human race. With characteristic certitude Emerson defined the role of the poet: 'He stands among partial men for the complete man.' Poetry, like language, develops with the civilization from which it springs and of which it is a central part. Embodied in poetry is the influence of each successive culture from which it drew its inspiration and to which it gave expression. The unbroken stream of poetry carries resonances of the growth and decay of civilizations, the vicissitudes of wars, the effects of migrations and trading, the influences of religious belief. It expresses the aspirations and disappointments of the human race. As an art form, the phenomenon of poetry has developed in concert with the progress of mankind and, in early societies, we see the beginnings of poetry.

The remains of the earliest human beings, unearthed in Java, China and elsewhere, are thought to be at least half a million years old. Although Palaeolithic cave art demonstrates the superb skills of the early artists who decorated the walls of their rock shelters and caves, the culture had not yet invented writing. The span of time from that remote era to about 5000 BC is, therefore, usually referred to as prehistoric, or preliterate.

Early Civilization

Poetry had its beginnings in the East with four gifted races, each with a distinguished culture, who flourished more than 4,000 years ago. The *Hamitic* people founded an empire in Egypt under great dynasties of kings; accounts of their deeds have come down to us in hieroglyphic inscriptions. The *Semitic* race which conquered Chaldea, uniting Sumer and Akkad, left records of their civilization on tablets of cuneiform inscriptions. The *Turanian* race founded a vast kingdom in China, where they evolved a sophisticated system of art, and a highly articulate literature. The *Aryans* were a pastoral expansionist people who flourished in India, with a fully developed language and a tradition of highly talented bards. (*see* Chapter 11 – India, p.235).

It was along the banks of rivers that the first civilizations were found: Mesopotamia straddled the Tigris and the Euphrates; Egypt stretched along the Nile; India arose along the Indus and the Ganges; and

China expanded eastwards from the region of the Wei and the Hwang Ho.

The lower areas of land enclosed by the Tigris and Euphrates rivers – in what is now Iraq – were known in ancient times both as Babylonia and Mesopotamia (from the Greek, meaning 'between rivers'). The delta of this river system was called Sumer.

If the skill of writing and the advent of the city reveal the emergence of civilization, then the people of Sumer deserve the credit for having created the first civilization in world history. It was the Sumerians, speaking a non-Semitic language, who are credited with evolving the cuneiform system of writing and the earliest significant poetry. They are also considered to have invented wheeled vehicles and the plough. Writing leaves a record of poetry enabling later generations to appreciate both the extant poems and their preceding oral tradition.

The discovery in Egypt of cylinder seals similar in shape to those used in Sumer attests to contact between these two areas towards the end of the fourth millennium BC. There is a strong possibility that the Mesopotamian and Egyptian systems of writing were related.

The Beginnings of Western Culture

With a clear indebtedness to the Egyptians and Mesopotamians, the inhabitants of Crete, Troy, and Mycenae created a wealthy, sophisticated commercial culture. But in 1250 BC the Mycenaeans went to war against the Trojans, their power collapsed and the Aegean World was plunged into the so-called Dark Age. Then, around the 10th century BC a historic change occurred in this region; the Bronze Age gave way to the Iron Age throughout the Mediterranean area. In what we now call Greece, a culture arose which was to form the foundation of Western Civilization. By the 5th century BC, its accomplishments were such that subsequently this period has been regarded as one of the great eras of human achievement. Significantly, at this time in India, Buddhism was developing into a major spiritual and cultural force.

Poetry in Ancient Greece

During the first 300 years of the Iron Age, the epic poems known as the *Iliad* and the *Odyssey* were composed. Because these works deal with heroic themes, the early Iron Age has also been called the Heroic Age. As the years passed, Greek myth and religion became a mixture of folk-tales, primitive customs and traditional rituals that arose during the Heroic Age but, at the time, had not been structured into a coherent system. This task was undertaken by the poet Hesiod. The Greek people had always turned to their deities for explanations of natural phenomena and for an understanding of those psychological characteristics that they had come to recognize as part of themselves. But questions of social morality required human rather than divine solutions. For this, the Greeks looked to art and literature, rather than to prayer, for guidance and instruction.

Within this context, the vast scale of the poet's work is succinctly expressed in the celebrated remark: 'Homer gave the Greeks their heroes; Hesiod their gods.' It seems clear that, by quality of imagination and nobility of purpose, these men of genius defined the identity of a civilization. Their influence on ancient literature (prose as well as poetry) was persistent and profound. Epics by bardic poets depicted the exploits of warriors and heroes in long poems embodying a blend of history and legend. In the Heroic Age, especially in times of war, these poets helped to cultivate a sense of tribal identity and national pride; in periods of peace they extolled the virtues of farming and artisan craftsmanship.

The history of humanity is graced by the presence of the Greeks, the first people to be conscious of man's powers and his potential. They confronted the old world with reason and were aware of the ever-present mysterious and ineffable. We who are their descendants exult in their ascendancy and are mindful of our debt to them.

European Poetry and its Perspective

Centuries later, poetry in Europe during the Middle Ages reflects a turn away from activity in the outer physical world to an inner realm of dream, vision, and speculation. The visionary poet, writing in allegory (*see* Glossary), deals with the origins and ends of things and with punishments and rewards. Divine intervention and displeasure are no longer wreaking havoc and indulgence of whim upon hapless victims of 'Fate'. With the development of Christianity, men are held to be responsible for their sinful behaviour and they develop a sense of guilt. Rewards and punishments are set out like a tariff in allegorical descriptions which chart the journey of the soul.

Humanism Enters Poetry

With the Renaissance, poetry expresses and celebrates the arrival and development of humanism (*see* Glossary). This leads later to an exploration of human psychology, so ably presented by Shakespeare in his sonnets and his use of soliloquy in the great plays. From this important precursor, there developed the more tenuous spiritual psychology of W.B. Yeats and T.S. Eliot.

Searching for Beginnings

The unfolding of poetry, this most careful art, began in the Ancient World. Poetry, like existence itself, is an ever-present force in human civilization. Time, man's measure of elapsed existence, is just one dimension of poetry's development. With the perspective of chronology we can look into the past for significant early examples of the poet's art.

1
The Ancient World

THE SO-CALLED 'Ancient World' was the place where very early examples of poetry originated. Mesopotamia (with Assyria to the north and Babylonia to the south) was the geographical region where the square-tipped reed was busy and clay tablets were receiving the cuneiform impressions of poetry some 4,000 years ago.

Epic of Gilgamesh

The most famous of all Sumerian rulers was Gilgamesh, who ruled at Uruk around 2700 BC. A series of legends accrued to his name, one of which developed into a superb early work of poetic expression.

Originally composed in the Sumerian language (c2000 BC), the *Epic of Gilgamesh* was eventually inscribed on clay tablets (in their own tongue) by Babylonians, Hittites, and others. The hero of the epic, Gilgamesh, was purportedly a king of ancient Erech who sought to gain the secret of immortality. An account of his travels, which was widely known in its time, includes the story of a cataclysmic flood. In its details which are recorded on Tablet XI, it bears a striking resemblance to the biblical story in *Genesis*. There is however a major difference. In the epic the deities inflicting the flood are, somewhat improbably, impelled by annoyance at being disturbed in their sleep by noisy mortals – in contrast to the God of the Hebrews who acts from moral disapproval. The most complete version of the great myth is the Akkadian copy. Its tablets were found in the library of the Assyrian monarch Assurbanipal.

Here are some lines from the *Epic of Gilgamesh* taken from Tablet XI:

> Utnapishtim said to him [Gilgamesh]:
> I will reveal to you, Gilgamesh, a hidden matter –
> It is a secret of the gods that I will tell you.

The secret to be imparted is, in fact, an instruction:

> Man of Shuruppak, son of Ubar-Tutu,
> Tear down your house, build a ship!
> Give up your possessions and seek *life*.
> Despise property – keep the soul alive!
> Take aboard the ship the seed of all living things.

The epic goes on to describe a flood of cosmic proportions, a deluge that inundates the Earth:

The gods were frightened by the deluge;
They cowered like dogs crouched against the wall.
Ishtar cried out like a woman in travail –
The sweet-voiced mistress of the gods moaned aloud.

★

On Mount Nisir the ship came to a halt –
The mass of rock holding the ship fast.
For a fifth, and a sixth day – Mount Nisir held the ship fast
Allowing no motion.
When the seventh day arrived,
I set free and sent forth a dove which later returned.

★

Then I released and sent forth a raven.
The raven departed and seeing the waters reduced
Began to eat, circle, caw and did not return.
Then I released all creatures to the four winds
and offered a sacrifice –
I poured a libation on the mountain-top.

Based on a translation by E.A. Speiser

Egyptian Poetry

To the west of Sumer lay Ancient Egypt, where many poets were at work. Nothing now remains with which Egyptian religious poetry can be compared; Babylonian (the only contemporary poetry) is entirely different in concept and viewpoint. There seems no doubt that from the earliest times in man's history, poetry of many kinds existed – as an oral tradition. There is no known record of a true poem in Egypt until the Sixth Dynasty. Egyptian poetry uses four main poetic elements in common use at the time:

1 *Parallelism of members*, that is repetition of the same idea in different words, for example: 'Thy word is a lantern unto my feet and a light unto my path.' Its chief Egyptian use is in epithets applied to the Deity: 'King of kings', 'Lord of lords', 'Ruler of rulers'.
2 *Rhythm* was used, but because the Egyptians wrote without vowels or vowel-points, it is difficult to know where stress should fall.
3 *Alternate solo and refrain*. When used in religious poetry, it is often in the form of a litany with the priest chanting solo and the people answering with a refrain in chorus. Such litanies are found in the early Pyramid Texts. (Psalm 136 is a good example of a similar litany used later in the somewhat derivative Hebrew religious poetry.)
4 *Paronomasia* (play on words or punning) occasionally occurs in Egyptian poetry, but the absence of vowels makes it difficult to recognize.

Rhymed verse and alliteration are unknown in the poetry of Egypt.

The Pharaoh (Āmenhotep IV) who ruled from 1379 to 1362 BC, single-handedly attempted a total reform of Egyptian religious and political life. He replaced the multitude of deities of traditional religion with just one – the Sun God Āton – and changed his own name to Ākhenaton ('the servant of Āton'). The image worshipped is frequently described as being the 'sun disc', yet the inscriptions make it clear that the Āton was regarded by the king as being the creative force of the Universe that was manifested by the sun. The god itself had no image. To make his changes more effective, and to elude the influences of the priests at the royal court of Thebes, Ākhenaton moved the capital to a new location – known today as Tell el-Amarna. His sweeping and revolutionary religious reforms gave rise to a new lightness, naturalism, grace, and elegance in art. But these reforms were not to last long. The belief in a single god, who ruled the Universe, threatened the priests who had a vested interest in preserving the old polytheistic traditions. As a result, after his death, Ākhenaton's successors branded him a heretic and fanatic, excising his name from any monuments that had survived him. These upheavals prepared the ground for a new tranche of fine poetry. It was during this period of the New Kingdom (1570-1185 BC) that a remarkable work of poetry was composed. To give some flavour of the theology behind the change, here are some lines from the beautiful *Hymn to Āton* found on the walls of the tomb of Eye:

You appear full of beauty on the horizon of heaven –
You, the living Āton, origin of life!
When *you* are risen on the eastern horizon,
Every land is filled with your beauty

★

When you are set beyond the western horizon,
The land is in darkness – as though in death.

★

Darkness is a shroud; the earth is in stillness,
For he who made it rests in his horizon.
At daybreak, when you rise at the world's edge,
When you shine as the Āton by day,
Darkness is dispelled as you give your rays.

★

Creator of seed in women,
You who make fluid into man,

★

You are life-force, you your very self,
For we live only through you.

Based on a translation by J.A. Wilson

Egyptian religious poetry is almost entirely anonymous. An exception is the *Hymn to Thoth* by Haremheb, a professional writer in the Court of Ākhenaton:

Hymn to Thoth

Praise to Thoth, child of the Sun, as Moon arising in beauty,
Lord of brightness, Light of the gods, all praise and worship are thine.

★

Judge of mankind to whom the laws of the gods are entrusted for
 enforcement.

★

Obtaining truth at the Weighing of Souls, you weigh every heart in
 the balance;
Just and exact are the scales of the Lord, facing the doer with the deed.

★

Time and Eternity wait upon your Word,
The Word which abides for ever.

Translation from the *Journal of Egyptian Archaeology*

Poetry and the Biblical Tradition

One of Egypt's geographical neighbours on the shores of the Red Sea was Israel. The earliest Hebrew poetry dates from the period 1350-1090 BC and is largely Egyptian both in outlook and form. From the year 1000 BC to 961 BC King David was on the throne and it was around this period that the formation of the Scriptures into written form occurred. It was the beginning of the Iron Age in the region; during the reign of Solomon the iron-tipped plough was developed and the armies used iron war chariots. This era was the height of ancient Israel's cultural power. After the death of Solomon a civil war resulted in the split of the Northern Kingdom (Israel) away from the Southern Kingdom (Judah). At this time a major body of poetry was about to be brought together – the *Psalms of David.*

The *Psalms*

The *Psalms* are believed to have been compiled around 950 BC. The 150 psalms in the *Bible* are Hebrew poems composed, for the most part, to be sung at religious ceremonies, or services, in Solomon's time. This ancient Hebrew poetry has a characteristic and distinctive style; its essence is *parallelism*. Parallelism means, very simply, that a thought expressed in a line (or a series of lines) is re-expressed in different words in successive lines. It is a common device in chants and other ritual pieces. *Antithetical parallelism* is where the idea expressed in one line is contrasted in its successor. The very first poem in the *Psalms* uses both types of parallelism:

Blessed is the man
 that walks not in the counsel of the wicked;

nor stands in the way of sinners,
 neither does he sit in the seat of scoffers.

But his delight is in the law of the Lord,
    That law on which he meditates day and night.

He is like unto a tree
    planted by a river of water
yielding its fruit in due season.
    Such a tree is of a leaf that does not wither;
In all he does, he prospers.

The wicked are not so;
    but rather, are like chaff driven away by wind.
The wicked shall not survive the judgement,
    neither will sinners flourish in the congregation of
        righteous people.

The Lord knows the way of the righteous;
    He will ensure that the way of the wicked shall perish.

Based on the translation in the Authorized Version

In the *Old Testament*, after the wisdom of the *Proverbs* and the strictures of *Ecclesiastes*, comes the majestic poetry of Solomon's song.

Song of Solomon

The *Song of Solomon*, one of the books of the *Old Testament*, is a love idyll, sometimes interpreted as an allegory of the union between the Deity and the body of His followers.

We will be glad and rejoice in thee,
    We will remember thy love more than wine;
Those who are upright love thee. I (iv)

I have compared thee, O my love,
    To a company of horses in Pharaoh's chariots. I (ix)

Stay me with flagons, comfort me with apples:
    For I am sick with love. II (v)

The flowers appear on the earth;
    That time of the singing of birds is come,
And the voice of the turtle is heard in our land. II (xii)

I charge you, O ye daughters of Jerusalem,
    By the roes [bucks] and by the hinds of the fields,
That ye stir not up, nor awake my love,
    Until he please. III (v)

Thy breasts are like two young roes that are twins,
    Feeding among lilies. IV (v)

Awake, O north wind; and come thou, south;
    Breathe through my garden that its spices may
        emit their fragrance.
Let my beloved come into the garden,
    To taste the pleasing fruits. IV (xvi)

Make haste, my beloved, thou who are
    Like unto a roe or to a young hart
Upon the mountains of spices. VII (xiv)

Based on the translation in the Authorized Version

In whatever way the import of this poetry is interpreted, its beauty of imagery is superlative.

The theological culture of Israel would provide the ethical ideal of a tradition that was to persist for some 3,000 years. The development of poetry, however, was to continue elsewhere – beyond the northern shores of the Mediterranean Sea – in Greece. The earliest great era of poetry in which we might expect to find master poets at work is the thousand or so years in which the Greeks and Romans evolved their civilizations. An approximate but convenient representation of this period (which was pervaded throughout by Greek influence) is set out below:

Development of Greek and Roman Culture	
Prehistoric or Heroic Age	c3000-700 BC
The Greek Period	c700-325 BC
The Hellenistic Period	c325-90 BC
The Roman Period	c90 BC-AD 50
The Roman Empire	cAD 50-AD 450
Early Byzantine Period	cAD 500-AD 600

2
The Greeks

AN EXAMINATION of the Graeco/Roman periods in greater detail is helpful since they formed the context within which some important poets were at work. The next figure expands the outline of events in the Prehistoric Period:

GENERAL HISTORICAL EVENTS – PREHISTORIC PERIOD

Bronze Age		3000 BC-
	Mycenaean Period.	
c1184	Fall of Troy.	
Dark Age		
1100	Collapse of Mycenaean Empire.	-1000 BC
Iron Age, also called *Heroic Age*		1000 BC-
1000	Development of Iron Age culture at Athens.	
900-700	Greeks begin colonizing in East and Italy.	
776	First Olympic Games.	700 BC

Notes:

1 Mycenae lies in the north-east corner of the Argive plain, nine miles from the sea; the name *Mykene* is not Greek but Carian. The city was first inhabited at the beginning of the Bronze Age (3000 to 2800 BC), but the culmination of its power and prominence occurred between 1400 and 1150 BC.

2 Between the years 900 and 700 BC the Homeric epics *Iliad* and *Odyssey* were being compiled.

3 During the 8th century BC Hesiod's *Works and Days* and the *Theogony* were composed.

Throughout the first era (Prehistoric or Heroic periods) the most outstanding literary achievements were the works of Homer and Hesiod.

Homer the man is an entirely unknown poet. The date by which his great poems received their final shape is conjecturally put somewhere between the 12th and the 9th century BC. The *Iliad* is an epic of warfare and debate full of energy, splendour, and tragic pathos. The charm of the *Odyssey* emanates from its narrative account of wondrous adventure, its descriptions of social life, and certain scenes of tender and delicate beauty. The two epics are different but akin in that their heroes and principals are presented as ideal men. Moreover, both stories combine divine and human action. Homer was essentially an oral poet whose writing is imbued with freshness and simplicity. His sureness of touch is maintained at a high level and his work has the dignity and finished eloquence necessary in the literary epic. Matthew Arnold (1822-88) summarized the Homeric style as, 'swiftness; plainness in thought, nobility of diction'.

The later poetic *genera* developed from three principal themes: worship of the gods; private life; the life of the community.

Heroic poetry aimed at the creation and perpetuation of a heroic ideal; the epic style adorns all that it touches. As the *rhetor*, Dio of Prusa, says of Homer: 'he praised almost everything – animals and plants, water and earth, weapons and horses'. He mentioned nothing without somehow honouring and glorifying it. Even the one man whom he abused, Thersites, he called 'a clear-voiced speaker'.

The *Iliad* (15,693 lines) is an account of the ten-year Siege and Fall of Troy and, within that context, the story of Achilleus (Achilles). He is the tragic hero: magnificent, but human and imperfect. His tragedy is the result of free choice by a will that falls short of omniscience and is disturbed by anger. Any extract can do no more than give a flavour of the essence of an epic like the *Iliad*, but the following lines show how Homer, making use of homely simile, temporarily detaches his epic narrative from its usual heroic war-like imagery:

> But just as at that time when the woodcutter makes ready his supper in the wooded glens of the mountains, when his arms and hands have grown weary from cutting down the tall trees, and his heart has had enough of it, and the longing for food and for sweet wine takes hold of his senses; it was at that time that the Danaans, by their manhood, broke their battalions.
>
> Translated by Richmond Lattimore

The central figure of the *Odyssey* is Odysseus, King of Ithaca, favourite of the grey-eyed goddess Athene. It is thought that the *Odyssey* (12,110 lines) was put into its present form by one man who used existing Ionian poems and added to them. The story describes a series of adventures: the ten-year homeward journey of Odysseus from the smoking ruins of conquered Troy; the land of the Lotus Eaters; the cave of the man-eating giant; the island of Circe the Witch; the Underworld; the rock of the Sirens, the hazard of Scylla and Charybdis; the Sun God's pastures; the grotto of Calypso the Nymph – and home at last, into the arms of his faithful Queen Penelope.

The lady to whom the wandering Odysseus returns was 'circumspect' Penelope – 'she, shining among women'. Early in the epic poem, *Antinous* (II.116) describes the being of Penelope:

> Athena has bestowed on her
> Wisdom of mind and excellence of skill
> In manifold beautiful devices
> Beyond all others.
>
> Based on a translation by J.W. Mackail

Only imagination can conjure an image of this epic lady, but in the Acropolis Museum, Athens are many sculptures of Archaic Greek maidens (*Korai*) who bear contemporaneous resemblance to high-born ladies of Homer's era.

No extract from the *Odyssey* can catch the grandeur of the whole, but the following lines show its clarity of descriptive detail and a glimpse of the interaction between mortals and the Divine World:

> Then resourceful Odysseus spoke in turn and answered him: 'Never fear, let these concerns not trouble your thinking; but let us go to the house which lies here next to the orchard, for there I sent Telemachos on ahead, with the oxherd and the swineherd, so that they could most quickly prepare our dinner.'
>
> So he spoke, and the two went into the handsome dwelling; and when they had come into the well-established dwelling place, there they found Telemachos, and the oxherd and swineherd, cutting up a great deal of meat, and mixing the bright wine.
>
> Meanwhile the Sicilian serving-maid bathed great-hearted Laertes in his house, and anointed him with olive oil, then threw a handsome mantle about him. Also, Athene, standing by the shepherd of the people, filled his limbs out, and made him taller and thicker to behold than he had been. He stepped forth from the bath, and his son looked on in amazement as he saw him looking like one of the immortal gods to encounter.
>
> So he spoke to him and addressed him in winged words, saying: 'Father, surely some one of the gods who are everlasting has made you better to look upon for beauty and stature.'
>
> Translated by Richmond Lattimore

From the outset, Odysseus is a man equipped to manage adroitly almost any situation. In coping with Circe's enchantment Odysseus is aided by a god. Unable to subdue him with either supernatural powers or womanly wiles, Circe surrenders herself, imploring him to come to her bed. He avoids submitting to her destructive power but this does not mean that her positive feminine values must be rejected. On the contrary, the heroic individuality of Odysseus is in part defined by his capacity to encounter the essence of the female principle without being overwhelmed by it.

Homer's own term for a poet is *aoidos*, 'singer'. Although his lengthy poems would take many hours to sing, they were capable of achieving complex literary and psychological effects. Nothing like this influence had existed in the more anecdotal and episodic songs of his predecessors.

The Homeric Epic differs from all other Greek poetry (and from all poetry with which most of us are familiar today) in one major respect: many of its compositional elements are phrases, not individual words; two examples are 'the wine-dark sea' and 'grey-eyed Athene'. This device generates lines, or parts of lines, which are virtually ready-made. Homer made much use of this formulaic fixed phrase-unit, the compound-epithet, relating it by association with a major god or hero. He structured the device according to the amount of space remaining to be filled in each hexameter (verse consisting of six feet). For example, in the *Odyssey*, the hero is described variously and repeatedly as: 'god-like Odysseus', 'resourceful Odysseus', 'much-enduring Odysseus', 'the great Odysseus', 'the long-suffering Odysseus'. With such descriptive compound-epithets the poet wooed his listeners and supported the singer's memory. For example, from his innovative and resourceful stock of phrases he drew 10 or 20 times on such adjectives as 'swift-footed' and 'silver-footed'. Thus rhythm combined with familiarity held the wrapt attention of his hearers.

The Supremacy of Homer

The poet Homer is a master. In the *Odyssey* he rarely loses control over detail or structure during his long narrative. Tension is subtly modulated, incidents are developed powerfully and then expanded into an eloquent, persuasive and imaginative epic. Characters are progressively created by similes, epithets, speeches and actions, to emerge as 'men' who have since lived on in the imagination of the human race. Whatever the arguments over attribution, the greatness of the *Iliad* and *Odyssey* is indisputable.

The mythical content of the *Odyssey* has led some critics to attempt an allegorical understanding of Homer's work. But such an interpretation of Greek literature could not develop until philosophy had begun to acquire a degree of independence, and an abstract, that is non-mythical, language of its own. Despite this, many admirers of the wisdom and inspiration of Homer and Hesiod, who value the ideas of the developing philosophy, have sought to find similar ideas expressed in an earlier poetry. The modern view is that deliberately written allegories are rare in Greek, and are never extensive; therefore any attempts to accord such a treatment to Homer are spurious.

In the *Republic*, Plato alludes to the description of Homer as 'educator of all Greece'. In the 6th century BC the Greek philosopher and poet, Xenophanes, said of Homer that he was 'the source from which all men have taken their wisdom since the beginning of time.' This appraisal was widely endorsed when subsequently his two great works formed the basis of education and culture throughout the Greek and Roman world. Ideas evolved, but admiration for Homer was to continue undiminished. Nor was reverence for this master poet restricted to the ancient world. In *The Divine Comedy* (*Inferno IV*), Dante described Homer as the greatest of all poets. In the *Parnassus* fresco in the Vatican, Raphael depicts him placed prominently to the left of Apollo. Homer's influence continued through to the 20th century and was an inspiration for James Joyce's important novel, *Ulysses* (the Latin form of Odysseus).

The Homeric Hymns

Mention should perhaps be made of the so-called *Homeric Hymns*. These were preludes and mythical tales in honour of the gods of various sanctuaries, written in the diction, style and verse forms of the epic poets.

They were not the work of great poets, but were nevertheless written by skilled versifiers with a useful competence. Here is an example; it is the *Hymn to the Delian Apollo*,★ intended to be recited at the religious festivals on the sacred island to celebrate the birth of the god in Delos. The momentous event of the god's birth is described with a distant charm and an economy of words:

> And as soon as Eilithyia the goddess of sore travail set foot on Delos, the pains of birth seized Leto, and she longed to bring forth; so she cast her arms around a palm tree and kneeled on the soft meadow, while the earth laughed for joy beneath her. Then the child leapt forth into the light, and all the goddesses raised a cry.
>
> Translated by D.M. Garman

Hesiod (8th century BC) is the earliest identified Greek poet after Homer. Very little is known of Hesiod the man, and most of that is gleaned from 'asides' in his *Works and Days*. Born in the shadow of Mount Helicon, he lived most of his life in Ascra on land inherited from his merchant father. He was probably a bachelor whose main occupation was writing poetry. He won a poetry prize at Euboea during the funeral games of Amphidamas:

> I won the contest with a song and took off an eared tripod; and this I set up as an offering to the Muses of Helicon, where they first had made me a master of melodious singing.
>
> Translated by Richmond Lattimore

The principal works of Hesiod are the *Theogony* and the *Catalogue of Women* (or *Eoiai*). The latter survives only in fragments, but to it are attached, as excursus, the *Shield of Herakles* and the *Works and Days*. The scale and sweep of his vision were matched by succinctness. In his *Theogony* Hesiod describes the sequence of Creation simply and concisely:

> First Chaos came, then broad-bosomed Earth,
> The everlasting seat of all that is,
> And Love.

In his *Works and Days*, Hesiod depicts a world very different from that of the Homeric nobility. The land of Greece always demands hard and constant labour from its country people and, as Herodotus the Greek historian (c484–432 BC) puts it, 'Poverty is native to Greece.'

The poetry of Hesiod contains much ancient peasant wisdom and alludes to mysteries of the earth in words which bring to life the very grass at the roadside, the richness of the multi-hued earth and the harsh life of men who work the soil. His lines record ageless precepts on the conduct of everyday life and the worth of supportive neighbours, willing to assist with problems:

★ In Greek and Roman mythology Apollo is god of the sun, prophecy, music, healing, and poetry. The ascriptions in this list are integral; their focus is the god and from thence to the art of poetry, contributing to its wholeness as an art.

neighbours come as they are to help;
your relatives will dress first!

Hesiod speaks for the hard-pressed peasants of his own day; he was interested in social justice and how to survive a harsh world with grace and comfort. Hesiod is no less an educator than Homer. In his *Works and Days*, a key concept is *arete* ('virtue; the activity of reason'). 'Best of all', says Hesiod, 'is the man who considers everything for himself and sees what is going to be right in the end.' Before presenting his separate precepts Hesiod defines the aim of work as *arete*.

Because he alludes to the gods who guard justice and morality in a context of moral rightness and lawful rule, he was called *Vates* (sacred bard). In a sense, Hesiod was the first theologian and therefore to some extent the first philosopher. Homer was neither, as is acknowledged by Socrates and Plato. Herodotus recognized in Homer and Hesiod the main authors of Grecian beliefs, noting how they set out the names, generations and attributes of the gods, together with appropriate forms of worship. But it was Hesiod's masterly hand that definitively systematized the generation and genealogy of the gods, a pantheon taken only partially from Homer.

The general reader of the *Theogony*, while admiring particular episodes such as the story of Prometheus, may not discern a coherent purpose or much sign of a unified structure in the poem. The genealogical catalogues seem encyclopaedic but dull, and for a fuller appreciation of this poem the reader benefits from the help of later scholars.

The complex grouping of Hesiod's catalogue of events resolves into three major categories:

Level	*Example*
Divine	Zeus' conflict with Kronos
Human	Invocation of the Muses
Physical	Rivers, Moon, Stars

The manifest totality derives from two primal powers:

Void	*Earth*
(Chaos)	(Gaia)

In other religious systems of the world this fundamental duality would be variously expressed: 'Unmanifest and Manifest; 'Undifferentiated and Differentiated'; 'Purusha and Prakriti'; 'Heaven and Earth', etc. From these dual forces, Hesiod establishes a pattern of progressive differentiation. He describes a process of proliferation stimulated by an immanent, creative energy which he calls *Desire* and which he sees as a primordial cosmic power.

Two other myths in the *Theogony* – the birth of Aphrodite and the story of Prometheus – account for, and develop, the theme of male dominance in the human cosmos under the dispensation of Zeus. Since Zeus' power is based on politics, his distinctive attribute is not strength but statesmanship. This quality Hesiod calls *metis* ('cunning' or 'wisdom'), although the word cannot be satisfactorily translated. Zeus is said at one point to be 'full of immortal wisdom'.

Hesiod is not ponderous when dealing with moral issues such as attempts to evade poverty by seizing what belongs to others, or mistreatment of friends, family or the helpless. Here is an extract from the *Works and Days*:

> Goods are not to be grabbed; much better if God lets you have them. If any man by force of hands wins him a great fortune, or steals it by the cleverness of his tongue, as so often happens among people when the intelligence is blinded by greed, a man's shameless spirit tramples his sense of honour; lightly the gods wipe out that man, and diminish the household of such a one, and his wealth stays with him for only a short time. It is the same when one does evil to guest or suppliant, or goes up into the bed of his brother, to lie in secret love with his brother's wife, doing acts that are against nature; or who unfeelingly abuses fatherless children, or speaks roughly with intemperate words to his failing father who stands upon the hateful doorstep of old age; with all these Zeus in person is angry, and in the end he makes them pay a bitter price for their unrighteous dealings.
>
> Translated by Richmond Lattimore

Hesiod's Power as a Poet

Hesiod, in the prelude to the *Works and Days*, declares to his brother that he will tell the *truth*. This deliberate purpose is something new, not found in Homer. Hesiod's poetry is thus a noble characterization of the man himself as the Greek poet-prophet who seeks, through his deeper insight into the structure of the world, to lead mankind along the right path.

In an age when science was rudimentary, technology simple and spiritual knowledge undeveloped, the poet Hesiod used myth as a medium for explaining how things are and for the assertion of a recommended code of conduct. The word *myth* (from the Greek *muthos*) means: 'word, speech, tale, legend'; 'fictitious traditional story or legend embodying ancient or primitive beliefs in, and interpretation of, religious or supernatural phenomena such as the gods, lesser deities and the force of nature'.

The *Theogony*, like all mythical poetry, is part of an existing structured tradition; a system of hereditary stories once believed to be true by a particular cultural group and accepted as an explanation (in terms of supernatural beings) of why things happen as they do. It was also used to establish rules by which people should conduct their lives. Hesiod imaginatively reinterprets a series of existing myths linking them with human experience. In this way he describes the basic structure of the cosmos, together with the primal conflict occurring in the divine milieu. He offers explanations and furnishes details authoritatively. For instance, he describes how the Olympian Muses 'honour Zeus both at the beginning and at the end of their song'.

In his introductory invocation of the Muses he says that they appeared to the shepherd Hesiod and told him what to sing. This has to be interpreted by us in a later age as either a literary artifice or a mandate from the gods to speak on their behalf as a prophet of religious truth. There was no orthodox *corpus* of Greek religion as such; therefore, in his *Theogony*, Hesiod was under no constraint either to conform or to maintain orthodoxy. Instead he was able to offer a creative reinterpretation which imaginatively reorganizes old myths and augments them with new ideas. The material with which he worked is thought to have been drawn from three main sources:

The Homeric literature
Greek local and tribal tradition
Ancient and Near East mythology*

Greek Drama

Before considering Greek lyric poetry, mention must be made of the great poet-playwrights and the immense achievement of Greek drama. The word *drama* means 'doing', and perhaps there is a link here with the persistent fatalistic themes of the great Greek plays.

The festivals of ancient Greece were events at which sacrifices and offerings were made; there was also dancing, drinking, and great merriment. There were many different gods and each one had a festival. The god Dionysus had four annual festivals in Athens, and the link with him is seen in three different types of Greek plays:

Satyric-plays	Satyrs were strange wood-creatures in Greek legends.
Tragedies	*Tragedy* from the Greek word meaning 'goat-song'.
Comedies	*Comedy*, from a Greek word, means 'revellers' or 'the song of the merry-makers'. Their function was to welcome the god into the city.

Tragedy

Tragedy is thought to have sprung from a performance which was entirely lyric. Numbers in the chorus varied (according to the play's requirements) from 12 to 15 singers. Exceptionally, in the earliest extant play of Aeschylus, it is thought that the chorus numbered 50 singers.

* This third source is disputed by some authorities. For later generations, in the words of Northrop Frye (1957), '... the typical forms of myth become the conventions and genres of literature.' In the *Shield of Heracles* Hesiod seems to have imitated Homer's description of the 'Shield of Achilles'. In its turn, Hesiod's *Works and Days* appears to have provided a model on which Virgil, in part, framed his *Georgics*. Such examples confirm the continuity of themes in poetry, which persists uninterrupted to the present day. The vast range of Hesiod's vision, his transformational and innovative creativity, but above all his use of language, reveal his status as a master poet.

Thespis, an Attic poet considered to be the father of Greek tragedy, won the prize (a goat) when tragedy was first offered at the Great Dionysia in about 534 BC. Cleverly, Thespis introduced an individual actor who, prologue-like, explained to the audience what was about to happen and had exchanges with the chorus-leader. (The Greek word for 'actor' meant 'answerer'). Thespis was perilously inventive in the matter of facial disguise. He is reputed to have treated his actors' faces with white lead and then covered them with cinnabar (a red oxide of mercury). Later, and less dangerously, he introduced masks of unpainted linen.

Aeschylus (526-456 BC) introduced a second actor, and the two could now speak in dialogue and present scenes by themselves without involving the chorus.

Sophocles (496-406 BC) introduced a third actor. In the 5th century BC there were only three *performers* in a play; there could be more than three *characters*, provided they were not all on stage at the same time. An actor had merely to change his costume and *persona* (mask) to become another character.

Euripides (485-406 BC) was the last of the great writers of Greek tragedy whose works have survived to the present day. He and Sophocles often competed with each other in the Festival of the Great Dionysia. The scenes of a tragedy consisted of set speeches and, later, the addition of dialogues. Scenes were separated by choral odes of considerable length and high excellence as lyric poetry. The following extract is from *Trojan Women*:

CHORUS: Far away,
Over these waters,
The soft surf encircles
The island of Salamis,
Where the ceaseless sound of bees is heard
Murmuring among the flowers.
It was Telamon, the king, ruled there.
And from his throne he would look
Across a little bay
To Athens' holy hill,
Where the goddess first bestowed on man
The green branch of the olive:
A shining crown from heaven
Which is now the glory of that city.
But Telamon left his island,
Sailed from the shores of Salamis,
Left that peaceful land,
And lent his strength in battle
To the warrior, Heracles;
Together they came,
And sacked the town of Troy.
Yes, once before,
In those far-off days,

Our city was destroyed by war.
For a vow had been broken:
Our king had promised him
Two matchless, white, immortal steeds,
But failed to keep his word.
For this
The armies of Greece set sail.
And at the mouth
Of our beautiful river Simois
They shipped their oars.
The canvas was furled.
The cables made fast.
And Heracles, the archer,
Brought on shore
His mighty bow,
And the arrows
Which the god's hand guided to their mark.
One shaft was bent at Laomedon's heart,
And the debt was paid.
But not content
They sent
The red breath of fire
Roaring over the walls,
Brought down the stones
Apollo's hands had laid.

Next, the Chorus speak of Hecuba and describe their own plight:

CHORUS: Tears cannot wash away her shame,
Nor pity mollify her grief.
My fingers that followed the flying shuttle
May be busy again, but not in Troy.
They will not even let us see
The graves of our dead sons.
Our fate is worse –
We are to be raped.
The curse of god strike the Greeks that night!

Trojan Women, Translated by Neil Curry

Comedy

Another festival of Dionysus was the *Lenaea*, a winter event held in Athens. In this, comedy took precedence over tragedy and five comic playwrights, each with a single play, competed for a prize. The three most prominent names in Greek comedy are **Aristophanes** (c450-380 BC), **Menander** (?343-291 BC) and **Philemon** (?361-?263 BC). Philemon was a rival of Menander, defeating him several times in contests. Unfortunately, only fragments of his work remain.

We have many of the plays of these great poets of tragedy and comedy; they are still staged frequently and have continuing relevance. They should, preferably, be read or heard in their entirety, but some morsels follow. In his *Prometheus Bound*, Aeschylus refers to:

> Multitudinous laughter of the waves of ocean … Translated by Herbert Weir

Sophocles in his *Antigone* acknowledges what was to be remarked by his many successors down the ages:

> Wonders are many, and none is more wonderful than man.
> Translated by R.C. Jebb

Euripides, in *Hippolytus*, shapes the old excuse of the human race:

> 'Twas but my tongue, 'twas not my soul that swore.
> Translated by Gilbert Murray

Although no translation quite conveys the spirit of the original, here is the celebrated 'Welcome to the Nightingale' from the *Birds* by Aristophanes:

> O dear one, tawny sprite, dearest of birds!
> Singer in tune with all my songs, nurtured
> with me, nightingale!
> You are here, yes you are here, and into our eyes you have
> shone, bringing your sweet voice to us all!
> Come, you who set the fair-tuned flute
> to the music of spring; come dancers, let the
> anapaest measure begin!
> Based on the translation by J.A. Symonds

Aristophanes had the distinction of earning a tribute from Plato:

> The graces once made up their mind
> A shrine inviolate to find:
> And thus they found, and that with ease,
> The soul of Aristophanes.

A fragment from an unknown play by Menander shows the originality and insight of the Greeks, who sometimes foreshadow poetry yet to come in the Middle Ages:

> When thou wouldst know thyself, what man thou art,
> Look at the tombstones as thou passest by:
> Within those monuments lie bones and dust
> Of monarchs, tyrants, sages, men whose pride
> Rose high because of wealth or noble blood,
> Or haughty soul, or loveliness of limb;
> Yet none of these things strove for them 'gainst time:
> See thou to this, and know thee who thou art.
> Translated by J.A. Symonds

This fragment from the missing works of Philemon indicates the quality of what has been lost to us:

> Have faith in God and fear; seek not to know him;
> For thou wilt gain nought else beyond thy search;
> Whether he is or is not, shun to ask;
> As one who is, and sees thee, always fear him.
>
> Translated by J.A. Symonds

Developments in Greek Poetry

In primitive societies the poet was regarded as the instrument of an external power which possessed him and spoke through his voice. The poet is at least a seer, if not a prophet. He is an agent of unseen incalculable forces. He may depend upon inspiration, but he sees what others do not see; he articulates arcane knowledge, sometimes in dark mysterious words. Frequently, neither the knowledge nor the poet's words are considered to be his own. His statements require interpretations and may carry more than one meaning. It was not without good reason that the Delphic Oracle delivered its mysterious messages in verse; the Greeks had always accepted that poetry was an inspired activity.

Different Forms of Poetry

The Greeks had different words for various kinds of poetry: *epos* (epic poem); *aoide* (song); *molpe* (song combined with dance). The word which combined all aspects as one was, perhaps surprisingly, *sophia*, 'wisdom', meaning, in part, 'skill'. This was the term applied to all the fine arts from poetry to sculpture. For the Greeks poetry, of all the arts, embodied a quality so unusual and so important that they could not but relate it to a superior order.

A variety of forms in poetry evolved with the maturing of Greek civilization. Growth of trade, a series of major wars, the emergence of city-states and the expansion of spiritual awareness, produced genres and configurations which later generations of poets gradually developed. The major Greek forms are:

1 *Epic poetry* (of which the *Iliad* and the *Odyssey* are the supreme examples).
2 *Elegiac* (earliest examples are verses of martial elegy by Callinus of Ephesus, 600 BC). The elegiac couplet is a hexameter followed by a pentameter.
3 *Iambic* (the common rhythmic form: a short syllable followed by a long one).
4 *Lyric poetry* (originally wholly or partly sung to music).

Iambic poetry, like the Elegiac form, was an Ionian composition which first appeared around 700 to 650 BC. These two companion forms are ideally suited for expressing individual thought and feeling on any subject; moreover, neither requires great poetic skill. Originally both forms were lyric, that is, wholly or partly sung to music, but even before the 5th century BC the connection with music began to diminish and finally became lost altogether. Many scholars consider the generic term *lyric* to include iambic, true lyric, lyric monody and choral lyric. Representative poets under this collective heading are:

Archilochus of Paros
Callinus of Ephesus
Semonides of Amorgos
Hipponax of Ephesus
Tyrtaeus of Sparta
Mimnermus of Colophon
Solon of Athens
Phocylides of Miletus
Xenophanes of Colophon
Theognis of Megara
Terpander of Antissa (Lesbos)
Bacchylides of Ceos
Alcman of Sparta
Stesichorus of Himera
Ibycus of Rhegium
Sappho of Mytilene
Alcaeus of Mytilene
Anacreon of Teos
Hybrias of Crete
Praxilla of Sicyon
Corinna of Tanagra
Simonides of Ceos
Pindar of Thebes

Certain writers predominate:

Archilochus was a Greek poet and soldier who lived in the 7th century BC. He had a remarkable talent for presenting conversation and character; the ancients ranked him next to Homer. He is the earliest known poet to write in the first person and amazingly, although writing in the Heroic Age, admits to discarding his shield on the battlefield while getting out of a tight corner:

Some Saian mountaineer
Struts today with my shield.
I threw it down by a bush and ran
When the fighting got hot.
Life seemed somehow more precious.
It was a beautiful shield.
I know where I can buy another
Exactly like it, just as round.

Again on the subject of shields, but this time Archilochus writes with a level of realism that conveys just what it was like to be in the thick of things on the battlefield:

There are other shields to be had,
But not under the spear-hail
Of an artillery attack,
In the hot work of slaughtering,
Among the dry racket of the javelins,
Neither seeing nor hearing …

Translations by Guy Davenport

The poet's brother-in-law perished in a shipwreck, and he wrote a 'consolation' in the form of an elegy, containing the following couplet:

> Since weeping will not cure my grief,
> Pleasure and feasting cannot make it worse.

To a courtesan whose nick-name, Pasiphile, means 'dear to all', he wrote a charming couplet:

> Fig tree of the rocks, where many rooks delight to feed,
> How sweetly, Pasiphile, you make your guests at home.

But it was with Neobule, the daughter of a well-known Parian citizen, that Archilochus fell in love. Here he writes of his passion for her:

> Hair and breast steeped in perfume, she would awaken desire in an old man … Wretched am I, unable to breathe, overwhelmed with desire, and the gods stabbing me to the bone with hideous suffering … Now am I tamed by the longing that turns the bones to water: no longer am I moved by feasting or the delights of poetry … Translations by D.M. Garman

We know little in detail of **Sappho**, who probably lived from about 612 to c580 BC. It is known that she married Cercolas and had a daughter, Cleis. She wrote in simple but superbly articulated stanzas and is recognized as a poet of importance, despite the fact that only relatively few poems and fragments have been found. In an epigram within the *Anthology* attributed to Plato, Sappho is referred to as the 'tenth Muse'.

Here is part of a poem to Aphrodite, the Goddess of Love – verses vividly alive and displaying her famed lyricism:

> Come to me from Crete to this holy temple,
> Aphrodite. Here is a grove of apple
> trees for your delight, and the smoking altars
> fragrant with incense.
>
> Here cold water rustles down through the apple
> branches; all the lawn is beset and darkened
> under roses, and, from the leaves that tremble,
> sleep of enchantment
> comes descending. Here is a meadow pasture
> Where the horses graze and with flowers of springtime
> now in full bloom, here where the light winds passing
> blow in their freshness.
>
> Translated by Richmond Lattimore

Lament for a maidenhead

First Voice Like a quince-apple
ripening on a topmost
branch in a tree top

not once noticed by
harvesters or, if
not unnoticed, not reached.

Second Voice Like a hyacinth in
the mountains, trampled
by shepherds until

only a purple stain
remains on the ground.

Translated by Mary Barnard

In her famous *Ode*, the passionate sincerity of feeling in certain lines is such that they were widely imitated in Rome (by Catullus and Lucretius), and many Greeks are said to have known them by heart:

In my eyes he is the equal of the gods,
He who sits close to your side,
Savouring the sweetness of your voice
And the charm

Of that laugh that pierces my heart,
Till it beats in my very lips.
I have only to see your face,
And my voice cracks.

My tongue goes dry in my mouth,
Fire burns beneath my skin,
And my ears grow suddenly deaf,
My eyes blind.

My whole body is drenched with sweat,
I tremble from head to foot;
My cheeks turn green as the grass,
And I feel I shall die.

Translated by D.M. Garman

Sappho directed an 'academy' for young women which she herself called 'the house of the servants of the Muses'. Her pupils learned music, dancing, and poetry. They were with a teacher who considered the best education to be one inspired by love. Their names float down to us like delicate and charming shadows from her poetry: Gyrinno, Atthis, Anactoria, Gongyla, Arignota:

You have done well to come: I have been longing for you.
Like a spring of water you well up in my soul, aflame
with desire. Welcome, my Gyrinno!

Translated by D.M. Garman

An epitaph indicates apt, compressive skill:

This is the dust of Timas, who died before she was married
and whom Persephone's dark chamber accepted instead.
After her death the maidens who were her friends, with sharp
iron cutting their lovely hair, laid it upon her tomb.

Translated by Richmond Lattimore

Sappho could be direct, incisive, factual, as here:

> Some say a company of cavalry
> or of infantry, others that
> the swift oars of our fleet
> are the finest sight
> on dark earth; but I say
> that whatever one loves, is.
>
> Based on the translation by Mary Barnard

Sappho's poetry is so distinctive that, when some scraps of verse were found in the wrappings of a mummified crocodile, they could be confidently attributed to her.

Historical Context

The poetry of Sappho had been written during a most productive phase of Greek cultural development. After 750 BC the Greek civilization was thriving and its people began to establish colonies throughout the Mediterranean; cities were established in Egypt and on the Black Sea. Around 700 BC the Greeks adapted the Phoenician alphabet for their own language. In the 6th century when Sappho was writing her poetry, the development of pre-Socratic Schools of philosophy began: Materialists, Pythagoreans, Dualists and Atomists. Towards the end of this century, playwriting competitions were inaugurated.

After 525 BC the first official versions of the Homeric epics appeared. These later events, and others, occurred during the Age of Colonization and the later Archaic Period – as indicated in the following figure:

General Historical Events – The Greek Period		
Age of Colonization		750 BC-
750-600	Greeks settle colonies throughout Mediterranean, from Egypt to Black Sea.	
7th century	Archilochus, *Poems*.	
Archaic Period		
Early 6th century	Sappho, *Poems*.	
c590	Solon reforms Athenian constitution.	
546	Persian Empire expands to seize Greek colonies in Asia Minor.	
490	Start of Persian Wars; King Darius defeated at Marathon.	
c490 BC	*Critian Boy* (Sculpture where archaic smile is superseded by more natural expression). Turning point between Archaic and Classical Periods.	480 BC

Role of Poetry

The sheer variety of Greek poetry during this period illustrates its functional place in Greek life. The work of Pindar demonstrates this.

The date of **Pindar**'s birth is uncertain, but it was around 520 BC. The fact that so much Greek poetry survives is a miracle; but equally, there is the corresponding tragedy of the amount which has been lost. Pindar's work is an example. Ancient scholars collected his works into 17 books, which contained: hymns, paeans, dithyrambs, processional songs, maiden's songs, dance songs, encomia, dirges and victory songs. A mere four books survive, containing 45 authentic odes, together with a number of fragments.

An understanding of the nature and traditions of Greek aristocratic society will help us to appreciate how some of Pindar's subjects – victory in a chariot race or an athletic contest for example – could inspire poetry of such seriousness and deep feeling.

The poetic structure and majesty of his formal odes is celebrated. Their qualities of force, vividness, and loftiness of style are expressive of an intensely Hellenic spirit. They show mastery of rhythm and metre, together with diction of a quite individual imagination. Here is how Pindar begins his ode for Aristocleides of Aigina, Winner in the Pancration:

> O Divine Muse, our mother, I pray thee come unto this
> Dorian isle Aigina now stranger-thronged for the
> sacred festival of the Nemean games; for by the waters
> of Asopos young men await thee, skilled to sing sweet
> songs of triumph and desiring to hear thy call.
>
> Translated by Ernest Myers

In his *Olympian Ode II* for Theron of Acragas, winner in the chariot-race, Pindar writes a statement (much quoted) on the relationship between knowledge and words:

> Many swift arrows have I beneath my bended arm within my quiver, arrows that have a voice for the wise, but for the crowd they need interpreters. His art is true who of his nature hath knowledge; they who have merely learnt, strong in the multitude of words, are but as crows that chatter vain things in strife against the divine bird of Zeus. Translated by Ernest Myers

Praxilla of Sicyon was a lyric poetess of the 5th century BC who wrote hymns, dithyrambs and drinking-songs. She is represented here by two fragments which indicate her love of simple things and her skill in conveying unaffected natural realism. In her *Hymn to Adonis* she portrayed Adonis in the Underworld being asked what were the fairest things he had left behind on earth; he replied:

> Loveliest of what I leave behind is the sunlight, and loveliest after that the shining stars, and the moon's face, but also cucumbers that are ripe, and pears, and apples.

Here, the poem is concerned with the living:

> Girl of the lovely glance, looking out through the window,
> your face is virgin; lower down you are a married woman.
>
> Translations by Richmond Lattimore

Simonides was a lyric poet and epigrammist from the Aegean island of Ceos, who is thought to have lived from about 556 to 468 BC. In the field of choral work he is remembered chiefly for his dirges and victory songs; his style seems to have been simple and elegant. Of his epigrams most, if not all, were prepared for tombs or other monuments. With his impassioned chanted poetry (called dithyrambic) he was successful in many Athenian competitions. Simonides lived mostly in Athens but was a well-travelled and renowned professional poet who will here be represented by one of those timeless ironic comments from an inscribed epitaph:

> Traveller, take this word to the men of Lakedaimon:
> We who lie buried here did what they told us to do.
>
> Translated by Richmond Lattimore

Philetas of Cos (*Philitas* in Coan inscriptions), was born around 320 BC. He became the tutor of Ptolemy II, that is, Philadelphus. (Ptolemy was the formal name of all the Macedonian Kings of Egypt.) He was also tutor to Theocritus and Zenodotus (the first head of the library at Alexandria). Zenodotus was described by Strabo as 'poet and scholar in one'. Philetas' great reputation as a poet among his younger contemporaries may have rested partly on his status as the inaugurator of the scholar-poet tradition, which was continued by the Alexandrians. Like Philetas, many poets during this era were both academician and librarian.

In Whibley's *Companion to Greek Studies* (Cambridge, 1916) we read, as though casually, in passing, 'Philetas of Cos, whom Ovid imitated, and whom Propertius preferred to Callimachus.' Philetas, although a key figure in ancient literature is, alas, now known only through tantalizing scraps and allusions. He is remembered principally for his elegies and is represented here by two such pieces:

> Past fifty and cloyed at last,
> Nikias, who loved to love,
> Hangs up in the temple of
> Kypris her sandals, her long
> Uncoiled hair, her shining bronze
> Mirror that never lied to her,
> Her rich girdle, and the things
> Men never mention. Here you can
> See the whole panoply of love.
>
> Translated by Kenneth Rexroth

This tombstone heavy with grief announces
'Death took little Theodota's tiny life',
And the little one says to her father, 'Don't be unhappy,
Theodotos. Men are always having bad luck.'

Translated by Peter Jay

Theocritus of Syracuse, whose life may have spanned the years 310-250 BC, was an accomplished craftsman who succeeded in nearly every genre to which he put his hand. He is considered to be the father of pastoral poetry, and his knowledge of flora and the countryside in his bucolic poems reveals his level of familiarity and observation.

Those dew-moist roses and that bushy thyme
are sacred to the Muse of Helicon.
But yours, Apollo, is the dark-leaved bay
which sanctifies your shrine on Delphi's height;
this horned white goat chewing the terebinth
shall stain your altar with his blood.

His work conceals his considerable learning. He has a dramatic talent coupled with an empathetic insight into people and their emotions (for example, the revealing monologue of a jilted girl). There is gentle humour, but above all there is a felicity and melody in his use of language. This is how Theocritus begins *The Marriage-Song of Helen and Menelaus*:

And so in Sparta long ago the maids,
With blooms of hyacinth among their locks,
Before the newly limned bride-chamber
In the palace of the fair-haired Menelaus,
Began their dance (twelve girls, the city's pride,
The flower of Spartan maidenhood); at that time
The younger son of Atreus wooed and won
Helen, the darling of the Tyndarids,
And took her to his bower. With one accord
They sang, with measured beat and woven steps,
While loud rang the halls with the marriage-lay.

Translations by J.H. Hallard

Pre-Socratic Criticism of Poets

Greek poets were not without their critics. **Xenophanes** was a poet and philosopher, born about the year 570 BC. What we know for certain is that Xenophanes led a wandering life from the age of 25 and was still active and writing poetry at the age of 92. Subjects in the surviving fragments of his work include: theology, philosophy, satirical attacks. He assailed traditional accounts of the gods and was particularly contemptuous of anthropomorphism:

> If cattle and horses had hands …
> horses would draw the forms of gods
> like horses, and cattle like cattle.

Here is another in similar vein:

> The Ethiopians make their gods black and snub-nosed; the Thracians say theirs have blue eyes and red hair.
>
> Translations by John Burnet

Xenophanes was somewhat sceptical of human knowledge. He held that God is – one; ungenerated; unmoving. We still have a fragment of an elegy in which he ridiculed Pythagoras and the doctrine of transmigration:

> And now I will turn to another tale and point the way … Once, they say, Pythagoras was passing when a dog was being beaten and he said, 'Stop! don't beat it! It's the soul of a friend – I recognize the voice.'
>
> Based on a translation by John Burnet

Xenophanes was no detractor of the power of human thought:

> But without toil he swayeth all things
> by the thought of his mind.
>
> Translated by John Burnet

What is most striking about this shrewd poet-philosopher is the nobility of his religious feeling and the acuity with which he criticizes polytheism. He was a convinced monotheist:

> Among gods and men there exists but one god, the supreme, who neither in body or spirit resembles mankind. And he abides ever in the self-same place, moving not at all.
>
> Translated by John Burnet

Although Xenophanes considered that the gods (far from having created mankind as Hesiod contends) were mere inventions of the human imagination, he was no atheist. He continued to worship a supreme being and deplored the deeds of the gods as presented by some poets. His argument is that, in Greece, children's intelligence and sensibility are developed first by studying the works of Homer and other classical poets. Yet the *Iliad* and the *Odyssey* are full of legends and fictions, that is, of falsehoods. The poets describe the gods as tricksters, criminals, parricides and adulterers. In expressing these views and holding his central belief in monotheism, Xenophanes is a direct precursor of Plato.

Plato's Criticism of Poets

Before following the Greek spirit to Rome we will consider the censoriousness of Plato (c429-347 BC) towards poets (and musicians). His complaint was that poets and prose-writers declare that virtue is honourable but painful, while vice (perhaps conventionally considered disgraceful) is often pleasant. In the *Republic*, Plato (a disciple and companion of Socrates until his death in 399 BC) claims that writers condone and applaud successful wickedness and speak with ill-disguised contempt of the unhappiness and bad luck of the virtuous.

It is clear that the Greeks had been gradually waking up to the blasphemous immorality of their traditional anthropomorphic mythology. Such tales as Homer and Hesiod relate about the gods, says Socrates, must not be recounted to our alumni. In support of his criticism he lays down three canons of sound theology:

> God [the gods] is author of good only.
> God never deceives.
> He never changes.

Although widely approved, poetic representations of the terrors of the future world are also deprecated by Plato because they engender an unphilosophical fear of death that is generally unsuitable, particularly to the soldier. The censure is extended to other immoral and unedifying passages in Homer describing the conduct of heroes and demigods of old. But Plato ingeniously adds that we cannot yet proscribe teaching by poetry simply so that the unjust may be happier than the just – 'which would beg the question of our entire argument!' Plato's criticism was the chief source of the Greek Christian Fathers' polemic against pagan mythology, but the detail of his censure of Homer has lost much of its interest for modern readers. To some extent Plato is censuring too absolutely the medium for its message and the poet for the content of his story.

Allegory has been invoked in defence of Homer against Plato's criticism since, in the words of Heracleides (a Greek philosopher of the 4th century BC and a disciple of Plato), Homer was impious if he did not allegorize. Plato anticipates this evasion by pointing out that the young who are unable to distinguish the directly literal from the allegorical will, nevertheless, still have their unschooled minds indelibly impressed.

One difficulty with poetry, as we learn in Plato's *Protagoras*, is its associated ambiguity. The poets cannot be interrogated retrospectively on the meaning of what they are saying; interpretation of meaning, therefore, is a dispute which can never be decided. Plato also attacked the use by poets even of *positive* philosophical allegory, on the grounds that although the poet's authority might be identified with an authentic teaching, the allegory was still no substitute for reasoned argument. In the terms of true principles of education, Plato identifies three aspects of the poet's teaching:

(1) material content; (2) form; and (3) spirit.

In a discussion, from which Aristotle's *Poetics* borrows much, Plato makes distinction between the equable flow of epic narrative and the more vivid imitative speeches which provide the source of mimetic art in Attic tragedy. All art is, broadly speaking, mimetic in that it expresses character and feeling but, says Plato, imitation of *anything but the good* is dangerous for the stability and unity of the soul. Plato argues that the tone, temper and rhythm of the poetry we read (and its aesthetic quality) *should* conspire for good rather than evil, so that the soul from our earliest years is drawn into a likeness and sympathy with the beauty of reason.

Clearly, Plato is advocating censorship, albeit from the highest of motives. To take an example from another tradition, a casualty of such a stern doctrine would be India's much-loved legends describing Krishna's boyhood pranks and deceits (a bad example for children). Greek and Roman mythology would be made poorer, if not destroyed, by Plato's uncompromising absolutist stand for truth. However, it should be remembered that, despite his sweeping condemnation of poets, in another context Plato alludes to the ephithet often applied to Homer – 'educator of all Greece'.

As always with Plato, in the *Dialogues* there is balance and reason. In the *Symposium* there is an allusion to 'the poets who were children and prophets of the gods.' In *Lysis* 'the poets are to us, in a manner, the fathers and authors of wisdom …' In the *Timaeus*: 'poets can imitate only what they have experienced'; and vindication of these inspired writers is made with the important statement in the *Symposium*: 'poets are creators in their souls and (like legislators) bring forth conceptions of wisdom and virtue'.

The Loss of Greek Independence

At the beginning of the 5th century BC (in 499 BC) the Greek cities of Asia Minor, with Athenian support, rebelled against their Persian masters. The Persian King, Darius, succeeded in checking this revolt, but when he later led a punitive expedition against mainland Greece, his army was defeated by the Athenians at the Battle of Marathon. Athens, in the 5th century BC, was the political and cultural centre of Greece. The arts were flourishing and there was a search for reason and order. The aim of life was perfect equilibrium; everything in due proportion, nothing in excess. A celebrated Greek proverb of the time was: 'Nothing too much.'

Tragically, the Greeks were unable to sustain their ideals in practice. This proved fatal to their independence and they became vulnerable to colonization by another great civilization with different ideals – Rome. The next figure indicates the direction taken by events:

General Historical Events

Classical Period		478 BC-
480	Xerxes' second expedition against Greece; wins at Thermopylae; sacks Athens. Greeks defeat Persians decisively at Salamis.	
479	Greek Victories at Plataea and Mycale. End of Persian Wars.	
478	Formation of Delian League; beginning of Athenian Empire.	
461	Pericles comes to prominence in Athens.	
454	Treasury of Delian League moved to Athens.	454
Golden Age		450-
443-430	Pericles in full control of Athens.	
429	Pericles dies of plague that devastates Athens.	
423	Peloponnesian War begins.	
413	Renewed outbreak of Peloponnesian War.	413
Late Classical Period		404-
404	Fall of Athens and victory of Sparta.	
331	City of Alexandria founded.	323
Hellenistic Period		
323-281	Wars of Alexander's successors.	323-
146	Romans sack Corinth; Greece becomes a Roman province.	146 BC

The genius which flowered as the Greek spirit was reflected in poetry as it underwent the usual ascent and fall of great civilizations:

Surge and Decline of the Greek Spirit

The prehistoric or Heroic age (extending to the first Olympiad, 776 BC).

Early growth of poetry and prose before the supremacy of Athens in Hellas (776 BC to the date of the Athenian League – 477 BC)

The flowering of the Greek genius, the supremacy of Athens, from the end of the Persian wars to the age of Alexander (479-323 BC)

Athenian decline, reaching its demise with Alexander's death (413-323 BC)

Asia and Egypt are Hellenized. In Rome and Byzantium the Greek spirit, still vital, extends its life on foreign soil.

Notes:

1 Alexander the Great, of Macedonia, lived from 356 to 323 BC, dying of fever at the age of 33.

2 In the year 146 BC, the Romans sacked the city of Corinth; Greece became a Roman province. In due course the cultural achievement of Classical Greece was absorbed and reborn in Rome.

3
The Romans

IT COULD BE SAID that the Romans poured most of their energy into political and military affairs, but culturally (and in many other ways) Rome was a worthy successor to the Greeks. Artistically, it drew its initial productive impulse from Greek civilization, but the outcome had a native inspirational vigour that flourished in its own right. It was at the time of the decisive contests with Carthage (c250 BC) that the Romans, with the help of mature models obtained from Greece, first began the development of a national literature. Fortuitously, Roman copies of the works of antiquity became an invaluable record-source when, subsequently, the Greek originals had been lost. As to poetry, this had a life and development of its own which we shall explore. To help set the context, an outline of certain major events in Roman history is given in the following figures:

GENERAL HISTORICAL EVENTS

Beginnings		
753	Founding of city of Rome (traditional date).	753 BC-
c700	Development of Etruscan culture.	
Roman Republic	*Conquest of Italy and Mediterranean*	509 BC-
	Expulsion of Etruscans and founding of Roman Republic.	
264-241	First Punic War: Roman conquest of Sicily, Sardinia, Corsica.	
218-201	Second Punic War: Roman conquest of Spain.	
146	Destruction of Carthage: Africa becomes a Roman province. Sack of Corinth: Greece becomes a Roman province.	
60	First Triumvirate: Pompey, Caesar, and Crassus.	
58-56	Caesar conquers Gaul.	
46-44	Caesar rules Rome as dictator until assassinated.	
43	Second Triumvirate: Antony, Lepidus, and Octavian.	31 BC

From the power base of the Republic the Roman expansionist forces moved out to establish a far-reaching empire:

General Historical Events – Roman Empire		
31	Battle of Actium won by Octavian.	31 BC-
30	Death of Antony and Cleopatra.	
27-14 AD	Octavian under name of Augustus rules as first Roman emperor.	
Birth of Jesus; crucified cAD 30.		BC .... AD-
AD 14-68	Emperors: Tiberius, Caligula, Claudius, Nero.	
70	Capture of Jerusalem by Titus.	
307-337	Reign of Constantine.	
330	Founding of Constantinople.	
409-455	Vandals and Visigoths invade Italy, Spain, Gaul, Africa.	
476	Romulus Augustulus abdicates as the last Western Roman emperor.	AD 476

For about 100 years the Roman Empire, as it now was, enjoyed a period of stability, but the seeds of disintegration were inherent in a political system unable to move with the times. Despite the establishment of Constantinople, with Constantine as sole ruler of the Empire after AD 324, the Roman Empire in the West collapsed under the assaults of the Vandals and Visigoths. The Roman Empire of the East was to rule from Byzantium for another thousand years, coming to its end with the fall of Constantinople in AD 1453.

Roman Poetry – Beginnings

The poetry of Rome was not the vestigial creative spirit of Greece lingering on as a pale, moribund reflection. It had a vigorous individuality of its own and breathed into the Greek forms a distinctive new life.

By the time Rome was founded (its traditional date is put at 753 BC), Greek civilization had already passed through its Bronze Age and was well into its Iron Age. Troy had long fallen; the Mycenaean Empire had flourished and faded; Homer had lived and was gone. The foundations of Greek culture were some 2,000 years old.

It is believed by some scholars in Italy that there was an early indigenous poetry which flourished about the 5th century BC, after the founding of Rome. The theorists believe that this native poetry disappeared under the influence of Ennius and that his immediate predecessor, Naevius, was the last of the genuinely native minstrels. We will leave this debate in the hands of such scholars as W.Y. Sellar who, in his *The Roman Poets of the Republic* (1889), Oxford, deals with this question in depth.

Greek Influence on Roman Literature

Critics of early Roman literature sometimes claim that it is largely imitation and translation of a Greek model. This is substantially true. As a source, Greek literature was extremely rich and varied. This lent an important dimension to the Roman work, but the Latin writers and poets brought their own vigour and originality to the literary forms absorbed from the Greeks. By the 3rd century BC the Greeks had already invented and developed to a consummate degree almost every conceivable literary form: epic, drama (both tragedy and comedy), elegy, epigram, lyric, history, pastoral, oratory, treatise, philosophic dialogue. Not only Roman but all subsequent Western European literatures are ultimately indebted to Greece for their literary forms.

Latin and Roman Poetry

Against its background of Roman history, the native poetry, albeit heavily influenced by Greek models, flourished with an inherent vitality. The history of Roman poetry may be divided into four major periods:

• Naevius, Ennius, Lucilius etc	c240 to c100 BC
• Lucretius, Catullus (last age of the Republic before Civil War between Caesar and Pompey)	c100 BC to c50 BC
• The Augustan age	27 BC-AD 14
• The whole period of Empire after Augustus	Last Roman Emperor deposed in AD 476

It is a curious fact that Latin has no native word which means either 'poet' or 'poem'. *Vates* is, properly, a seer; *poeta* is a later borrowing from Greek; *carmen* means a formula (whether or not it is in verse). Within this grouping come charms, proverbs, prophecies, prayers and other compositions of brevity. In Latin, as in other languages, these tend to be rhythmic even if not actually in verse. There was also a form of popular poetry called *satura* which was sometimes sung.

Satire

Satura (satire) had existed from early times in Italy. Of all the types of Roman poetry, satire was least indebted to the works of the Greeks. As a form it was so free and personal that its character changed with each satirist. The name *satura* comes from *satur*, 'full', indicating a miscellany or medley: full of different things. A plausible modern suggestion is that the form comes from the Etruscan *satir*, 'speech'. Satire certainly had a distinctly Etruscan origin and was essentially speech. *Saturae* were in verse of differing kinds. Some were in dialogue, others were sung, and the pieces could be dramatic in character.

The greatest of the Roman satiric poets was Decimus Junius Juvenalis, now known as Juvenal (c60 to c140). Like Martial, who knew him well, he was miserably poor. The chief impetus to his satire seems to have been a bitter sense of failure and injustice. He was a Roman lawyer and satirist of Roman vices under the Empire, who early in his career wrote a lampoon which ruined him. Here are three typically cynical statements:

Everything at Rome has its price.

★

Honesty is commended – and starves.

★

Death alone discloses how very small are the puny bodies of men.

In contrast, here is an important statement about a positive attitude to death:

> Your prayer must be for a sound mind in a sound body. Pray for a bold spirit, free from all dread of death; one that reckons the closing scene of life among Nature's kindly boons.
>
> Translations by Lewis Evans

Next a comment about the uneasy relationship between acquisitiveness and an accompanying compromise of morals:

> There is nothing a woman does not allow herself, nothing she thinks shameful, when she has surrounded her neck with green jewels and attached great pendants to her stretched ears.

One of Juvenal's vivid remarks is spoken with the voice of experience:

> What groin does not an alluring, dissolute voice stimulate? It has fingers.

In this next statement, Juvenal makes a profound and useful observation:

> If we have wise foresight, thou, Fortune, hast no divinity. It is we that make thee a deity, and place thy throne in heaven.
>
> Translations by Richard Jenkyns

Juvenal's style was admired and imitated by Boccacio and Byron among others.

Five books containing 16 satires are still extant, and in Juvenal Roman literature has one of its more original, imaginative, and penetrative poetic minds.

Epigram

This poetic form is examined in some depth in Chapter 13 – Poetry's Figurative Element.

The word *epigram*, which is of Greek origin, means 'inscription' and is, invariably, a metrical inscription. During about a thousand years of development the poetic epigram never wholly lost its original meaning; its popularity carried it through four phases: Archaic, Hellenistic, Graeco-Roman, and Byzantine.

By the nature of the form, which began with inscriptions on votive offerings, tombs, and occasionally signposts, we have only a meagre record of this skilful use of language and comment. There is nothing extant by which to estimate the literary worth of Marsus, Pedo and Gaetulicus, who were acknowledged by Martial to be his models. We are fortunate, however, in having examples of work by Martial himself and Catullus.

Marcus Valerius Martialis, now commonly called **Martial**, was born in Spain in about AD 40, at Bibilis near Saragossa. Apparently, he preferred to shift for himself rather than seek gainful employment or recognition from the schools, government, or law-courts of his day. He did, however, win popularity, patronage, and a name which to this day is still synonymous with the epigram.

Soon after AD 98 Martial left Rome and returned to Spain to live at leisure near his native Bibilis, as is described by Palmer Bovie (1963), 'on a country estate provided for him by a sympathetic duenna in whom Roman sensibility combined with the liberal generosity of a provincial grandee.' Of this lady, Martial wrote:

> Who would think, Marcella, that you were a burgess of iron-tempering Salo,* that you were born in my native land? So rare, so sweet is your quality! The Palatine will declare, should it but hear you once, that you are its own ... You bid my longing for the Queen City be allayed: you by yourself make a Rome for me!
>
> Book XII, Number xxi, translated by Walter C.A. Ker

He was by turns scathing, tender, obscene, ironic; but although he could be wounding, he would often deliver his barbs with a genial malice. Here is an example of Martial's sexual humour:

> If from the baths you hear a loud applause
> Know that it's Maron's 'yard' that is the cause.
>
> Based on a translation by James Michie

Although Martial used no rhyme, some translators have introduced it because, in English, it conveys wit more readily:

> You see that fellow with the shaggy hair,
> Ranting about old heroes and their might,
> Whose gloomy scowl gives all the girls a scare?
> Don't go by looks – he was a bride last night.
>
> Based on a translation by Rolfe Humphries

> What good's a farm so far from anywhere?
> One thing, at least. I don't see Linus there.
>
> Translated by Rolfe Humphries

* Diminutive of Salonis

If you are poor, you'll always be that way;
Only the rich get richer in our day.
One who gives presents to a rich old man,
You for instance, Gaurus – do not doubt it –
Is telling you as plainly as he can.
Please drop dead and hurry up about it.

Translated by Rolfe Humphries

Here, to conclude, is the assessment of Pliny the Younger in a letter to Cornelius Priscus:

> I have just heard of the death of poor Martial, which much concerns me. He was a man of acute genius, and his writings abound in both wit and satire, combined equally with candour. When he left Rome I complimented him by a present to defray the charges of his journey, in return for the little poem he had written about me.

The eleven-line poem (which Pliny had memorized) began:

Go wanton Muse, but go with care,
Nor meet, ill-tim'd, my Pliny's ear.
He, by sage Minerva taught,
Gives the day to studious thought,
And plans that eloquence divine,
Which shall to future ages shine,
And rival, wond'rous Tully,* thine.

Translated by Rolfe Humphries

Fables

Popular stories, parables and fables have always been extensively circulated among peoples of widely differing civilizations. In fables, the story-teller invents adventures for talking animals and birds, which express and communicate motives, emotions, and behaviour that serve as models for human beings, teaching simple wisdom. There are no fables in the Homeric poems, but a few occur in Greek poetry as early as the 8th or 7th centuries BC. Hesiod has a story of a hawk and a nightingale in his *Works and Days*.

The name inseparable from the genre of fables is **Aesop**, the reputed author of *Aesop's Fables*. He is said to have lived about 620-560 BC and to have been born a slave. Although he created many new stories, a number of the fables in his collection have since been traced to earlier sources.

The first extant collection of fables in Latin verse was made by **Phaedrus**, a Roman poet who lived early in the 1st century AD. He was born a slave in Macedonia but lived most of his life at Rome, where he became a freedman of the emperor Augustus. Many of the fables were based on earlier Greek versions but some are Phaedrus' own creations.

* 'Tully' is Cicero Marcus Tullius (106-43 BC), the great Roman orator, philosopher, and statesman.

Most of these attractive stories are simple, concise, and effective; improving tales with a lively charm, characteristic of the genre.

About the year AD 400 the Roman **Avianus** composed 42 fables in Latin verse. Although the work was of poor quality, commentaries and quotes from it indicate that it was popular.

Centuries later, in Europe, French and English versions were to perpetuate these stories.

Drama

Whereas in Athens, the winning *protagonist* (leading actor) was something of a national hero, the Romans generally had little respect for the acting profession. Their word for a company of actors was *grex* – which also means 'a flock of sheep'. The producer, who was called *dominus gregis* or 'master of the flock', was also usually the chief actor.

Playwrights did not have an easy time with Roman audiences, who were a mixture of citizens and slaves, women and children. If a popular rival attraction occurred at the time a play was about to be presented, it had to take its chance along with jugglers, acrobats, boxers and the rest. The crowds knew parts of popular plays so well that on one occasion, when an actor missed his cue, it is reported that twelve hundred voices chorused the words!

The Romans enjoyed rhetoric and spectacle; they also had a keen appreciation of satire and repartee. These features were prominent in their drama. (*Drama*, from the Greek *drama*, means 'a deed; action performed on the stage', so it includes every type of stage presentation.)

Tragedy

It has been said of the Roman writers of tragedy that to achieve dignity, they sacrificed simplicity – as if a favourable judgement depended upon the weightiness of their lines! This criticism certainly applied to the outstanding Roman tragedian **Seneca** (?4 BC-AD 65). The plays were widely read and greatly admired, both in his lifetime and long afterwards, but they do exhibit a certain ponderousness. Here is a line from *Thyestes*, ii, chorus:

> On him does death lie heavily who, but too well known to all, dies to himself unknown.
>
> Translated by Miller

Seneca was a lawyer and an influential councillor of Nero in the early years of his power. Later Nero turned against him; the Emperor finally accused him of complicity in the conspiracy of Piso and by order of Nero he took his own life. His most important works are philosophic essays, but he was also the author of nine tragedies. These are marked by violence, bloodshed, bombast, and characters of little individuality or differentiation. Like many aristocratic Romans, Seneca despised the theatre as it then was. He therefore wrote his plays to be read aloud for selected audiences, not for the stage.

Seneca wrote plays which were reputed to have caused the old Roman drama to degenerate into mannerism and epigram. Even so, his work is cited by Quintilian and Martial as 'a case where a small output conferred ample fame'. Martial's apparent approval of Seneca's work might have been the frequency with which, amid the heavy verbiage, appear such epigrammatic morsels as:

> He who is alarmed at empty fears, deserves to suffer from real ones.
>
> Fortune favours the bold, but she tramples on the coward.

There is a philosopher's realism about the line:

> It is already a matter of necessity for you to bear what
> Fortune has marked out for you.

In the following, there is an unexpected delicacy:

> A placid sleep spirited away the old man's existence.

Seneca's plays had a strong influence on the tragic drama of Italy, France, and, especially, Elizabethan England.

Naevius wrote seven tragedies of which only fragments survive. **Ennius** translated many of Euripides' especially the *Hecuba* and the *Medea*.

Undoubtedly it was comedy which proved to be the enduring strength of Roman dramatic literature in satire, epigrams, and plays.

Comedy

The era in which Roman epic and tragic poetry thrived was also the time when Roman comedy was popular. The prominent poet-playwrights in this genre were Naevius, Plautus, Caecilius and Terence.

Naevius was born c270 BC. He was spirited and outspoken – for which he was first imprisoned, then exiled. He was chiefly valued by his contemporaries for his *Punic War*, an account of the campaign in which he served. In the epitaph which he is said to have composed for himself, Naevius declares that since *he* is dead they have forgotten how to speak Latin at Rome:

> If deities immortal their tears for men might shed,
> Our native Latin Muses would weep for Naevius dead;
> For since we laid our poet in Hades' treasure-store,
> The true old Latin language is heard in Rome no more.

Only fragments of his comedies remain, but even in these there are many puns and double meanings:

> I don't want to return her love … I want it available to me, for always.

Many such lines of his were reproduced by his successor, Plautus.

Naevius was an outspoken political critic. His celebrated attack on the Metelli and their consulship was veiled but evident in a verse from one of his comedies:

Fato Metelli Romae fiunt consules.
By Fate the Metelli are made consuls at Rome.

With its ambiguous word *fate*, suggesting 'by chance' or 'to the misfortune (of Rome)', this injudicious remark was met by Metellus, consul of 206 BC:

Dabunt malum Metelli Naevio poetae.
The Metelli will give misfortune to the poet Naevius.

The adversity threatened by Metellus resulted in Naevius being cast into prison. A recurring note of independence and liberty keeps appearing in his plays:

We will speak with the tongues of freedom at the feast of Freedom's god.

I have always prized Freedom far above wealth.

His plays contain lines which echo his own reputation for outspokenness:

I hate folk who mutter: say plainly what you mean.

'Naevius had', as W. Beare (1950) put it, 'taken the first steps towards creating a new drama which would deal with the vital interests of the Roman people; but the heavy hand of the State was to confine Latin playwrights to frivolous or foreign themes.'

Plautus (?254–184 BC) translated works from the Greek New Comedy, never hesitating to augment or extend where he thought fit, and inserting frequent puns and topical allusions. The principal ground for his reputation was his skilled use of language. For instance, he fully exploited Latin for terms of endearment and abuse, producing lively dialogue and clever repartee. Shakespeare and Molière (and other English and European playwrights) adapted his plays or modelled their own upon his.

Here are some exchanges from his plays:

GRIPUS: Then you are a beggar?
LABRAX: You have touched the point with a needle. *Rudens*

MEGADORUS: Oh, your words rattle round my poor bones,
And shatter my skull. Sister dear, you speak stones!
Adularia: The Pot of Gold

ENCLIO (*aside*): All these promises mean something; he is gaping for my gold.
Stones in one hand, bread in t'other! no! I'm not to be cajoled!

> I will never trust a rich man when he is so monstrously civil; though he strokes you down so gently, he would send you to the devil. *Ibid.*

> You'd prove truth itself a liar ... *Captivi*

Finally, his epilogue from the same play:

> Gentlemen, this play's been written on the lines of modesty;
> Here are found no wiles of women, no gay lovers' gallantry;
> Here are no affiliations, and no tricks for getting gold;
> No young lover buys his mistress whilst his father is cajoled.
> It's not often nowadays that plays are written of this kind,
> In which good folk are made better. Now then, if it be your mind,
> And we've pleased you and not bored you, kindly undertake our cause,
> And modestly award the prize with heartiest applause. *Ibid.*

Translations by E.H. Sugden

Terence (?195-159 BC) was a slave from Africa, educated by his master Terentius Lucanus, and freed. He enjoyed noble society, and his daughter married a patrician. He was considered by Julius Caesar to be a polished dramatist of exemplary style. Terence was also valued for the urbane and humanitarian style of his plays. Although criticized for lack of humour in his work, he was deeply interested in the complexities of life and the contrasts to be found in human character.

We cannot fail to be struck by the genius displayed by a young foreigner who was able so to absorb the spirit of his adopted language as to rank among its purest exponents. Although his plays draw heavily on Greek sources for their plots, there is originality in Terence's subtlety of plot development, his enlargement of character, and his economy of dialogue. He avoided the coarser fun which would have won easy popularity with his audience. He was curiously tender in his treatment of courtesans in his plays. Above all, he preferred to be true to life rather than follow rigidly the conventions of the comic stage and he writes more like a philosopher than a comic playwright.

Here are some morsels and lines from his plays:

> It is my view that the most important thing in life is never to have too much of anything. *Andria* (Woman of Andros)

> The quarrels of lovers are the renewal of love. *Ibid.*

> I am a man. Nothing human is a matter of indifference to me. *Heauton Timorumenos*

> *Fortis fortuna adiuvat* – Fortune aids the brave. *Phormio*

> So many men, so many opinions; to each, his own is law. *Ibid.*

Translations by William Ritchie

Briefly, in passing, mention must be made of Statius **Caecilius**, who died in 168 BC. Not Roman but an Insubrian Gaul, he was a manumitted slave or freedman. His work was praised by contemporaries for the emotional power of the writing and for the structure of the plots, despite the fact that they were largely derived. According to both Varro and Gellius (quoting Volcacius Sedigitus), the ancients rated Caecilius highly – above or equal to Terence. Unfortunately none of his plays survives but fragments indicate that he had a broad sense of fun reminiscent of Plautus.

The End of Roman Theatre

Under the emperors theatre thrived; the splendid stone buildings were often full. However, with the spread of Christianity throughout the Empire, theatre-going was heavily criticized as immoral, and attendances declined. In the 6th century Justinian the Christian emperor closed the theatres – he was married to Theodora, a mime actress whose stage disrobing act had been very popular. The fall of the Roman Empire led to the period in the arts known as the Dark Ages.

Latin and Roman Poets

During the period in which Latin and Roman poetry developed, the more notable lyric and epic poets were: Ennius, Lucretius, Catullus, Horace, Virgil, Tibullus, Propertius, Ovid.

It has been said that Roman poetry without Quintus **Ennius** would be a column wanting a base; in a more lively metaphor, he has been called the Chaucer of Roman literature by Professor H.J. Rose (1936). He was the earliest of the great epic poets of Rome (c239-169 BC) and was the pre-eminent founder of Latin literature. The poet could speak his native Oscan, Greek and Latin and, as a man of Hellenic culture, adapted many Greek dramas into Latin plays. His favourite model was Euripides. His epic chronicles, *Annales* (Annals), occupied his last 20 years and for the Romans the language in these Annals was consecrated and magical. Here, for the first time, a Greek metrical scheme is used to write Latin verse. The work, in 18 books, is a poetical history of Rome from its legendary beginning to the time of the author. It was the starting point of the national literature and foreshadowed its development. A typical nationalistic thought expressed in the *Annals* and, therefore, valued by his fellow countrymen is:

> The Roman state endures by its ancient customs and its manhood.

Although Ennius was known to later Romans as the father of Roman poetry, almost all his works are lost.

The Republic – Final Phase

Lucretius and **Catullus** were regarded by their contemporaries as the greatest poets of the last age of the Republic. They also best represent the poetry of that time to modern readers.

Lucretius (99-55 BC), whose full name was Titus Lucretius Carus, was a Roman philosophical poet. He was the celebrated author of the unfinished *De Rerum Natura* (*On the Nature of Things*), a didactic poem in six books containing a complete cosmology based on the philosophy of Democritus and Epicurus. He had a fierce dislike of conventional superstition, a strong predisposition for intellectual liberty, and a deep sense of awe in the presence of nature.

Beginning with an invocation to Venus, the creative power of nature, this is how Lucretius opens his great poem *On the Nature of Things*:

BOOK I

Mother of Aeneas's sons, joy of men and gods, Venus the life-giver, who beneath the gliding stars of heaven fillest with life the sea that carries the ships and the land that bears the crops; for thanks to thee every tribe of living things is conceived, and comes forth to look upon the light of the sun. Thou, goddess, thou dost turn to flight the winds and the clouds of heaven, thou at thy coming; for thee earth, the quaint artificer, puts forth her sweet-scented flowers; for thee the levels of ocean smile, and the sky, its anger past, gleams with spreading light. For when once the face of the spring day is revealed and the teeming breeze of the west wind is loosed from prison and blows strong, first the birds in high heaven herald thee, goddess, and thine approach, their hearts thrilled with thy might. Then the tame beasts grow wild and bound over the fat pastures, and swim the racing rivers; so surely enchained by thy charm each follows thee in hot desire whither thou goest before to lead him on.

Translated by Cyril Bailey

Roman Lyricism

Gaius Valerius **Catullus** lived from about 84-54 BC and is the first eminent name in the history of Roman lyricism. Of the Roman poets who succeed him in lyricism – Horace, Tibullus, Propertius and Ovid – no one else is quite so expressive of personal feeling.

Among his works are 25 short poems describing the course of his relationship with a woman he calls Lesbia. Catullus loved her and eventually, after a long and painful struggle with himself, broke away from her spell. The poems describe a range of emotions and reactions, from the ecstasy of its early stages to the disillusionment and despair of its final phase. The clarity of his style perfectly complements the direct expression of emotion. The poems, although personal, are the vehicles of experiences we recognize as universal. In them, Catullus switches with ease from sadness to joy; from the beautiful to the sordid; from intense and charming lyrics to short poems and savage epigrams. He died while still a young man in the Rome of Cicero, Pompey and Caesar, after a life of creativity and amatory adventures. For Catullus, the emotion of love was life itself:

51

He is changed to a god he who looks on her,
godlike he shines when he's seated beside her,
immortal joy to gaze and hear the fall of her sweet laughter.

All of my senses are lost and confounded;
Lesbia rises before me and trembling
I sink into earth and swift dissolution seizes my body.

Limbs are pierced with fire and the heavy tongue fails,
ears resound with noise of distant storms shaking
this earth, eyes gaze on stars that fall forever into deep midnight.

109

My life, my love, you say our love will last forever;
O gods remember
her pledge, convert the words of her avowal into a prophecy.
Now let her blood speak, let sincerity govern each syllable fallen
from her lips, so that the long years of our lives shall be
a contract of true love inviolate
against time itself, a symbol of eternity.

Translations by courtesy of Thames & Hudson

Quintus Horatius Flaccus (**Horace**) lived from 65-8 BC. He was a Roman lyric poet and satirist who was educated in Rome and Athens. Among his works are two books of satires, one book of epodes (*see* Glossary), four books of odes, two books of epistles and *Ars Poetica* (a letter dealing with the principles of poetic composition, especially with the drama).

Two thousand years have not dimmed the freshness, vigour, delicacy, and charm of the Odes of Horace. It is not what Horace says, but the way he says it, which carries the charm. He takes the thin, and some might say barren, Latin vocabulary and by his skill conjures images – as in making use of proper names to manifest pictures; for example, ointment is described as Achaemenian nard, the laurel as Apolline. By bringing Greek metrical measures across into Latin, he creates a variety of musical effects hitherto not known in Latin poetry. As a master of lyric form Horace is unexcelled among Roman Poets; in content many of his Odes represent the highest order of poetry.

Whenever he deals with moral law in his poetry, Horace speaks with conviction and sincerity, displaying significant depths of reason and reflection. On the other hand, his treatment of love (the favourite subject of his lyric poet contemporaries) appears to lack passion and has led some later critics to challenge his eminence as a poet. Here (to refute that charge and demonstrate his descriptive powers) is the opening of Horace's Ode 25 from Book I. The poet chides Lydia and bids her consider the future, especially as her charms are already faded:

Less often now do riotous youths
Shake your shutters with repeated blows;
No longer do they steal your slumbers
from you; and the door that once
right willingly moved on its hinges
now hugs its threshold. Less and
less often you hear such plaints
as: 'sleep you, Lydia, while I,
your lover true, die throughout the
livelong night?' Your turn will come,
and you, a hag forlorn in deserted
alley, will weep o'er your lovers'
disdain …

Based on a translation by C.E. Bennett

Horace's critical censure at the appropriation of land by the rich is the subject of Ode 15 in Book II:

Soon I foresee few acres for harrowing
Left, once the rich men's villas have seized the land;
Fishponds that outdo Lake Lucrinus
Everywhere; bachelor plane trees ousting

Vine-loving elms; thick myrtle-woods, violet-beds,
All kinds of rare blooms tickling the sense of smell,
Perfumes to drown those olive orchards
Nursed in the past for a farmer's profit;

Quaint garden-screens, too, woven of laurel-boughs
To parry sunstroke. Romulus never urged
This style of life; rough-bearded Cato
Would have detested the modern fashions.

Small private wealth, large communal property –
So ran the rule then.

Translated by James Michie

Ode 7 of Book IV is poetically beautiful, but profoundly melancholy. Horace notes that the changing seasons come and go but return again, whereas man, when he departs, ends in dust and shadow:

Now are the snows all fled, and the grass returns to the fields,
    Tresses return to trees;
Earth to her annual changes (her beautiful changes) yields;
    The bed of the river receives
The chastened floods. The nymphs and their sisters with naked grace
    Dare lead the dance of spring.
Nothing immortal: so warns the year and kindly day
    Which time is ravishing.
Frosts melt, and hard on the heels of spring will summer tread,
    Which soon, too soon, must die.
Autumn will all of her lavish and fruit-laden bounty spread
    Where soon dull winter will lie.

Translated by Helen Rowe Henze

Despite the superb work of scholars, the Odes remain doggedly difficult to translate. Their architectural perfection, elusive humour, and bewildering and subtle shifts of mood have defied attempts to catch their quality. Perhaps that is as it should be: the essential spirit is in the original, like an absolute that no relative representation can simulate or hold.

Virgil

The Greeks were not alone in having a language capable of expressing higher levels of human thought and aspiration. Latin is an inflected and syntactically complex language, and its written form was gradually developed until it could handle, with equal power, Cicero's rhetoric and philosophy, Martial's epigrams and Virgil's subtle poetry.

Few poets have for so long received the unbroken esteem and affection of humanity as Publius Vergilius Maro, whom we know as Virgil (70-19 BC). His voice expressed a spirit of hope and gladness in the Roman world, not least because by resonance he secured a connection retrospectively with the era of the heroic Greeks. There is the obvious link through his epic poem, the *Aeneid*, but T.S. Eliot also ascribes to him a determining role in the creation and refinement of Augustan 'classicism', reflecting the classical norms of Periclean Athens. Virgil is perhaps the most significant poet of ancient Rome, a superb writer of epic, didactic, and idyllic poetry. In his *Aeneid*, with its splendour of diction and grandeur of rhythm, he demonstrates his consummate mastery of language. It is a measure of his literary greatness that much of the later Latin literature, prose as well as poetry, contains countless Virgilian quotations, adaptations and allusions – just as the English literature of the past 300 years is replete with Shakespearean references.

In the *Aeneid*, at the very opening of his subject, Virgil reveals that his purpose is to show the origin 'of the long glories of majestic Rome'. The epic poetic architecture of the *Aeneid*, with its embellishment augmenting the structural detail, was considered a work which resonated with the spirit of the Roman Empire. It was dubbed the *Imperial Poem* and fostered as a great national work. Copies rapidly proliferated, and Virgil's fame and popularity were firmly established during his own lifetime.

For readers without Latin some lines from the *Aeneid* will be offered in English prose translations which avoid certain monotonies that, despite Virgil's intricate and consummate art, managed to creep into the original. Two Victorian translators of the works of Virgil, James Lonsdale and Samuel Lee (1874), worked valiantly to retain a sense of rhythm in the sentence structure; and where in the Latin the sound of the words is an echo of the sense (as frequently occurs in Virgil), they attempt to produce the same result in English.

BOOK IV

393–449. Aeneas continues to prepare his fleet for the voyage. Dido again and again implores him to stay. She begs her sister to beseech him to remain at least for a short time, but Anna's intreaties are fruitless.

But pious Aeneas, though he longs to soothe and comfort her sorrow, and to divert her pain by his words, often sighing, and staggered in resolution by strong love, nevertheless begins to execute the commands of heaven, and revisits his fleet. Then indeed the Trojans set themselves to the work, and launch the lofty ships all along the shore. The keel is careened and floated, and they bring leafy oars, and unshaped timber from the forests, in their eagerness for flight. You might observe them in the act of departing, and flocking out from all quarters of the city. Even as when ants, mindful of the winter, ravage a huge heap of corn, and store it up in their abode, the black troop moves across the plains, and over the grass they incessantly carry in the plunder along the narrow way; some with all their force push on with their shoulders mighty grains of corn, some keep the line together, and punish the slothful; the whole path is alive with the work. What was then your feeling, Dido, when you discerned such a sight, or what sighs did you heave, when from the height of your citadel you saw before you the long line of the shore full of life, and beheld the whole surface of the sea beneath your eyes made tumultuous with such loud clamours? Wicked love, what is there to which you do not drive the hearts of men? She is driven to resort again to tears, again to strive to win him by intreaty, and humbly to surrender her pride to love, lest she leave any course untried, and so die in vain.

When Helenus gave Aeneas instructions on the safest sea route to Italy, he also gave firm rules for Aeneas' consultation with the Sibyl at Cumae, rules which Virgil has Aeneas recall when he appears at the grotto of Apollo's prophetess. This time, the translation is by C. Day-Lewis (1904-72):

BOOK III

Now when you are safely there, close to the city of Cumae
And the haunted lake Avernus deep in a soughing wood,
You will find an ecstatic, a seeress, who in her antrum
communicates
Destiny, committing to leaves the mystic messages.
Whatever runes that virgin has written upon the leaves
She files away in her cave, arranged in the right order.
There they remain untouched, just as she put them away:
But suppose that the hinge turns and a light draught blows
through the door,
Stirs the frail leaves and shuffles them, never thereafter cares she
To catch them as they flutter about the cave, to restore
Their positions or reassemble their runes; so men who have
come to
Consult the Sibyl depart no wiser, hating the place.
Here you must not grudge time spent, although it delays you –
However impatient your friends may grow, however fine
The weather for sailing, however strong the sea calls you –
Time spent in approaching the Sibyl, asking an oracle of her,
Praying that she will graciously open her mouth and prophesy.

Lines 441-57

The *Georgics* earned Virgil the name 'prince of didactic poets'. The great practicality of the verses is enhanced by their consistent quality as poetry. In these delightful treatises on agriculture, he imparts so much of his own enthusiasm that our thoughts enlarge with his imagery and our emotions stir with his warmth. Virgil wrote the *Georgics* at the urging of his patron Maecenas in order to rekindle in the hearts of the Romans a love for their primary source of wealth, agriculture – which at that time had seemed in peril of decline.

Each of Virgil's many translators draws out a particular strength or nuance of the poet's thought. The following translation reaches the bedrock of his profound but uncomplicated philosophy:

> Happy is the man, who, studying nature's laws,
> Through known effects can find the secret cause –
>
> His mind possessing in a quiet state,
> Fearless of Fortune, and resigned to Fate!
>
> *Georgics*, Book II, Translated by Dryden

For comparison, these same lines are rendered by C. Day-Lewis, who condenses the text, but in doing so unfortunately diminishes the philosophy:

> Lucky is he who can learn the roots of the universe,
> Has mastered all his fears and fate's intransigence.

The *Aeneid* combines three elements: the exaltation of Augustus; the legendary story of Rome's origin; and the evocation of the luminaries and key events in Roman history. Above all is the theme *pius Aeneas*: Aeneas is the embodiment of the man of duty – duty to God and duty to man. If Virgil had a motto of his own it was perhaps: *His will is our peace.*

In the *Eclogues* Virgil describes country life but is using pastoral poetry simply as a device to disguise his own personality and to clothe in poetic allegory incidents and circumstances of his own day. Although the pastoral genre, of which Virgil was the originator, has been considered unreal (principally because of the excesses of later writers), the *Eclogues* continue to be read for their distinctive vitality and characteristic charm.

There are, in *Eclogue* IV, some lines which have brought Virgil's reputation forward, through time, to our present day. This is because they bear an uncanny resemblance to prophecies in the *Old Testament*, particularly those of Isaiah which foretold the coming of the Messiah. The relevant lines are summarized in prose:

> Let my pastoral song rise higher and be worthy of Pollio.* In his consulship the golden age shall come round again and a godlike child be born, who shall rule a world of universal peace and innocence. Nature will

* Gaius Asinius Pollio (76 BC-AD 5) was made Consul in 40 BC. He was himself a poet. In his youth he was an associate of Catullus and his circle; later he enjoyed the friendship of Horace. Pollio suggested to Virgil that he should write a *carmen bucolicum*.

do homage to the infant child, and serpents and poisonous herbs will disappear.

Eclogue IV, Virgil
Translated by James Lonsdale and Samuel Lee (1894)

Subsequently, when the Roman Empire had become the Holy Roman Empire, these seemingly prescient lines caused Virgil to be regarded by the medieval church as a prophet among the Gentiles. Moreover, monks in the Middle Ages were allowed to read Virgil, a pagan writer, not least because his serene waves of hexameters were considered a model of good Latin. It was not surprising, therefore, that it was he who was chosen by one of the greatest poets of the Middle Ages, Dante, to be his guide through the circles of *Hell* and the terraces of *Purgatory* in *The Divine Comedy*.

With masterly succinctness his epitaph expresses the essentials of his life:

Mantua begat me, but Calabria
Robbed me of life; now Naples holds my bones;
I sang of pastures, farms and warriors.

In recent years Virgil has become controversial. For T.S. Eliot, the *Aeneid* is the classic of Western society; for Robert Graves, the poet is a negative artist whose influence outweighs his merit. As for Virgil's alleged negativity, the poet saw life as essentially tragic, and the prevailing mood of the poem is one of melancholy and regret for the sadness of human lives and the inevitability of human suffering. As for his being overrated, a succession of great poets (Dante, Tasso, Milton, among others) considered Virgil their master.

Roman Love Poetry

Tibullus and Propertius

Quintilian (rhetorician and teacher of Oratory in Rome, from AD 68) pointed out that some critics rated Propertius first among elegiac poets, although he himself would place Tibullus first and Propertius second. Tibullus and Propertius both wrote love poetry in the same form, the elegiac metre (one hexameter line alternating with a shorter pentameter line). There were similarities of subject: both had a mistress to whom significant passionate poems were addressed. Each mentions a minor woman but is preoccupied with contending for the favours of the principal woman in his life. Each becomes expert at expressing the experience of being in love. Both evoke richly described pastoral imagery – particularly Tibullus. In short, Tibullus is the quiet, clear, craftsmanlike poet; Propertius, one who is daring, difficult, experimental.

Albius **Tibullus** (?54–?18 BC) was a Roman elegiac poet of whose work only two books have come down to us. One sentence, often quoted, poignantly connects us with the man:

BOOK I

Te spectem, suprema mihi cum venerit hora,
Te teneam moriens deficiente manu.
Let me behold thee when my last hour is come,
thee let me hold with my dying hand.

Tibullus is addressing Delia. He goes on:

Thou wilt weep for me, Delia, when I am
laid on the bed that is to burn;
Thou wilt give me kisses mingled with
bitter tears.

★

Do thou hurt not my spirit; but spare
thy loosened hair and spare thy soft cheeks, Delia.
Meantime, while Fate allows, let us
be one in love.

Sextus **Propertius** (born c51 BC) is known for his elegiac verse dealing with the varying phases of ecstasy and disillusionment in love. Many critics have held to the view that he is a love poet of far greater veracity than the other elegiac poets of Augustan Rome. It is as the lover of the beautiful and talented Hostia (the 'Cynthia' of the poems) that he is celebrated. However, his perception and wit do more than present the miseries of love as he exercises his skills of narration and powerful satire. This is how he begins his description of Cynthia's spell over him:

BOOK I

Cynthia began my griefs, when her bright eyes
Took me, then first sex-bitten for her prize.
Love dashed my lordly stare to earth that day:
His foot was on my head, the conqueror's way,
Until he taught me, graceless god, distaste
For a well-ordered life, and girls who're chaste;
And still my year-old madness does not cool,
Though all my prayers find heaven unmerciful.

★

It's fair! – I fled from Cynthia, breaking free;
And now I talk to lonely birds at sea.
Cassiope will never glimpse my sail;
The shore rebuffs me, and no prayers prevail.

★

Would Cynthia's whims have been as hard to bear
(Unfeeling was she, yet a girl so rare)
As the wild shores, wood-fringed, I gaze on here.

★

II

To write of love whence has my impulse sprung?
Whence comes my book, soft-rounding on the tongue?
It's not Apollo, nor Calliope
Sings thus: my lady makes my poetry.
If gay with Coan dyes she walks the town,
A book will issue from her Coan gown.

Here, in Book IV, is how Propertius ends his long poetic statement:

My speech is ended: you that mourn for me
Rise, and as witnesses support my plea,
Till life's reward is given by grateful earth –
Or heaven which sometimes opens wide to work.
May I be found deserving, and pass on
To where my glorious ancestors have gone.

Translated by A.E. Watts

Hostia (Cynthia) was a courtesan, and Propertius was in a doomed relationship, but perhaps he would not have had it otherwise, since it inspired his poetry. Nevertheless, we have his amazing poems, and as with the paintings of Toulouse-Lautrec in a later age, we have on record aspects of their era which lift the human activity – however debased – into an appreciation that arouses our compassion.

And if my strength fail, at least my boldness will be a title of honour; in great enterprises the very 'I would' is enough. Translated by J.S. Phillimore

Ovid

Publius Ovidius Naso was born at Sulmo, a city about 90 miles east of Rome, in 43 BC, the year of the second triumvirate (Augustus, Antony and Lepidus). He knew Tibullus and Propertius well. His works fall naturally into three groups.

- The amatory poems which were the works of his youth; they include the *Heroides*, verse-letters purportedly written by deserted ladies to their former lovers;
- The mythological, which includes the *Metamorphoses*;
- His last works, which were, in effect, laments.

Although the *Heroides* are not works of genius (their language is nearly always artificial, frequently rhetorical, often diffuse), nevertheless they exemplify the engaging kind of art that disarms criticism and wins our interest. Their theme is the universal one of love, and particularly of woman's love; moreover, of woman's love in misfortune. They do not have the realism of the poetry of Tibullus or Catullus and should not be judged as attempts at naturalistic art.

Perhaps the *Heroides* are best enjoyed as adroit and genial treatments of literary themes, imbued with enough human warmth to rouse in the benevolent reader empathy and a sympathetic perception of these people's lives. Figures from Homer and Virgil possess qualities that confer on them the semblance of reality: Penelope is faithful, Briseis forgiving, Dido filled with despair, and Helen vain. The poet has endowed each of his heroines with that most human of qualities, a heart submissive to the power of love.

The *Amores*, *Heroides* and *Ars Amatoria* (*Ars Amoris*) were widely known in the Middle Ages, influencing the convention of courtly love – and the poet Chaucer. These poems were the product of Ovid's late youth and sprightly middle age. He was a little uneasy about them, if we adduce as evidence the contrived frequent expostulations of the Muses exhorting *him* to a loftier use of his talents.

Ovid's major work, the *Metamorphoses*, is a narrative poem recounting classical legends, describing miraculous changes of form and many other events, which occur during a time-span from the creation of the world to the lifetime of Julius Caesar.

Chaucer, Spenser and Shakespeare were influenced by the spirit and the substance of Ovid's work. From the *Metamorphoses*, Shakespeare extracted and parodied the story of Pyramus and Thisbe in *A Midsummer-Night's Dream*. In *The Tempest*, he has Prospero address the forces of magic in a passage strongly reminiscent of Medea's invocation to natural and unnatural powers in the seventh book. Here first are the words of Ovid:

And she raised
Her arms to the stars, three times, and turning thrice,
Thrice sprinkled her head with quick-caught running water,
Thrice cried a wailing call, and knelt, and prayed:
'O Night, most true to mysteries, O stars
Whose gold with the moon's silver shines and follows
The fires of day, O Hecate, triple goddess,
Witness and helper of magic art and charm,
O Earth, provider of the herbs of magic,
O winds, O little breezes, O streams, O mountains,
O lakes, O groves, O gods of the groves, O gods
Of night, come, help me, help me, help me!
You have before this, when I wanted, seen me
Make streams return to their sources, while their banks
Wondered; you have seen me still the angry oceans,
Rouse the calm waters, drive the clouds away
Or marshal them together, exile winds,
Recall them; you have seen me break the fangs
Of serpents with my charms and incantations,
Root up the rocks from the soil, root up the oak-trees,
Move forests, shake the mountains, make earth rumble,
Call ghosts from graveyards.

Translated by Rolfe Humphries (1954)

For comparison, here are Prospero's words from *The Tempest*:

Ye elves of hills, brooks, standing lakes, and groves;
And ye, that on the sands with printless foot
Do chase the ebbing Neptune and do fly him
When he comes back; you demi-puppets, that
By moonshine do the green sour ringlets make
Whereof the ewe not bites; and you, whose pastime
Is to make midnight mushrooms; that rejoice
To hear the solemn curfew; by whose aid, –
Weak masters though ye be – I have bedimm'd
The noontide sun, call'd forth the mutinous winds,
And 'twixt the green sea and the azur'd vault
Set roaring war: to the dread-rattling thunder
Have I given fire and rifted Jove's stout oak
With his own bolt; the strong-bas'd promontory
Have I made shake; and by the spurs pluck'd up
The pine and cedar; graves at my command
Have wak'd their sleepers, op'd, and let them forth
By my so potent art.

Act V, Scene i

With terse economy Ovid, in the *Metamorphoses*, creates many a succinct aphorism, for example: 'Plenty makes me poor.'

Hugh Latimer (c1485-1555) Bishop of Worcester (who was burnt at the stake by Mary Queen of Scots), gave a (seventh) sermon before Edward VI in 1549. It contained a sentence of Ovid's which Latimer himself had translated; it reads like a beautiful proverb:

The drop of rain maketh a hole in the stone, not by violence,
but by oft falling.

Ovid said of the *Metamorphoses*:

And now I have finished the work, which neither the wrath of Jove,
nor fire, nor the sword, nor devouring age shall be able to destroy.

Astrology into Poetry

Marcus **Manilius** is a writer of uncertain date who set himself to explain the whole theory of astrology in Latin verse. He composed five books (which included arithmetic calculations) into hexameters comparable in quality to Ovid's. It has been said of him that, at his best, he reminds us of Lucretius, but one critic rather carpingly said of his style that 'the language is inexcusably crabbed and the metre has the regular and monotonous flow of the age'. He is not a great poet but it is perhaps significant that A.E. Housman, the classical scholar and poet, produced a text and commentary in five volumes, 1903-30 (with Latin notes). A line of Manilius is inscribed upon Benjamin Franklin's statue:

Eripuit caelo fulmen, mox sceptra tyrannis.
He snatched the thunderbolt from heaven, soon the sceptre from tyrants.

Post-Augustan Poetry

This era of poetry contains a large number of borrowings and many formal pieces of variable merit. It may, therefore, be appropriate simply to make some general remarks about the period and its poetry.

The opinion of scholars on the intrinsic worth and merit of Latin poetry has, over time, undergone a major fluctuation of opinion. From Europe's revival of learning until the end of the 18th century, the poets of ancient Rome – particularly of the Augustan age – were considered exemplars of the literary art. Their work was given to students of higher education for study, translation and imitation; the poetry was extensively quoted by moralists, humourists and essayists. Then gradually, as later poets came to be more fully appreciated and there was greater familiarity with Greek literature, from which so much Roman poetry developed, the earlier excessive deference abated. Finally, changes in taste and the attractiveness for scholars of the Greek epic and lyric poets, has led almost to disparagement of the Latin poets. Furthermore, there was an inherent feature of Roman education which had produced a debilitating effect on poetry – the development of rhetoric (the art of oratory). This had become so important to Rome that it was having a detrimental effect on true and accurate expression, as we shall see in the next section.

Quintilian

The Spanish-born rhetorician and teacher of oratory in Rome from AD 68 ruefully compared the ease of expression of the uneducated with the anxious self-criticism inhibiting many of those who had received an elaborate training in the art of speech. Moreover, he noticed that too strong a concentration on the *art of writing* could lead to avoidance of the direct and cogent; a tendency to resort to the far-fetched and stilted. Students should not be altogether blamed for this. One teacher in the time of Augustus, when presented with work he considered too unambiguous and straightforward, would say 'darken it'.

In Quintilian's day it was considered that authors had merit only if their writing required interpretation. This produced its counter-reaction. Augustus himself referred deprecatingly to what he called the 'Asiatic style', that is, 'a flow of words without meaning'. One problem affecting much ancient poetry was the over-use of ornament, particularly the way in which figures of speech were employed. It was widely believed that writing of distinction could be achieved by the adoption of certain tricks of style. This fallacy was compounded by the utterances of rhetoricians whose art had scant regard for truth. As long as a case was being eloquently and effectively made, or a theme was being treated with elegance, distortion or factual inaccuracy were considered unimportant.

Lucan

Marcus Annaeus Lucanus (AD 39-65) was a Roman poet born at Cordova in Spain. His sole extant work is an epic of ten books, *Pharsalia*, which described the Civil War between Caesar and Pompey. For a time he enjoyed Nero's favour, but lost it as his literary reputation grew. Finally, the jealous Nero forbade his public recitals. Lucan subsequently joined a conspiracy against Nero, was betrayed and condemned to death, but committed suicide.

Lucan's narrative poetry, which is relentlessly bleak and ironic over thousands of lines, cannot but seem wearisome. Occasionally he touches felicity with his thought or words:

> The abode of God, too, is, wherever is earth and sea and air, and sky and virtue. Why further do we seek the Gods of heaven? Whatever thou dost behold and whatever thou dost touch, that is Jupiter.
>
> Translated by Bishop Nicholas Ridley (c1500-55)

Lucan offered this further critical advice:

> O luxury, prodigal of wealth, never content with what comes cheaply, and ambitious hunger for foods sought over land and sea, and pride in a smart table, learn how cheaply life may be maintained, and how little nature asks for.
>
> Translated by Richard Jenkyns

The Shift Away from Rome

So ended the great *scena* which some call 'the glory that was Rome'. It was responsible for monsters like Caligula and Nero, but it also produced the enlightened Roman emperor Marcus Aurelius. The peace and prosperity of the Aurelian years were believed by Gibbon to have been the happiest age of the human race. He wrote, 'In the second century of the Christian era, the Empire of Rome comprehended the fairest part of the earth, and the most civilized portion of mankind.' Marcus Aurelius had the eye for detail of a poet:

> We should remark the grace and fascination that there is even in the incidentals of Nature's processes. When a loaf of bread, for instance, is in the oven, cracks appear in it here and there; and these flaws, though not intended in the baking, have a rightness of their own, and sharpen the appetite.
>
> *Meditations*, 2nd century

The rule of Rome in the West was now ended, but the survival of Roman law and the Latin tongue, the Roman Church and the Holy Roman Empire, were to perpetuate the Roman tradition.

In the East the reign of Justinian (AD 527-565), the Eastern Roman emperor in Constantinople, was running its course. The early Christian era had given way to the Byzantine era, but the Christian crusaders on their way to the Holy Land had not yet sacked Constantinople.

Augustine of Hippo had written *The Confessions* (AD 397) and *The City of God* (AD 413 to 426), but what of the state of poetry during this time? The poet-historian searching for evidence of master poets must now turn to Western Europe.

After the exotic flowering of the aesthetic spirit in the civilizations of Greece and Rome, there was a resting period in Europe rather like winter in the natural world: the buds were formed, ready to burst, but a fresh impulse was needed. This waiting time in Europe is often called the Dark Ages, and the impulse awaited was the Italian Renaissance. To see this period in context, it is necessary to consider its relationship with what has gone before and what is to come. Thus far, Classical Greece and its aftermath extended from the beginning of the Classical Period to the Roman sacking of Corinth when Greece became a Roman province (about 480 to 146 BC). The Roman Empire and its demise extended from the founding of Rome to the abdication of the last Western Roman emperor (about 753 BC to AD 476). The Byzantine World stretched from the early Christian era to the capture of Constantinople by the Ottoman Turks (about AD 64 to 1453).

We turn our attention now to Western Europe, which was experiencing the so-called Dark Ages, that period in Europe from the end of the Roman Empire to the beginning of the Middle Ages (early 5th century to about 1200).

4
Poetry in the Shadows

The Dark Ages

LITERATURE, particularly poetry, reflects the events of the culture from which it springs. Such an event was the withdrawal of Roman legions from England to defend Rome from barbarians, in the early 5th century. This left the country exposed to attack by Picts and Scots in the North and Germanic invaders on the East coast. The Angles, Saxons and Jutes drove the Celts back to Wales and Cornwall. In the mid-5th century they founded settlements which developed into the kingdoms of Kent, Sussex, Wessex, East Anglia, Mercia and Northumbria.

From sporadic fighting among the kingdoms Northumbria emerged dominant, and in the late 7th century an outstanding centre of learning was established at Durham with Bede and Alcuin. Bede or Baeda (c672-735) was the pupil of Benedict Biscop of Northumbria, who founded the two famous Benedictine monasteries of Wearmouth and Jarrow. Alcuin of York (735-804) eventually became adviser to Charlemagne and head of his palace school. A native Anglo-Saxon literature developed at Durham, and throughout the 8th century religious poetry flourished in Northumbria.

In due course, Mercia rose to supremacy and towards the end of the 8th century the Danes raided the coasts and, having landed an army, began to settle. This era (5th to 8th century) became known as the Dark Ages and was considered to be a period of intellectual darkness, supposedly characteristic of the time. Not least, the years between the end of the Roman Empire and the beginnings of Provençal song were considered dark simply because we are ignorant of much that took place during that period. As to poetry, very little Old English verse has survived, although at its best it is highly accomplished, with a sober intensity and an epic character.

The Angles and Saxons were of Germanic stock, and their tongue, Anglo-Saxon or Old English, stems from the Germanic group of languages. It was the vernacular of England for seven centuries. A taste of its power may be had from a poetic description of a ruined Roman city, possibly Aquae Sulis (Bath). The Anglo-Saxon poet muses on the long-since dead builders of the city:

Shattered the showershields, roofs ruined,
age under-ate them,
And the wielders and wrights?
Earthgrip holds them – gone, long gone,
fast in gravesgrip while fifty fathers
and sons have passed.

Translated by Michael Alexander

Old English poetry was one of the glories of Europe during the period prior to the Norman Conquest. Here is 'The Wife's Complaint', a fragment of dramatic soliloquy, from *Wulf and Eadwacer* in the Exeter Book. It illustrates the expressive power of the language *before* Chaucer and Shakespeare developed it:

Trouble in the heart now:
I saw the bitterness, the bound mind
of my matched man, mourning-browed,
mirk in his mood, murder in his thoughts.

The harshness of the Dark Ages and early feudal conditions is evident from the surviving literary works. This is rendered all the more stark and vivid by the language in which these works were written. Although Latin remained the language of the Church and the international language of scholars, more and more writers began to use the native or local tongues of Europe. Norman French and Latin influenced Anglo-Saxon (Old English) and transformed it into Middle English. With the growing sense of national identity in all countries, the vernacular came to be used increasingly. In a notable example, the Anglo-Saxon Low German dialect gave its characteristic expression to a major poem – *Beowulf*.

Beowulf

Before the great era of Elizabethan poetry came into being, many developments in the English language had taken place. Moreover, because it had a vernacular literature written in the Anglo-Saxon period, England has the longest continuous literary history of any country in modern Europe. In an examination of the role of the poet in this great literary development, perhaps the work with which to begin is that masterpiece of Old English secular verse, *Beowulf*. It is an Anglo-Saxon epic (c700) of unknown authorship in alliterative verse and heroic style. The story is set in 6th century Denmark (or southern Sweden, as it now is) and tells how the hero, Beowulf, defeats the monster Grendel and his mother, but is himself killed destroying a dragon.

This lively epic poem is preserved in a late 10th century manuscript. It was probably composed, or at least reworked, in the 8th century by a Christian poet sympathetic to pagan ideals of honour and courage. Certain obscurities in the poem are partly the result of an intense compression of style and partly an assumption of knowledge in the hearers which nowadays we do not necessarily have. There is a sense, as with Homer, of being present at the dawning of mankind – as if the human race was just becoming conscious. The poet takes great pride in the inventive skill of the people he describes. There is, as in Homer, a naive and fresh delight in everything made or used by man. It is as though human initiative were a recent and delicious phenomenon; as if the mind were seeing everything anew. In this, as in other Anglo-Saxon poems, there are glimpses of a bleak unfriendly world in which the centre of light and comfort is the high-roofed wooden mead-hall where lord and warriors sit round the central hearth in conversation, drinking and listening to bard and storyteller. The stressed alliterative verse of Anglo-Saxon poetry is clearly the product of an oral court minstrelsy. It was intended to be recited by the *scop*, the itinerant bard and minstrel who frequented the halls of kings and chiefs and who sometimes found continuous service with one master. The word *scop* derives from the Old English meaning 'jester, one who scoffs'. He was in fact a professional entertainer, poet and singer. The *scopas*, as well as being preservers of the Old English oral tradition, composed much of the poetry they recited.

Beowulf divides into two main parts. The first deals with the visit of Beowulf, nephew of King Hygelac of the Geats (the Geats probably occupied what is now southern Sweden), to the court of King Hrothgar of Denmark. The ageing Hrothgar had long been plagued by a man-eating monster, Grendel, who came regularly to the king's great hall of Heorot to prey on his warriors. It was to slay this monster that Beowulf came to Denmark. He fights with and mortally wounds Grendel in Heorot. Grendel's mother, who lives at the bottom of a pool on the moors, comes to take revenge for the death of her son, and Beowulf follows her home and, after a desperate struggle, slays her. He and his companions then leave for home, laden with honours and gifts from the Danish king.

The second part takes place 50 years later, when Beowulf has long been King of the Geats. A dragon guarding a hoard of treasure has been disturbed and has been wreaking slaughter throughout the land. Beowulf, to save his country from the dragon's ravages, undertakes to fight it, and though he succeeds in slaying it, he is mortally wounded. The poem ends with an account of Beowulf's funeral, at which his body is burned on an elaborate pyre, amid the lamentations of his warriors.

The poem is in the unrhymed alliterative verse characteristic of Anglo-Saxon poetry. Its 3,182 lines are divided into 42 *fits* (songs) preceded by an introduction of 52 lines. The following extract, with characteristic realism, reflects the central role of the sea in this epic tale:

> The ship surged forward, and butted the waves in deep waters;
> it drew away from the shores of the Scyldings.
> Then a sail, a great sea-garment, was fastened
> with guys to the mast; the timbers groaned;
> the boat was not blown off its course
> by the stiff sea-breezes. The ship swept
> over the waves; foaming at the bows,

the boat with its well-wrought prow sped
over the waters, until at last the Geats
set eyes on the cliffs of their own country,
the familiar headlands; the vessel pressed forward,
pursued by the wind – it ran up onto dry land.

The harbour guardian hurried down to the shore;
for many days he had scanned the horizon,
anxious to see those dear warriors once more.
He tethered the spacious sea-steed with ropes
(it rode on its painter restlessly)
so that the rolling waves could not wrench it away.
Then Beowulf commanded that the peerless treasures,
the jewels and plated gold, be carried up from the shore.
He had not to go far to find the treasure-giver
Hygelac son of Hrethel, for his house and the hall
for his companions stood quite close to the sea-wall.

Translated by Kevin Crossley-Holland

The poetry has a dignified seriousness, but also tenderness, with an undercurrent of melancholy and fatalism, as in this example:

So the King hardy in war, sat on the headland and from
that place, the Geat's gold-giving friend spake words of
greetings to his hearth-companions. His spirit was sad,
restless to depart; the Fate immeasurably near which was
to wait upon the aged man, to seek the treasure of his
soul, to part asunder life from the body; not for long
after this did the spirit of the prince remain enwrapped
in flesh.

Translated by Kevin Crossley-Holland

On the surface, *Beowulf* is a heroic poem celebrating the exploits of a great warrior whose character and actions are offered as a model of aristocratic virtue. It reflects the ideals of that period we call the Heroic Age, and its resemblance to the *Odyssey* in this respect has often been remarked. The grave courtesy in which men of rank are received and dismissed, the generosity of rulers, the loyalty of retainers, the appetite for fame through deeds of courage and endurance, the solemn boasting of warriors prior to and after performance, the interest in genealogies and pride in a noble heredity – all these aspects are found in both epic poems. *Beowulf* is an important work, being the only surviving epic of the Anglo-Saxon age and the first masterpiece of English literature. It portrays the conflict between good and evil, together with the function of heroism, and is an expression of the Anglo-Saxon imagination and beliefs. It affirms the continuity of the human spirit in a world where everything else is transient.

Some importance attaches to **Caedmon**, who flourished during the late 7th century, since he is considered to be the earliest English Christian poet. He was a herdsman who, according to Bede, was instructed in a dream to sing of 'the beginning of created things'. He obeyed, afterwards writing from memory verses which were previously unknown.

So the Dark Ages gradually gave way to the Middle Ages, where the development of poetry was to receive a powerful fresh impetus.

The Middle Ages

In the year 735 there occurred the death of the Venerable Bede, author of the *Ecclesiastical History of the English People* and other religious writings. In 785 Alcuin wrote his *Sacramentary*. After 814, the Carolingian monasteries adopted the *Rule* of St Benedict. In 1098 the *Song of Roland* was written down after 300 years of oral tradition. The general historical period constituting the context of these and other literary events, is shown in the following figure:

General Historical Events		
Early Middle Ages		
	Era of the Franks	AD 650-
714-741	Charles Martel, grandfather of Charlemagne, becomes first ruler of the Frankish kingdom.	
741-768	Pepin the Short, father of Charlemagne, rules.	-768
	Carolingian Period	768-
768	Charlemagne ascends the Frankish throne.	
800	Charlemagne crowned Holy Roman emperor at Rome.	
814	Death of Charlemagne.	
987-996	Hugh Capet brings about the French termination of Carolingian succession.	1000
	Romanesque Period	1000-
1066	William the Conqueror invades England.	
1096-99	The First Crusade; Christians capture Jerusalem.	-1140
Gothic Period		
1202-4	Fourth Crusade; sack of Constantinople by Crusaders.	
1291	Fall of Acre, last Christian stronghold in the Holy Land.	
1348-67	Universities based on the Paris model are founded at Prague, Vienna and Cracow.	1400

Note: During the 13th century there arose a genre of secular poetry centred on *Goliardic* verse. Bishop Golias was the mythical patron of the Latin poets of the Middle Ages, a figure feted in the lively and often licentious verse of this period for his intemperance and immorality. With his name providing their identity, these poets came to be called Goliards and their poetry Goliardic. The greatest of these medieval authors of satiric and ribald verse in Latin was the Archpoet, whose *Confession of Golias* is considered the most representative poem of the Goliards. It was addressed to the Archbishop of Cologne, and it sums up the pursuits and attitudes of the wandering scholars of the Middle Ages.

From 1267 to 1273, Thomas Aquinas laboured on his *Summa Theologica*, and less than 30 years later (c1303-21), Dante was beginning work on *The Divine Comedy*. From 1385 to 1400 Chaucer was writing *The Canterbury Tales*. This was a span of 200 years during the history of poetry when two acknowledged masterworks of poetry came into being.

The Middle Ages (medieval era) is the period of European history characterized by feudal social and economic organization and the international dominance of the Church. The age had a distinctive culture. In broad terms its time may be said to extend from the fall of the Roman Empire (about 476) to the capture of Constantinople by the Turks (1453). In England the Middle Ages is usually considered to be the period from 409 to 1485. That is, from the Anglo-Saxon *heptarchy* (Greek: 'seven governments'), when (as was mentioned earlier) England was divided into an alliance comprising Kent, Sussex, Wessex, Essex, East Anglia, Mercia and Northumbria, to the accession of Henry VII. It is the earlier part of this period (until about 1200) that is still sometimes referred to, pejoratively, as the Dark Ages.

After the Norman conquest in the 11th century, learned men, courtiers, and the nobility all spoke and wrote either in Latin or in Norman French. Anglo-Saxon fell into disuse as a literary language, with one notable exception, the *Anglo-Saxon Chronicle*. Begun in Alfred's time, perhaps earlier, it is not only the principal work in Anglo-Saxon prose but is believed to be the earliest original prose composition in any medieval popular language. This instance apart, Anglo-Saxon became simply the spoken tongue of the common people. Although it is sometimes referred to as Old English, it is very different from the English language of later times. Only after a long period during which sounds, endings and inflections underwent considerable alteration, together with the enrichment by imported vocabulary from French and Latin, did the language of the people come to be used as a literary medium. Even books on English grammar were in Latin. It was, therefore, not until the 13th century and the second half of the 14th that with Langland and Chaucer the great period of English medieval literature was reached.

Medieval and courtly literature first appeared in France in the course of the 12th century in response to new tastes and attitudes developing in high society. This new approach centred on the spiritual and psychological idea of courtly love (*amour courtois*). According to this widespread convention of the Middle Ages, the knight regarded his lady with deep veneration and unquestioning devotion. It was characterized by an elevated gallantry of conduct and accompanied by exaggerated physical effects such as loss of sleep and appetite, etc, swooning when he was in her presence or brooding over her indifference. It had reached its height at the court of Eleanor of Aquitaine (?1122-1204), and by the time of Guillaume de Lorris, who flourished in the period around 1230, its source-potential for romance had been largely realized.

The Mystery of Allegory

Romance of the Rose

The *Romance of the Rose* (*Roman de la Rose*) is in two parts, each by a different author. **Guillaume de Lorris** was the French poet who wrote the first part, supposedly between 1225 and 1230. This section emphasizes the psychology of chivalric love from an aristocratic point of view, effectively combining the pervading theme of courtly love with allegory, in a style subsequently much imitated.

The word *romance* comes from the Middle English *roma(u)nce*, Old French *romans*, etc, and means 'something written in the popular tongue, not in Latin'. From this developed the notion of 'a tale (of chivalry, etc), a novel'. The poem *Roman de la Rose* consists of over 20,000 lines and is an elaborate allegory on Ovid's *Art of Love*, beneath which can be discerned an accurate depiction of medieval life.

The narrator-poet is accosted by Dame Idleness, who conducts him to the Palace of Pleasure, where he meets Love. She is surrounded by Sweet Looks, Riches, Jollity, Courtesy, Liberality, and Youth, all of whom spend their time in dancing, singing, and other amusements. By this retinue the poet is led to a bed of roses, where he chooses one and attempts to pluck it. At once an arrow from Cupid leaves him swooning on the ground, and he is thereupon borne away from the place and separated from the flower of his choice.

When recovered, he is alone and at once resolves to return to his rose. Welcome accompanies him, but at every turn he is obstructed by Danger, Shameface, Fear and Slander. Reason counsels him to abandon the pursuit, but he refuses. As a result, Pity and Liberality assist him to reach the rose he has selected, and Venus allows him to touch it with his lips. At this point, Slander conjures Jealousy, who seizes Welcome and incarcerates the lover within a stout castle; the key he puts into the keeping of an old hag.

The poet-lover mourns his fate, and at this point the first part of the poem comes to an end.

When viewed with the hind-sight of modern psychology, the *dramatis personae* and sequence of events in this poem convey a worldly understanding of the course of ordinary love-relationships. The whole poem is structured on the evocation of real mental states, operating within an imaginative idealization. Even so, there is in the imagery, a balance of clarity and brightness, together with a delicate particularity, that keeps it just within the frame of human reference:

> Clear was the water, and as cold
> As any well is …
>
> And with that water, which ran so clear,
> My face I wash.

Translated by Charles Muscatine

Jean de Meung or **Jean de Meun** (the pseudonym of Jean Clopinel), was writing around 1270 and he completed the *Romance of the Rose* in what some think of as a totally alien manner. He introduces realistic middle-class attitudes and bitingly satirizes women and the evils of society as he sees them.

In this second part (which is much longer), written about 1280, the same characters appear, but the spirit of the poem is altogether different. The poet's interest is in life as a whole, rather than in the phenomenon of love. He is a satirist and directs his invective especially towards women. The realistic style has long been remarked, as has the anti-feminist and anti-clerical satire. Jean de Meun's work contains copious borrowings from Ovid, the ascetic Church Fathers, and the *fabliaux* (ribald and often obscene stories of the Middle Ages – an important component of the literature of the common people). Together, these elements enable the poet to produce a huge structure of erotic and philosophical poetry. The procedure followed in the poem is the creation of a thin allegorical line of action in which the lover finally obtains the Rose, but the action is interrupted by a series of long didactic monologues from various characters. To take a single illustration, the personification Reason characteristically distinguishes and defines a number of differences in application of love:

- the indisposition of courtly eroticism,
- the loving friendship of others,
- charity as it relates to true justice,
- protective love.

Romaunt of the Rose

It may be of interest to note that a 15th-century English version, the *Romaunt of the Rose*, is often published with Chaucer's works and it is probable that the first 1,700 lines or so *are* by Chaucer. Jean de Meun is a direct textual source for Chaucer, and this influences the English poet's work in very specific places. To take a single example, Chaucer's *The Wife of Bath* has the longest prologue of *The Canterbury Tales*, and the Wife delivers doctrinaire feminist and materialistic principles in full voice and being. Her realism is an extension of Jean de Meun's skilful transformation of a stock figure (the Duenna) into a realistic character with a down-to-earth delivery of tenets and opinions.

Pearl

An important 14th-century manuscript in the British Library contains the mystical, alliterative verse-sequence, *Pearl*. It is one of the great medieval religious poems – an elegy, deeply moving in human terms, and a narrative of enlightenment and consolation. Like so many allegories, it is difficult to interpret and has been the subject of much debate and many theories.

To constitute an *allegory* a poem *must as a whole and with consistency* describe in a metaphorical image an event or process. Moreover, the main narrative and all crucial details should be integral. The poem *Pearl* meets these criteria and in addition contains several minor allegories. Nothing is known of the poem's author, and attempts at identification are unconvincing. However, scholars agree that the sophisticated form and concept of the poem suggest that he was either of the court or subject to its influence.

Pearl laments the death of a child, considered by surmise to be the poet's daughter Margaret. (The French *Marguerite* translates as 'pearl' or 'daisy'.) It describes, through a dream, her happiness in heaven. The pearl and the daisy, both symbolically signifying virginity, recur throughout the poem, and there are allusions to the *Bible* and medieval theology. As a symbol of that which is pure and precious, the pearl appears many times in medieval literature. It almost certainly derives from the celebrated parable of 'the pearl of great price' in the Gospel of Matthew. It is noteworthy that St Aldhelm (c640-709), English abbot and bishop, describes holy maidens as *Christi Margaritae, paradisi gemmae*.

The poem cannot be dated with any precision but was probably written 1360-95; the manuscript date is not later than about 1400. The dialect of the *Pearl* is now generally thought to have belonged to the North West Midlands.

Pearl

I

Perle, plesaunte to prynces paye
To clanly clos in golde so clere,
Oute of oryent, I hardly saye,
Ne proued I neuer her precios pere.
So rounde, so reken in wyche araye,
So smal, so smothe her sydez were,
Quere-so-euer I jugged gemmez gaye,
I sette hyr sengeley in synglere.
Allas! I leste hyr in on erbere;
Purz gresse to grounde hit fro me yot.
I dewyne, fordolked of luf-daungere
Of that pryuy perle wythouten spotte.

Sythen in that spote hit fro me sprange,
Ofte haf I wayted, wyschande that wele,
That wont watz whyle deuoyde my wrange
And heuen my happe and al my hele.
That dotz bot thrych my hertz thrange
My breste in bale bot bolne and bele;
Set thoyght me neuer so swete a sange
As stylle stounde let to me stele.
For sothe ther fleten to me fele,
To thenke hir color so clad in clot.

O moul, thou marrez a myry inele,
My priuy perle wythouten spotte.

This extract, edited by E.V. Gordon, is from the manuscript in the British Library.

Here are the same two stanzas presented in a modern translation by J.R.R. Tolkien, who has striven to retain the rhyme and alliterative schemes of the original:

Pearl of delight that a prince doth please
To grace in gold enclosed so clear,
I vow that from over orient seas
Never proved I any in price her peer.
So round, so radiant ranged by these,
So fine, so smooth did her sides appear
That ever in judging gems that please
Her only alone I deemed as dear.
Alas! I lost her in garden near:
Through grass to the ground from me it shot;
I pine now oppressed by love-wound drear
For that pearl, mine own, without a spot.

Since in that spot it sped from me,
I have looked and longed for that precious thing
That me once was wont from woe to free,
To uplift my lot and healing bring,
But my heart doth hurt now cruelly,
My breast with burning torment sting.
Yet in secret hour came soft to me
The sweetest song I e'er heard sing;
Yea, many a thought in mind did spring
To think that her radiance in clay should rot.
O mould! Thou marrest a lovely thing,
My pearl, mine own, without a spot.

Twenty such stanzas, totalling some 1,200 lines of moving and beautiful poetry, constitute a narrative which incorporates a scriptural vision and provides a means for insight into higher truths. As poetry, it is considered by many to be the equal of Chaucer.

Sir Gawain and the Green Knight

In the 14th century an unknown medieval poet, thought to be a contemporary of Chaucer, wrote an unusual poem called *Sir Gawain and the Green Knight*. Gawain's name may be derived from the Welsh *Gwallt-advwyn*, 'of the bright hair' or 'of the splendid hair', reinforcing a pagan mythological link between Gawain and the sun. It is a weird romance, relating how Gawain beheads the Green Knight in single combat, having promised to meet him after an interval of 12 months at the Green Chapel. During that period Gawain has been severely tested by the sexual allure of the Green Knight's wife. This occurs in the long Third Part, where hunting scenes and the temptations are interspersed. By this constructional device the poet keeps the three main characters in view and interacting. During three vital days the scenes in the castle and those out in the hunting field are connected by the Exchange of Winnings (a ritual bargain that each would give the other whatever he acquired each day). The gains of the chase diminish as those of Gawain increase and the peril of his testing mounts. His faithfulness to the knightly vow of chastity contributes to his ultimate success in combat. The following extract indicates the nature of the temptation the knight has to contend with:

> While the hende knight at home holsumly sleeps
> Withinne the comly cortaynes on the colde morn.
> Bot the lady for luf let not to slepe,
> Ne the purpose to payre that pyght in hir hert,
> Bot ros hir up radly, rayked hir thider
> In a mery mantyle mete to the erthe,
> That was furred ful fyne with felles wel pured;
> No houve good on hir hed, bot the hawer stones
> Trased aboute hir tressour by twenty in clusters;
> Hir thryven face and hir throte throwen all naked,
> Hir brest bare before and bihinde eke.
> She comes withinne the chamber dor and closes hit hir after,
>
> Wayves up a wyndow and on the wye calles,
> And radly thus rehayted him with hir rich wordes,
> With chere:
> 'A! mon, how may thou slepe,
> This morning is so clere!'
> He was in droupying depe,
> Bot then he con hir here.
> The lady lovely come laghande swete,
> Fel over his fayr face and fetly him kyssed.
> He welcomes hir worthily with a wale chere;
> He sey hir so glorious and gayly atyred,
> So faultles of hir fetures and of so fyne hewes,
> Wight wallande joy warmed his hert.
> With smothe smylyng and smolt thay smeten into mirthe,
> That all was blysse and bonchef that brek hem bitwene
> And wynne.
> Thay laused wordes good,
> Much wele then was therinne;
> Grete peryl bitwene hem stode
> Nif Mary of hir knight mynne.

The rendering in modern English that follows is by Brian Stone:

> While harmoniously at home the honoured knight slept
> Between the comely curtains in the cold morning.
> But the lady's longing to woo would not let her sleep,
> Nor would she impair the purpose pitched in her heart,
> But rose up rapidly and ran to him

In a ravishing robe that reached to the ground,
Trimmed with finest fur from pure pelts;
Not coifed as to custom, but with costly jewels
Strung in scores on her splendid hairnet.
Her fine-featured face and fair throat were unveiled,
Her breast was bare and her back as well.
She came in by the chamber door and closed it after her,
Cast open a casement and called on the knight,
And briskly thus rebuked him with bountiful words
Of good cheer.
'Ah sir! What, sound asleep?
The morning's crisp and clear.
He had been drowsing deep,
But now he had to hear.
The lovely lady advanced, laughing adorably,
Swooped over his splendid face and sweetly kissed him.
He welcomed her worthily with noble cheer
And, gazing on her gay and glorious attire,
Her features so faultless and fine of complexion,
He felt a flush a rapture suffuse his heart.
Sweet and genial smiling slid them into joy
Till bliss burst forth between them, beaming gay
And bright;
With joy the two contended
In talk of true delight,
And peril would have impended
Had Mary not minded her knight.

Here is the same translator's description of a second visit to the sleeping knight by the Green Knight's lady:

'Good morning, Sir Gawain,' the gay one murmured,
'How unsafely you sleep, that one may slip in here!
Now you are taken in a trice. Unless a truce come
between us,
I shall bind you to your bed – of that be sure.'
The lady uttered laughingly those playful words.
'Good morning, gay lady,' Gawain blithely greeted her.
'Do with me as you will: that well pleases me.
For I surrender speedily and sue for grace,
Which, to my mind, since I must, is much the best course.'
And thus he repaid her with repartee and ready laughter.
'But if, lovely lady, your leave were forthcoming,
And you were pleased to free your prisoner and pray to
him to rise,
I would abandon my bed for a better habiliment,
And have more happiness in our honey talk.'
'Nay, verily, fine sir,' urged the voice of that sweet one,
'You shall not budge from your bed. I have a better idea.
I shall hold you fast here on this other side as well

And so chat on with the chevalier my chains have caught.
For I know well, my knight, that your name is Sir Gawain,
Whom all the world worships, wherever he ride;
For lords and their ladies, and all living folk,
Hold your honour in high esteem, and your courtesy.
And now – here you are truly, and we are utterly alone;
My lord and his liegemen are a long way off;
Others still bide in their beds, my bower-maidens too;
Shut fast and firmly with a fine hasp is the door;
And since I have in this house him who pleases all,
As long as my time lasts I shall, lingering in talk,
take my fill.
My young body is yours,
Do with it what you will;
My strong necessities force
Me to be your servant still.'

A third time the lady comes to him, and after he has again declined her amorous advances he accepts her girdle, the cincture of her gown.

A girdle of green silk with a golden hem,
Embroidered only at the edges, with
hand-stitched ornament.

She reveals its persuasive virtue:

For the man that binds his body with
this belt of green,
As long as he laps it closely about him,
No hero under heaven can hack him to pieces,
For he cannot be killed by any cunning on earth.

It is significant that the knight is tempted *three* times. In the *New Testament* Christ was tempted three times and Peter denied Him thrice. Despite the mystery and strangeness of the allegorical ambience, Gawain emerges as a credible, real person. His personal characteristics determine his behaviour and the web of circumstances with which he has to contend. The allegory shows the man striving for an ideal against events which play on his human vulnerability: situations which he has incurred because he is what he is.

How he fares and the manner of it is an absorbing tale, veiled in the mystery of allegory. The poem, written in alliterative verse with a short rhyming refrain after each strophe (stanza), is in a Northern English dialect strangely different from Chaucer's London sounds. Christian and pagan elements are merged in the complex symbolism of a rich and absorbing poem. An extraordinarily subtle and accomplished piece of work, it is one of the most important poems of the English Middle Ages.

The Green Man who is such an important character in the poem is a recurring image of Western art. In the allegorical poem of Sir Gawain, the Green Knight has green skin, hair and clothing. He rides a green horse and bears a holly bush in his hand. He appears during a feast at the Round Table and demands that one of the knights should strike his head from his shoulders. Gawain accepts the challenge and decapitates the Green Knight who, with his head under his arm, rides out, challenging Gawain to meet him in a year's time so that he may perform the same service for him.

Representation of the Green Man in churches and cathedrals is usually the portrayal of just a head (which accords with the Gawain allegory). The head often depicts an older man. As William Anderson (1985) has pointed out, some words of Virgil which he applied to another god: *cruda deo viridisque senectus* ('a god's old age is hardy and green') could well apply to the Green Man. When woods and forests dominated the English landscape, fear of trees (especially of grotesquely shaped older specimens) was widespread. It is a short step from a 'presence' believed to be tree spirit or woodland demon – to the Green Man.

An interpretation of the Gawain allegory is suggested by philosophy. The Green Man may be seen as a metaphor representing the loving natural force which vivifies us all, as well as impelling the sap in leaves and branches. Worship is mankind's response to perceived bounteousness; a love for nature reflecting back the warmth, direct contact and delicacy of response, measured towards us. Moreover, if the human being is to transcend the limitation of believing that the physical body is 'what I am', then the 'head' which holds this erroneous idea must be struck off. 'The mind is both what binds and what liberates,' says an old scripture. The head spoils what is natural by unwarranted interference. In the allegory, the Green Knight demands to have his head removed and offers the same favour in return. When they meet on New Year's Day, Sir Gawain's virtue appears to save his head, but a small cut inflicted on his neck by the Green Knight serves as a reminder that he must continue to be careful in future.

The Vision of Piers Plowman

Another poem characteristic of its period (somewhere between 1362 and 1399) is *The Vision of Piers Plowman* or, to give the poem its fuller title, *The Vision of William concerning Piers the Plowman*. There are three versions of *Piers Plowman*: in manuscripts at Trinity College, Cambridge, the British Library, and the Bodleian Library. The **A** text, begun between 1367 and 1370, consists of a Prologue and 12 Passus (sections or divisions of the poem). The **B** text, which reworks and develops material from **A**, is about three times as long. The **C** text is a partial revision of **B** and dates from about 1385. A recommended version of the **B** text, with excellent notes, was published by A.V.C. Schmidt, Fellow of Balliol College, Oxford (1978).

Piers Plowman is a long allegorical and satirical poem, written in Middle English alliterative verse. The whole consists of nearly 15,000 verses arranged in 20 groups. It has, perhaps, four or five authors, although the first section is now ascribed to William **Langland** (c1332-c1400). Writing and revising the poem seems to have occupied at least 25 years of his life, as he twice reworked the manuscript. Little is known about the life of William Langland. Most of the information we have is inferred from a literary portrait, refracted through the fictional persona of the dreamer/narrator of his poem. In one manuscript of the **C** text, there is a biographical note identifying Langland as the son of Stacy de Rokayle of Shipton-under-Wychwood, in Oxfordshire. He spent most of his life in London.

Piers, the subject of the poem, is in the early parts a simple pious English labourer; later in the poem he is Christ Himself. The poet supposes himself falling asleep on the Malvern Hills and dreams he sees visions of an allegorical character whose activities have a bearing on the vices of the times. Writing in the dream-vision mode released medieval poets from such narrative genre limitations as time and space. Langland makes full use of this freedom, using a series of dream-vision sequences, two of which are dreams within dreams. The poet explores the nature of charity and patience by the imaginative use of a metaphoric tree image. He perceives the corruption of the Church as a threat to Unity and sees what counters that threat – the development of human charity and the saving power of Grace. More than 50 copy-manuscripts are extant, indicating that the work enjoyed considerable popularity with clerics and the educated middle classes of the 15th-century. Scholars consider that the poem's depth, intensity, and richness of organization make it comparable with Dante's *Divine Comedy*.

A major theme of the poem is the true purpose of life and its value. Although Christians tend to be vulnerable to an over-involvement in the world, Langland perceived obsession with wealth to be the specific problem of his day. Certainly it was very evident that the Church was becoming increasingly prepossessed with wealth and property. Another important subject is the spiritual condition of people as a whole and the belief that their redemption must proceed through four stages: sermon; confession; pilgrimage; pardon.

A further theme is the essential requirement that truth be both understood intellectually *and* lived. This develops as action following simple understanding obtained by learning.

Langland was an imaginative writer whose verses spoke directly to the common people of his own day. It is said that the 14th-century poor folk, although illiterate, had learnt many of his verses by heart – no doubt recognizing the accuracy of the poet's description of their plight:

> The needy are our neighbours, if we note rightly;
> As prisoners in their cells, or poor folk in hovels,
> Charged with children and overcharged by landlords,
> What they might spare in spinning they must spend on rental,
> On milk, or on meal to make porridge
> To still the sobbing of the children at mealtime.

Also they themselves suffer much hunger.
They have woe in winter time, and wake at mid-night
To rise and rock the cradle at the bedside,
To card and to comb, to darn clouts and wash them,
To rub and to reel and put rushes on the paving.
The woe of these women who dwell in hovels,
Is too sad to speak of or put into rhyme…

Translated by Henry W. Wells

The dream-vision form of poetry was common in medieval England and occurs in both accentual-syllabic and alliterative verse. Accentual-syllabic verse uses the syllable as a determining feature, rather than stress or quantitative measure; for example:

Treasure to live by to their lives end.*

Figures of Speech in Medieval Poetry

Alliteration is the repetition of consonant or vowel sounds of two or more words in sequence. It is dependent on sound, regardless of spelling, and was one of the chief characteristics of the old Teutonic poetry. In Anglo-Saxon (Old English) and in Middle English, it preceded the use of rhyme at the end of a line. Chaucer was an adroit practitioner of this technique, but from Piers Plowman, here is an example of consonant alliteration:

I shope me in shroudes, as I a sheep were
In a summer season when soft was the sun.

Langland employs puns frequently in a serious, responsible, and illustrative way; he also makes imaginative use of expanded metaphor and thematic imagery, and employs Latin to enrich his English poetry. He creates delicately expressed rhythms, using a wide repertory of verbal expression and word-play of all kinds, as he strives to make the spiritual visible. Langland's poetry beautifully combines the grand and the homely; at times he touches the sublime. His principal contemporaries in alliterative verse were Chaucer and Gower, but certain of his qualities invite comparison with Shakespeare. T.S. Eliot acknowledged the mastery of Langland in the opening of his final poem *Little Gidding* (*Four Quartets*), which echoes both the beginning of Langland's *Prologue* and his ecstatic lines on the Holy Ghost in Passus XVII:

Midwinter spring is its own season
Sempiternal though sodden towards sundown,
Suspended in time, between pole and tropic.

With this gesture, Eliot reveals his powerful awareness of the nature of poetic tradition.

* See also Gerard Manley Hopkins – sprung rhythm.

A Psychological Awakening

Chaucer

The great poet tends to be in advance of his contemporaries by transcending the standpoint of his age; his very learning, experience, and talents are an expression of his era and its poetic development. Such a poet is Geoffrey Chaucer (1342-1400), whose works established the southern English dialect as the literary language of England. Thomas Hoccleve, a contemporary poet, called Chaucer 'the first findere of our fair language', for until that time Norman-French was still spoken at Richard II's court.

While it is possible to discern early signs of the Renaissance spirit in the work of Petrarch and other Italian writers of the 14th century, Chaucer reflects the culture of his immediate past. The new spirit with its esteem for the individual, so evident in Petrarch, is absent in Chaucer, who is still very much a medieval man. He was born in London, the son of a vintner. In his boyhood he seems to have been attached to the household of Lionel, Duke of Clarence. There are many uncertainties concerning his early life, but it is known that he was at the wars in France in 1359, was taken prisoner, and was ransomed by the King, Edward III.

He married, perhaps in 1366, Phillipa de Roet. An attendant to the Queen, she was connected through her sister to John of Gaunt, who became Chaucer's patron. By 1368 Chaucer had become one of the King's esquires. He was soon spending time abroad on official business for the Monarch, several times travelling to France and Italy. Substantial records exist of Chaucer's career in royal service, both as a member of court and as a diplomat. He was also appointed Controller of Customs in the Port of London in 1374 and was made Clerk of the King's Works in 1389. Despite his official duties, he found the time for writing.

Of the works of Chaucer, the greatest and most famous is *The Canterbury Tales*, begun about 1386. His version of the story of *Troilus and Criseyde* is the only one of his longer works brought fully to completion. Lesser works include: *The Book of the Duchess*; *The House of Fame*; *Anelida and Arcite*; *The Parliament of Fowls*; *Boece* (*Boethius*); *The Legend of Good Women*; *The Romance of the Rose* (a fragmentary translation); *A Treatise on the Astrolabe*; and a number of shorter poems, some only doubtfully attributed to him.

The original story of *Troilus and Cressida* appears first in the 6th century AD and after various modifications appears in Boccaccio's *Il Filostrato*, where Pandarus first appears. This version was the basis for Chaucer's narrative. Cressida or Criseyde, daughter of Calchas, a Greek priest, is beloved by Troilus. They vow eternal fidelity to each other, and as pledges of their vow Troilus gives the maiden a sleeve, while she gives the Trojan prince a glove. Hardly has the vow been made when an exchange of prisoners is agreed. Diomede yields up three Trojan princes and, incredibly, receives Criseyde in their place. Criseyde vows to remain constant, and Troilus vows to rescue her. She is led away to the Grecian's tent and before long has given her affections to Diomede, even inviting him to wear the sleeve given by Troilus in token of his love. Hence Criseyde has become a byword for infidelity; as the whole plot turns on her unfaithfulness, the emphasis on it is inescapable. Her sin, from the medieval standpoint, is reprehensible, and Chaucer the medieval poet-creator cannot excuse her; but the poet, the man of universal human understanding, feels compassion for her lack of strength:

> Ne me ne list this sely womman chyde
> Ferther than the story wol devyse.
> Hir name, allas! is publisshed so wyde,
> That for hir gilt it oughte y-now suffyse,
> And if I might excuse hir any wyse,
> For she so sory was for hir untrouthe,
> Iwis, I wolde excuse hir yet for routhe.
>
> Book V, lines 1093-9 (Skeat's 1901 edition)

In the language of our own day:

> I will not take pleasure in chiding this wretched woman
> Further than is necessary to relate her story.
> Her name is, alas, now so widely publicized,
> That it is enough to punish her guilt,
> And if I might in any way excuse her,
> For she was so sorry for her insincerity,
> Certainly I would do so, for compassion's sake.

In Chaucer's portrayal Criseyde suffers, fully aware of her weakness even as she resists it. But she needs love: Troilus is far away and the 'chivalrous' Diomede close at hand. For all her grace and tenderness, she surrenders to her need and becomes 'slydinge of corage'. Chaucer makes Troilus a man of high valour and Diomede hardy, strong, and chivalrous. He renders the dilemma powerful and the participants real.

Near the end of this fine work, Chaucer describes what happens to Troilus after his death:

> And whan that he was slayn in this manere,
> His lighte goost ful blisfully is went
> Up to the holownesse of the seventh spere,
> In convers letinge every element;
> And ther he saugh, with ful avysement,
> The erratik sterres, herkeninge armonye
> With sownes fulle of hevenish melodye.
>
> And doun from thennes faste he gan avyse
> This litel spot of erthe, that with the see
> Enbraced is, and fully gan despyse
> This wrecched world, and held at vanitee
> To respect of the pleyn felicitee
> That is in hevene above; and at the laste,
> Ther he was slayn, his loking doun he caste;

And in him-self he lough right at the wo
Of hem that wepten for his deeth so faste;
And dampnel al our werk that folweth so
The blinde lust, the which that may not laste,
And sholden al our herte on hevene caste.
And forth he wente, shortly for to telle,
Ther as Mercurie sorted him to dwelle. –

Swich fyn hath, lo, this Troilus for love,
Swich fyn hath al his grete worthinesse;
Swich fyn hath his estat real above,
Swich fyn his lust, swich fyn hath his noblesse;
Swich fyn hath false worldes brotelnesse.
And thus bigan his lovinge of Criseyde,
As I have told, and in this wyse he deyde.

Book V, lines 1807-34 (Skeat's 1901 edition)

Here is the sense of these lines in modern English:

And after he had been slain in this manner,
His light spirit blissfully ascended
To the inner space of the seventh sphere
On the other side of all the elements;
And there he viewed and pondered
The wandering stars, hearing their harmony
With their sounds of heavenly melody.

And down from thence intently he began to contemplate
This little spot of earth surrounded by the sea,
And began roundly to condemn
This miserable world, and urged vanity
To hold in honour the simple felicity
That is in heaven above; and finally
He looked down to the place where he was slain;

And within himself laughed at the grieving
Of one that weeps for his own death so intensely;
He condemned those deeds of ours that follow
The blind lust which does not last,
And instead urged us to centre our hearts on heaven.
Then forth he went, shortly to render his account there,
For Mercury had decreed that there he should dwell.

Such need had Troilus for love,
Such was his great worthiness;
So exalted was his royal bearing,
So great his lust, so fine his nobility;
Such effect had this false world's brittleness,
That thus began his loving of Criseyde
As I have related, and in this manner he died.

Influenced by Petrarch, Dante, and Boccaccio, Chaucer was responsible for the major innovation of introducing French and Italian styles of prosody which soon superseded the native alliterative verse. In metre, rhyme and verse-form he displays a consistent skill, rendered the more striking when compared with the work of his English contemporaries.

Intuitive and sympathetic, Chaucer's irony does not preclude tenderness; his cynicism is always friendly. He has a keen eye for detail and writes with vivid realism. His humanity gives his work a timeless relevance. For instance, his question in *The Wife of Bath's Tale* from *The Canterbury Tales,* would promote lively discussion in a modern mixed group, as surely as in a boisterous crowd of medieval pilgrims:

> What thing is it that women most desire?

Chaucer's answer:

> Wommen desiren to have sovereyntee
> As wel over hir housbond as hir love,
> And for to been in maistrie hym above.

That is:

> Women desire the self-same command
> Over husbands as over lovers,
> And to be in the position of mastery.

The Wife of Bath had scant regard for wives who did not master their husbands. Chaucer expands on this in *The Shipman's Tale* in lines given to a merchant's 'wyf of excellent beautee':

> And wel ye woot that wommen naturelly
> Desyren thinges sixe, as well as I.
> They wolde that hir housbondes sholde be
> Hardy, and wyse, and riche, and ther-to free,
> And buxom to his wyf, and fresh a-bedde.

That is:

> For you well know that women naturally
> Desire six things, just as I do;
> They want their husband to be
> Sturdy and prudent, rich and generous,
> Obedient to his wife and inventive in bed.

All Chaucer's heroes regard love, when it comes upon them, as the most beautiful of absolute disasters: an agony as much desired as bemoaned, ever to be pursued, never to be betrayed. In theory, it was for a husband to command and for a wife to obey. But Chaucer is saying that many women desire the right, as much as men, to assert their own identity and to dominate the opposite sex. The deliciousness of the compromise achieved by well-matched lovers avoids the misery of 'hen-pecked' husbands and abased women. Chaucer deals with this and other important matters – with consummate mastery – in his *Canterbury Tales*.

The Wife of Bath's Tale is based on an interesting old story, *Weddynge of Sir Gawen and Dame Ragnell*. In it the knight has to choose between having his old and ugly wife

> beautiful by day, or
> beautiful by night ...

This is to be interpreted as a choice between ideal love or physical love. Chaucer alters the application of the choice in the story to a different pair of alternatives:

> ugly and faithful, or
> beautiful and unfaithful ...

The knight in the tale chooses neither alternative but elects to offer the decision to the lady herself. This unselfish surrender of his male dominance gives them both the opportunity to obtain shared and mutual benefit:

> Cheseth youreself which may be best pleasance,
> And moost honour to yow and me also.

His choice results in his having the lady both beautiful *and* faithful. His acknowledgement of her individual integrity and equality as a person – in short, his own surrender of ego – results in mutual receiving within a relationship of unity.

In Chaucer's day love was considered to be, at least in the context of the ideal, a good in itself. Although love uniting man and woman fell far short of divine love, human love had a high place in the aristocratic man's list of virtues.

Dr T. Whittock (1968) sees Chaucer's *Canterbury Tales* as a Christian work of art in which the sequence of recurring themes takes on the nature of a debate on death, marriage, the role of women, truth or deception in art, the perception of evil in the Creator's plan, temporal imperfection, and the hidden mystery of God's being. Chaucer was not a moralist; he was a court poet writing during a period of high religious sensibility for the diversion of a range of people, some of inferior education and culture. His poetry, especially *The Canterbury Tales*, contained descriptions of human behaviour opposed to *trouthe* and *sothfastnesse* ('steadfastness'). To deal with this he provided clues as an unobtrusive guidance to his hearers and readers. For example, *The Shipman's Tale* is about a merchant's wife and her adulterous relationship with a monk. The misbehaving pair are likeable people and Chaucer introduces into his narrative certain danger signals. The monechal misdemeanours proceed from 'a young monk, well-made and bold' who says the mass 'hastily' and dines rather too richly:

> He brought with him a jug of Malmsey wine
> And also one of sweet Italian juice,
> With these a brace of birds as was his use.

Moreover,

Whenever he stayed there, carefully attending
To what should please; he poured out tips like wages,
Forgetting not the meanest of the pages.

Chaucer is careful to tell us that a 'mayde child' in the woman's care is allowed to be present while the monk and his temptress come to terms and she is handled and kissed:

A little girl was there for company
Beside her, under her authority,
Still subject to the rod ...

Undeterred by this the monk seizes the merchant's wife:

And on the word he caught her by the flanks
Clasping her closely, giving her a riot
Of kisses, saying softly, 'keep things quiet ...'

Translated by Nevill Coghill

As ever, Chaucer brings matters to a neat conclusion, ending with 'Amen'.

Despite the earthy realism and the astounding range of human types he presents, Chaucer introduces his great work with disarming simplicity. Here are the opening lines of the Prologue to his *Canterbury Tales*:

Whan that Aprille with his shoures sote
The droghte of Marche hath perced to the rote,
And bathed every veyne in swich licour,
Of which vertu engendred is the flour;
Whan zephirus eek with his swete breeth
Inspired hath in every holt and heeth
The tendre croppes, and the yonge sonne,
Hath in the Ram his halfe cours y-ronne,
And smale fowles maken melodye,
That slepen al the night with open ye,
(So priketh hem nature in hir corages):
Than longen folk to goon on pilgrimages.

For comparison, the lines are given here in a modern translation by Nevill Coghill:

When the sweet showers of April fall and shoot
Down through the drought of March to pierce the root,
Bathing every vein in liquid power
From which there springs the engendering of the flower,
When also Zephyrus with his sweet breath
Exhales an air in every grove and heath
Upon the tender shoots, and the young sun
His half-course in the sign of the Ram has run,
And the small fowl are making melody
That sleep away the night with open eye
(So nature pricks them and their heart engages)
Then people long to go on pilgrimages.

Even in its incomplete state and with its somewhat uneven structure, *The Canterbury Tales* is nevertheless a brilliant evocation of contemporary personality-types. Chaucer amply met the Horatian maxim: 'He has borne every point who has mingled the useful with the sweet, at the same time delighting and instructing the reader.' With its splendour of language, it is undoubtedly the major work in English of its period and one of the glories of English literature.

Chaucer sums up the ideas, attitudes, and literary themes of the Middle Ages and imbues his work with the warmth of a discernible personality. His verse structuring is masterly and a key factor in his poetic creativity. A cursory reading of his work is enough to confirm the apparent ease and simplicity of his poetry. Closer examination reveals how cunningly he has concealed the pains taken with the verse. For instance, in *The Canterbury Tales*, adapting his verse form the better to individualize his characters. His works are written with comedy, realism and insight; they breathe the spirit of the age. Chaucer's founding role in the establishment of an English literary tradition is fittingly emphasized by the eventual creation of Poets' Corner around his tomb in Westminster Abbey.

A New Realism

Whether or not we agree with Edith Sitwell's declaration that 'Poetry is the deification of reality,' if poets have the lucid grasp of structure to match their clarity of vision her statement appears to be true. One such was a French poet of the late Middle Ages, François de Montcorbier known as François Villon.

François Villon

T.S. Eliot, in a eulogy to Dante delivered in 1950 at the Italian Institute, London, compared Dante's directness of speech with that of Chaucer and Villon. Villon has long been celebrated for his technical competence, his vigour, and his realism, together with the pathos and the expressive lyric power of his poetry. He is known principally for his *Petit Testament*, *Grand Testament*, *Ballade des Pendus*, and his *Ballade des Dames du temps jadis*.

Villon was born in 1431. He came from a poor family with well-to-do relatives, from one of whom he took the name by which he is best known. He held both Bachelor's and Master's degrees from the Sorbonne. Often involved in student brawls in the Latin Quarter, he was arrested several times for complicity in murders and robberies. In 1462 he was sentenced to be hanged, but later the punishment was changed to banishment for ten years. Immediately thereafter, the poet disappeared. This is hardly surprising, for Villon had been tortured at the command of both Church and State. (It was customary to torture malefactors in order to obtain confessions.)

It is on record in Villon's own words that he 'was beaten like cloth in a stream' in the few years prior to 1457. He is unlikely to have been so treated for assiduity in his studies. Open profligacy and much violence were present when Villon left the University with his degrees. The Hundred Years War was over, famine and pestilence had abated, and pleasure-seekers everywhere sought stimulation. Student brawls and horseplay threatened people and property; and, as ever, the line between 'student prank' and 'criminal act' was difficult to draw. However, what matters is to read the poetry, rather than make potentially misleading assessments of stature from facts of a poet's life. Villon's works are what earn him distinction among poets. A glimpse of his realism comes from these extracts:

The Small or First Testament

En ce temps que j'ay dit devant,
Sur le Noel, morte saison,
Que les loups se vivent de vent
Et qu'on se tient en sa maison,
Pour le frimas, pres du tison,
Me vint ung vouloir de brisier
La tres amoureuse prison
Qui souloit mon cuer debrisier.

At the aforesaid time, towards Christmas, the dead season, when wolves are famished and when we stay indoors near the coals because of the frost, there came upon me a desire to break forth from the strong prison of love which had long been crushing my heart.

Translated by Geoffrey Atkinson (1930)

Villon has the poetic intuition to ask questions rather than provide answers. 'Where are my gay companions of former years?' he asks in a question less well-known but no less beautiful than the celebrated, 'Where are the snows of yester-year?' In 15th-century France with its harshness, violence, and loathsome diseases, death was never far away. Villon remembers and reviews the many people he had known and concludes: 'Death seizes all, without exception.' After listing many, some of great importance, he ends: 'Such as these, the wind bears away.'

The following lines from *The Testament* reveal Villon's matter-of-fact realism:

No angel's son am I, I own,
Who weareth on his radiant head
A diadem or starry crown.
God keep his soul, my father's dead;
His body's in an earthy bed …
My mother's too will die one day
And knows her days are numbered,
Nor will her son live on for ay.

All men must die, I am aware,
– The rich and poor, the frocked and lay
The wise and foolish, foul and fair,
The thin and fat, the grave and gay;
And pranked out ladies pass away;
Of whatsoe'er degree withal,

Bejewelled, stiff with ruff and stay,
Cold death will seize them, one and all.

This rendering into English *and* metre by Alan Conder is exemplary. A comparison with Geoffrey Atkinson's careful literal translation appearing further on in these pages, when matched against the original medieval French, beautifully illustrates the relative merits of opting for the spirit or the letter when translating.

Old age accompanies the phenomenon of death and in *Les regrets de la belle Heaulmiere* Villon writes in the person of a withered old woman in her eighties who tottered about the environs of Notre Dame. He was aware that this 'gnarled and shrivelled crone' had once been a young woman of legendary beauty. She was for him a symbol of the tragedy of the human condition and the ever-present immanent death awaiting us all. We take up the poem at stanza six as she asks:

> What has become of that smooth brow, that blonde hair, those arched eyebrows, that wide space between my eyes, that pretty look, with which I used to capture the most circumspect; that fine straight nose neither large nor small, those little close-set ears, that dimpled chin, clear pretty face, and those beauteous vermilion lips?
>
> Those lovely slender shoulders, long arms, and pretty hands, little breasts, full hips, set high, smooth, and made for lists of love; that wide back, that 'dainty little thing,' resting on large firm thighs, within its pretty little garden?
>
> My brow wrinkled, hair grey, eyebrows gone, eyes completely dulled, which used to cast glances and laughter, whereby many passers-by were struck; my nose bent and far from beauty, my ears rough and pendulous, my face whitened, lifeless, and colourless, my chin wrinkled, and my lips flabby …
>
> This is the lot of human beauty! Arms shortened and hands knotted, all humped at the shoulders; breasts, ah, yes, all shrivelled; the same with hips as with paps; and the 'dainty little thing,' ugh! As for my thighs, they are thighs no longer, but shrunken hams, and spotted like sausages.
>
> Thus we poor silly old crones look back with regret, among ourselves, to our happy days – crouching on our haunches, huddled together like balls of wool, by a little fire of flax-sticks, soon lighted and soon extinguished – and formerly we were so dainty! Thus it goes with many, both men and women.
>
> Translated by Geoffrey Atkinson

Chaucer in *The Monkes Tale* reminded us that 'Full wise is he that can himselven know.' Plutarch remarked in his *Lives – Demosthenes*: 'If the "Know thyself" of the oracle were an easy thing for every man, it would not be held to be a divine injunction.' The scholar-poet François Villon concurs, with his characteristic directness:

> I know when flies are in milk, I know a man by his clothes, I know fair weather from foul, I know the apple by the apple tree, I know the tree from seeing its gum, I know when things are the same, I know who is working or idling, I know all things except myself.

I know a doublet by the collar, I know a monk by his long robe, I know the master by his servant, I know the nun by her veil, I know when a thief is talking 'cant', I know silly people richly fed, I know wine by the cask it is in, I know all things except myself.

I know a horse from a mule, I know their burden and their load, I know Beatrice and Ysabelet apart, I know chips and counters which add up to a total, I know a vision from a nap, I know the Bohemian schism, I know the power of Rome, I know all things except myself.

Prince, to conclude, I know all things, I know ruddy people from pallid people, I know Death which swallows all, I know all things except myself.

Translated by Geoffrey Atkinson

In an age when poets were straitjacketed by the Church and much verse was dictated and informed by Christian doctrine, Villon's writing stands apart for its authenticity and realism. He offers us a cogent and unsparing description of the human condition as it really is. T.S. Eliot said of him: 'There are those who remain in one's mind as having set the standard for a particular poetic virtue, as Villon for honesty ...'

Some 32 years after Villon's death, Clement **Marot** (1495-1544) was born. Imbued with similar cogency of expression, Marot makes a Faustian plea – not to the Devil, but to Love:

Of Himself

No longer am I what I was,
Nor ever shall I be again;
My spring is gone and summer has
Leapt lightly through the window pane.
To call thee 'Master' I was fain;
I've served but thee of gods above.
I'd doubly serve, with might and main,
Could I be born again, O Love!

In a further Epigram, Marot deals with the timeless 'knowing negotiation' and 'stage-management' of feminine acquiescence:

Of 'Yea' and 'Nay'

A sweet 'Nay' with an equally sweet-smile
Is ladylike, – an admirable trait.
But I would charge you with a lack of guile,
Were you, when importuned, to murmur 'Yea';
Not that I'd suffer grievous pain – nay nay, –
To have the tempting fruit that I so covet;
But I would wish that while you did give way,
You'd say to me: 'No, No, you shall not have it!'

Translated by Alan Conder

Before leaving this rich seam of French poetry we should consider briefly Pierre de **Ronsard** (1524-85). Ronsard was of noble birth, and in his early years was a page at the court of Francis I. He served in a diplomatic capacity in Scotland and England until an unfortunate illness left him deaf. He was a man of powerful intellect and wide learning. He is best known for his light and graceful amorous verse, especially in the form of the sonnet and the ode. He was celebrated as the greatest French poet of his day and exerted an important influence on the Elizabethan writers of sonnets. Here are two poems by Ronsard. The first, a reproof of biting potency:

Cold Kisses

On my return (I think of it with dread!)
You met me with a kiss of ice, like those
A loveless maid on her betrothed bestows,
As freezing as the kisses of the dead.

As dry, as ardourless, as void of savour
As those that frosty Dian gave of old,
Or a girl her grandam gives. Pray, why so cold?
What! have my lips then such a bitter flavour?

'Twere well for you to imitate the dove,
That, beak to beak, doth at the season's call
Love warmly with long kisses on a bough.
And so, I beg you, see to it from now
That when you kiss, your lips will taste of love,
Or, pray you, Mistress, kiss me not at all.

Translated by Alan Conder

Here is another example of a poet urging his mistress to be less circumspect, bearing in mind the inexorable effects of time:

When You Are Old …

When you are old and sit by candle-light
At evening near the fire and spin away,
You'll chant my verse and, marvelling, you'll say:
'Ah, Ronsard sang my beauty when 'twas bright.'
Hearing the tidings that you tell of me,
Your drowsing maids will waken at my name,
Extolling you and your immortal fame,
For you will share my immortality.
While I in darkness 'neath the myrtles rest,
A ghost, my body shed, among the blest,
You'll huddle by the hearth all bowed and grey,
And o'er my love and your disdain you'll sorrow.
Live now, love; heed me, wait not till to-morrow,
But cull life's roses while 'tis yet to-day.

Translated by Alan Conder

While the French poets of the late Middle Ages were continuing with the well worn themes of medieval life and courtly love, major changes (with powerful implications for poetry) were well under way in Italy.

5
Humanism and Spirituality

Renaissance Italy

IN THE LATER Middle Ages the Italian cities lost for the most part their political independence and their communal institutions. However, as a result of the economic prosperity won in the previous period and continued in this, they generated and patronized a host of writers, scholars, and artists. This great output of cultural activity became the Italian Renaissance. Major family dynasties like the Medici were influential in this stimulation and patronage of the Arts.

It could be said that the spiritual essence of the religious, moral, and political structure of the Middle Ages found its essential expression in three principal ways:

- Philosophy — The encyclopaedic *Summae* of Albertus Magnus and Thomas Aquinas.
- Art — The French Gothic cathedrals of the 12th and 13th centuries.
- Poetry — *The Divine Comedy* of Dante.

The late Middle Ages and the next great civilizing development in Europe had certain quite specific characteristics. The artistic, literary, and scientific revival or rebirth (Renaissance) which originated in Italy in the 14th century influenced the rest of Europe in a variety of ways for the next two centuries. Its principal themes were:

- The spread of humanism.
- A return to classical values.
- The beginning of scientific investigation.

The term 'Renaissance' was given currency in the 19th century by Jacob Burckhardt (1818-97), the Swiss historian, who emphasized the contrast between the Church-centred culture of the Middle Ages and the new sense of primacy given to personality, prevalent in 14th-century Italy.

The learned men of the new period (Late Middle Ages and Renaissance) called themselves *humanists* (from *humanista*), which was student slang for teachers of grammar, rhetoric, and other 'humane studies'.

Humanism was the study of classical literature, but the aim was not so much to derive from it scientific or theological information as to concentrate on its literary and human interest. These scholars were impressed not only by the subject-matter of the ancients but also by the elegance of their Latin style.

The humanists were scholars of the classics, but they were more than scholars. They themselves wrote voluminous letters, speeches, poems, and treatises on grammar and rhetoric, history, politics, education, and religion. They proclaimed an ideal of eloquence – as professional rhetoricians they were convinced that classical models provided the best guides. With the growing sense of national identity in all countries, the vernacular came to be used increasingly – above all, in Italy.

Dante

At the very beginning of the use of the vernacular in literature, and the practice of humanism, stands the towering figure of Dante Alighieri (1265-1321). Dante was the son of a lawyer whose family belonged to the lower ranks of the nobility. Details of his early life are few, but it can be assumed that he received the best education then available. Like others of his background, he wrote poetry as a youth and familiarized himself with painting and music. He was particularly influenced by the thought of Aristotle; the painter Giotto was an intimate friend.

In 1274, when they were nine years old, Dante met Bice (Beatrice) Portinari and fell in love with her. They met only infrequently, but later, although Beatrice married Simone de' Bardi, Dante continued to idealize and idolize her. She died in 1290. Dante was married in 1292, his wife Gemma Donati eventually bearing him seven children.

By 1300 Dante had become prominent in the political life of Florence and had been appointed one of the six *priori* who governed the city. In 1301 a major dispute developed between the Neri (Black) and Bianchi (white) factions of the Guelph party in Florence. Pope Boniface was invited to mediate, and Dante went with two other councillors to Rome to meet the Pope. During his absence the Neri achieved dominance and Dante, whose sympathies were with the Bianchi, was fined, banished, and subsequently sentenced to be burnt alive. As a disaffected exile, he visited many Italian cities and travelled to France. Altogether he spent some 20 years deeply unhappy because he was unable to return to Florence. He died in Ravenna.

The Divine Comedy

Dante wrote two influential treatises on the merits of vernacular Italian as a literary language, but it was his *Commedia* (or *Divine Comedy*), begun about 1307, that secures his place among the master poets. In his bitter wanderings as an exile in the North of Italy he fashioned, and finally brought to conclusion, a long poem to which he gave the bitterly ironic title *The Comedy of Dante Alighieri, A Florentine by Birth but Not in*

Behaviour. Dante termed it *comedy* because he considered it to have a happy outcome. The adjective *divine* was added later, some say by Boccaccio, who in the next generation lectured on the poem in Florence and wrote one of the first biographies of the great poet. *The Divine Comedy* with its allegorical narrative is structured as a long poem containing a hundred *cantos* or divisions. (The Latin *cantus* means 'song'.) The work is in three parts: *Hell*, *Purgatory*, and *Paradise*. It narrates a journey in imagination to the other world, where Dante's guide initially is Virgil (whose own account of the realm of Hades in the sixth book of the *Aeneid* was familiar throughout the Middle Ages). Dante journeys through Hell and Purgatory, until finally he is conducted to Paradise by his great love, the lady Beatrice. *The Divine Comedy* reveals a scheme of the Universe, presented as a comprehensive moral, religious, and visionary journey through Hell, Purgatory, and Paradise. At the same time, this may be seen as the way of an individual soul, journeying from sin to purification. *The Divine Comedy* has been ranked by some with Plato's *Dialogues*, Shakespeare's *Plays* and the *New Testament* as an exemplar of the relationship between souls at the level of the divine.

Dante's poem is very long and vastly complex; it is also perhaps the most rigorously structured work of Western poetry. This work is Dante's spiritual testament, and in it he reveals his profound insight into human nature. It is written in the form of an allegory, for as T.S. Eliot remarked, Dante's is a visual imagination. He is an outstanding poet, and for him allegory necessitates clear visual images. He lived in an age when men readily saw visions, whereas in our own times such visualizations are, perhaps, expected only of the aberrant or psychologically disturbed. Accepting and expounding the full philosophy of the devout medieval Christian, Dante manages to avoid the abstractions of the medieval allegorist. He makes his ideas on good and evil the more convincing by having them spoken by historic personages known to his readers. With his visionary poetry, Dante created an impressive piece of work which constitutes a major statement of medieval faith and opinion.

The Divine Comedy is written in *terza rima*, a form of *iambic* rhythm, in lines containing 10 or 11 syllables, arranged in groups of three. Here are the opening lines of *Hell*, Canto I:

Midway this way of life we're bound upon
   I woke to find myself in a dark wood,
   Where the right road was wholly lost and gone.

Ay me! how hard to speak of it – that rude
   And rough and stubborn forest! the mere breath
   Of memory stirs the old fear in the blood;

It is so bitter, it goes nigh to death;
   Yet there I gained such good, that, to convey
   The tale, I'll write what else I found therewith.

How I got into it I cannot say,
  Because I was so heavy and full of sleep
  When first I stumbled from the narrow way;

But when at last I stood beneath a steep
  Hill's side, which closed that valley's wandering maze
  Whose dread had pierced me to the heart-root deep,

Then I looked up, and saw the morning rays
  Mantle its shoulder from that planet bright
  Which guides men's feet aright on all their ways;

And this a little quieted the affright
  That lurking in my bosom's lake had lain
  Through the long horror of that piteous night.

Translated by Dorothy L. Sayers

Although he is dealing with such a vast canvas, Dante includes many examples of earthy realism which heighten relevance for the reader:

There is no greater sorrow than to recall
a time of happiness in misery.

The Divine Comedy – Hell

You shall discover how salty is the taste of
another's bread,* and how hard a path is the
going down and going up of another's stairs.

The Divine Comedy – Paradise

Poets often take an image from the past and shape it to their present need; such borrowings can frequently be inferred from a singular word parallel. Dante's *Hell*, in the third Canto, contains the famous inscription over Hell's gate:

Through me men go into the city of grief,
through me men go to unending pain,
through me men go among the lost people …
all hope abandon, you who enter here.

David West (1991) noticed that in Plautus's comedy *Bacchides* (c190-185 BC) the testy old tutor, Lydus, standing outside the house of Bacchis where the ladies of pleasure are feasting, shouts:

Throw wide open, I beseech you, and unclose this door of Hell!
It deserves no better name; it doesn't need a sage to tell
He who enters must abandon every hope of temperance.

Translated by E.H. Sugden

Not unreasonably, David West asks, 'Can it be that Dante picked up his jewel from a pavement outside a brothel in Roman comedy?'

The clarity of Dante's images are revealed in his simple language. He uses few metaphors because their use tends to obscure allegorical image,

* To this day, Tuscan bread is unsalted.

but he did use some striking similes. A well-known example was remarked by Matthew Arnold – Dante is describing how the crowd in Hell looked at him and his guide in the prevailing dim light:

> *e si ver noi aguzzavan le ciglia,*
> *come vecchio sartor fa nella cruna.*
>
> and sharpened their vision (knitted their brows) at us,
> like an old tailor peering at the eye of his needle.

The power and beauty of *The Divine Comedy* has been recognized ever since it appeared. Many of Dante's contemporaries considered it to be divinely inspired. The vast encyclopaedia of human knowledge embodied in the work has, as if by metamorphosis, been transfigured into poetry itself. No English translation quite transmits the poetic magic adequately.

The New Life

La Vita Nuova (*The New Life*) is Dante's celebration of his intensely spiritual love for Beatrice. Its prose, lyric poems, and sonnets establish a landmark in poetic tradition extending from the medieval convention of courtly love, begun by the troubadour poets of Provence, and continued through the sonnets of Petrarch to the sonnet sequences developed in Elizabethan England. *The New Life* has by general consent found an almost ideal translator in Dante Gabriel Rossetti (1828-82), the English poet and painter of Italian parentage.

Dante's work was unusual in that he wrote in Italian (which has an inherent musicality) rather than Latin and waived certain time-hallowed poetic formalities. As reality displaces convention, so a creative freshness renders the work more original. The poetry is deeply felt but intellectually disciplined; it reveals how, within Dante's vision, human love aspires to and touches that of God. Here is a sonnet:

> With your companions you make fun of me,
> Not thinking, Lady, what the reason is
> I cut so strange a figure in your eyes
> When, raising mine, your loveliness I see.
> If you but knew, Pity no more could be
> Severe towards me in her usual guise.
> Finding me near you, Love his weapons tries,
> Gaining in boldness and temerity,
> And on my frightened spirits rains such blows
> That some he slays and others flee in fear,
> Till only he is left to look on you.
> Hence I am altered into someone new,
> Yet not so that I do not plainly hear
> My outcast spirits wailing in their woes.
>
> Translated by Barbara Reynolds

The Italian medieval poet considered pre-eminent before Dante was Guido Guinicelli or Guinizelli (c1274). His was the work from which

Dante drew early inspiration. But whereas Guinicelli perceived love to be overpowering and irrational, the destroyer of intellect and virtue, Dante believed love to be a choice made by reason and will. It was rational and purifying and reflects the love of God Himself – whose love can 'move the sun and other stars'.

As Italy's finest poet and one of the greatest writers the world has ever known, Dante may justifiably be considered the first major author of the modern tradition. Eliot said of Dante that no other poet has ever given closer attention than he to the technical problems of versification and language, and none has ever attained a greater mastery of the craft. His influence on Western writers from Chaucer onwards has been immense. In a sense, Dante is bringing to a close the great period of medieval culture, whereas Petrarch, at about the middle of the 14th century, is beginning the Italian Renaissance – a period of great genius and output in the fine arts; a time when painting and sculpture were to develop independently of architecture.

Petrarch

In 14th-century Italy there was intense human creativity in all arts, especially literature. With Dante's literary eminence already secure at the time of his death (1321), the reputation of Italian letters was further enhanced by two other outstanding Tuscan writers: Francesco Petrarch (1304-74) and Giovanni Boccaccio (?1313-75).

Petrarch (Petrarca in Italian) was born in Arezzo, a small town in Tuscany south of Florence, but at the age of eight moved with his family to Avignon. His early years were spent in the Papal court at Avignon, after which he was continually travelling. He described himself as *peregrinus ubique* ('wanderer everywhere'). He journeyed throughout Provence and Italy and visited cities as far apart as Paris and Prague; travelling was to become a major metaphor in Petrarch's writing. Indeed, transience was one of the Petrarchan themes most readily seized upon by Elizabethan writers like Wyatt (1503-42).

Petrarch was a diplomat, a classical scholar, and, by the age of 37, poet laureate. He wrote volumes of poetry and prose, conducted a prodigious correspondence, advised the rulers of the age, and had a wide circle of literary and artistic friends. Many of his writings are in Latin, including the epic poem *Africa*, together with treatises on philosophical and political subjects. Petrarch was largely responsible for the revival of interest in the literature of the Greeks and Romans, but his most influential legacy is an outstanding sequence of love poems in Italian, *Rime in vita e morte di Madonna Laura* – known simply as the *Canzoniere*. This collection was inspired by his spiritualized passion for an elusive lady, Laura, who was both the object of unrequited love for nearly 40 years and a metaphor for the poet's obsessional desire for personal glory and fame.

The poet fell in love with Laura in 1327, immediately after seeing her in church at Avignon. For the rest of his life the roots of his imagination drew on an imperishable but unattainable love. Petrarch poured out his adoration for Laura in more than 300 sonnets – the 14-line poems he so distinctively separated into an octave (eight lines) and a sestet (six lines). The poems inspired by this lady divide into those written during her lifetime and those mourning her untimely death. (She died in the plague of 1348.) They were never actually lovers but, as Petrarch writes in his *Secretum*, this was due more to her chasteness than to his – she was a married woman. For him, Laura was no mere literary abstraction: she was a woman of flesh and blood whom he genuinely loved. One of the characteristics of his poetry, in fact, is the palpable reality of Laura as a person. She never becomes (as Beatrice does for Dante) a symbol without earthly reality. Indeed, his *Canzoniere* offer much earthly wisdom, such as this old Italian saying: 'We lose our hair before our vices.'

His verses to Laura are written in the Tuscan dialect. Although conceived within the main tradition of courtly love, they are characterized by being a celebration of love liberated from allegory and mysticism. However, it must also be said that their elegant sophistication is sometimes at odds with the strength of passion being expressed.

To offer illustrative examples of Petrarchan sonnets is to attempt the near impossibility of enlightened selection. Moreover, it is obviously misleading to choose a few to represent all. Then there is the perennial problem of translation. That having been said, here is a sonnet, written while Laura still lived:

Canzoniere, 134

I find no peace, yet I am not at war,
I fear and hope, and burn and I am ice;
I fly above the heavens, and lie on earth,
I grasp at nothing and embrace the world.

One keeps me jailed who neither locks nor opens,
nor keeps me for her own nor frees the noose;
Love does not kill, nor does he loose my chains;
he wants me lifeless but won't loosen me.

I see with no eyes, shout without a tongue;
I yearn to perish, and I beg for help;
I hate myself and love somebody else.

I thrive on pain and laugh with all my tears;
I dislike death as much as I do life:
because of you, lady, this is the way I am.

Translated by Mark Musa

Petrarch is a major poet of the Renaissance and a lyricist who writes with great delicacy. He has a masterly capacity for modulating rhythmical phrasing to express a mood.

Here now is the languishing Petrarch; the following translation is preceded by the original for comparison:

Canzoniere, 116

Pien di quella ineffabile dolcezza
che del bel viso trassen gli occhi miei
nel di che volentier chiusi gli avrei
per non mirar giamai minor bellezza.

Lassai quel ch' i' piu bramo; et o si avezza
la mente a contemplar sola costei
ch' altro non vede, et cio che non e lei
gia per antica usanza odia et disprezza.

In una valle chiusa d'ogn' intorno,
ch'e refrigerio de' sospir miei lassi,
giunsi sol con Amor, pensoso et tardo;

ivi non donne ma fontane et sassi
et l'imagine trovo di quel giorno
che 'l pensier mio figura ovunque io sguardo.

116

Full of that ineffable sweetness which my eyes drew from
her lovely face on that day when I would gladly have
closed them so as never to look on any lesser beauties.

I departed from what I most desire; and I have so
accustomed my mind to contemplate her alone that it sees
nothing else, and whatever is not she, already by
ancient habit it hates and scorns.

In a valley closed on all sides, which cools my weary
sighs, I arrived alone with Love, full of care, and
late; there I find not ladies but fountains and rocks

and the image of that day which my thoughts image forth
wherever I may glance.

Translated by Robert M. Durling

After Laura's death the distraught Petrarch rouses himself from his earlier self-pity and writes:

Canzoniere, 267

O God! that lovely face, that gentle look,
O God! that charming way of hers, so proud!
O God! those words that any wild, harsh heart
could tame and turn cowards to courageous men!

And, O God, that sweet smile whence came the arrow
of death, the only good I hope for now!
Royal soul, the worthiest of all to rule,
if only you had not joined us so late:*

* In this context, 'late' means that this is a time when the world has grown more corrupt.

it is for you I burn, in you I breathe
for I am yours alone; deprived of you,
I suffer less for all my other pains;

with hope you filled me once and with desire
the time I left that highest charm alive,
but all those words were scattered in the wind.

Translated by Mark Musa

Petrarch's achievement as a lyric poet is particularly complex. As Robert M. Durling (1976) reminds us: 'Petrarch combines matchlessly rich expressiveness with a sometimes empty formalism; critical self-awareness with sentimentality and narcissism; daring originality with conservative respect for tradition.' The introspective self-analysing and the adulation of a womanly ideal as mistress and saint that occur in the *Canzoniere* were to become a fundamental influence throughout the 16th and 17th centuries.

Although his sonnets differ little from Dante's either in form or spirit, Petrarch's fame as a sonnet writer quickly outran that of his predecessor. The interest in Petrarch's sonnets did not end with his death; in fact, his influence over sonnet writing finally dominated Western Europe. 'Petrarchism' has come to mean the Petrarchan form of the sonnet and particularly the poet's attitude to his subject matter – praise of woman as the perfection of human beauty and the object of the highest expression of love. All over Europe, Petrarchism became a growing creative force which renewed the poetic art of the lyric. The figure of Laura represented the new ideal of woman, who personified wisdom, beauty, and virtue; she who illuminated, at its centre, the poet's life and art. It became a model for poetic language, demonstrating a new mode of expression, using sensitivity and elegance to convey the familiar with wit, grace, and power. The influence of this Italian poet and scholar over English Renaissance poetry is incalculable, but before considering Petrarch's effect on Elizabethan sonnet writing it will be helpful to consider the historical evolution of the sonnet form.

The Development of the Sonnet

One of the major channels by which the influence of the Italian Renaissance reached England was the sonnet.

The *quatorzain*, or poem of 14 lines, is said to have originated with Guittone d'Arezzo (c1235-94), who used it to express troubadour ideas on love. His courtship poetry extended in range from elevated, mystical love to the mannered wooing of an exalted lady. (The troubadour of that period was a singer who composed the melody, words, and verse-scheme for his song.)

Trobadors or troubadours were minstrels at work in the south of France from the 11th to the 13th century. Their name derives from the

Provençal verb *trobar*, 'to find; invent'. They wrote in the *langue d'oc*. Eminent troubadour poets were Bernart de Ventadour, Bertram de Born, Geoffrey Rudel, Piere Vidal, Guirat de Bornelh, and Guilhelm de Cabestanh. Similar minstrels appeared in the north of France, where they were called *trouveres*. They were active during the 12th to the 14th centuries. Their works were chiefly narrative poems. The troubadour brought news, could be hired to deliver messages of love, and created a receptive climate for poetry in the community.

In the first half of the 13th century, the influence of Provençal love poetry passed, via the cultured court of the Emperor Frederick II in Sicily, to the Italian city states. Here, it was taken up and developed by thoughtful, pragmatic people whose love poetry was serious and reflective – a marked contrast with the more lyrical, often trifling, poetry of the idle, feudal courts.

The sonnet was developed as a literary form, principally by Dante (1265-1321), who wrote and worked in Florence. All the sonnet literature of Europe looks back to Petrarch (1304-74), whose influence on our own earliest sonneteers was direct and seminal. The Petrarchan sonnet was a verse form characteristic of its age both in formal structure and in the vision it embodied. Its 14 lines formed an octave followed by a sestet, each sub-divided by syntax but linked by the rhyme scheme. These complementary verse units contain two sequential structures of thought embodying the Renaissance humanist vision.

For the Tuscan writers of the late 13th century (Dante, Guinicelli and others) the figure of the lady and the praises bestowed upon her were mere earthly symbols of transcendental beauty and ideal love. The development and refinement of the sonnet is a remarkable evolution of an art form, with its beginning in a sometimes rudimentary expression of desire through several transitionary stages, and culminating in the majestic expressions of psychology and love left to us by Shakespeare.

The sonnet tradition takes its descent from two strains of poetry: one native to the feudal courts of Provence, the other from the city-states of 13th-century Italy. Any reader of Provençal lyrics will recognize in them attitudes and images which have passed through Petrarch's writings into the literature of Western Europe.

The term *sonnet* derives from the Italian *sonnetto*, 'little sound' or 'song'. There are now three basic forms of sonnet:

(1) Petrarchan; (2) Spenserian; and (3) Shakespearean.

Petrarchan Sonnet

The Italian sonnet, as Dante and Petrarch used it, contained 14 lines arranged as shown below. The letter sequences indicate the rhyme-relationship of the final syllable in each line.

Octave eight-line rhyme scheme:
a b b a, a b b a

Sestet six-line rhyme scheme in one of three forms:
c d e, c d e
c d, c d, c d
c d e d e c

To illustrate the rhyme patterns, here is a sonnet by the great Renaissance painter Michelangelo in the Petrarchan form:

Why should I seek to ease intense desire *a*
With still more tears and windy words of grief, *b*
When heaven, or late or soon, sends no relief *b*
To souls whom love has robed around with fire? *a*
 Why need my aching heart to death aspire, *a*
When all must die? Nay, death beyond belief *b*
Unto these eyes would be more sweet and brief, *b*
Since in my sum of woes all joys expire? *a*
 Therefore because I cannot shun the blow *etc*
I rather seek, say who must rule my breast,
Gliding between his gladness and his woe?
 If only chains and bands can make me blest,
No marvel if alone and bare I go
An armed Cavaliere's captive and slave confessed.

Translated by J.A. Symonds

The rhyme scheme of the final syllables in each line is:

Octave	*a b b a, a b b a*
Sestet	*c d, c d, c d*

The Tudor poets who embraced this form were exploring new patterns from which, in the fullness of time, the Elizabethans were to garner their rich harvest.

Spenserian Sonnet

The rhyming scheme developed by and named after Edmund Spenser, is indicated below. The letter sequences indicate the rhyme-relationship of the final syllable in each line.

Quatrain:	*Rhyme pattern*:
First	*a b a b*
Second	*b c b c*
Third	*c d c d*
Final couplet	*e e*

This verse form is also sometimes termed the *link sonnet* from the way each quatrain's final rhyme picks up on the next. There is also a binding final couplet as used by Shakespeare. The following example is from Spenser's sonnet cycle, *Amoretti* (1595):

70

Fresh spring, the herald of love's mighty king,
In whose coat-armour richly are displayed
All sorts of flowers, the which on earth do spring,
In goodly colours gloriously arrayed;
Go to my love, where she is careless laid,
Yet in her winter's bower not well awake;
Tell her the joyous time will not be stayed,
Unless she do him by the forelock take;
Bid her therefore herself soon ready make,
To wait on love amongst his lovely crew;
Where every one, that misseth then her make,
Shall be by him amerced with penance due.
  Make haste, therefore, sweet love, whilst it is prime;
  For none can call again the passed time.

Elizabethan Sonnet

During the Elizabethan period in England a sonnet of another form evolved and was brought to perfection, following its beginnings in the Tudor period. Throughout the last 25 years of Elizabeth's reign the sonnet surged in popularity. Poetry radiated from her court, where culture required – in addition to policy and valour – acquaintance with the traditions of Italian and French literature. The sonnet form established in England was described by George Gascoigne in 1575:

> Sonnets are of fourteen lynes, every lyne conteyning tenne syllables. The first twelve do ryme in states of foure lynes by crosse metre, and the last two ryming together do conclude the whole.

From Wyatt and Surrey, on through Sidney and Spenser, the Elizabethan sonnet developed, flowered and culminated, reaching its full realization with Shakespeare. The principal English sonnet form, the Shakespearean pattern, contains its ideas or themes in three parallel quatrains, and concentrates its emotional impact or central meaning in the final couplet.

The most usual rhyming scheme for an Elizabethan sonnet is as follows:

Quatrain:	*Rhyme pattern*:
First	*ab a b*
Second	*c d c d*
Third	*e f e f*
Final couplet	*gg*

This is illustrated in a familiar sonnet by Shakespeare:

116

Let me not to the marriage of true minds
Admit impediments. Love is not love

Which alters when it alteration finds,
Or bends with the remover to remove:
O, no! it is an ever-fixed* mark,
That looks on tempests and is never shaken;
It is the star to every wandering bark,
Whose worth's unknown, although his height be taken.
Love's not Time's fool, though rosy lips and cheeks
Within his bending sickle's compass come;
Love alters not with his brief hours and weeks,
But bears it out e'en to the edge of doom.
  If this be error and upon me prov'd,
  I never writ, nor no man ever lov'd.

The Elizabethan sonnet, as a verse-form expressing the mood and lyrical outlook of an age, has suffered undeserved neglect. The sonnets of Shakespeare (1564-1616) are an exception; they are continually accorded close attention, undergoing constant examination of source, image, and meaning. They are unsurpassed for sustained elevation and power. No selection can do justice to the impressive cumulative effect of the whole sequence.

The Renaissance poetic tradition, begun by Petrarch, evolved through the Elizabethan era of lyric writers to reach its consummation in the genius of Shakespeare. The poets of the late 16th century were attracted by the possibilities inherent in the love sonnet and considerably extended its range. Unfortunately, they were unable to introduce a new central theme to replace the obsolete convention of courtly love. Instead, they substituted an endless repetition of sentiment and conceits which brought the sonnet into disrepute. An attempt to carry forward the development of the sonnet was made by Edmund Spenser, whose particular contribution was to substitute the Protestant-Platonic ideal of pure and virtuous courtship for the defunct theme of chivalric infatuation.

The Sonnet's Sequent History

Most subsequent major poets have attempted to write sonnets with, it must be said, varying degrees of success. The form is at its most vital when employed, not for academic reasons, but because it is the verse structure best suited to its theme, content, and meaning. It puts this verse form into context and increases our appreciation of the major sonnet writers, if we look retrospectively at its use from our present position.

The sonnet is considered by some to be outmoded and discredited, particularly after its use by Romantics, who used it as a vehicle for dreamy, diffuse sentiment. The vigour and spare beauty of an incisively written sonnet reveals the injustice of this fusty reputation.

* In Elizabethan poetry the syllable 'ed' was pronounced; for example, 'fixed' had two measures: 'fix-ed'. If one measure only was required, the word was compressed and an apostrophe employed, for example 'lov'd'.

Edward Thomas (1878-1917) wrote in a letter:

> Personally, I have a dread of the sonnet. It must contain fourteen lines and a man must be a tremendous poet or a cold mathematician if he can accommodate his thoughts to such a condition.

Such a rhyming scheme need not be a prescriptive tyranny; rather it is a structural matrix of benign discipline which both challenges and sustains the writer. Used adroitly, it focuses concentration and contributes to the trenchant qualities which are the hall-marks of sonnet excellence.

Rupert Brooke, during November and December of 1914, wrote his sonnet, *The Soldier*, the fineness and richness of which has been blurred somewhat by being so frequently quoted:

> If I should die, think only this of me:
> That there's some corner of a foreign field
> That is for ever England. There shall be
> In that rich earth a richer dust concealed.

The self-effacing 'think only this of me' seems to reflect the unthinking, artless way so many of the young men of that time volunteered to throw their lives away.

The sonnet was a fundamental form of Elizabethan poetry and, as such, should be viewed in the context of that era's poetic works. Sonneteering was an almost universal vogue at the end of the 16th century. 'A perfect sonnet is one of the most difficult of all forms of poetry,' said Sidney Lee (1904). 'Only the fullest command of the harmonies of language and the ripest power of mental concentration ensure success.' Lee, with justification, says that the majority of aspiring sonneteers are 'notable for little else than the uncouthness of their verbiage and their poverty of thought. They are mere wallowers in the bogs that lie at the foot of the poetic mountain.'

As was noted earlier in this section, the sonnet was adopted by English writers in the mid 16th century from the love poetry of the Italian Renaissance. By this time the form had been used in Italy for nearly 200 years.

6
The Renaissance Enters England

The Elizabethans

AFTER CHAUCER'S death in 1400, English poetry was moribund, if not dead, for the whole of the 15th and the first half of the next century. English literature in the 16th century, unlike the visual arts and music, was profoundly influenced by Renaissance thought. William Caxton (c1421-91) had introduced the printing press into England and, by the first half of the 16th century, books had become increasingly plentiful and relatively cheap. Literacy grew, and readers were keen to acquaint themselves with the developing ideas of their day.

The development of humanism flourished, and classical or Italian models were employed to express it. Sir Philip Sidney (1554-86) wrote a series of sonnets using Petrarch's form and rhyme scheme, as well as a romance called *Arcadia*. Edmund Spenser (c1552-99), the greatest non-dramatic poet of Elizabethan England, wrote *The Faerie Queene*, combining the romance of Ariosto and the Christian allegory of Tasso. Finally, the great English achievement in the Renaissance was drama. The classical models for this were the Latin tragedies of Seneca and the comedies of Plautus and Terence. The wider availability of these plays through the introduction of printing created a demand that dramatists like Marlowe and Shakespeare were to satisfy magnificently. At the same time, prosperity and leisure prompted a surge of creativity in madrigals and musical composition.

In 1557 a remarkable book called *Songs and Sonnets, written by the Right Honourable Lord Henry Howard, late Earl of Surrey, and other* was published by Richard Tottel. It is usually known simply as Tottel's *Miscellany* and contains work by several identifiable poets – notably courtiers from the court of Henry VIII – and some anonymous pieces.

The collection forms a natural and convenient entry point into a study of Elizabethan poets and the sonnet as a verse form. In the *Miscellany*, the debt to Petrarch was acknowledged in two anonymous sonnets. The first opened with this tribute:

O Petrarch, head and prince of Poets all
Whose lively gift of flowing eloquence
Well may we seek, but find not how or whence
So rare a gift with thee did rise and fall,

> Peace to thy bones, and glory immortal
> Be to thy name!

The second began:

> With Petrarch to compare there may be no wight
> Nor yet attain unto so high a style.

The two principal poets in the *Miscellany* were Surrey and Wyatt (the 'other' of the original title). Both wrote their main literary works between 1530 and 1540, but none of it was published before 1557, when it appeared in the *Miscellany*.

The poet credited with having introduced the sonnet into England was Thomas **Wyatt** (1503-42). Born in Kent and educated at Cambridge, he was in the service of Henry VIII and went on many official missions to foreign countries. He was knighted in 1537. Sir Thomas Wyatt was stimulated by his contact with Italian literary men during his diplomatic service and he soon began to translate and emulate the work of Petrarch. Some of Wyatt's verse displays ease and mastery; other examples reveal stiffness and puerility. However, he does initially seem to have chosen the most conceited sonnets of Petrarch to imitate.

George Saintsbury (1845-1933), the distinguished English literary critic and writer on the history of English and French literature, says of Wyatt: 'He had a great deal to learn ... and the strange turns and twists which the poet gives to his decasyllables suggest either a total want of ear, or such a study in foreign languages that the student had actually forgotten the intonation and cadences of his own tongue.' His rebuke is turned, however, by an example like the following:

> *The lover having dreamed the enjoying of his love,*
> *complaineth that the dream is not either longer or truer:*
>
> Unstable dream, according to the place
>   Be steadfast once, or else at least be true.
>   By tasted sweetness, make me not to rue
> The sudden loss of thy false feigned grace.
> By good respect in such a dangerous case
>   Though brought'st not her into these tossing seas
>   But mad'st my sprite to live, my care to increase,
> My body in tempest her delight to embrace.
> The body dead, the sprite had his desire:
>   Painless was th' one, the other in delight.
>   Why then, alas! did it not keep it right,
> But thus return to leap into the fire?
> And where it was at wish, could not remain?
> Such mocks of dreams do turn to deadly pain.

Wyatt could at times be exquisite in the lyric measures at which he excelled, but the labour of writing sonnets seems always to have been too great to allow fineness. Grandeur he never commanded: he could be powerful or poignant, but not majestic.

E.K. Chambers (1866-1954) wrote of him that 'The deeper accents of emotion, with much else that is the soul of literature, come back with Wyatt.' In the best poems of Wyatt there is freedom, movement, life. It has been said of him that for those who like their poetry lean, sinewy and a little sad, Wyatt is a pre-eminent poet. E.M. Tillyard (1929) says that, because he experimentally used a liberality of rhyme, 'Technically Wyatt almost invented the Shakespearean form.'

Henry Howard, Earl of **Surrey** (c1518-47) was the son of the Duke of Norfolk. He was cousin to both Anne Boleyn and Catherine Howard, and a courtier of Henry VIII. Although his early reputation was that of a wise and sober young man, he later spent a number of periods in prison for various misdemeanours and was finally beheaded for treason. While in prison, he wrote most of the poetry for which he is renowned. This was published after his death, together with works by Sir Thomas Wyatt. As well as *Songs and Sonnets* he also translated *The Aeneid* into blank verse, the first known use in English of this form.

Surrey was fortunate to have as his model a poet as magnificently inventive as Virgil. Even so, it shows sound critical perception on his part to have realized that fidelity to those forms was essential if his blank verse was to be aesthetically interesting and agreeable. (Blank verse by its very nature may easily become slack and nerveless.) It was said of Surrey by G.F. Nott (1815): 'He reformed that rude and diffusive mode of writing which was common to all our poets who preceded him.' An appreciative comment by Maurice Evans (1955): 'He banished the aureate and the alliterative once and for all, and established a standard of clear, controlled language which was what the century needed above all things.' Here is an example of Surrey, a master of the architecture of verse, whose ear for the cadence of successive lines results in such an integrated poem.

Complaint that his lady, after she knew of his love,
kept her face alway hidden from him:

I never saw my lady lay apart
Her cornet black, in cold nor yet in heat,
Sith first she knew my grief was grown so great;
Which other fancies driveth from my heart,
That to myself I do the thought reserve,
The which unwares did wound my woeful breast.
But on her face mine eyes mought never rest
Yet, since she know I did her love, and serve
Her golden tresses clad away with black.
Her smiling looks that hid(es) thus evermore
And that restrains which I desire so sore.
So doth this cornet govern me, alack!
In summer sun, in winter's breath, a frost
Whereby the lights of her fair looks I lost.

Since Wyatt and Surrey both took Petrarch as their model, it is instructive to compare their work with the inspirational original:

140

Amor, che nel penser mio vive, e regna,
E'l suo seggio maggior nel mio cor tene;
Talor armato nela fronte vene;
Ivi si loca, et ivi pon sua insegna,
Quella ch'amare, e sofferir ne'nsegna,
E vol che'l gran desio, l'accesa spene
Ragion, vergogna, et reverenza affrene;
Di nostro ardir fra se stessa si sdegna?
Onde Amor paventoso fugge al core,
Lasciando ogni sua impresa; et piang, et trema;
Ivi s'asconde, et non appar piu fore.
Che poss'io far, tremendo il mio signore,
Se non star seco infin a l'ora estrema?
Che bel fin fa chi ben amando more.

Wyatt, who introduced Petrarch's poetry to England, produces a loose translation with some clumsiness:

The long love that in my thought I harbour,
And in my heart doth keep his residence,
Into my face presseth with bold pretence,
And there campeth displaying his banner.
She that me learns to have and to suffer,
And wills that my trust, and lust's negligence
Be reined by reason, shame, and reverence,
With his hardiness takes displeasure.
Where with love to the heart's forest he fleeth,
Leaving his enterprise with pain and cry,
And there him hideth, and not appeareth.
What may I do, when my master feareth,
But in the field with him to live and die?
For good is the life, ending faithfully.

Surrey, although influenced by Wyatt, is considered to be less literally accurate but more dexterous and poetic in execution:

Love that liveth and reigneth in my thought,
That built his seat within my captive breast;
Clad in the arms wherein with me he fought,
Oft in my face he doth his banner rest.
She, that me taught to love, and suffer pain;
My doubtful hope, and eke* my hot desire
With shamefast cloak to shadow and refrain,
Her smiling grace converteth straight to ire.
And coward Love then to the heart apace
Taketh his flight; whereas he lurks, and plains
His purpose lost, and dare not show his face.
For my Lord's guilt thus faultless bide I pains.

* Eke: 'to increase, add to'.

Yet from my Lord shall not my foot remove?
Sweet is his death, that takes his end by love.

The greatest non-dramatic poet of Elizabethan England, Edmund **Spenser** (c1552-99), was influenced by Ariosto (1474-1533) and by Torquato Tasso (1544-95), Ariosto's Italian successor in the production of massive epic poems. Spenser's most celebrated poem is *The Faerie Queene*, an allegorical, chivalric, epic romance originally conceived in 12 books, of which only the first six and fragments of a seventh were written. His other works include *The Shephearde's Calendar*, *Epithalamion*, *Prothalamion*, and many sonnets.

The last 20 years of the 16th century – which was a productive period of poetic development and of vigorous and prolific writing – is the period in which Spenser is the dominant figure. He was educated at Merchant Taylors', and at Pembroke Hall, Cambridge, where in May 1569 he joined as a sizar (an undergraduate receiving expenses from the college). He fulfilled seven years of residence, first taking his Bachelor's Degree in 1573, and then his Master's three years later. Thereafter he seems to have moved to the North to stay with friends and spend a year or two there, falling in love and writing his lady, as heroine, into *The Shephearde's Calendar*. This remarkable work brought Spenser immediate and well-deserved recognition, setting him at once at the head of the English poets of his day.

In 1580 Spenser became private secretary to Lord Grey and went with him to Ireland, where he resided for some 10 years. During this time he made several visits to England. On 1 December 1589 the first three books of *The Faerie Queene* were entered at Stationers' Hall, and were published in the spring of the next year. (The fourth, fifth, and sixth books appeared in January 1596.) On 11 June 1594 he married Elizabeth Boyle. In 1595 he published the beautiful *Amoretti* or love sonnets, together with the still more beautiful *Epithalamion*, describing his courtship and marriage.

In 1598 he was named Sheriff of Corke. A few weeks later the Irish Rebellion broke out, and Spenser's house was sacked and burnt, resulting in the death of one of his children. After the tragedy, he returned to this country and died in Westminster on 16 January 1599.

Spenser enriched poetic diction by introducing into his work archaisms, dialect words and foreign loanwords. In *The Faerie Queene* he perfected a new nine-line stanza form which became known as the Spenserian stanza. In its nine lines, eight iambic pentameters (five-stress lines) are followed by an alexandrine (six-stress line). The line-endings are rhymed as follows:

a b a b b c b b c

The form was later employed by Byron, Shelley, and Keats, but is suitable only for long narrative poems. *The Faerie Queene* is the story of

12 Knights, representing 12 virtues, who were to be sent on adventures from the court of Glorianna, Queen of Fairyland. The poem is incomplete, but nevertheless contains some 4,000 stanzas, that is, 36,000 lines. As a poem, it has its artificialities but it carries a powerful sense of unity and flowing eloquence. Spenser has been called the poet's poet, a description earned by the sheer poetic qualities of his work; an apparent absence of effort; the colour, the sound-effects; the cadences of his phrasing, his verse-language. George Saintsbury (1907) said of it that '*The Faerie Queene* is the only long poem that a lover of poetry can sincerely wish longer.'

The poem is sometimes political, more often religious or moral, and veiled allusions to Queen Elizabeth I are not difficult to find. Certainly the beauty, grandeur, and drama of the poem were inspired by her reign. They are expressed in poetry unsurpassed for its wealth of imagery, melodic line, and flexible stanzas. A flavour of the poet's chivalric sensitivity in this epic piece may be gained from the first stanza from Canto III of Book I:

> Nought is there under heaven's wide hollowness,
> That moves more dear compassion of mind,
> Than beauty brought to unworthy wretchedness
> Through envy's snares, or fortune's freaks unkind.
> I, whether lately through her brightness blind,
> Or through allegiance, and fast fealty,
> Which I do owe unto all womankind,
> Feel my heart pierced with so great agony,
> When such I see, that all for pity I could die.

Although Spenser's name tends to be irrevocably linked with *The Faerie Queene*, some of the sonnets in the *Amoretti* (among Spenser's later works) are comparable with the best of Sidney's and hardly below the finest of Shakespeare's.

Sonnet 88

> Since I have lacked the comfort of that light,
> The which was wont to lead my thoughts astray,
> I wander as in darkness of the night,
> Afraid of every danger's least dismay:
> Nor ought I see, though in the clearest day,
> When others gaze upon their shadows vain,
> But the only imagine of that heavenly ray
> Whereof some glance doth in mine eye remain,
> Of which, beholding the idea plain,
> Through contemplation of my purest part,
> With light thereof I do myself sustain,
> And thereon feed my love-affamished heart.
> But with such brightness whilst I fill my mind
> I starve my body, and mine eyes do blind.

Sonnet 75

One day I wrote her name upon the strand,
But came the waves and washed it away.
Again I wrote it with a second hand,
But came the tide and made my pains his prey.
'Vain man,' said she, 'that dost in vain assay
A mortal thing so to immortalize,
For I myself shall like to this decay,
And eke my name be wiped out likewise.'
'Not so,' quoth I. 'Let baser things devise
To die in dust, but you shall live by fame.
My verse your virtues rare shall eternize,
And in the heavens write your glorious name.
Where when as death shall all the world subdue,
Our love shall live, and later life renew.'

In Sonnet 30 of his *Amoretti* Spenser asks a question:

My love is like to ice, and I to fire:
how comes it then that this her cold so great
is not dissolv'd through my so hot desire,
but harder grows the more I her entreat?

The answer comes in the final couplet:

Such is the power of love in gentle mind
that it can alter all the course of kind.

But, making clear the worth of the incomparable 'she', in the final couplet of Sonnet 35, he writes:

All this world's glory seemeth vain to me,
and all their showers but shadows saving she.

From Italy came the doctrine of love and beauty spiritualized into a passion of excessive refinement. Poets sought a great patroness to whom they could address elaborate, perhaps fanciful, protestations which were combined with a genuine lover's natural reserve and respect. They sought a 'Laura' of cruel chastity and perfect beauty. Desire pushed against a Christian 'thou shalt not' and longed to move through the physical, earthly beauty to the Platonic ideal *Beauty* itself.

It manifests in the timeless struggle between duty and passion, reason and desire.

Humanism in England

The development of humanism in England undoubtedly influenced Erasmus of Rotterdam (1466-1536), who was brought into contact with humanist ideas during his visits here. In addition to teaching at Cambridge, Erasmus formed a warm personal friendship with the English statesman Sir Thomas More (1478-1535), who became Lord Chancellor in 1529. Moreover, John Colet (c1466-1519), the English theologian and humanist, collaborated with More and Erasmus prior to his appointment as Dean of St Paul's Cathedral. These ideas, and the use of classical or Italian models to express them, influenced such men as Sir Philip Sidney.

Sir Philip **Sidney** (1554-86), poet, soldier, and statesman, was born at Penshurst in Kent. Educated at Shrewsbury School and Christ Church, Oxford, he attended the court of Queen Elizabeth I and spent several years in Europe, often as the Queen's representative. Sidney embodied that perfect balance of grace and accomplishment which made him the delight of all who knew him. His biographer wrote:

> I lived with him and knew him from a child, yet I never knew him other than a man with such steadiness of mind, lovely and familiar gravity, as carried grace and reverence above greater years; his talk ever of knowledge and his very play tending to enrich his mind.

It was said of Sidney, by William of Orange, that he was the ripest and most valuable counsellor at Elizabeth's court. In 1580, having temporarily incurred the Queen's displeasure, Sidney withdrew from the court, at which time he wrote his *Arcadia*, a romance in prose and poetry. He produced and circulated privately among his friends *An Apologie for Poetrie* (sometimes called *The Defence of Poesie*) and the sequence of sonnets and songs, *Astrophel and Stella*. Lady Penelope Rich *née* Devereux (1562?-1607) was the loved lady of the sonnet sequence. Restored to favour and knighted, he embarked on a military campaign in the Low Countries, where he received a bullet wound in the thigh, which became infected. According to a traditional story, he characteristically declined a cup of water, giving it to a dying soldier with the words, 'Thy need is greater than mine.' A month later, at the age of 32, he died. Dr John James, who was at Sidney's bedside when he died, wrote in his journal that night: 'Few ages have ever brought forth his equal, and the very hope of our age seemeth to be utterly extinguished in him'. His work was not published until after his death, when it became apparent that he was among the best poets of his era. His *Apologie* is one of the most notable examples of literary criticism in the language. Here is an example of Sidney's quality in a sonnet, which fittingly concludes a sequence by its noble combination of Christian and Platonic themes:

From Certaine Sonnets

Leave me, O Love, which reachest but to dust,
And thou, my mind, aspire to higher things.
Grow rich in that which never taketh rust;
What ever fades but fading pleasure brings.
Draw in thy beams, and humble all thy might
To that sweet yoke where lasting freedoms be;
Which breaks the clouds and opens forth the light,
That doth both shine and give us light to see.
O take fast hold: let that light be thy guide

In this small course which birth draws out to death,
And think how evil causeth him to slide
Who seeketh Heav'n, and comes of heav'nly breath.
  Then farewell World; thy uttermost I see.
  Eternal Love, maintain thy life in me.

The underlying theme of this poem seems to be that, if beauty is to be enjoyed without concomitant suffering, the courtier should, using reason, transcend desire for the body and aspire to beauty alone. Using love to mount higher, he will no longer contemplate the particular beauty of one woman, but rather the universal beauty that adorns all bodies. Just as love attracts from the particular to the universal beauty, so mind is drawn to the universal intellect. Thus united with divine love, and understanding all things intelligible, the soul perceives unveiled pure divine beauty.

Sadly, as mentioned earlier, Sidney died at the age of 32 (when Shakespeare was just 22). Sidney sometimes writes in the rhyme-scheme that came to be known as the Shakespearean sonnet form. He also naturally uses the conventions of poetic imagery which were an inherited tradition. As a result we seem to observe an apparent anticipatory glimpse of Shakespeare in these two sonnets:

39

Come Sleep; O Sleep, the certain knot of peace,
The baiting place of wit, the balm of woe,
The poor man's wealth, the prisoner's release,
Th' indifferent judge between the high and low.
With shield of proof, shield me from out the press
Of those fierce darts despair at me doth throw.
O make in me those civil wars to cease,
I will good tribute pay if thou do so.
Take thou of me smooth pillows, sweetest bed,
A chamber deaf to noise and blind to light,
A rosy garland, and a weary head.
And if these things, as being thine by right,
  Move not thy heavy grace, thou shalt in me,
  Livelier than elsewhere, Stella's image see.

90

Stella, think not that I by verse seek fame
Who seeks't who hop'st who lov'st but only thee,
Thine eyes my pride, thy lips my history,
If thou praise not, all other praise is shame.
Nor so ambitious am I, as to frame
A nest for my young praise in laurel tree;
In truth, I swear I wish not there should be
Graved in my epitaph a poet's name.
Nor if I would, could I just title make
That any laud thereof to me should grow;

Without my pains, from others, wings I take,
For nothing from my wit or will doth flow,
  Since all my words thy beauty doth indite
  And love doth hold my hand and makes me write.

The range and originality of Sidney's art is extraordinary. He experiments with a great variety of rhyme schemes and, indeed, carries the English sonnet forward from its Petrarchan birth to its pre-Shakespearean maturity.

A poet and dramatist who should receive mention in the context of Elizabethan poetry is Samuel **Daniel** (1562-1619). After travelling extensively in France and Italy (c1586), he was employed as tutor to the son of William Herbert, Earl of Pembroke, the patron of Shakespeare.

Daniel collaborated with Spenser and Drayton in a late-Elizabethan project to compile a historical epic about the Wars of the Roses, called *The Civil Wars*. This huge unfinished work had been intended to assist in the creation of a sense of national identity. It is, however, his sonnets which constitute the major portion of his writings. He took the inevitable haughty, unattainable lady, Delia, and published a collection of sonnets, *Delia* (1592). Probably the best known of all his sonnets is that containing the lines:

Care-charmer Sleep, son of the sable Night,
Brother to Death, in silent darkness born!

Interestingly both Homer and Hesiod called sleep 'brother of death'. Daniel 'borrowed' from Petrarch as much as he emulated him. Petrarch's sonnet to *Laura in Heaven*:

Due gran nemiche inseme erano agiunte,
Bellezza, et Onesta, con pace tanta …

becomes, in Daniel's Sonnet 6:

Chastity and Beauty, which were deadly foes,
Live reconciled friends within her brow.

He maintains, in Sonnet 39, the required respectful distance from the idealized source of his aspiring love:

Although my careful accents never mov'd thee
Yet count it no disgrace that I have lov'd thee.

For all but the greatest Renaissance poets, the sonnet was less an exploration of the phenomenon of love than an attempt to transform a moment of passion into a polished artefact. Daniel, in his *Defence of Ryme*, praises the sonnet as the vehicle with which to structure the 'unformed Chaos without fashion' of our imagination into 'an orbe of order and forme'.

In this example Daniel asks a poet's rhetorical question; then answers himself with a lover's response.

Sonnet 17

Why should I sing in verse, why should I frame
These sad neglected notes for her dear sake?
Why should I offer up unto her name
The sweetest sacrifice my youth can make?

Why should I strive to make her live for ever,
That never deigns to give me joy to live?
Why should m'afflicted Muse so much endeavour
Such honour unto cruelty to give?

If her defects have purchas'd her this fame,
What should her virtue do, her smiles, her love?
If this her worst, how should her best inflame?
What passions would her milder favours move?

Favours (I think) would sense quite overcome,
And that makes happy lovers ever dumb.

The poet Michael **Drayton** (1563-1631) was born at Hartshill, Warwickshire, but little is known of his life. He is of principal interest here for his collection of sonnets, gathered under the title *Idea's Mirror*, which appeared in 1594. This consisted of 51 sonnets, mainly in the Petrarchan mode. The sequence was continuously revised, with additions appearing in 1602, 1605, and the final version (containing 64 sonnets) in 1619.

Drayton felt it important not to have so many 'whining' sonnets. In a poetic preface to his 1619 edition of his sonnets he writes:

No far-fetch'd sigh shall ever wound my breast,
Love from mine eye a tear shall never wring,
Nor in Ah-mees my whining sonnets dress'd.

Whereas Spenser's *Amoretti* were entirely within the charmed circle of love, Drayton's sonnets spill over into the world beyond the inner sphere controlled by love. He is very keen to display his wit – as though for a protection against love. Here is one such example:

To the Senses

When conqu'ring love did first my heart assail,
Unto mine aid I summon'd ev'ry sense,
Doubting, if that proud tyrant should prevail,
My heart should suffer for mine eyes' offence;
But he with beauty first corrupted sight,
My hearing brib'd with her tongue's harmony,
My taste by her sweet lips drawn with delight,
My smelling won with her breath's spicerie:
But when my touching came to play his part,
(The king of senses, greater than the rest)
He yields love up the keys unto my heart,
And tells the other how they should be blest.
And thus by those of whom I hop'd for aid
To cruel love my soul was first betray'd.

Michael Drayton outlived Shakespeare by some 15 years and was publishing work up to the penultimate year of his life. In a sense, he brought a sceptical and healthy realism to the growing prevalence of wan complaining lovers, which had gone beyond the blending of Christian and Platonic idealism to become a mere convention.

After the innovative skill and the developing excellence of sonnet writers, from Tottel's *Miscellany* of 1557 to Drayton's *Idea's Mirror*, it is the moment to turn to the place of poetry on the stage.

An outstanding playwright who preceded and influenced Shakespeare (and others), was Thomas **Kyd** (1558-94). He is chiefly known for his 'revenge play', *The Spanish Tragedy*, which was immediately successful when presented in the late 1580s. Kyd is known to have written *Pompey the Great* (not printed until 1595), and two other plays are attributed to him: *The Tragedy of Solyman and Perseda* and a version of *Hamlet* which preceded Shakespeare's. *The Spanish Tragedy* is unusual among Elizabethan plays in that scholars have been unable to trace a source for its plot. Horatio, son of Hieronimo, is murdered while sitting within an arbor with the lady Bel-Imperia. Balthazar, the rival of Horatio, commits the murder with the assistance of Bel-Imperia's brother Lorenzo. The murderers suspend the dead body from a tree in the garden, where the father of the murdered Horatio – roused by Bel-Imperia's cries – discovers it and becomes consumed with revenge. He recounts his distressful tale to anyone who will listen:

> But night, the coverer of accursed crimes,
> With pitchy silence hushed these traitors' harms
> And lent them leave, for they had sorted leisure
> To take advantage in my garden-plot
> Upon my son, my dear Horatio:
> There, merciless they butchered up my boy.
>
> ★
>
> Where shall I run to breathe abroad my woes,
> My woes whose weight hath wearied the earth?
> Or mine exclaims, that have surcharged the air
> With ceaseless plaints for my deceased son?
>
> Act IV, Scene iv

The opening lines of the play are spoken by an apparition, the Ghost of Andrea, who deftly explains who Don Andrea was while living:

> When this eternal substance of my soul
> Did live imprisioned in my wanton flesh,
> Each in their function serving other's need,
> I was a courtier in the Spanish court.
>
> Act I, Scene i

Kyd is graphically realistic and economical in his use of words in ordinary description. Here an officer describes a military tactic:

Our battles both were pitched in squadron form,
Each corner strongly fenced with wings of shot;
But ere we joined and came to push of pike,
I brought a squadron of our readiest shot
From out our rearward to begin the fight:
They brought another wing to encounter us.

Act I, Scene ii

Later in the play a page-boy enters with a casket and uses soliloquy to explain his motivation. This short episode is in prose:

My master hath forbidden me to look in this box, and by my troth 'tis likely, if he had not warned me, I should not have had so much idle time; for we men's-kind in our minority are like women in their uncertainty: that they are most forbidden, they will soonest attempt. So I now.

(The page proceeds to open the casket.) Act III, Scene v

Kyd was powerfully influenced by the Roman dramatist Seneca, and certain dramatic devices he employs have come either directly from Seneca's works or from imitators such as Giraldi Cinthio (1504-73).

The Spanish Tragedy has always been analysed for the many examples of emulated Senecan convention and dramatic technique. In the following example we see how Kyd handled the Senecan device of *stichomythia* (line-by-line dialogue), a usage which lacked life in the hands of most earlier and contemporary playwrights:

LORENZO: Sister, what means this melancholy walk?
BEL-IMPERIA That for a while I wish no company.
LORENZO: But here the prince is come to visit you.
BEL-IMPERIA: That argues that he lives in liberty.
BALTHAZAR: No madam, but in pleasing servitude.
BEL-IMPERIA: Your prison then belike is your conceit.

Act I, Scene iv

Something of the lady's spirit is evident even in these brief lines of Bel-Imperia. This sparseness gives an actor ample opportunity to develop and open out the role.

Kyd employs an extraordinary range of dramatic styles and theatrical devices in his successful stage-play. *The Spanish Tragedy* is remarkable for the deft and integral way in which the author has brought his thematic material to dramatic life. Kyd is particularly adept at co-ordinating intricate features of dramatic structure. The swift and sure way in which he communicates necessary information – especially in the early scenes – and the way the play moves forward, as a whole, contributed to its immediate contemporary success.

Ben Jonson was paid for revisions to *The Spanish Tragedy* and some have suggested that Webster or Shakespeare or Dekker contributed lines during further revision. Whatever the truth of such speculation, this play deserves its place as one of the first important English tragedies.

Thomas Kyd was one of the best-known tragic poets of his time, and his work showed an advance in the construction of plot and development of character. His achievement, however, was about to be eclipsed by the master dramatist of all time – William Shakespeare.

Shakespeare

Ben Jonson said of Shakespeare, 'He was not of an age but for all time.' Shakespeare was a poetic being whose consummate expressive genius not only mirrored the spirit and people of his age, but transcended both. Dryden and Dr Johnson considered him to be 'the largest and most genuine progeny of common humanity'. To this Coleridge added his assessment that the characters created by Shakespeare were 'ideal realities'. The sheer breadth of his imagination constitutes an unequalled measure of the human dimension. This high evaluation of Shakespeare's greatness has been undiminished even in our own times. Igor Stravinsky (1882-1971) the Russian-born composer, gave his succinct assessment: 'Shakespeare; not quite God.'

A wide-ranging assessment on this scale has to be based on something very substantial, and an examination of Shakespeare's achievement reveals the genius upon which the renown is based. William Shakespeare (1564-1616), the son of John Shakespeare, a well-to-do tradesman and farmer, was born in Stratford-upon-Avon, Warwickshire. It is known that William's father and mother could not write, and this fact makes it likely that they would have wanted their eldest son to attend the free grammar school of Stratford. If so, he would have studied – among other subjects – Latin, Rhetoric and the plays of Terence. Little has been recorded of the poet's life and nothing is known of Shakespeare's late boyhood. In November 1582 a marriage licence was issued to William (then 18 years of age) and Anne Hathaway (then 26). She was the daughter of a well-to-do local farmer, an old friend of William's father. In May 1583, a daughter, Susanna, was born; she was always to be his favourite child. Twins, a boy and a girl (Hamnet and Judith) were born to the couple some 21 months later; they were baptized early in February 1585.

In 1587, a year before the invasion attempt by the Spanish Armada, Shakespeare left Stratford for London. He made contact with James Burbage (a man of considerable importance in theatrical and literary circles) and became a trusted friend and fellow actor in the leading theatrical company, the Lord Chamberlain's Men (called the King's Men after 1603). Shakespeare became a sharer (one of seven) in the Blackfriars theatre which was constructed upon part of the site of the dissolved monastery. It was a highly successful business venture. Shakespeare also benefited in the wills of several actors. In 1594 the construction of the Globe theatre was in progress on the Bankside (Southwark), a theatre built at the cost of the Blackfriars theatre sharers. The Globe opened in 1595, its motto: *Totus mundus agit histrionem* ('All the world's a stage').

In the beginning of 1598 – some 12 years after leaving Stratford – we find Shakespeare owning one of the finest houses, New Place, in one of the best parts of Stratford. He also bought property in London.

In 1601 the father of Shakespeare died and was buried at Stratford-upon-Avon. At that time five of his eight children were living: William, Gilbert, Joan, Richard, and Edmund. Shakespeare's mother, Mary, died and was buried at Stratford in September 1608.

One of the last acts of Shakepeare's life was the bestowing of his daughter Judith's hand upon Thomas Quiney, a vintner and wine-merchant of Stratford. In the late spring of that year Shakespeare became ill. His son-in-law, Dr John Hall, had been married to Susanna Shakespeare for more than eight years and it is likely that he attended his father-in-law in his last illness. On 23 April 1616 – the day of his 52nd birthday – Shakespeare died. Adverse inference is often drawn from the bequest in his will of his 'second best bed' to his wife. It should be remembered, however, that it was the marriage bed and consequently of more significance to William and Anne than the 'best bed' – which in those days was normally reserved for guests. As Shakespeare's wife, Anne was entitled by law to live out the remainder of her life at New Place; she also had a legal right to one third of her husband's various properties, so she was well provided for. Anne Shakespeare died in August 1623 and was buried beside her husband in the chancel of Holy Trinity Church.

Shakespeare's Poetry

In some 30 years there came the whole Shakespeare canon: plays, sonnets, lyric and narrative poetry. However, the collected works were not published until seven years after his death when they were brought together by his fellow actors, Heminge and Condell, to preserve 'the memory of so worthy a friend'. In a preface to the plays they wrote, 'His mind and hand went together, and what he thought, he uttered with that easinesse, that we have scarse received from him a blot in his papers.' When this First Folio edition was published in 1623, Martin Droeshout's engraved portrait was prefixed as a frontispiece. Ben Jonson accompanied it with these words:

> This Figure, that thou seest here put,
> It was for gentle Shakespeare cut;
> Wherein the Graver had a strife
> With Nature, to out-doo the life;
> O, could he but have drawne his wit
> As well in brasse, as he hath hit
> His face; the Print would then surpasse
> All, that was ever writ in brasse.
> But, since he cannot, Reader looke
> Not on his Picture, but his Booke.

Shakespeare is known principally as a poet-dramatist and this survey of his work will begin with the plays. They not only contain his greatest poetry but it is in that myriad world of character-types and events that Shakespeare transcends his time and place to become relevant for every age. His artistry and technique as poet-dramatist emerge as we see how he deals with plot, events and people. The words he gives to his players speak directly to us and to our condition.

Most of the plots for Shakespeare's plays were derived from traditional medieval legend, contemporary chronicles, classical literature, and existing dramas of his own day – particularly material drawn from Plutarch's *Lives* and Holinshed's *Chronicles*. The work is distinguished by a more profound understanding and conception of characters than is found in any of his fellow dramatists. His poetry is superior, having great variety, delicacy, sensitivity, and dramatic appropriateness. The lyric and narrative poetry is fairly conventional, but the sonnets and songs from the plays are distinguished by a combination of imagination, precision, and deep sincere emotion.

Shakespeare's greatness as an artist resides above all in the total impact which each of his plays makes upon us in performance, and the extent to which his work is relevant to each successive generation. Perhaps this is because he explores the great problems of human existence – the many forms and aspects of love and forgiveness; the possibilities and consequence of human error, particularly flaws of character in great men; the mystery of death and the transience of this human existence. All this is achieved with a subtlety and a directness which remain miraculous through countless readings and successive performances. As William Hazlitt expressed it, 'If we wish to know the force of human genius we should read Shakespeare.'

He is universally acknowledged to be the finest writer in the English language and one of the greatest ever in any tongue. The later plays illustrate his growing interest in psychological motivation rather than the simple sequence of events. By means of the *soliloquy*, the playwright indicates not so much what the characters do as why they do it, a 'thinking aloud' which reveals the inner workings of the character's mind. He expressed an understanding of the human being which has withstood the analysis of philosophers and psychologists ever since.

In four major plays, *Hamlet*, *Othello*, *King Lear* and *Macbeth*, the dramatic truth, poetic beauty, and profundity of meaning achieved reaches an artistic perfection matched only by the best examples of Classical Greek drama.

Shakespeare was writing at a crucial point in the development of English society, when Elizabethan man was moving through the transition from the medieval age to the modern. He creates in his character-dramas an individual human being responding to a particular set of circumstances, but he reveals the thoughts and feelings, and the living essence, of the person in a manner that confers universal recognition. Although it is simplistic to distinguish a single characteristic for each of Shakespeare's four great archetypes, namely: Hamlet, Lear, Macbeth and Othello, this is done here in order to emphasize the thoroughness with which the poet-dramatist explores these limiting attributes.

Date	*Individual*	*Characteristic*
c1600	Hamlet	Doubt
c1604	Othello	Passion
c1605	King Lear	Pride
c1605	Macbeth	Ambition

Hamlet

Shakespeare's *Hamlet* is based on a rudimentary story by the 13th-century Danish chronicler, Saxo Grammaticus. Hamlet discovers to his horror that Claudius, his uncle, and Gertrude, his mother, now reigning together as king and queen, have been responsible for the death of his royal father. He puts aside Ophelia, whom he loves, and, feigning madness, dedicates himself to revenge. While Hamlet is vacillating, Laertes, the brother of Ophelia (who has lost her reason and drowned herself), challenges him to a 'friendly' duel. Encouraged by the King, Laertes uses a poisoned foil, but because of an accidental exchange of weapons during the fight, both men receive fatal wounds. On realizing the treachery, the dying Hamlet at last kills the King.

Schlegel (1767-1845), the German poet, scholar, and critic, wrote: 'the whole play is intended to show that calculating consideration exhausts … the power of action'.

In Machiavelli's, *The Prince* (1532), it was asserted that 'whoever desires to govern a state must begin by assuming that all men are bad and ever ready to show their vicious nature.' Shakespeare softens the harshness of the Machiavellian assessment by ameliorating judgement and distinguishing nature from nurture (conditioning), to give the individual the benefit of any doubt:

> So, oft it chances in particular men,
> That for some vicious mole of nature in them,
> As, in their birth, – wherein they are not guilty,
> Since nature cannot choose his origin, –
> By the o'ergrowth of some complexion,
> Oft breaking down the pales and forts of reason,
> Or by some habit that too much o'er-leavens
> The form of plausive manners; that these men,
> Carrying, I say, the stamp of one defect,
> Being nature's livery, or fortune's star,
> Their virtues else, be they as pure as grace,
> As infinite as man may undergo,
> Shall in the general censure take corruption
> From that particular fault: the dram of eale
> Doth all the noble substance of a doubt,
> To his own scandal.
>
> *Hamlet*, Act I, Scene iv

The language in this powerful play is succinct, cogent, and witty.

> A little more than kin, and less than kind.

These are Hamlet's first words in reply to his uncle-stepfather's reference to him as cousin and 'son', and they indicate the perplexity of the young man whose family relationships have been set awry. His uncle (if a ghost is to be believed) has murdered his father – the late king; Hamlet's mother has married the murderer.

Hamlet has given his word to the ghost that the sepulchral command to wreak revenge will take precedence in his brain. The Prince perceives the royal court of Denmark to be a prison, rotten to the core with intrigue, spying, drunkenness, and immorality.

Whether his madness is feigned or not, he behaves with an 'unkindness' bordering on animality, with total absence of feeling.

> … now could I drink hot blood,
> And do such bitter business as the day
> Would quake to look on …
>
> Act III, Scene ii

His cruelty brings about the rejection, insanity, and death of the young girl who loves him. This and other acts produce an inversion of a central belief of Shakespeare's, that only love and forgiveness can generate 'kindness'.

In the 'play within the play' which Hamlet has set up to test the King's conscience, the Player King says:

> *'Now, what my love is, proof hath made you know;*
> *And as my love is siz'd, my fear is so.*
> *Where love is great, the littlest doubts are fear;*
> *Where little fears grow great, great love grows there.'*
>
> Act III, Scene ii

The love referred to here is flawed. It is said in the *New Testament* that: 'Perfect love casteth out fear'; so its inversion, a 'great love' that turns the 'littlest doubt' into 'fear', attracts a large question-mark. Hamlet is preoccupied with his thoughts and, as he himself later says, '… there is nothing either good or bad, but thinking makes it so …'

Although discussion and analysis abound concerning Hamlet's psyche and his inability to act decisively, he never fails to convince dramatically. His unpredictability, procrastination, and inactivity, his endless reflection, rationalization, and 'reasons' for not acting, are universally recognizable. The events take place within a revenge play constructed around the chief character's reluctance to take revenge. When he does finally move into action there is a bloodbath, as though delay compounded the retribution. It is a coherent play, full of paradox; a most profound commentary on the mind of man and the complexities of human life.

> The time is out of joint; O cursed spite,
> That ever I was born to set it right!
>
> Act I, Scene v

Hamlet deplores his situation and his wretched response to it. Sir John Davies (1569-1626), English lawyer and a poet known for the vigour of his writing, said: 'I know myself a man, which is a proud and yet a wretched thing.' Shakespeare, in *Hamlet*, considers man's ultimate potential; then contrasts it questioningly – with dust:

> What a piece of work is a man! How noble in reason! how infinite in faculty! in form, in moving, how express and admirable! in action how like an angel! in apprehension how like a god! the beauty of the world, the paragon of animals! And yet, to me, what is this quintessence of dust?
>
> Act II, Scene ii

This seemingly exaggerated description has to be viewed in the context of his having been given, as a man, choice, reason, and free-will!

With mind rich in fancy, having fullness of soul; born rather for feeling than action, more for contemplation than deed – an artist and scholar rather than warrior, hero, or statesman – Hamlet with superior level of mind discerns true principle. This principle, perhaps the noblest pronounced by Shakespeare, is in essence:

> Rightly to be great
> Is not to stir without great argument,
> But greatly to find quarrel in a straw
> When honour's at the stake.
>
> Act IV, Scene iv

Hamlet, even with *his* fine intelligence, expresses but cannot implement, this principle. His is a tender, nervous manifestation, less coarse than the natures surrounding him in the Danish court. He is invested with a knowledge and insight not traditionally part of the muscularity of the old heroic age.

This play is Shakespeare's most comprehensive study of the individual. As well as being a prince, Hamlet is, significantly, a student of philosophy and seems to prefer the seclusion of contemplation at Wittenberg to the bustle of the court. As the play proceeds, Hamlet becomes increasingly alone in an alien political milieu. In the world of Elsinore, with its roistering courtiers and intrigue, he strives to balance his understanding of philosophy with his experience of life. He is disillusioned with mankind generally but not with Horatio – a fellow philosopher:

> for thou hast been
> As one, in suffering all, that suffers nothing,
> A man that fortune's buffets and rewards
> Hast ta'en with equal thanks; and bless'd are those
> Whose blood and judgement are so well co-mingled

> That they are not a pipe for fortune's finger
> To sound what stop she please. Give me that man
> That is not passion's slave, and I will wear him
> In my heart's core, ay, in my heart of heart,
> As I do thee.
>
> Act III, Scene ii

This state of balance, this equanimity of blood and judgement to which Hamlet himself aspires unsuccessfully, he recognizes as a noble ideal in man. In turn, Horatio acknowledges Hamlet's eminence in his elegant farewell:

> Now cracks a noble heart. Good-night, sweet prince,
> And flights of angels sing thee to thy rest!
>
> Act V, Scene ii

King Lear

The immediate source for *King Lear* was Holinshed, who in turn derived it from Geoffrey of Monmouth's *Historia Britonum*. In Shakespeare's version of the story, King Lear in his old age divides his kingdom between his daughters Goneril and Regan, who profess great love for him but then harass him into madness. Cordelia, left portionless, succours him and comes with an army to dethrone her sisters, but is captured and slain. Lear dies over her body.

In the play Shakespeare presents, in juxtaposition, political power and individual behaviour within the context of the overarching moral order to which both are subject:

The Moral Order

Macrocosm	*Microcosm*
The State	The individual

In modern terms, Lear is a hyperactive old man on the brink of senility but, infuriatingly, he retains the superficial logic of seemingly normal behaviour based on decades of habit. He cannot bear to be questioned or contradicted; for him, obedience equals love (which he craves) and opposition is total betrayal.

In this play, Shakespeare is indicating the sacredness of order, rule, and self-rule, but at a level so deeply rooted in human morality as to be beyond religion. Even Regan says, 'he has ever but slenderly known himself'. The upheaval of the elements is a tangible metaphor for what Lear has done and what has been done to him. He, in his blind arrogance, has destroyed the kingdom of which he is absolute ruler; as for his courtiers, they have lost the sense of awe that should accompany the person of the king, whatever he may be like as a man. No such loss has occurred for the blinded Duke of Gloucester, who retains the conventional loyalty: 'O let me kiss that hand,' he cries. 'Let me wipe it first … It smells of mortality,' says Lear.

Within the dark world of *King Lear*, humanity is stripped bare of its pretensions, and Lear, the supreme egoist and autocrat, without the trappings of pampering power, discovers his formerly submerged humanitarianism.

Lear is obdurate and implacable. He has made a fool of himself, but his pride will not let him retract. He fails to show responsibility in office. Granville-Barker described him as 'a massive fortress of pride', a man devoid of judgement and moral sensitivity. His autocracy has bred in him only worldly values.

> LEAR: Dost thou call me fool, boy?
> FOOL: All thy other titles thou hast given away; that thou wast born with.
> Act I, Scene iv

He is a ruler who yields absolute power to ordinary nature (symbolized by his two eldest daughters). Disillusioned by their treatment of his impotence, he breaks into incoherent ramblings and empty threats as he realizes his powerlessness. Stripped of temporal power and thus naked, defying nature's wildest forces (the storms), he becomes a crazed lonely man. Lear's anguished plea: 'O let me not be mad, not mad, sweet heaven,' suggests that sanity is heaven; madness, hell.

> I am a very foolish, fond old man,
> Fourscore and upward, not an hour more or less;
> And, to deal plainly,
> I fear I am not in my perfect mind.
> Act IV, Scene vii

Lear drifts towards spiritual catastrophe, but in the exhaustion of near madness, he comes at last to a clear vision of the condition of ordinary man. In his humbled state he recognizes the falsity of pomp and power: 'Robes and fur gowns hide all.' Once devoid of that power, Lear in the innocence of moral freedom and with a mystic's clarity, gains the vision of mature spiritual development. Lear has to lose power to realize how it should be properly exercised. This powerful message is a key theme of the play and is a further reminder that Shakespeare's tragic characters are more than ordinary people.

Macbeth

The tragedy of *Macbeth* by Shakespeare is based on an episode in Scottish history recorded in Holinshed's *Chronicles*. The victorious general, Macbeth, is hailed by three mysterious witches as Thane of Glamis, prospective Thane of Cawdor, and future King of Scotland. His companion, Banquo, is foretold by the witches that his children shall be kings.

Macbeth is soon made Thane of Cawdor, and impelled by his own and Lady Macbeth's ambition, he murders King Duncan, is proclaimed King, and accomplishes the murder of Banquo. Banquo's ghost appears at a great banquet unseen by any but Macbeth, and one disaster follows another. Lady Macbeth, tormented by conscience, walks in her sleep, trying to wash from her hands imaginary blood-stains, and finally takes her own life. The witches have assured Macbeth that 'none of woman born' can kill him and that he will not die till Birnam Wood be removed to Dunsinane. He is finally slain in battle by Macduff, a man 'from his mother's womb untimely ripped'; the moving wood seems to manifest when the soldiers of Macduff, during their march to Dunsinane, are commanded to conceal their numbers by carrying boughs from the forest. Duncan's son is proclaimed King.

The play is a concise and compelling account of a man's decline from increasing worldly success into a doomed state of evil. When Macbeth appears at the beginning of the play, he is a widely acclaimed and admired general. During the fight he had displayed the valorous qualities of a great soldier; a man of action but deficient in the intellectual culture of a Hamlet. He seems to express a wilder past in an age when society is aiming at milder manners.

Macbeth, as a play, embodies an important preternatural thread deriving from the concept *wierd*. This all-important word is related to *weorthan* ('to be, become or happen'). It means: 'what is, what happens, the way that things happen; fate, personal destiny, death'. Shakespeare's 'weird sisters' are descended from the *fatal sustren thre*' of mythology. The modern adjective *weird* is a weaker derivative of the Old English word *wierd*.

Having succumbed to the witches' siren song, Macbeth begins to act as though he has acquired a permission from the dark powers and a promise of their supernatural backing in his bid to usurp power. A question arises about his state of being: Was he ripe for these supernatural solicitings or did they take him by surprise? Irrespective of Macbeth's strength or weakness, evil-doing is often a lonely business; its energy needs frequent recharging and the perpetrator needs constant reassurance. Macbeth has the witches and Lady Macbeth on hand for both. The witches personify the then popular belief in evil geniuses and adverse persecutors of mankind – a darker race of beings who, as external manifestations, can be blamed for evil even if they cannot rationally be held ultimately responsible. Macbeth lusts for power and has an overweening ambition for political control, but his wife, Lady Macbeth, says of him:

> Yet do I fear thy nature;
> It is too full o' the milk of human kindness,
> To catch the nearest way; thou wouldst be great,
> Art not without ambition, but without
> The illness should attend it; what thou wouldst highly,
> That thou wouldst holily; wouldst not play false,
> And yet wouldst wrongly win.
>
> Act I, Scene v

To achieve his goal Macbeth must murder the very centre of order and harmony, symbolized by the King. In Shakespeare's plays, divinity is the natural ambience of the kings; we see how the King is revered and held in a kind of sacred awe. It is in this setting that the full monstrosity of a king's murder is realized. This unnatural act brings yet another vivid mental picture into Macbeth's mind, and the unrest and disharmony that he anticipates will follow. It translates into concern for its ill effect upon the sweet nourishment of restful sleep.

> Methought I heard a voice cry, 'Sleep no more!
> Macbeth does murder sleep', the innocent sleep,
> Sleep that knits up the ravell'd sleave of care,
> The death of each day's life, sore labour's bath,
> Balm of hurt minds, great nature's second course,
> Chief nourisher in life's feast. –
>
> Act II, Scene ii

In his conference with the 'murderers', Macbeth has all but declared himself an atheist and mocked at a hereafter, and is now in a state of religious anxiety. He is seized with a piteous melancholy that shocks even his hardened wife as he confesses that he could not say 'Amen' to the prayers of Duncan's attendants.

After more murders, the situation is summarized by Macbeth himself:

> … I am in blood
> Stepp'd in so far, that, should I wade no more,
> Returning were as tedious as go o'er.
>
> Act III, Scene iv

With his Queen dead, Macbeth reviews human life and exclaims:

> To-morrow, and to-morrow, and to-morrow,
> Creeps in this petty pace from day to day,
> To the last syllable of recorded time;
> And all our yesterdays have lighted fools
> The way to dusty death. Out, out, brief candle!
>
> Act V, Scene v

We learn from the murderer himself how he sees his present position:

> I have liv'd long enough: my way of life
> Is fall'n into the sere, the yellow leaf;
> And that which should accompany old age,
> As honour, love, obedience, troops of friends,
> I must not look to have; but, in their stead,
> Curses, not loud but deep, mouth-honour, breath,
> Which the poor heart would fain deny, and dare not.
>
> Act V, Scene iii

As James Gregson (1983) so aptly put it, 'Macbeth's clear-sighted recognition of the stages of his moral decline, his capacity to convey his situation with pitiless vigour and vividness, are what have sustained the play'.

They have tied me to a stake; I cannot fly,
But bear-like I must fight the course.
Act V, Scene vii

Having defied the whole moral order, Macbeth has called down upon himself a great besieging force. Finally, he sees the weird sisters for what they are, creatures:

That keep the word of promise to our ear,
And break it to our hope. Act V, Scene vii

In this masterpiece, a human soul is seen moving inexorably through an initial innocent nobility, the temptation of ambition, the commission of the murderous crime of regicide, the aridity of disillusionment and the ultimate torment that precedes damnation. Macbeth achieved power, but sovereignty eluded him.

Othello

In his great play, *Othello*, Shakespeare presents a tale of passion which leads to jealousy of such magnitude that it drives the lover to destroy the object of his love. This unbearable deed is not the act of a man intoxicated, feverishly excited; nor is it the deed of an unstable man driven by a sudden fit of uncontrollable rage. The destructive lover is of steadfast disposition and noble character. Not only does Shakespeare make this totally credible, but ensures that the tragic lovers have our sympathy as events move to their inexorable conclusion.

In Shakespeare's version of the well-known story, Othello, a Moor and commander of the Venetian military, elopes with Desdemona. Her outraged father accuses him of necromancy, but Desdemona refutes this. The Moor, sent to expel the Turks from Cyprus, wins a signal victory. On his return, Iago, Othello's 'ancient' (ensign or lieutenant), works upon his feelings, arousing jealousy by convincing him that Desdemona has played him false with Cassio. Othello murders her, but on learning how he was duped by Iago, slays himself.

In the tale from which Shakespeare took his story, *Hecatommithi* (1566) by Giraldi Cinthio, the intended message is unequivocally stated by Desdemona: 'I fear,' she says 'that I must serve as a warning to young maidens not to marry against the will of their parents; an Italian girl should not marry a man from whom nature, heaven and mode of life have wholly separated her.' Othello at the outset is a majestic figure of great reputation, more fair than black, and of royal blood.

Shakespeare's Desdemona loves the Moor for his virtues and marries him against the wishes of her family. Othello, accused of bewitching her, defends himself:

She lov'd me for the dangers I had pass'd,
And I lov'd her that she did pity them.
This only is the witchcraft I have us'd.
Act I, Scene iii

Later, following society's acceptance of his marriage, Othello exclaims to Desdemona:

> If I were now to die,
> 'Twere now to be most happy, for I fear
> My soul hath her content so absolute
> That not another comfort like to this
> Succeeds in unknown fate.

She replies:

> The heavens forbid
> But that our loves and comforts should increase
> Even as our days do grow! Act II, Scene i

That such a stable relationship founders indicates either a latent instability in one of the lovers, or the intervention of evil. Shakespeare masterfully contrives both.

The Moor is by nature a man of powerful passion which manifests as courage, enthusiasm, and love. But latent in this emotional chemistry is jealousy. Our word *jealousy* (Old Friesian *gelos*, Latin *zelus*) carries the sense, 'zeal' and 'emulation'. The dictionary gives: 'Eager to uphold, solicitous for, guarding carefully.' Here is the essence of Othello. Dictionary meanings also give clues to the character of Iago: *envious*: 'feeling ill-will on account of another's happiness, etc.' Iago, with that hatred which seems to defy rational explanation, jealously resents his master:

> He hath a daily beauty in his life
> That makes me ugly ... Act V, Scene i

It is with the poison of jealousy that Iago infects Othello and brings him down. Shakespeare, with sub-plots, shows how jealousy links with reputation, self-esteem, and threat to honour – Othello is a military commander of renown.

Cassio, Othello's lieutenant, was a necessary pawn in Iago's scheming and has now fallen from grace. His anguished cry reveals its effect on him and is a pointer to an aspect of character which contributes to Othello's vulnerability, after he has begun to doubt his wife's fidelity:

> Reputation, reputation, reputation!
> 'O! I have lost my reputation. I have lost the
> immortal part of myself. Act II, Scene iii

Othello's spirit, his range of sight, his power of mind and his cool determination avail him nothing, as the sick-minded Iago works on his sensibilities. He is easy prey, with his silent reserved nature and his tendency to brooding thought. Othello has the inclination, so common in rugged characters, to yield himself to soft compliant dispositions, to the apparent honesty of the hypocritical Iago, to the pliable Cassio, and entirely to the gentle Desdemona. His trusting confidence, once established, was seemingly without limits.

The three principals in the play have certain characteristics that make the tragedy inevitable:

Characteristics of Vulnerability

Desdemona	Naive, trusting innocence; carelessness of the relationship.
Othello	Excitable nature; trusting; deficient in reason; obsessed with honour.
Iago	Has the skill of perfect dissimulation. He is consumed with envy and is a compulsive schemer.

Shakespeare's play demonstrates that it is from circumstances and the nature of men that good and evil, happiness and unhappiness, fortune and misfortune arise.

Iago begins at the beginning, enraging Desdemona's father:

Call up her father;
Rouse him, make after him, poison his delight,
Proclaim him in the streets, incense her kinsmen.

⋆

... an old black ram
Is tupping your white ewe.

⋆

... your daughter and the Moor are now making
the beast with two backs.

Act I, Scene i

Desdemona's unassertive vulnerability is evident from a description of her by Brabantio:

A maiden never bold;
Of spirit so still and quiet, that her motion
Blush'd at herself.

Act I, Scene iii

Desdemona may appear unassuming in public but she was evidently a spirited match for her military commander in their loving relationship:

Enter OTHELLO *and* Attendants
OTHELLO: O my fair warrior!
DESDEMONA: My dear Othello!

Act II, Scene i

Her attractiveness to Othello is evident in his own description:

Thou cunning'st pattern of excelling nature.

Act V, Scene ii

Othello undertakes the murder of Desdemona with the calmness of a judge. He feels compelled to 'punish' her, not in wrath but from a sense of honour: it is the *cause* which urges him.

> It is the cause, it is the cause, my soul;
> Let me not name it to you, you chaste stars!
> It is the cause. Act V, Scene ii

Passion, in its sense of powerful enthusiasm tempered with strong feeling, produces almost a sense of duty to kill her. His sorrow 'strikes where it doth love'. He justifies this:

> An honourable murderer, if you will;
> For nought did I in hate, but all in honour.
> Act V, Scene ii

In the words of G.G. Gervinus (1875), Othello 'regards himself as the chastening judge of her shame and the physician of his own honour.' Finding himself rashly mistaken, he punishes himself with the same rational coolness. Othello, suggesting an epitaph for himself, includes:

> … speak
> Of one that lov'd not wisely but too well.
> Act V, Scene ii

Sadly, that statement applied even more fittingly to the lovely Desdemona, a rich 'pearl' he 'threw away'.

Shakespeare's Plays as Poetry

Nineteenth-century critics tended to think of the Plays as representations of the ordinary real world, like journalistic accounts of contemporary events. This approach culminates, perhaps, in the brilliant but somewhat eccentric work of A.C. Bradley, who in *Shakespearean Tragedy* (1904), asks such questions as, 'Where was Hamlet at the time of his father's death?' 'Did Emilia suspect Iago?' 'Was the fainting of Lady Macbeth a simulation?' This 19th-century approach is to treat the plays almost as novels.

Later critics have been inclined to evaluate the Plays as poetry. Each play – creating a particular world through poetry – uncannily conveys a strong sense of reality. Shakespeare anticipates 'modern' psychology by some 400 years. Certain patterns of observation, analysis, and inference coalesce to constitute an artistic wholeness. Sub-plots, the use of metaphor and other aspects of 'imagery', all contribute to 'a theatre in the mind' based on poetry.

The Sonnets

In the spring of 1593, when Shakespeare was 29 years old, his first signed work, *Venus and Adonis*, dedicated to his patron Henry Wriothesley, third Earl of Southampton, was published. One year later, Shakespeare published a second poem, *The Rape of Lucrece*, also dedicated to Southampton, with whom a deep friendship was developing. The dedication reads:

> *The love I dedicate to your Lordship is without end; whereof this pamphlet without beginning is but a superfluous moity. The warrant I have of your honourable disposition, not the worth of my untutored lines makes it assured of acceptance. What I have done is yours, what I have to do is yours, being part in all I have, devoted yours. Were my worth greater my duty would shew greater, meantime as it is, it is bound to your Lordship; to whom I wish long life still strengthened with all happiness.*

Southampton was delighted with the two poems, which were published by Richard Field, Shakespeare's friend from Stratford. Field had taken over the firm of his famous late master, Vautrollier, and married his widow Jacqueline, now known as Jacklin Field. The relevance of this will appear later.

Shakespeare was encouraged and favoured by the Earl of Southampton. On the death of his father, the young Southampton, then aged eight, had been made a royal ward; he was inordinately rich, a graduate of Cambridge, and a favourite of the Queen. Undoubtedly, such a friendship would have exercised an enormously important shaping influence on the young developing poet. The first edition of the *Sonnets* (1609) has a dedicatory reference to a 'Mr WH' as 'the only begetter of these ensuing sonnets'. Two men are considered by historians to be the most likely owner of these initials:

1 Henry Wriothesley, as well as being Shakespeare's patron and friend, was some nine years younger than Shakespeare and, while he was not particularly handsome, it was the fashion to praise the beauty of a person admired or loved. It must also be sadly acknowledged that in those and earlier times poets and composers had virtually to grovel to their patrons – in print – in order to obtain preferment.

2 The Earl of Pembroke's name was William Herbert. Even younger than Southampton, he was extremely dissolute but a generous patron of the arts. It is known that Mary Fitton, Maid of Honour to Queen Elizabeth and reputed to be a dark beauty, was Pembroke's mistress.

It is also just possible that 'Mr WH' was no more than the *procurer* of the manuscript for Thomas Thorpe – who published it without Shakespeare's authority – rather than the *inspirer* of the poems. Several contemporaries whose names match the initials have been suggested but none is remotely convincing.

As well as the mystery of the male owner of the initials 'WH' there is the intriguing identity of the unknown 'dark lady' of the Sonnets.

1 Shakespeare had friends among the aristocracy and was a frequent visitor to the court. Although there is not a shred of evidence to support it, there is the possibility that the poet may have desired Mary Fitton. Was she the 'dark lady'?

2 Some historians have suggested that Jacklin Field, the French wife of Shakespeare's printer, was the mysterious lady who broke her bed-vow (Sonnet 152).

The characters alluded to in the *Sonnets* are archetypes as well as the dramatic counterparts of actual people: the fair youth; a stolen mistress (40-2); a rival poet (83-6); a dark beauty loved by the author (127 *et seq*).

Two writers have, plausibly, each been suggested as the rival poet. George Chapman (?1559-1634), English poet and dramatist – *see* Martin Seymour-Smith, *Shakespeare's Sonnets* (1963). Another, convincingly argued by Robert Gittings in *Shakespeare's Rival* (1960), is Gervase Markham (?1568-1637); the latter, not least because he wrote *The English Arcadia* (1607; a poem in continuation of Sidney's *Arcadia*).

If the *Sonnets* are autobiographical they enshrine the central mystery of Shakespeare's life. The theme is love and betrayal. Intensive work by scholars has failed to identify any of the enigmatic characters positively.

Although W.H. Auden tended to the view that the *Sonnets* are private writings, like musings in a diary with no intended audience, this seems hardly tenable. In 1598 a Cambridge schoolmaster and cleric, Francis Meres, then living in London and on familiar terms with some literary men, said that Shakespeare's sonnets were in circulation among his 'private friends'. If it is THE *Sonnets* that Meres meant, Martin Seymour-Smith believes the plain implication to be that they were not for *general* circulation.

Turning now to the content of the *Sonnets*, J.B. Leishman, Senior Lecturer in English Literature in the University of Oxford and Fellow of St John's College, is of the opinion that English sonnets, in genius and craftsmanship, fell far below those of the Italians and the French. He writes:

> Indeed, despite his immense genius and immense achievement, Shakespeare's own craftsmanship, sometimes even in his finest sonnets, is too often slovenly; there are too many inversions merely for the sake of rhyme, too many syllables supplying expletives such as 'do', 'did' and 'doth' and too many rhymes on the final syllable of weak past participles, such as remember-ed. Perfection still remains perfection, even though it be Shakespeare himself who sometimes falls short of it.

As an antidote to idolatry of Shakespeare and as literary criticism, the censure levelled by Leishman is justified, but for many it will seem a somewhat carping slight. The Italian and French craftsmanship often produced work barren of credibility and realism; Shakespeare 'reads' more satisfyingly because he engages more than the intellect of the reader.

Martin Seymour-Smith (1963), in his scholarly edition of the *Sonnets*, writes:

> It should be clear from the first eighteen sonnets that at the outset Shakespeare was ambitiously setting out to write a successful sequence in the accepted style of his day. But by Sonnet 20 the situation and consequently the whole poetic atmosphere, has changed ... technique and procedure have ceased to matter ...

Although Shakespeare's desire and regard incline upon the friend, the poet's love immeasurably transcends its immediate object. He appears to denigrate his own afferent love, deeming it too unworthy to have elicited a fuller loving response from the other. In several sonnets he even reaches towards that universal being – that friend that transcends what is merely of this world:

Sonnet 53

What is your substance, whereof are you made,
That millions of strange shadows on you tend?
Since every one hath, every one, one shade,
And you, but one, can every shadow lend ...

Sonnet 30

But if the while I think on thee, dear friend,
All losses are restor'd and sorrows end.

In the *Sonnets*, as in no other poems, we are brought very close to ourselves. Shakespeare seems to be alluding to the essential self *behind* the personal self (which is a construction based on the ego). The poet's reference to 'thee, dear friend' might be to the essential self in us all which never changes, is unaffected by events; that witnessing awareness which each individual knows has always been present – since birth.

The *Sonnets* were printed in 1609 and the bulk of them appear to have been written between 1593 and 1596. It is perhaps significant that *Romeo and Juliet* is also assigned to the period 1594–5.

Shakespeare is the *nonpareil* of poets. The *Sonnets* are his spiritual biography. From these poems emerges the profile of a most sensitive spirit, able to express nuances of passion from platonic admiration of a friend to the torments of jealousy; from light buoyancy to deep sorrow; from sensual ecstasy to darkest repugnance. Shakespeare's sonnets are the most disputed and analysed collection of poetry in the English language. This is hardly surprising. They are personal and intimate poems, written to individuals, which would reveal much about Shakespeare's life if only certain facts could be indisputably established. The problems of identity and events raised by the *Sonnets* are considerable: a personal story, so fragmentary and yet so intimate, is not likely to have left many traces in any kind of records.

In a brief examination of certain aspects of the *Sonnets* we will take some preliminary help from another major English poet. In his *On Poetry and Poets* (1953) T.S. Eliot distinguished three 'voices' of poetry:

First voice	The poet *talks to himself*, or nobody in particular.
Second voice	The poet *addresses someone else* generally or particularly.
Third voice	The poet *creates a character speaking in verse*.

Here is an example of Shakespeare speaking in Eliot's notional 'First voice':

Sonnet 94

They that have power to hurt and will do none,
That do not do the thing they most do show,
Who moving others, are themselves as stone,
Unmoved, cold, and to temptation slow;
They rightly do inherit heaven's graces,
And husband nature's riches from expense;
They are the lords and owners of their faces,
Others but stewards of their excellence.
The summer's flower is to the summer sweet,
Though to itself, it only live and die,
But if that flower with base infection meet,
The basest weed outbraves his dignity:
  For sweetest things turn sourest by their deeds;
  Lillies that fester smell far worse than weeds.

G.K. Hunter (1953) makes an interesting observation on the dramatic technique used by Shakespeare in his sonnets. In them, one heart relates to another or others, which sets up a system of tensions between forces presented as persons. This interests the reader in a manner akin to drama. In contrast, in the odes of Keats and Shelley, solitary imaginings are presented as though of universal significance.

A sonnet, which begins in an imperative dimension, clearly addresses a notional listener (Eliot's 'Second voice'):

Sonnet 90

Then hate me when thou wilt; if ever, now;
Now, while the world is bent my deeds to cross,
Join with the spite of fortune, make me bow ...

Here is another example in Eliot's 'Second voice'. Clearly not a meditation or soliloquy, but a message rhetorically addressed to another:

Sonnet 87

Farewell! thou art too dear for my possessing,
And like enough thou know'st thy estimate;
The charter of thy worth gives thee releasing;
My bonds in thee are all determinate.
For how do I hold thee but by thy granting,
And for that riches where is my deserving?
The cause of this fair gift in me is wanting,
And so my patent back again is swerving.
Thyself thou gav'st, thy own worth then not knowing,

Or me, to whom thy gav'st it, else mistaking;
So thy great gift, upon misprision growing,
Comes home again, on better judgement making.
  Thus have I had thee, as a dream doth flatter,
  In sleep a king, but waking, no such matter.

When the poet creates a character speaking in verse (Eliot's 'Third voice'), there is a marked loss of intimacy and authenticity of feeling. In a work of such inward reflection as Shakespeare's *Sonnets* there are almost no examples. The last one in the series meets the definition but seems little more than a shallow contrivance:

Sonnet 154

The little Love-god lying once asleep
Laid by his side his heart-inflaming brand,
Whilst many nymphs that vow'd chaste life to keep
Came tripping by, but in her maiden hand;
The fairest votary took up that fire
Which many legions of true hearts had warm'd;
And so the general of hot desire
Was, sleeping, by a virgin hand disarm'd.

Of the notional 'three voices of poetry', Eliot concludes his essay:

> I think that in every poem, from the private meditation to the epic or drama, there is more than one voice to be heard. If the author never spoke to himself, the result would not be poetry, though it might be magnificent rhetoric; and part of our enjoyment of great poetry is the enjoyment of *overhearing* words which are not addressed to us. But if the poem were exclusively for the author, it would be a poem in a private and unknown language, and a poem which was a poem only for the author would not be a poem at all.

Shakespeare's command of figurative language is outstanding. Here are two sonnets which show the poet in full flight as the creator of metaphor:

Sonnet 15

When I consider every thing that grows
Holds in perfection but a little moment,
That this huge stage presenteth nought but shows
Whereon the Stars in secret influence comment;
When I perceive that men as plants increase,
Cheered and check'd e'en by the self-same sky,
Vaunt in their youthful sap, at height decrease,
And wear their brave state out of memory;
Then the conceit of this inconstant stay
Sets you most rich in youth before my sight,
Where wasteful Time debateth with Decay,
To change your day of youth to sullied night;
  And, all in war with Time for love of you
  As he takes from you, I engraft you new.

Sonnet 18

Shall I compare thee to a summer's day?
Thou art more lovely and more temperate:
Rough winds do shake the darling buds of May,
And summer's lease hath all too short a date:
Sometimes too hot the eye of heaven shines,
And often is his gold complexion dimm'd:
And every fair from fair sometime declines,
By chance, or nature's changing course untrimm'd;
But thy eternal summer shall not fade,
Nor lose possession of that fair thou ow'st,
Nor shall death brag thou wander'st in his shade,
When in eternal lines to time thou grow'st;
  So long as men can breathe, or eyes can see,
  So long lives this, and this gives life to thee.

Shakespeare is no irrational romantic. In the following sonnet extract he anticipates the beloved's ardour cooling – indeed turning away:

Sonnet 49

Against that time when thou shalt strangely pass,
And scarcely greet me with that sun, thine eye,
When love, converted from the thing it was,
Shall reasons find of settled gravity …

In the crucial 'triangle' poem, as indeed in the whole sonnet sequence, it is not clear whether or not a personal experience underlies these statements, or if it is the correlative of characters in action, as it is in the plays.

Sonnet 42

That thou hast her, it is not all my grief,
And yet it may be said I lov'd her dearly;
That she hath thee, is of my wailing chief,
A loss in love that touches me more nearly.
Loving offenders, thus I will excuse ye:
Thou dost love her, because thou know'st I love her;
And for my sake even so doth she abuse me,
Suffering my friend for my sake to approve her.
If I lose thee, my loss is my love's gain,
And losing her, my friend hath found that loss;
Both find each other, and I lose both twain,
And both for my sake lay on me this cross:
  But here's the joy; my friend and I are one;
  Sweet flattery! then she loves but me alone.

The reason why the *Sonnets* are referred to as the greatest love poems in the language is also the reason why Shakespeare is the greatest poetic dramatist. The 'I' who speaks in the poems is mysteriously without identity. No one knows if it is Shakespeare or not. There is a lack of self-assertion; in fact, to be positive, there is a selflessness that transcends the personal in favour of the universal.

What the eyes see outwardly is of secondary importance to what, inwardly, the seer knows: this is insight. Sidney in the fifth sonnet of *Astrophel and Stella* speaks of this deeper love and the penalty of veering from it:

> It is most true, that eyes are form'd to serve
> The inward light, and that the heavenly part
> Ought to be King, from whose rules those who swerve,
> Rebels to Nature, strive for their own smart.

In one sonnet, Shakespeare goes further and considers what is, and what is not, love:

Sonnet 116

> Let me not to the marriage of true minds
> Admit impediments. Love is not love
> Which alters when it alteration finds,
> Or bends with the remover to remove.

The theme of marriage, alluded to in this way, has been traced back by Douglas Hamer (1974) to an anonymous 5th-century *arian* (prayer) and thence to a homily *Matrimonium non facit coitus, sed voluntas* – 'Marriage is not made by the coition of two bodies but by the union of two minds!'

Shakespeare in his sonnets expresses, as a lover, two emotions which have come straight through from the Italian Renaissance: an abject humility, and a serene confidence in the power of poetry and love. But in the process the strained conventionality of the feudal courtier is enlarged into the self-disclosure of a warm human being.

It is perhaps necessary to say something about Shakespeare's love and high admiration for the gentle man, whom he exhorts to procreate. The poet foreshadows a double dimension of immortality in Sonnet 17:

> But were some child of yours alive that time,
> You should live twice – in it and in my rhyme.

As to the charge of homosexuality, nowhere in his plays does the poet give any indication that it has any importance in his interpretation of life. In the *Sonnets*, with great precision, Shakespeare makes clear that platonic love for the young man does not imply a physical bond. In a reference to 'Nature's' handiwork he writes:

Sonnet 20

> But since she prick'd thee out for women's pleasure,
> Mine be thy love, and thy love's use their treasure.

The young man's *love's use* is the treasure of women, and in Sonnet 10 the young man is urged to:

> Make thee another self, for love of me.

In Sonnet 74, the poet says:

... my body being dead;
The coward conquest of a wretch's knife,
Too base of thee to be remembered.

Whereas Marlowe was stabbed to death, Shakespeare was not – another indication that the *Sonnets* should not be regarded unequivocally as autobiographical.

In giving immortality to what he loved, Shakespeare immortalized himself:

Sonnet 81

The earth can yield me but a common grave,
When you entombed in men's eyes shall lie.
Your monument shall be my gentle verse,
Which eyes not yet created shall o'er-read;
And tongues to be your being shall rehearse,
When all the breathers of this world are dead.

The Concept 'Love'

Such is Shakespeare's contribution to poetry, drama, and verse-philosophy that he enlarges our understanding of the very concept, 'Love'. He carried forward the Renaissance ideal but opens love's human dimension very wide: this he achieves by his understanding of human psychology and by his vocabulary and range of literary figures – such as the metaphor. Shakespeare provides *the language* with which love can be explored and in which its behaviour might be explained.

Love is not love
When it is mingled with regards that stand
Aloof from the entire point.

King Lear, Act I, Scene i

The word *love* is from the Old English *lufu* meaning 'connected with'. The Sanskrit *lubh* means 'to desire' and the Latin *lubet*, 'it pleases'. These three etymological roots contain elements of the phenomenon ordinarily thought of as 'love'. Thomas Chatterton in *The Revenge* offers his definition:

What is love? 'tis nature's treasure,
'Tis the storehouse of her joys;
'Tis the highest heaven of pleasure,
'Tis a bliss which never cloys.

The concept 'free' is associated in the English language with love. The benign phase of a human loving relationship demonstrates this with the lover wanting to free the beloved from discomfort, constraint, and limitation. The lover desires to give everything, including the self. There is much to do with surrender here – for both genders – which in the ultimate is the yielding of the ego.

The human expression of love spans the whole spectrum of physicality, intellect, and the emotions. Love has a vital spiritual dimension. Its operation is central to the continuing evolution of consciousness in mankind. Indeed, for many, love defines the growing point of human development. That point is the centre which is everywhere, excluding nothing but including everything.

As might be expected, Shakespeare enables us to enlarge considerably the scope of enquiry. In his plays, he distinguishes between the kinds of human heterosexual attraction generalized as 'love'. Five such levels suggest themselves:

- Love — A universal transcendence of relative separation.
- Platonic love — An asexual attraction transcending ordinary physical sexuality.
- Aesthetic attraction — Mind-influenced attractant chemistry – for example, love of beauty.
- Appetite — A chemistry-driven tension to compel the satisfaction of a natural need – for example, hunger, procreation.
- Lust — Old English, *lystan*: to desire passionately; long for with excessive sexual passion.

From hundreds of examples in the plays, there are differences in the *level* of response and its *measure*. On love, no personal limitation can be placed, it being a universal. It is an unmeasured giving of the self, as exemplified in *Romeo and Juliet*:

JULIET: My bounty is as boundless as the sea,
My love as deep; the more I give to thee,
The more I have, for both are infinite.

Act II, Scene ii

Platonic love is a philosophical resonance; an asexual response, emanating from the love of wisdom, to which we find reference in another Shakespeare play:

HAMLET: Give me that man
That is not passion's slave, and I will wear him
In my heart's core, ay, in my heart of heart,
As I do thee.

Act III, Scene ii

It is usual for an aesthetic dimension to inform the perception of the lover for the beloved, particularly early in the relationship. Not an overestimation; rather a response to the essential self in the other:

ROMEO: O! she doth teach the torches to burn bright.
It seems she hangs upon the cheek of night

Like a rich jewel in an Ethiop's ear;
Beauty too rich for use, for earth too dear!
Romeo and Juliet, Act I, Scene v

An appetite determines that a need be satisfied. Cleopatra, the mistress *par excellence*, understands this:

ENOBARBUS: Age cannot wither her, nor custom stale
Her infinite variety; other women cloy
The appetites they feed, but she makes hungry
Where most she satisfies.
Antony and Cleopatra, Act II, Scene ii

Lust is the expression used for intense sexual desire when its presence attracts censure:

MRS FORD: I think the best way were to entertain him with hope, till the wicked fire of lust hath melted him in his own grease.
The Merry Wives of Windsor, Act II, Scene i

In *Measure for Measure*, Shakespeare shows what can happen when repressive forces have interfered with these natural responses. Angelo seems to have a fear of sexuality and is described as:

… a man whose blood
Is very snow-broth; one who never feels
The wanton stings and motions of the sense.
Act I, Scene iv

When a glimmer of warmth flickers uncertainly, he panics:

What's this? What's this? Is this her fault or mine?
Act II, Scene ii

Isabella also seems to have a fear of sexuality which appears as virtue mixed with self-involved pride:

… were I under the terms of death,
Th' impression of keen whips I'd wear as rubies,
And strip myself to death, as to a bed
That longing hath been sick for, ere I'd yield
My body up to shame.
Act II, Scene iv

That her later statement uses the royal plural is no coincidence:

Then Isabel, live chaste, and, brother, die;
More than our brother is our chastity.

In a further statement she says, improbably:

O! were it but my life,
I'd throw it down for your deliverance
As frankly as a pin.
Measure for Measure, Act III, Scene i

In *King Lear* Shakespeare portrays the King as an egoist and autocrat, imperiously demanding a public declaration of filial love from his three daughters:

> Which of you shall we say doth love us most?
>
> Act I, Scene i

Cordelia answers with exactness and an unfortunate ungraciousness:

> I love your Majesty
> According to my bond; nor more, nor less.
>
> Act I, Scene i

With Shakespeare's poetic skill, seemingly any metaphor can yield poetry about love. For instance, in *Romeo and Juliet*, at first sight there might seem little affinity in linking borrowed terms of falconry with Juliet's condition, as she urges 'love performing night' to arrive in advance of its time. But in fact the metaphor is totally appropriate and provides her with language which is laden with sexual overtones:

> Hood my unmann'd blood, bating in my cheeks,
> With thy black mantle; till strange love, grown bold,
> Think true love acted, simple modesty.
>
> Act III, Scene ii

The verb 'unmann'd' carries two meanings. Juliet as yet has no husband; and in falconry, an untrained (unmann'd) hawk would flutter its wings (bate) when taken out of doors unless a hood were pulled over its head.

The image links at once with Juliet's sexual inexperience and with her sexual eagerness. Blood 'bating in my cheeks' is the beating-pulse impelled blood, and this heartbeat rhythm pulses in her language: 'Come night, come Romeo, come thou day in night'. She entreats night to come so that it will dissipate shyness and allow her unfamiliarity to be superseded by boldness. This is boldness not based on experience but inspired by innocence. It exemplifies that 'true love acted' which *is* 'simple modesty'. Shakespeare conveys all this in three lines of poetry!

Shakespeare is not just a magnificent poet: he is an able communicator who uses words with a powerfully effective economy. Juliet, asked by her mother to consider well the proposed suitor for her hand, Paris, underscores her childlike obedience to the wishes of her parents in three superbly wrought lines:

> I'll look to like, if looking liking move;
> But no more deep will I endart mine eye
> Than your consent gives strength to make it fly.
>
> Act I, Scene iii

Upon learning Romeo's family name, she expresses surprise and dismay – again, note the intense compression of meaning and content in small compass:

My only love sprung from my only hate!
Too early seen unknown, and known too late!
Act I, Scene v

Another example showing Shakespeare's skill as poet: in an unwitting declaration of love to Romeo, Juliet muses on his name. Shakespeare has her begin a line but contrives Romeo's completion of it – as an expression of love's unity:

So Romeo would, were he not Romeo call'd,
Retain that dear perfection which he owes
Without that title. Romeo, doff thy name,
And for that name, which is no part of thee,
Take all myself.
Act II, Scene ii

At this point, Romeo steps from the shadows, continuing her line. He shares her wishful belief that their familial ties be lightly severed:

I take thee at thy word.
Call me but love, and I'll be new baptiz'd;
Henceforth I never will be Romeo.
Act II, Scene ii

Thus these two young lovers, whose story contrasts love and hate, develop the loving relationship that is to bring about their death, but reconcile the conflict that has long embittered and diminished their two families.

A question arising with Shakespeare is: What special conditions and opportunities could have come into conjunction to produce this master of dramatic composition and the poet craftsman who conceived the *Sonnets*? Part of the answer must lie in the cultural context in which Shakespeare worked, the Elizabethan Age. It was an era of special opportunity for a poet-dramatist. For the entire 16th century, England enjoyed a new stability and commercial prosperity. The Spanish Armada had foundered, suffering defeat; the threat from Spain had passed. The English language was moving through a phase of unprecendented development and enrichment. Music and literature were flourishing on the surging new currents of Renaissance thought. The theatres were thriving amidst intense rivalry and the pressure of competition. The most successful companies were invited to entertain Queen Elizabeth and her court. The works written for the court of James I (Elizabeth's successor) were impelled into further elaboration and development. Plays were required which reflected the increasing appreciation of and demand for real poetry – plays which had a high intellectual content with no loss of the 'common touch'.

Shakespeare had been brought up in the heart of rural England, had studied classical drama and comedy, and had developed the basis for a phenomenal command of the English language. His writing brought him into contact with aristocratic patrons, actors, theatre managers and the thronging variety of Elizabethan London.

The conciseness of his great tragedies, their richness and magnificence of language, the delight in the sound of words – all denote the master dramatist at work. He explores the many forms of love, varieties and consequences of human error, the mystery of death – all with consummate subtlety pervaded by the directness of truth. His very last works examine the borderline between tragedy and comedy with a sophistication unique to his own or any other age. His achievement remains miraculous transcending innumerable readings and performances, continuing to provide inspiration to generations of artists and writers.

7
Metaphysical Poetry

Metaphysics

At the still point of the turning world.

THUS, IN *Burnt Norton* – the opening section of *Four Quartets* – T.S. Eliot speaks of the mysterious *locus* which is 'neither flesh nor fleshless; neither from nor towards'. Eliot continues: 'at the still point, there the dance is, but neither arrest nor movement. And do not call it fixity.' The poet insists that, 'Except for the point, the still point, there would be no dance, and there is only the dance.' This enigmatic, secret *something, somewhere* is often conveniently, but somewhat lamely, designated 'metaphysical'.

In *The Big Questions* (1986) Robert Solomon says that philosophy – metaphysics in particular – is an interpretation of the world: our attempt to make sense of it and determine what in it is real. A modern dictionary describes *metaphysics* as the branch of abstruse study concerned with the nature and theory of knowledge – an area of considerable uncertainty. The term *metaphysics* derives from the title given to a group of Aristotle's writings by the philosopher Andronicus of Rhodes in the 1st century BC. Aristotle said that the forms of things are in themselves and have no separate existence. For him, metaphysics was simply 'beyond physics'. The Greek word *metaphusika* means the works of Aristotle 'after the *Physics*'.

In his *Introduction to Metaphysics*, Heidegger writes: 'Language is the primordial poetry in which a people speaks being.' Poetry has always dealt with those areas that philosophers, using only intellect, cannot penetrate. Kant thought an investigation of this kind impossible because, he insisted, our minds can cope only with the phenomenal world of appearances. Ayer, in *Language, Truth and Logic* (1936), used the word *metaphysics* as a pejorative term to indicate the meaninglessness of much traditional philosophy. Despite this, philosophy is still generally considered to fall under the three main headings: Ethics, Epistemology, and Metaphysics.

The term *metaphysical poets* was first used by John Dryden (1631-1700) in his dedication to *A Discourse Concerning the Origin and Progress of Satire*. As a descriptive label it is not entirely appropriate, since it implies that metaphysical poetry is concerned with the enquiry into the nature of the soul, which it is not. Dryden was a poet, dramatist, and critic. He was also the literary dictator of the Restoration period, and so his use of 'metaphysical' had an impact.

For the poet, an important device for dealing with the metaphysical is the metaphor, but this is not without its difficulties. One of these is the matter of interpretation. An extreme example makes the point. It occurs in the Gospels, with Christ's statement at the Last Supper, 'This is My body which is given for you; do this in remembrance of Me.' This is a prime example of uncertainty of meaning in religion. For many Christians this is *metaphor* at its most profound; for others it is a central *fact* of their faith. This crucial difference of interpretation gives two points of view: for Protestants it is a simple act of remembrance; for Catholics it is the reality of transubstantiation. One action has produced two quite different perceptions. Mere simplicity in such statements does not assist meaning:

> For, of the soul, the body form doth take,
> For soul is form, and doth the body make.
>
> Spenser

In Spenser's lines the proposition is clear enough. The question is, what does 'soul' mean? Our word *soul* comes from the Old English *sawol*, the principle of life in man or animals. It was also considered to be the principle of thought and action in man, commonly regarded as an entity distinct from the body – the spiritual part of man in contrast to the purely physical. The idea of the soul as the immaterial and immortal part of man surviving death as a ghost or spirit is an ancient and widespread belief. For Aristotle, the soul is essentially the internal principle of movement and sensibility which holds bodies together and gives them life; but this vital principle or 'soul' does not survive the death of the body, even though the intelligent soul of man does possess a portion of 'active reason' which is immortal and is, perhaps, to be identified with God.

In the domain of poetry, the description 'metaphysical' refers to a style rather than to subject matter and, in this context, the poems reflect attitudes to experience. Characteristically, the poetry is highly complex and bears greatly compressed meanings. When referring to concepts of religion, it does so by means of:

- conceits, sustained at length;
- by a frequent avoidance of smooth and regular metre (for dramatic and oratorical effect);
- by unusual syntax or unconventional imagery drawn from philosophy, religion, and theology.

In contrast to the philosophers' inventive conceptualizing and analysis, the poet proceeds towards understanding with feeling and insight.

Where beauty or a meaning is inexplicable, the poet leads us in the direction of essentials, towards the inward mystery of things. Since 'dream delivers but dream' and there is no end to illusion, the major poet in his creative visualizing reveals a mind poised on the razor's edge between insight and illusion – and reflects the insight. As the dictum has it, 'As I am, so I see.' Shakespeare's level of being – about which we can only speculate on the evidence of his writing – showed an outstanding knowledge of the human condition. His understanding seems far beyond his time, immersed as he was in the Renaissance tradition and Elizabethan England's superstitions, primitive science, and religious orthodoxy. He was, however, endowed with a sensibility, subtlety of comprehension, and insight not shared by other poets.

It was in a reaction against those 'others' that a new generation of poets sought to initiate a shift in direction. They began a movement within poetry that left Shakespeare's achievement intact but moved the expression of spiritual insight into another phase. This shift was to begin with Donne and would continue through to Yeats and Eliot. It entailed a lift in spiritual expression that transcends orthodox science and religion – going where they cannot follow – into the realm of metaphysics. It begins with a poet who became a priest.

John **Donne** (c1572-1631) was born in London. He was educated privately and then at both Oxford and Cambridge. He was a Roman Catholic in early life, but was converted to Anglicanism in 1614 and ordained in 1615. He had originally intended to become a lawyer but abandoned this to sail with Essex to Cadiz and later with Raleigh to the Azores. On his return to England he became secretary to Sir Thomas Egerton, Lord Keeper of the Great Seal, and while in his employ wrote his longest poem, *The Progress of the Soul.* In 1602 he imprudently and secretly married Egerton's niece, which angered Sir Thomas and led to his dismissal – and a brief imprisonment. His marriage produced 12 children. Two years after his ordination (1615) his wife died; in 1621 he was appointed Dean of St Paul's.

Donne's poetry, including his early ironic and erotic verse and his later religious poems, is marked by intellectual power, deep learning, and intense emotion. His imagery, to which the adjective 'metaphysical' was applied, is powerful and striking. Dr Johnson invented the term 'metaphysical school', applying it to Donne as the notional leader of the movement and to those poets whose work he influenced. Ben Jonson, the least gushing of critics towards his contemporaries, said of John Donne that he was 'the first poet of the world in some things'. Thomas Carew's famous description was:

> A king who ruled as he thought fit
> The universal monarchy of wit.

Donne writes direct, vigorous poetry – amorous, religious, and mystical – which is argumentative and colloquial in tone and carries dramatic immediacy. Its combination of agile thought and intense feeling is best seen in the metaphysical poems, where sensibility and thought merge into an image always ingenious and appropriate. His poems have addressed widely differing areas of human experience, ranging from passionate frank discussions of sexual love to profound meditations on human mortality and the nature of the soul.

Donne's love poetry reads as if it stems from two different men: one cynical, scornful of Petrarchan themes deifying women; the other, a man articulating profoundly felt expressions of love – given and returned. His poem, *Woman's Constancy*, begins with cynicism:

> Now thou hast loved me one whole day,
> Tomorrow when thou leavs't, what wilt thou say?

The same man could write:

> If yet I have not all thy love,
> Dear, I shall never have it all.

He well understood the 'now' and eternity of love:

> Only our love hath no decay;
> This no tomorrow hath, nor yesterday,
> Running it never keeps from us away,
> But truly keeps his first, last, everlasting day.

Donne expressed a range of extreme views about love. At one level a neo-platonic attitude; the notion that through his mistress's celestial beauty the lover receives a moral enlightenment which leads his thoughts away from bodily desires. At the other extreme, an ironic sarcasm which seems to hold woman in contempt. He also wrote of holding a balance which acknowledges the essential need to accept both spirit *and* sexuality. He enters a passionate plea for the body to be allowed its part in their union: 'Else a great prince in prison lies.'

In *The Flea*, Donne writes as if with the deliberate intention of scandalizing his readers: as though the lover had no other concern than seduction and physical gratification by securing the surrender of his partner's virginity. His poem opens with the peremptory demand:

> Mark but this flea, and mark in this
> How little that which thou deny'st me is;
> Me it sucked first, and now sucks thee,
> And in this flea, our two bloods mingled be;
> Confess it, this cannot be said
> A sin, or shame, or loss of maidenhead,
>   Yet this enjoys before it woo,
>   And pampered swells with one blood made of two,
>   And this, alas, is more than we would do.

The poet demolishes any opposing reluctance by relentlessly sustained reasoning and outrageous sophistry.

The Sun Rising contains many characteristic features of Donne's poetic writing. The scathing opening lines are an insulting outburst, carrying enough censure to deal with forward children, troublesome wenches and meddling older people:

> Busy old fool, unruly sun … Saucy
> pedantic wretch …

This rebukes the impudence and petty-mindedness of the sun and its mistaken sense of duty. Having dealt with the sun's ill-mannered intrusion, the poet indicates, as would a Mercutio, the routine duties that await the source of the world's light and warmth:

> … go chide
> Late schoolboys and sour prentices;
> Go tell court huntsmen that the king will ride;
> Call country ants to harvest offices.

The last line of the first verse of the poem contrasts the torpor of harvesters reluctantly turning out for work, with the leisurely self-indulgent activity of two lovers in the private world of their room. Short syllables and many words, have the effect of slowing time:

> Love, all alike, no season knows, nor clime,
> Nor hours, days, months, which are the rags of time.

The second verse arrogantly questions the validity of the sun's power, the 'beams so reverend and strong', but the poet's boastful comparison with the beauteous light the sun has intrusively encountered is so well expressed that the poet's complacency becomes a measured statement of unshakable assurance:

> If her eyes have not blinded thine,
> Look, and tomorrow late, tell me
> Whether both the Indias of spice and mine
> Be where thou left'st them, or lie here with me.

The sense of totality felt by the lovers in the single world of their unity is no mere perception, but a fact:

> She is all states, and all princes I:
> Nothing else is.

The strength and power of the statement is its brevity:

> Shine here to us, and thou art everywhere.

Here is the metaphysical poet, emphasizing that 'here, now' is everywhere and beyond time.

This is the poem in full so that its integral structure can be appreciated:

Busy old fool, unruly sun,
Why dost thou thus
Through windows and through curtains call on us?
Must to thy motions lovers' seasons run?
Saucy pedantic wretch, go chide
Late schoolboys, and sour prentices;
Go tell court huntsmen that the king will ride;
Call country ants to harvest offices.
Love, all alike, no season knows nor clime,
Nor hours, days, months, which are the rags of time.

Thy beams so reverend and strong
Why shouldst thou think?
I could eclipse and cloud them with a wink,
But that I would not lose her sight so long.
If her eyes have not blinded thine,
Look, and tomorrow late tell me
Whether both the Indias of spice and mine
Be where thou left'st them, or lie here with me.
Ask for those kings whom thou saw'st yesterday,
And thou shalt hear, all here in one bed lay.

She is all states, and all princes I,
Nothing else is.
Princes do but play us; compared to this,
All honour's mimic, all wealth alchemy.
Thou, sun, art half as happy as we
In that the world's contracted thus;
Thine age asks ease, and since thy duties be
To warm the world, that's done in warming us.
Shine here to us, and thou art everywhere;
This bed thy centre is, these walls thy sphere.

In his later, religious life, Donne uses his understanding of the dissolving of the ego by love to express his longing to be possessed by the Deity:

Holy Sonnet XIV

Batter my heart, three-personned God, for you
As yet but knock, breathe, shine and seek to amend;
… for I
Except you enthral me, never shall be free,
Nor even chaste, except you ravish me.

As James Winney (1970) reminds us, the 19 *Holy Sonnets* were written in the dark period of Donne's life following the death of his wife (1617), which not only deprived him of his deepest comfort but profoundly altered his outlook. His disturbance of spirit after his wife's death reflects his loss of a vital sense of security; he now looks to God for an assurance of love.

Metaphysical Poets

To designate a few writers *Metaphysical Poets* is to make an artificial distinction. The concept *metaphysics* has a philosophical significance usually absent in their poems. The term *metaphysical* in the context of the history of poetry is used to denote a poetic tradition and a group of poets who wrote under the influence of John Donne. The names which come most readily to mind in this connection are:

George Herbert	(1593-1633)
Henry Vaughan	(1622-95)
Andrew Marvell	(1621-78)

A fuller list would include:

Thomas Traherne	(1636-74)
Richard Crashaw	(1612-49)
Francis Quarles	(1592-1644)
Abraham Cowley	(1618-67)
John Cleveland	(1613-58)

The Metaphysical Poets were reacting against the lingering death throes of the Elizabethan sonnet, which in the late 16th century was manifesting as feeble and over-conventionalized work. However, in their turn, Cowley and Cleveland reduced the effectiveness of their own style by their use of far-fetched and over-wrought conceits.

A characteristic of the Metaphysical Poets is the way they relate one thing to another. The relations they perceive emphasize the logical rather than the sensuous or emotional. Experience becomes grist to the intellectual mill, and they constantly present the abstract with the concrete, the remote with the near, and the sublime with the commonplace. The logic of analysis is given the correlation of emotion. There is, to some extent, a return to the cruder, more homespun type of imagery found in the intellectual thought of the Middle Ages and the poetry of the mid-16th century.

Of the more eminent writers in this style, Marvell has been described by Bush (1962) as 'the finest flower of secular and serious metaphysical poetry'.

Andrew **Marvell** (1621-78) was a late representative of the English Metaphysical Poets. He is renowned for his combination of intellectual conceits with lyric grace. In 1650 he became tutor to Lord Fairfax's daughter; then, in 1653, tutor to Cromwell's ward. During the rule of Cromwell's government, Marvell was assistant to John Milton, then Latin Secretary of the Commonwealth. Among his best known poems are *The Garden*, *To His Coy Mistress* and *Bermudas*; *Ode upon Cromwell's Return to Ireland*.

Interest in Marvell revived in the 20th century in literary circles, largely through the influence of the essays of T.S. Eliot. The main body of lyric poetry is to be found in *Miscellaneous Poems* of 1681, which contains his best known verse.

Here is a celebrated example of Marvell's work:

To His Coy Mistress

Had we but World enough, and Time,
This coyness Lady were no crime.
We would sit down, and think which way
To walk, and pass our long Love's Day.
Thou by the Indian Ganges side
Should'st Rubies find; I by the Tide
Of Humber would complain. I would
Love you ten years before the Flood:
And you should if you please refuse
Till the Conversion of the Jews.
My vegetable Love should grow
Vaster than Empires, and more slow.
An hundred years should go to praise
Thine Eyes, and on thy Forehead Gaze.
Two hundred to adore each Breast:
But thirty thousand to the rest.
An Age at least to every part,
And the last Age should show your Heart.
For Lady you deserve this State;
Nor would I love at lower rate.

After this courtly extravagance comes a poetic but metaphysical reference to time, the arch-enemy of lovers:

But at my back I always hear
Time's wingèd Chariot hurrying near:
And yonder all before us lie
Deserts of vast Eternity.
Thy Beauty shall no more be found;
Nor, in thy marble Vault shall sound
My echoing Song: then Worms shall try
That long preserv'd Virginity:
And your quaint Honour turn to dust;
And into ashes all my Lust.

Instead of the courtly couplet there now follows a sardonic urging to compliance:

The Grave's a fine and private place,
But none I think do there embrace.

Marvell ends with logic and passion:

Now therefore, while the youthful hew
Sits on thy skin like morning dew,

And while thy willing Soul transpires
At every pore with instant Fires,
Now let us sport us while we may;
And now, like am'rous birds of prey,
Rather at once our Time devour,
Than languish in his slow-chapt pow'r.
Let us roll all our Strength, and all
Our sweetness, up into one Ball:
And tear our Pleasures with rough strife,
Through the Iron gates of Life.
Thus, though we cannot make our Sun
Stand still, yet we will make him run.

The writers of verse who are somewhat grandly designated *Metaphysical Poets* might have been more accurately called simply the 'Religious Poets'. One poet rightly not included in any list of Metaphysical Poets – he was altogether too religiose – is Milton.

John **Milton** (1608-74) was trained at Cambridge University in the Anglican faith but he became a Puritan in religious and political belief. Many critics have remarked upon their difficulty in believing that anyone could have loved John Milton the man, but what of his poetry? Descriptions of the poet and his work vary from exalted acclaim to damning with faint praise. A typical encyclopaedic entry reads: 'one of the best-known and most respected figures in English literature.' The same entry goes on to say of the poetry: 'At best, his poetry is marked by intense moral preoccupation, dramatic power, lofty eloquence, and an effective use of sonorous, dignified blank verse.'

Some critical admirers have ranked Milton with Shakespeare, so what is to be made of statements like the following:

> It is true [said George Saintsbury] that *Paradise Lost* is alone in its kind of greatness; and *Paradise Regained* is not far behind it, though curiously it has never had quite so high a position in public esteem.

> For pure poetry [writes J. Hislop] one must turn to his 'minor' poems but Milton's lyrics and sonnets are peculiarly his own.

Thomas Carlyle, 1838, in his *Lectures on the History of Literature*, wrote:

> Milton's sympathies were with things rather than men … He has no delineations of mind except Satan … I wish, however, to be understood not to speak at all in disparagement of Milton; far from that.

Samuel Taylor Coleridge, 1833, *Table Talk*, August 18, said:

> In *Paradise Lost* – indeed in every one of his poems – it is Milton himself whom you see; his Satan, his Adam, his Raphael, almost his Eve – are all John Milton; and it is a sense of this intense egotism that gives me the greatest pleasure in reading Milton's works. The egotism of such a man is a revelation of spirit.

Another critic wrote:

> The description of the garden of Eden, in the fourth book of *Paradise Lost*, is magnificent but vague. The pomp of language and profusion of image leaves on the imagination no definite picture. ... Such landscapes in poetry, entirely projected by the imagination and answering no scene on earth, are, like the composition pictures, which some painters delight in, only splendid failures.
>
> John Campbell Shairp, *On Poetic Interpretation of Nature* (1877)

This by a later critic:

> As he grew older the taste of Milton grew more austere. The change in the character of his ornament is deeply marked when we ascend from the alpine meadows of *Paradise Lost* to the peaks of *Paradise Regained*, where the air is so highly rarefied that many readers find it difficult to breathe.
>
> Edmund Gosse, *Short History of Modern English Literature* (1897)

Milton's work brings together something of the spirit of the Renaissance and Puritanism. His philosophical and theological ideas are often contradictory and their expression tends to be weighed down by the effects of much book learning. For many he holds a high place in literature, but the critical attacks of recent detractors show how wide apart are his admirers and adverse critics. Milton is renowned for the 'grand style' and the 'great theme' but as for the poetry – it seems that readers will continue to be polarized at the critical extremes.

The Wider Dimension

The so-called Metaphysical Poets were a small number of 17th-century poets who were religious in sensibility but who, apart from Donne and Marvell, wrote unremarkable verse. The artificiality of dubbing a small historical group of poets 'metaphysical' becomes obvious when considering the work of Shakespeare and T.S. Eliot. To widen the dimension of metaphysics and philosophy in poetry it is necessary to define terms.

A deep level of perception, capable of addressing truth, is possessed by those poets throughout history who are truly capable of dealing with the intangible, but their writing is sometimes obscure. Ambiguity is not an essential requirement of metaphysical poetry, nor is it inevitable. Incisive poetry which unfolds with a clear ordered logic can address and reconcile the difference between ephemeral changing appearance and the permanent unchanging reality which supports everything. In Eliot's words, 'The poet is constantly amalgamating disparate experiences and forming new wholes.'

Man experiences the Universe dualistically; he sees himself and everything else as two or more different entities. With the essential unity of nature seemingly riven, relationships with everything have to be formed and maintained. There is a perceived need to make whole the self; to bring it into harmony and unity with the total order of the Universe.

Poetry, with its roots in experience, offers more than a furtherance of self-analysis. The Elizabethan sonnet sought the re-integration of spirit and nature through the alchemy of sexual love and the transcendental power of personal integrity. It was also able, metaphysically, to address and consider cosmic destiny.

In our own age the human predicament is still an apparent separation from the unity of spirit and nature. Yet the notional individuality of which we are so certain is but a reflection of the ultimate oneness of an absolute being (the all-inclusive Universe pervaded by its own Creative Intelligence) in which there is no separation, notional or otherwise. In order to be what we are, we have to transcend what we are not. The notional separation from the unity of everything is only a concept, based on our experience of a separate physical body and social identity. Once this is realized, the perceived individuality is seen to be at one with the whole creation. Poetry is especially well placed for this ameliorative, uniting function. As we saw earlier, the sonnet, with 450 years of tradition behind it, is the perfect vehicle for philosophy. You will remember that Shakespeare, in a sonnet, addresses the beloved 'other' as his own reality – which he sees everywhere:

Sonnet 53

What is your substance, whereof are you made,
That millions of strange shadows on you tend?
Since every one hath, every one, one shade,
And you, but one, can every shadow lend.

To perceive the divine as external to ourselves is to be separate and in duality. The essential person, which embodies the divine spark, outgrows personality, becomes the self-transcendent being and, in a likeness of unity, manifests spirit and nature as one. Eliot conducts us on this journey, showing us the material world and its spiritual counterpart, moving easily between the two. In *Prufrock* he offers us an invitation:

Let us go then, you and I,
When the evening is spread out against the sky
Like a patient etherised upon a table …

His intention:

To lead you to an overwhelming question …
Oh, do not ask, 'What is it?'
Let us go and make our visit.

In *Four Quartets*:

Footfalls echo in the memory
Down the passage we did not take
Towards the door we never opened
Into the rose-garden.

Burnt Norton

And the end of all our exploring
Will be to arrive where we started
And know the place for the first time
Through the unknown, remembered gate.

Little Gidding

Eliot is a gentle guide. Although we are in no doubt about the esoteric knowledge we are being led towards, the poet seems to reassure us, as if in Dr Johnson's benign words, 'I will not instruct you in the things you do not know, but remind you of those things you do know.'

The period from 1637 to 1789, called The Enlightenment, saw the growth of Natural Science and the search for 'natural law'. As for poetry, Milton's *Paradise Lost* (1667) might be considered the last great work of the humanism of the Renaissance. The light verse of the age was excellent, and when concerned with love (as it often was) it had a lyric touch – and usually a sense of proportion. Thomas Gray's *Elegy written in a Country Churchyard* (1751), perhaps because of its innate patriotism and commmon touch, was a work later acceptable even to the reactionary first generation of 19th-century Romanticists. However, Romanticism was 200 years ahead, and was preceded by the stimulating and witty so-called Augustan Age.

The Augustan Age

As the contentions and enthusiasms of the mid-17th century receded, English cultural society settled into the relative stability and prosperity of the Augustan Age. The reign of Queen Anne (1702-14) produced a civilization with its own perspective on what constituted good society – wit, restraint, and good taste, which required subordination of personal idiosyncrasy to a social norm. In London, the coffee houses replaced the court as the meeting place of men of culture. Also, there flourished the Scriblerus Club – an association that included Jonathan Swift, John Gay, John Arbuthnot (physician in ordinary to Queen Anne), and Alexander Pope.

The English poet and satirist Alexander **Pope** (1688-1744) was the literary dictator of his age (in some ways he was a successor to Dryden). He was also regarded as the epitome of English neo-classicism.

In late childhood Pope contracted a tubercular infection of the vertebrae which inhibited his growth: he attained a height of only four feet six inches. Perhaps as a result of his invalidity he refined his writing skills and developed penetrating and perceptive powers of observation. Here he comments on the delicate structure of the spider's web:

The spider's touch, how exquisitely fine!
Feels at each thread, and lives along the line.

He wrote a mock heroic piece *The Rape of the Lock*, published in 1712 but enlarged and republished in 1714, which contained this line of compressed import:

What dire offence from am'rous causes springs,
What mighty contests rise from trivial things!

Pope translated the *Iliad* (1715-20) and the *Odyssey* (1725-26). It was a subscription enterprise undertaken with two others which served to render him financially secure.

He had a lifelong woman friend to whom he left his property – Martha Blount. Perhaps she was in mind when he wrote lines which express a rather special avowal of service in love, made in his *Eloisa to Abelard* (1717):

No, make me mistress to the man I love;
If there be yet another name more free,
More fond than mistress, make me that to thee!

Influenced by the philosophy of his friend Bolingbroke (English statesman and orator), Pope published a series of moral and philosophical poems, *An Essay on Man* (1733-4). Here are some lines which indicate the poet's perceptive observation:

Know then thyself, presume not God to scan,
The proper study of mankind is man.

★

Behold the child, by nature's kindly law
Pleased with a rattle, tickled with a straw …

★

Scarfs, garters, gold, amuse his riper stage,
And beards and pray'r-books are the toys of age:
Pleased with this bauble still, as that before;
Till tired he sleeps, and life's poor play is o'er.

★

Order is Heav'n's first law.

In a composite allusion to re-incarnation and an illusory 'heaven', he wrote:

Go like the Indian, in another life
Expect thy dog, thy bottle, and thy wife.

★

All our knowledge is ourselves to know.

An Essay on Man I

When, at the age of 23, Pope had published *An Essay on Criticism* he gave the English language truisms which were to enjoy continuing currency:

To err is human, to forgive, divine.

★

Men must be taught as if you taught them not,
And things unknown proposed as things forgot.

★

For fools rush in where angels fear to tread.

★

Still pleased to teach, and yet not proud to know.

★

All are but parts of one stupendous whole,
Whose body nature is, and God the soul.

Pope's, often spiteful, attacks on his contemporaries earned him the nickname 'the Wicked Wasp of Twickenham'. Perhaps he was putting into effect what he had stated so aptly in *An Essay on Criticism*:

True wit is nature to advantage dressed,
What oft was thought, but ne'er so well expressed.

Here finally, is how Pope's celebrated wit was lavished 'on the collar of a dog which I gave to his Royal Highness':

I am his Highness' dog at Kew;
Pray tell me, sir, whose dog are you?

After the acerbity of Pope and his contemporaries, literature was to be imbued with a softer-edged philosophy. The natural world and the beauty of life were to receive a powerful charge of emotion, from Romanticism.

8
Ideals and Dreams

The Romantic Movement

DURING THE LATE 18th century and the early half of the 19th, far-reaching revolutionary political changes were occurring in many areas of the world. A parallel upheaval in literature occurred, which contributed its own dimension to what became known as the Romantic Movement. Its adherents reacted against the restrictions of the classical style, valuing instead the importance of imagination, the free expression of emotion, and the beauty of life and nature. English Romantic poetry written in the first half of the 19th century represents a high point in the history of English literature. The following poets, with their spiritual characteristic, were prominent in the Romantic Movement in England:

Blake	The earliest poet of the group; a fundamental Christian.
Wordsworth	A poet with a pantheistic 'natural piety'.
Byron	A writer who explored the passionate and the demonic.
Keats	Sensitive responses to eternal problems – art, life, death.
Shelley	An atheist whose poetry connected extremes of feeling.
Coleridge	Poet and critic; apologist for the Church of England.

William **Blake** (1757-1827) was born in Soho, the third child of a well-to-do hosier. He was one of the strangest and most variously gifted figures in the history of English art and writing. He reported that from early boyhood he had seen visions of God and of His angels. While at school he learned relatively little and was apprenticed to an engraver at the age of 14. He married Catherine, the uneducated daughter of a Battersea market-gardener, when they were in their early 20s; they had no children. Catherine became a patient and devoted companion who accepted her husband's visions with equanimity. On one occasion she said, 'I spend very little time in Mr Blake's company; he is usually in Paradise!' They used to sit peaceably naked together in the back yard of their lodgings in Hercules Buildings, Lambeth. Blake was a poet and artist who earned his living by engraving illustrations for books, and although failing to find popular success, the life enjoyed by the visionary poet seems to have been blessed with self-sufficiency. He had a universal way of seeing and believed in the sanctity of human passion:

The pride of the peacock is the glory of God.
The lust of the goat is the bounty of God.
The wrath of the lion is the wisdom of God.
The nakedness of woman is the work of God.

Despite the fact that most of Blake's contemporaries suspected that he was a little mad, his peculiar genius did not go unrecognized. Viewed with the hindsight of modern psychological understanding, Blake can be perceived to have seen that warfare could be interpreted as a form of repressed sexuality:

I am drunk with unsatiated love
I must rush again to War for the
Virgin has frowned and refused.

He was morally indignant about the institutions of State and Church, convinced that their repression and religious hypocrisy had brought about a fallen world. His religious extremism led to isolation and disregard.

As the caterpillar chooses the fairest leaves on which to lay
her eggs, so the priest lays his curse on the fairest joys.

Blake saw the American and French revolutions as releasing the energies of humanity, so long repressed by the forces of absolutism, institutionalized religion, and sexual inhibition.

Embraces are comminglings:
from the Head even to the Feet;
And not a pompous High Priest
entering by a Secret Place.

Some lines of Blake's were held by A.E. Housman to be among the purest and most intense he wrote:

Truly, my Satan, thou art but a Dunce
And dost not know the Garment from the Man:
Every harlot was a Virgin once,
Nor canst thou ever change Kath into Nan.
Though thou art worshipp'd by the names Divine
Of Jesus and Jehovah thou art still
The Son of Morn – in weary night's Decline,
The Lost Traveller's Dream, under the Hill.

These lines have beauty, mystery, and a sardonic relish. Blake is one of the most intellectually challenging of English poets, and his work reveals a unique insight into the pieties and idealogical deceptions of his time. Blake's moral indignation is an aspect of a metaphysical quest for spiritual harmony beyond the material world. As well as idiosyncratic prophetic writings and drawings, he wrote some striking poetry:

Tyger! Tyger burning bright
In the forests of the night,
What immortal hand or eye
Could frame thy fearful symmetry?

He also wrote the gloomy poem that was made, so effectively, into a song by Benjamin Britten:

O Rose, thou art sick!
The invisible worm
That flies in the night,
In the howling storm,

Has found out thy bed
Of crimson joy,
And his dark secret love
Does thy life destroy.

Blake has a capacity for beholding with the mind's eye a vast and limitless vision; 'seeing with my inward eye' as he put it.

To see a World in a Grain of Sand,
And a Heaven in a Wild Flower,
Hold Infinity in the palm of your hand,
And Eternity in an hour.

Auguries of Innocence

In his preface to *Milton* he asks some vivid, penetrating questions:

And did those feet in ancient time
Walk upon England's mountains green?
And was the holy Lamb of God
On England's pleasant pastures seen?
And did the Countenance Divine
Shine forth upon our clouded hills?
And was Jerusalem builded here
Among these dark Satanic Mills?

Blake's wit is often heavy with irony:

When Sir Joshua Reynolds died
All Nature was degraded
The King dropped a tear into the Queen's ear,
And all his pictures faded.

On Art and Artists

The following acerbic statement refers to the so-called 'golden rule': 'Do as you would be done by' – a paraphrase of the *New Testament* verse, *Matthew* vii.12.

He has observ'd the golden rule,
Till he's become the golden fool.

Miscellaneous Epigrams

Some of Blake's simple statements have a philosophical profundity:

> A fool sees not the same tree that a wise man sees.

Spiritual dissent was a commonplace in the 18th century, but it took genius to confer upon it that strangeness and elevation to the level of pure joy which Blake's poems and pictures express.

William **Wordsworth** (1770-1850) was born in Cumberland, the son of a law-agent. His mother died when he was only eight – his father five years later. In 1787 he went to Cambridge; a year later he visited revolutionary France. He returned in 1791, staying a year. During this time, Wordsworth had a love affair with Annette Vallon, a surgeon's daughter at Blois, who bore him a daughter. After his return to this country having left Annette behind, he suffered considerable distress when England went to war with France in 1793. He married Mary Hutchinson of Penrith in 1802; they had and lost both a son, Thomas, and a daughter, Dora.

Wordsworth rejected artificiality and stylization, so that his poetry would communicate directly in easily comprehensible terms. This gives his work an impressive, stubborn authenticity of tone which he achieves by use of a primitive or simplistic literary form. An example is *We are Seven*. Wordsworth was clearly moved by a child who, too young to learn the significance of bereavement in the family, continues to respond 'we are seven'.

> A simple child
> That lightly draws its breath,
> And feels its life in every limb,
> What should it know of death?
>
> 'But they are dead; those two are dead!
> Their spirits are in Heaven!'
> 'Twas throwing words away; for still
> The little Maid would have her will,
> And said, 'Nay, we are seven!'

Keats called Wordsworth's style, in poems such as *The Prelude* and *Tintern Abbey*, his 'egotistical sublime'. In this mood he is profoundly introspective, but unfortunately his spiritual earnestness increasingly declines into orthodox piety. By 1830 his achievement was generally acknowledged, and in 1843 he was made poet laureate. As James Smith in *Scrutiny* (1938) remarked:

> Wordsworth's poetry is not only an extensive, it is a difficult country.

Amid tracts of seemingly mediocre verse there are some outstanding images. In one, the introspective poet speaks of the isolation of walking in the beautiful wilderness of his native Cumberland:

> I wandered lonely as a cloud ... *Daffodils*

Here is another such simile shaped from observation:

Poised, like a weary cloud in middle air.

The misty vapourous gatherings in the skies seemed to stimulate thought as he watched them with delight, forming and dissolving.

Although Wordsworth's description of the sounds of song-birds is the usual 'warble' or 'trill', there is nothing conventional about the 'faint wail' or 'angry barking' of the lone eagle; nor in the 'iron knell' of the flying raven.

As well as this acute ear for sound Wordsworth could hear the silence beyond silence:

... silent hills and more than silent sky.

In *The Prelude* he speaks of 'The self-sufficing power of Solitude'. Sometimes, this somewhat sombre poet displays a touch of humour:

O Cuckoo! Shall I call thee bird,
Or but a wandering voice?

To the Cuckoo

Noticing the reflexive leaping of spring lambs, Wordsworth uses a metaphor of medieval imagery:

And while the young lambs bound
As to the tabor's sound.

Wordsworth accepts philosophically that he cannot command the distinction between the extraordinary and the ordinary:

There was a time when meadow, grove and stream,
The earth, and every common sight,
    To me did seem
      Apparelled in celestial light,
The glory and the freshness of a dream.
It is not now as it hath been of yore; –
    Turn wheresoe'er I may,
    By night or day,
The things which I have seen I now can see no more.

Ode, Intimations of Immortality

It is clear that, by this stage, the poet has lost something very special in his whole approach to nature and his relations with it:

Whither is fled the visionary gleam:
Where is it now, the glory and the dream?

Intimations of Immortality

In 1798 when he wrote *Tintern Abbey* he remembered the blessed time of his 17th year:

For nature then ...
To me was all in all.

At the height of his creative career Wordsworth discovered that nature, in which he had invested unquestioning trust as his poetry's inspirational source, had withdrawn from him. We can distinguish two distinctive periods in Wordsworth's life:

- a youthful visionary power which operated through nature;
- later, a living presence which inspired him with devotion and was perceived as the 'soul of all his moral being'.

With remarkable psychological insight, Wordsworth saw that 'The Child is father of the Man'.

> Heaven lies about us in our infancy!
> Shades of the prison-house begin to close
> Upon the growing boy ... *ibid.*

> As if his whole vocation
> were endless imitation ... *ibid.*

> Though nothing can bring back the hour
> Of splendour in the grass, of glory in the flower;
> We will grieve not, rather find
> Strength in what remains behind;
> In the primal sympathy
> Which having been must ever be ... *ibid.*

His meditative seeing enables us, through his words, to share with him an exceptional moment of stillness:

> It is a beauteous evening, calm and free,
> The holy time is quiet as a nun,
> Breathless with adoration.
> *It is a Beauteous Evening*

Wordsworth was capable of bringing the past and future together in the present, in a way which many mystics and 'seekers after truth' would have been glad to experience. He alludes to it in *Lines Composed a Few Miles Above Tintern Abbey*:

> How often has my spirit turn'd to thee!
> And now, with gleams of half-extinguish'd thought,
> With many recognitions dim and faint,
> And somewhat of a sad perplexity,
> The picture of the mind revives again:
> While here I stand, not only with the sense
> Of present pleasure, but with pleasing thoughts
> That in this moment there is life and food
> For future years.

Wordsworth considered the poet to be a person with special gifts, 'endowed with more lively sensibility, more enthusiasm and tenderness;

who has a greater knowledge of human nature, a more comprehensive soul.' In the preface to *Lyrical Ballads* he wrote: 'Poetry is the breath and finer spirit of all knowledge'.

In lines *Composed upon an Evening of Extraordinary Splendour*, he alludes to a connection of heaven with earth:

> ... From worlds not quickened by the sun
> A portion of the gift is won;
> An intermingling of Heaven's pomp is spread
> On ground which British shepherds tread.

It would be an injustice not to mention the influence of Wordsworth's sister, Dorothy, whose devotion to her brother is a constant theme in her own superb *Grasmere Journal*. He wrote of her: 'She gave me eyes, she gave me ears.' To take an example of shared experience from her journal entry for 15 April 1802:

> When we were in the woods beyond Gowbarrow Park we saw a few daffodils close to the water-side. We fancied that the lake had floated the seeds ashore, and that a little colony had sprung up. But as we went along there were more and yet more; and at last, under the boughs of the trees, we saw that there was a long belt of them along the shore, about the breadth of a country turnpike road. I never saw daffodils so beautiful ... and the rest tossed and reeled and danced, and seemed as if they verily laughed with the wind ... they looked so gay, ever glancing, ever changing.

Carlyle remembered Wordsworth in his last years as 'a right good old steel-grey figure'. In his portraits he had a look which makes him seem dour, withdrawn, disillusioned, yet his sister Dorothy tells us that he had 'a violence of affection' which showed itself in a thousand attentions:

> Little, nameless, unremembered, acts of kindness and of love.

His religious and political conservatism changed Wordsworth the young radical into a creature of the establishment. In 1842 he was awarded a civil list pension and in 1843 he succeeded Southey as poet laureate.

In the spring of 1850 Wordsworth caught a cold during a country walk; pleurisy developed, and he died on St George's Day, 80 years to the month after his birth. He is buried in Grasmere churchyard.

> Our birth is but a sleep and a forgetting:
> The Soul that rises with us, our life's Star,
> Hath had elsewhere its setting,
> And cometh from afar:
> Not in entire forgetfulness,
> And not in utter nakedness,
> But trailing clouds of glory do we come
> From God, who is our home.
>
> *Intimations of Immortality*

Lord **Byron** (1788-1824) was internationally the most famous of the English Romantic writers. George Gordon Byron was the only child of his father's second marriage. Born in London, he was educated at Harrow School and went from there to Trinity College, Cambridge. Byron was a remarkable person: a Regency man of fashion, libertine, political idealist and romantic hero. As well as being a poet, he invented a system of shorthand, was a Fellow of the Royal Society, and a student of religious mysticism. He generated an image, of 'the Byronic hero', who reappears throughout his work – a sad, melancholy young man, brooding in a melodramatic way upon something mysterious and evil in his background which he never explains.

On attaining his majority in 1809 Byron took his seat in the House of Lords but almost immediately set off with Hobhouse on an extensive tour of the Continent. He was away about two years and travelled to Constantinople, going via Portugal, Spain, Greece and Albania – then a particularly remote and wild region.

Every age reconstructs or deconstructs its image of Byron. However, the abiding impression is that he was a constant rebel against convention and deliberately encouraged the legend of wildness, evil, and debauchery that surrounded his name. His wife, Annabella Milbanke, contributed to this by her suspicions that he had indulged in an incestuous liaison with his half-sister Augusta.

> My sister! My sweet sister! if a name
> dearer and purer were, it should be thine.
>
> *Epistle to Augusta*

Byron's command of figurative language is exemplified here:

> She walks in beauty, like the night
>   Of cloudless climes and starry skies;
> And all that's best of dark and bright
>   Meet in her aspect and her eyes:
> Thus mellow'd to that tender light
>   Which heaven to gaudy day denies.
>
> *She Walks in Beauty*

The poet values moments of solitude:

> There is a pleasure in the pathless woods,
> There is a rapture on the lonely shore,
> There is society, where none intrudes,
> By the deep sea, and music in its roar:
> I love not man the less, but Nature more.
>
> *Childe Harold*

Childe Harold was the narrative poem that made Byron famous; *Don Juan*, his most important and longest work, was left incomplete at his death. His poetry is fluent and rhetorical – often satirical; his wit is sardonic but informed. For his narrative poems he characteristically chose exotic and adventurous Eastern subjects.

The mountains look on Marathon –
  And Marathon looks on the sea;
And musing there an hour alone,
  I dream'd that Greece might still be free.

Don Juan

After Shelley's drowning in 1822, Byron became restless and decided to commit himself to the cause of Greek independence. He left England and went to Greece to join in the struggle against the Turks. He contributed large sums of money to the Greek cause and, although he never fought with them, they still regard him as a hero. He died of fever at Missolonghi in April 1824. His reputation as a rake prevented his burial in Westminster Abbey, and there is no bust of him in Poets' Corner.

He was often critical of other poets and was especially dismissive of Wordsworth, whom he appeared to detest:

Who, both by precept and example, shows
That prose is verse, and verse is merely prose.

English Bards and Scotch Reviewers

On the other hand, Wordsworth complained that the whole third Canto of *Childe Harold* was plagiarized from *Tintern Abbey*, the borrowed sentiments being worked into 'a laboured and antithetical sort of declamation'.

Byron's urbane wit reveals his experience in that activity 'men call gallantry, and gods adultery', as is evident in the following quotations from his *Don Juan*:

  Merely innocent flirtation,
Not quite adultery, but adulteration.

★

  A little she strove, and much repented,
And whispering 'I will ne'er consent' consented.

★

  Man's love is of man's life a thing apart,
'Tis woman's whole existence.

★

  Think you, if Laura had been Petrarch's wife,
He would have written sonnets all his life?

Byron in his more reflective moments brings his irony to bear upon a more serious side of human activity:

Christians have burnt each other, quite persuaded
That all the Apostles would have done as they did.

Don Juan

He takes a compassionate view of godly wrongdoing:

> Thy Godlike crime was to be kind,
> To render with thy precepts less
> The sum of human wretchedness.
>
> *Prometheus*

As a theorist of poetry Byron is an urbane neo-classicist who rejects almost all of what we now call Romanticism, including his own contribution to it. In Europe he is regarded as a significant philosopher of Romanticism. Certainly he deals with the great themes of time and decay with a flippant world-weariness which is genuinely moving:

> ... in short, I
> Have squandered my whole summer while 'twas May.
>
> *Don Juan*

> I have not loved the world, nor the world me;
> I have not flatter'd its rank breath, nor bow'd
> To its idolatries a patient knee,
> Nor coin'd my cheeks to smiles, – nor cried aloud
> In worship of an echo; in the crowd
> They could not deem me one of such; I stood
> Among them, but not of them.
>
> *Childe Harold*

John **Keats** (1795-1821) was born in Moorfields, London. After education at a private school he began to study medicine at Guy's and St Thomas's hospitals, but abandoned this for poetry in 1816. His early work was harshly reviewed by critics, and this, together with the death of his younger brother Tom in December 1818, profoundly distressed him. Keats was living with his friend, Armitage Brown, when he met and fell passionately in love with Fanny Brawne:

> You have ravished me away by a power I cannot resist; and yet I could resist till I saw you; and ever since I have seen you I have endeavoured often to reason against the reason of my Love.
>
> Every hour I am more and more concentrated in you; every thing else tastes like chaff in my mouth.
>
> To Fanny Brawne, February 1820

There followed a period of intensive creativity, and it was during this time that many of his finest poems were written: *The Eve of St Agnes*, *The Eve of St Mark*, *La Belle Dame Sans Merci*, *Ode to a Nightingale*, *Ode on a Grecian Urn*, *Ode to Melancholy*, and *To Autumn*. *Lamia, The Eve of St Agnes and other poems* appeared in July 1820 and received much praise. In fact, this was his most successful publication.

Keats was an outstanding representative of Romanticism in English poetry. Among his familiars were Leigh Hunt, Hazlitt, Shelley, Lamb,

Coleridge, and Wordsworth. He influenced the Pre-Raphaelite Brotherhood, Tennyson, and the French Symbolists. His poetry was characterized by a youthful exuberance, an intense, sensuous pictorial vividness, a sense of symbolism. He was attracted to medieval and supernatural subjects.

In the poetry of Keats, poetic imagery is vivid and intense; his use of figurative language is particularly rich and evocative:

Season of mists and mellow fruitfulness,
Close bosom-friend of the maturing sun;
Conspiring with him how to load and bless
With fruit the vines that round the thatch-eaves run.

⋆

Then in a wailful choir the small gnats mourn
Among the river shallows, borne aloft
Or sinking as the light wind lives or dies.

⋆

The red-breast whistles from a garden-croft;
And gathering swallows twitter in the skies.

To Autumn

O, for a draught of vintage! that hath been
Cool'd a long age in the deep-delved earth,
Tasting of Flora and the country green,
Dance, and Provençal song, and sunburnt mirth!
O for a beaker full of the warm South,
Full of the true, the blushful Hippocrene,
With blended bubbles winking at the brim,
And purple-stainèd mouth;
That I might drink, and leave the world unseen,
And with thee fade away into the forest dim.

Ode to a Nightingale

Those lines, pulsing with ecstatic imagery, sweep through the awareness with a meditative dynamic, culminating in a seeming dissolving of individual experience – a merging into universal invisibility.

In a letter to John Taylor, Keats wrote that 'If poetry comes not as naturally as leaves to a tree it had better not come at all.' He further said that 'Poetry should surprise by a fine excess, and not by singularity.' He expressed a concern to Taylor that he had 'been hovering for some time between the exquisite sense of the luxurious and a love for philosophy …. I shall turn all my soul to the latter.' Certainly, Keats made an important contribution to aesthetics. He wrote to B.R. Haydon, the English historical painter to whom he had addressed a sonnet, 'It is true that in the height of enthusiasm I have been cheated into some fine passages; but that is not the thing.' The thing, apparently, was beauty.

I never can feel certain of any truth but from a clear perception of its beauty.

To George and Georgiana Keats, 4 January 1819

In *Endymion* he expounds the eternal nature of the Platonic Beauty: 'A thing of beauty is a joy for ever: its loveliness increases; it will never pass into nothingness.' He further expresses his profound aesthetic understanding in *Ode on a Grecian Urn* in words as familiar as a biblical text: 'Beauty is truth, truth beauty, that is all ye know on earth, and all ye need to know.' Keats also believed that the poet has no fixed abiding identity; rather, he has the ability to suspend his own egotism by the selfless act of yielding subjective imagination to objective reality.

In his last sonnet Keats addresses his words heavenwards:

> Bright star! would I were steadfast as thou art –
> Not in lone splendour hung aloft the night ...
>
> ★
>
> Pillowed upon my fair love's ripening breast
> To feel for ever its soft fall and swell,
> Awake for ever in a sweet unrest ...

Keats died of tuberculosis in Rome, although his friends somewhat unrealistically preferred to believe that he died of a broken heart because of the harsh criticism by *Blackwood's Magazine* of *Endymion*. He is buried there in the Protestant cemetery. Earlier he had written movingly to Fanny Brawne:

> I have left no immortal work behind me – nothing to make my friends proud of my memory – but I have loved the principle of beauty in all things.

Percy Bysshe **Shelley** (1792-1822) was born at Field Place, near Horsham in Sussex, the eldest child of a highly respectable Sussex squire and Member of Parliament. He was educated at Eton and University College, Oxford, from which he was sent down for circulating a pamphlet entitled *The Necessity of Atheism*. He went to London and later the same year eloped with 16-year-old Harriet Westbrook to Scotland, where they were married. Harriet bore Shelley two children, but increasing disappointment with her marriage finally caused her to drown herself in the Serpentine in Hyde Park. Shelley's second marriage was to Mary Wollstonecraft, daughter of the philosopher Godwin. He left with her for Italy, taking his two small children. They were accompanied by Mary's stepsister, Claire Clairmont, who took with her the daughter she had borne to Byron. It was in Italy that Shelley was to spend the rest of his life, and where he would write his most enduring poetry. He was drowned while sailing with two others, in a sudden squall in the Bay of Spezia, in July 1822.

In his *Life of Percy Bysshe Shelley* (1858) T.J. Hogg wrote:

> His features ... breathed an animation, a fire, an enthusiasm, a vivid and preternatural intelligence, that I never met with in any other countenance.

The hectic quality of much of Shelley's rhetoric betrays the idealism of a frustrated radical during a period of reaction. He contends that poets have wider sympathies than ordinary men and in his *Defence of Poetry* insists that 'poets are the unacknowledged legislators of the world'. Shelley's range is astonishing. Even in his early work he delineates a complete philosophical and moral system. His *Queen Mab* (1813) expresses his revolutionary faith in Godwin's aesthetic doctrines; *Alastor* (1816) is an evocation of the poet's sense of loneliness and his taste for death. The *Hymn to Intellectual Beauty* (1817) signifies a period of Platonism; *The Revolt of Islam* combines a story of incest with a statement of the ideals of liberty and justice.

Shelley was a man of considerable culture, independence of mind, and elevated idealism. Like Byron's, his writing has a measure of self-indulgent narcissism, but his is more elegant and idealistic. He is one of the greatest of all lyric poets, and although some verse is flamboyant, and at times even wildly extravagant, many lines are exquisite in their imagery and delicate sensibility.

> O wild West Wind, thou breath of Autumn's being,
> Thou, from whose unseen presence the leaves dead
> Are driven, like ghosts from an enchanter fleeing,
>
> Yellow, and black, and pale, and hectic red,
> Pestilence-stricken multitudes: O thou,
> Who chariotest to their dark wintry bed
>
> The wingèd seeds, where they lie cold and low,
> Each like a corpse within its grave, until
> Thine azure sister of the spring shall blow
>
> Her clarion o'er the dreaming earth, and fill
> (Driving sweet buds like flocks to feed in air)
> With living hues and odours plain and hill;
>
> Wild Spirit, which art moving everywhere;
> Destroyer and preserver; hear, oh, hear!
>
> *Ode to the West Wind*

Constantly preoccupied with intellectual issues, Shelley's idealistic fervour tends to be abstracted and internalized. For example, his desire for social justice becomes an insistence on personal selflessness. He comments with irony on the transience of earthly dominion in his poem *Ozymandias*.*

> I met a traveller from an antique land
> Who said: Two vast and trunkless legs of stone
> Stand in the desert.

* Ozymandias is the Greek approximate vocalization of *User-Ma'at-Ra* the throne-name of Ramesses II. In the Ptolemaic Period (331-30 BC), his cult supported its own priesthood. The chronicler, Diodorus of Sicily (about 600 BC) noted the statue's unbelievable size and quality – it was originally 66 feet high and weighed approximately 1,000 tons. This early traveller quotes a translation of the hieroglyphs inscribed on its base: 'King of Kings am I, Ozymandias. If anyone would know how great I am … let him surpass one of my works.' – Hecataeus of Abdera (3 BC). By the time Shelley was writing his poem, earthquakes and looting had reduced both the Ramesseum and its statue to a ruin.

'My name is Ozymandias, King of kings:
Look on my works, ye Mighty, and despair!'

Nothing beside remains. Round the decay
Of that colossal wreck, boundless and bare
The lone and level sands stretch far away.

Goethe observed that when Byron begins to think, he becomes a child. But Shelley remains true to Locke, who asserts that 'Reason must be our last judge and guide in everything.' This produces the incredible simile:

Like a Poet hidden in the light of thought ... *To a Skylark*

There is depth in the philosophical statement:

He gave man speech, and speech created thought,
Which is the measure of the universe.

Prometheus Unbound

In this next sequence Shelley, continuing this theme and speaking as a poet, indicates how language commands and structures thought:

Language is a perpetual Orphic song,
Which rules with Daedal harmony a throng
Of thoughts and forms, which else senseless
and shapeless were. *ibid.*

It seems that for Shelley, the supreme force in creation is Love:

Fate, Time, Occasion, Chance, and Change: to these
All things are subject but eternal Love. *ibid.*

In his attitude to nature, Shelley the atheist seeks a reconciliation between rational scepticism and metaphorical imagination, seeing it as the function of poetry to restore a sense of creative wholeness. *Mont Blanc* (1817) is his response to the sublime beauty of nature, but the sense of awe felt by the poet has to be accounted for without reference to God. He resorts to 'the human mind's imaginings' as a substitute. This results in language which is distinctly religiose, although his use of the concept 'spirit' steers the atheistic poet towards more neutral ground.

But above all other things,
  Spirit, I love thee –
Thou art love and life! Oh, come,
  Make once more my heart thy home.

Song: *Rarely, Rarely, Comest Thou*

Hail to thee, blithe Spirit!
  Bird thou never wert,
That from Heaven, or near it,
  Pourest thy full heart
In profuse strains of unpremeditated art.

To a Skylark

Shelley's figurative language is not the equal of Keats', but his imagery is often finely sensitive:

And in the warm hedge grey lush eglantine,
  Green cowbind and the moonlight-coloured may,
And cherry-blossoms, and white cups, whose wine
  Was the bright dew, yet drained not by the day;

And nearer to the river's trembling edge
  There grew broad flag-flowers, purple, pranked with white,

And starry river buds among the sedge,
  And floating water-lilies, broad and bright.

The Question

The works written in Italy include the poetical tragedy *The Cenci* (1819); *Prometheus Unbound* (1820), a philosophical drama and sublimation of his political preoccupations; *Epipsychidion* (1821), a vast love poem in honour of the ideal Woman; *Adonais*, a touching elegy on the death of Keats – and a personal confession. In his *A Defence of Poetry* Shelley reveals his poetic ideal and his conception of the poet's role:

Poetry is the record of the best and happiest moments of the happiest and best minds.

Glimpses of idealism and sadness occur throughout Shelley's poetry:

A traveller from the cradle to the grave
Through the dim light of his immortal day.
Familiar acts are beautiful through love.

Prometheus Unbound

The rapid, blind and fleeting generations of mankind.

The Witch of Atlas

In *Stanzas Written in Dejection, near Naples* Shelley wrote: 'I could lie down like a tired child, and weep away the life of care which I have borne and yet must bear, till death like sleep might steal on me.'

Samuel Taylor **Coleridge** (1772-1834) was born in the vicarage of Ottery St Mary, Devon, and educated at Christ's Hospital and Jesus College, Cambridge. In 1793, heavily in debt, he impulsively enlisted in the 15th Dragoons but was mercifully bought out by his brother. He returned to Cambridge but failed to take a degree. He left in 1794 and, with the poet Robert Southey, a close friend, settled in Bristol. A year later, he and Southey married the sisters Sara and Edith Fricker. In 1797 he began a deep and lasting friendship with Wordsworth and his sister Dorothy.

In 1804, with his marriage failing and nursing an addiction to opium, Coleridge travelled to the Mediterranean. After ten months in Malta as secretary to the Governor, he went on to Naples and Rome. He returned to England, living first in the Lake District and then in Highgate. Highly respected in his final years, at last financially secure and with his opium habit under control, he held weekly *conversazioni* at which he entertained friends and young disciples with his brilliant discourse on philosophy, poetry, and literary criticism.

Coleridge, known for the acuity of his intellect, was an early crusader for Unitarianism, that is, the denial of the Trinity, holding that God is one in person and substance. With Robert Southey he helped to plan the so-called Pantisocracy settlement – a scheme for an ideal social community in America, which failed to materialize through lack of financial backing. He became a keen student of German philosophy and literature, spending time at the University of Göttingen. He lectured extensively, was a brilliant conversationalist, and was interested in politics, drama and the history of the Christian religion. In conjunction with Wordsworth he published *Lyrical Ballads* in 1798, a principal composition of the English Romantic Movement.

His most famous poems are *The Rime of the Ancient Mariner*, *Kubla Khan* and *Christabel*, all of which are especially popular with schoolchildren. In the realm of literary criticism during the Romantic period, he had no significant rival. *The Rime of the Ancient Mariner* is a strange tale of a seafarer who sails the oceans of the world on a phantom ship.

> And a good south wind sprung up behind;
> The Albatross did follow,
> And every day, for food or play,
> Came to the mariner's hollo!
>
> 'God save thee, ancient Mariner!
> From the fiends that plague thee thus! –
> Why look'st thou so?' – With my cross-bow
> I shot the Albatross.
>
> *The Ancient Mariner* (I)

Not surprisingly, this very long, odd piece of work has attracted speculative psychological and literary analysis. The human experience on which Coleridge bases the poem is an almost pathological condition of depression, isolation, and self-worthlessness. This may explain or justify certain examples of verse containing repetition and rhyme which, at times, verges on doggerel.

> Alone, alone, all, all alone,
> Alone on a wide wide sea!
> And never a saint took pity on
> My soul in agony. *ibid.* (IV)

It might be said that much of Coleridge's poetry is dominated by hallucination and dreams. His *Kubla Khan*, written in a fantastic, magical, and dream-like style, was never completed.

In Xanadu did Kubla Khan
A stately pleasure-dome decree …

★

A damsel with a dulcimer
In a vision once I saw:
It was an Abyssinian maid,
And on her dulcimer she played,
Singing of Mount Abora.
Could I revive within me
Her symphony and song,

To such a deep delight 'twould win me,
That with music loud and long,
I would build that dome in air,
That sunny dome! those caves of ice!
And all who heard should see them there,
And all should cry, Beware! Beware!
His flashing eyes, his floating hair!

Weave a circle round him thrice,
And close your eyes with holy dread,
For he on honey-dew hath fed,
And drunk the milk of Paradise.

From a miscellany of his writings, the following are perhaps characteristic of his wit or idealism:

What is an Epigram? a dwarfish whole,
Its body brevity, and wit its soul.

Epigram

In *Work Without Hope* he poignantly highlights despair:

All Nature seems at work. Slugs leave their lair –
The bees are stirring – birds are on the wing –
And Winter slumbering in the open air,
Wears on his smiling face a dream of Spring!
And I the while, the sole unbusy thing,
Nor honey make, nor pair, nor build, nor sing.

Coleridge makes some tender statements:

Poor little Foal of an oppressed race!
I love the languid patience of thy face.

To a Young Ass

In *Biographia Literaria* he shows that he knows that a depth of understanding pervades good poetry:

No man was ever yet a great poet, without being at the same time a profound philosopher.

Yet he was down-to-earth and practical; in *Table Talk* 9 May 1830:

> Poetry is certainly something more than good sense, but it must be good sense at all events; just as a palace is more than a house, but it must be a house at least.

Of Shakespeare, Coleridge said, 'He is of no age – nor of any religion, or party or profession. The body and substance of his works came out of the unfathomable depths of his own oceanic mind.' Most of the work produced in the last years of his life consisted of essays and literary studies. In his final years, admission to his company was much sought after, and two examples of his wit and intelligence perhaps show why:

> When I was a boy, I was fondest of Aeschylus; in youth and middle-age I preferred Euripides; now in my declining years I prefer Sophocles. I can now at length see that Sophocles is the most perfect. Yet he never rises to the sublime simplicity of Aeschylus – a simplicity of design, I mean – nor diffuses himself in the passionate outpourings of Euripides.
>
> *Table Talk*, 1 July 1833

> This passage is what I call the sublime dashed to pieces by cutting too close with the fiery four-in-hand round the corner of nonsense.
>
> *Table Talk*, 20 January 1834

The Pathetic Fallacy of Ruskin

A particularly perceptive critic of the Romantic Age was John Ruskin (1819-1900), the English critic and essayist, who performed a service to poetry when he invented the concept and the phrase *pathetic fallacy* in 1856. This term signifies the attribution to natural objects of human capabilities and feelings. (Ruskin's new term had, as a concept, been defined centuries earlier by the Greeks as *prosopopeia*.) For Ruskin, as for master poets, 'truth' was a primary artistic criterion. His new term was derogatory and applied to descriptions of appearances which were rendered false 'when we are under the influence of emotion or contemplative fancy.' He illustrates his point with two examples:

> The spendthrift crocus, bursting through the mould
> Naked and shivering, with his cup of gold.

Coleridge's descriptive line from *Christabel*:

> The one red leaf, the last of its clan,
> That dances as often as dance it can.

Such passages, says Ruskin, even if beautiful, are false and 'morbid'. The term is now used more neutrally to cover examples of ascription of human traits to inanimate nature – a common phenomenon in descriptive poetry.

Romanticism Fades

Romanticism was born of progressive ideals and was, essentially, a revolution. As the promise of the French Revolution evaporated and expectation faded, the response of the Romantic poets was to become increasingly conservative and orthodox. Coleridge abandoned his political views and became a spokesman for the Church of England; Wordsworth's simple pantheism became stolid piety. Byron and Shelley vigorously maintained their adherence to the ideals inspired by the Revolution and reproached their former contemporaries for relinquishing their ideals.

The Post-Romantic Period

With the death of Lord Byron in 1824 an era came to an end. Moreover, Keats and Shelley were dead; Wordsworth and Coleridge were a spent force. As the *Westminster Review* said rather unfeelingly in 1831, 'They are all going or gone.' However, certain influences persisted so that initially, the Romantic era shaded itself gently into the Post-Romantic period. Browning was a self-proclaimed disciple of Shelley, and Tennyson's work shows the influence of Keats.

The period from 1824 to 1922 was a time of intense progressive change in poetry, and because several important developments were occurring in parallel, the overall picture is not easy to discern. This span of 98 years swirls with the concurrent and overlapping changes that began taking place after the death of Byron and which continued until the publication of T.S. Eliot's *The Waste Land*.

The Romantic Movement in terms of poetry, can be said to have begun with the publication of *Lyrical Ballads* by Wordsworth and Coleridge in 1798 and to have ended with the death of Byron in 1824. At Byron's death, Tennyson and Browning were in their teens, Clough and Arnold were children and Swinburne not yet born. Hood, Barham, and Praed exemplified the energy of English writing during the raffish and turbulent period of the 1830s, but their writing did not meet with the approval of Baudelaire, who remarked in his *Salon of 1846* that such writers looked outside themselves for the poetic landscape of human thought and conduct, 'but it was only to be found within'.

During the period ahead, poetry was to undergo radical changes to its infrastructure, inspirational ideas, and indeed to its very *raison d'être* as poetry. These changes are foreshadowed as follows:

- The Post-Romantics — Victorian poets from c1820 to c1900.
- Symbolism — At its height in French literature from 1870 to 1886.
- Imagism — Mainly in England and United States from 1909 to 1917.
- Georgian Poetry — This period from 1824 to 1922 includes the War Poets.

The Victorian Poets

Victorianism is not the term describing the Victorian Age, or the period when Queen Victoria reigned; rather, it is applied to a special attitude during a vaguely defined period, when the outlook of English people was determined by a set of mores, ideas, and aspirations.

The Romantic poets were never in doubt as to their role in art and in society. Their era was swept in by Revolution in France and a Europe in turmoil. Victorian poets had no such clear sense of purpose and function.

> Nay, if there's room for poets in the world
> A little overgrown (I think there is),
> Their sole work is to represent the age,
> Their age, not Charlemagne's, – this live, throbbing age,
> That brawls, cheats, maddens, calculates, aspires,
> And spends more passion, more heroic heat,
> Betwixt the mirrors of its drawing rooms,
> Than Roland with his knights at Roncesvalles.
>
> Elizabeth Barrett Browning, *Aurora Leigh* (1857)

Elizabeth Barrett Browning countered the Victorian passion for nostalgia, asserting that it was tantamount to escapism. The sentimental evocation of the Middle Ages and the Early Italian Renaissance was widespread in Art, particularly in the works of the Pre-Raphaelite Brotherhood. Its constituent ideas were 'Antique devoutness, Antique veracity and heroism', as Carlyle put it in *Past and Present* (1843). This dreamy, nostalgic other world could be, and was, imagined into existence as a palliative for a present which seemed squalid and over-industrialized.

There was a richness and variety in some Victorian verse, but much was technically poor and imbued with the cloying sentiment of the age. The principal Victorian poets are:

Tennyson	(1809-92)
Browning	(1812-89)
Arnold	(1822-88)
Clough	(1819-61)
Swinburne	(1837-1909)

Alfred, Lord **Tennyson** was born in a Lincolnshire country rectory and grew up deeply attached to English institutions. He was very patriotic and detested pacifism. For his poetry he drew upon Greek legend, Arthurian romance, and English country life. His poetic effects are pictorial and colourful; the images emphasize the sense of hearing and of sight. He watched nature attentively:

> As careful robin's eye the delver's toil …
>
> ★
>
> The rabbit fondles his own harmless face. *Aylmer's Field*

Tennyson's poetry tends to be dominated by reverie, nostalgia, longing and melancholy. The past is a preoccupation for most Victorian writers, but Tennyson's is an extreme case. He was a favourite target for the attacks of English and American poets of the late 19th and early 20th centuries who, in assailing Victorian standards, denounced Tennyson for sentimentality, insipidity, over-ornateness and narrow patriotism.

Among the vast tracts of Tennyson's fields of words there are these lines, taken from his heart-felt poem for his friend Arthur Henry Hallam, whose early death affected him deeply:

So many worlds, so much to do,
So little done …

★

God's finger touched him and he slept.

★

And from his ashes may be made
The violet of his native land.

★

'Tis better to have loved and lost
Than never to have loved at all.

In Memoriam

Tennyson's distinguished imagery and his metrical skills have tended to be more properly evaluated since his own day. At their level, the rhythm, alliteration and brevity of the following well-known lines are perfectly apt for their purpose:

Cannon to right of them
Cannon to left of them,
Cannon in front of them
Volley'd and thunder'd.

The Charge of the Light Brigade

The following lines were set to music by Benjamin Britten in an evocative and atmospheric song:

The splendour falls on castle walls
  And snowy summits old in story;
The long light shakes across the lakes,
  And the wild cataract leaps in glory.
Blow, bugle, blow, set the wild echoes flying,
Blow, bugle; answer, echoes, dying, dying, dying.

The Princess, Introductory Song

He arduously searched for the 'magic' word, but often hardened what could have been free and fluent by overburdening an epithet:

  She woke: the babble of the stream
  Fell, and, without, the steady glare
Shrank one sick willow sere and small.
  The river-bed was dusty-white;

  And all the furnace of the light
Struck up against the blinding wall.

The Lady of Shalott

But note how even a line heavy with 'literariness' reads and flows easily:

> Thridding the sombre boskage of the wood,
> Toward the morning-star.

As a final example, a stanza that Walter de la Mare considered to be 'the very consummation of Tennyson's gifts and one of the most gravely beautiful in English poetry':

> But such a tide as moving seems asleep,
> Too full for sound and foam,
> When that which drew from out the boundless deep
> Turns again home. *Crossing the Bar*

Robert **Browning**, the son of a clerk at the Bank of England, was born at Camberwell. Now a district of London, Camberwell in the early years of the 19th century lay amid green fields.

After his marriage to Elizabeth Barrett (theirs was one of the great romances of literary history) the pair lived in Florence. Following his wife's death the distraught Browning returned with his son to England. It was 17 years before he went to Italy again. When he did, he purchased a Venetian Palace on the Grand Canal; two happy and industrious years later he died, in Venice, on 12 December 1889.

Browning's poetry is distinguished by its learning, psychological analyses of character, and use of the dramatic monologue. Shelley was his idol, and this was acknowledged in such youthful poems as *Pauline* and *Paracelsus*. He had a morbid curiosity in the macabre, which probably contributed to his delayed recognition as the great Post-Romantic poet.

There need be no apology for including the oft-quoted opening of *Home-thoughts, from Abroad*, as anyone will acknowledge who has nostalgically read these lines while in unforgiving, arid places of the world:

> Oh, to be in England
> Now that April's there,
> And whoever wakes in England
> Sees, some morning, unaware,
> That the lowest boughs and the brushwood sheaf
> Round the elm-tree bole are in tiny leaf,
> While the chaffinch sings on the orchard bough
> In England – now!

What Browning venerates in nature is not beauty or sublimity (as did Wordsworth), but the pressure of life – in plant, insect, and bird – when spring returns expressing God's renewal of life's ecstasy.

In *Paracelsus* Browning makes a statement central to spiritual psychology:

> Truth is within ourselves; it takes no rise
> From outward things, whate'er you may believe.
> There is an inmost centre in us all,
> Where Truth abides in fullness, and around,

Wall upon wall, the gross flesh hems it in,
This perfect, clear perception, which is truth.
A baffling and perverting carnal mesh
Binds it, and makes all error; and to know
Rather consists in opening out a way
Whence the imprisoned splendour may escape
Than in effecting entry for a light
Supposed to be without.

His curiosity and delight in detail, combined with a sensuous richness, is sometimes reminiscent of Keats:

Most like the centre spike of gold
  Which burns deep in the bluebell's womb,
What time, with ardours manifold,
  The bee goes singing to her 'groom
    Drunken and overbold.

Browning offered a wide range of events and characters in his work. He possessed a gift for conceiving dramatic situations; to portray these he structured his poetry with a rich variety of forms and rhythms.

Matthew **Arnold** was, as well as poet, a literary critic and classical scholar. Most of his poetry was written in the early years of his life. He was a meditative philosopher in verse and, perhaps of all the major Victorian poets, the most obvious descendant of Wordsworth in style. For a Victorian he had an evenness of poetic temperament, or as Eliot put it in 1933, Arnold had 'neither walked in hell nor been rapt in heaven'. Nevertheless, he seemed clear enough about the poet's function. In his preface to *Poems* (1853) he held that the poet's main responsibility was to 'appeal to the great primary human affections; to those elementary feelings which subsist permanently in the race, and which are independent of time'. One image of Arnold's has gained wide currency:

And that sweet City with her dreaming spires,
She needs not June for beauty's heightening.

Thyrsis

From the *Scholar-Gipsy*, two more memorable images:

All the live murmur of a summer's day.

And here, full of life-weariness:

Tired of knocking at Preferment's door.

In these next lines the poet combines wit with a feline image to make his point:

Cruel, but composed and bland,
Dumb, inscrutable and grand,
So Tiberius might have sat,
Had Tiberius been a cat.

Poor Matthias, 1

Arnold was a realist:

> Nor bring, to see me cease to live,
> Some doctor full of phrase and fame,
> To shake his sapient head and give
> The ill he cannot cure a name.
>
> *A Wish*

Arnold was a poet with a clear view of what poetry should, and could be, but his inhibitions were strong and intrusive. His most persistent theme is the isolation of man in the modern world.

> Know, man hath all which Nature hath, but more,
> And in that *more* lie all his hopes of good.
>
> *To an Independent Preacher*

Arthur Hugh **Clough** was an English poet noted for his expression of melancholy and religious conflicts. *Amours de Voyage*, a poem he wrote in 1849, drew the censure of Walter Bagehot, who wrote that the poet has 'an unusual difficulty in forming a creed as to the unseen world; he could not get the visible world out of his head; his strong grasp of plain facts and obvious matters was a difficulty to him.' The poem is written in conversational hexameters which become irritating, his imagery is diffuse and unexciting, and the poem suffers from long-windedness. A work considered to be his masterpiece, *Dipsychus*, remained unfinished.

Here is Clough letting his wit sparkle in *The Latest Decalogue*:

> Thou shalt not kill; but need'st not strive
> Officiously to stay alive.
>
> Do not adultery commit;
> Advantage rarely comes of it.
>
> Thou shalt not steal; an empty feat,
> When it's so lucrative to cheat.
>
> Thou shalt not covet; but tradition
> Approves all forms of competition.

Another familiar image from the pages of poetry:

> That out of sight is out of mind
> Is true of most we leave behind.
>
> *That Out of Sight*

Finally, from his best work, *Dipsychus*, a piquant exclamation:

> Delicious. Ah!
> What else is like the gondola?

Algernon Charles **Swinburne** was associated with the Pre-Raphaelite Brotherhood and known for his rebellion against Victorian social conventions and religion. He was an intense admirer of Shelley, and his poetry was influenced by Greek legend, Roman classical literature, medieval romance, and Elizabethan drama. His writing is noted for its pagan spirit and amazing musical effects.

Swinburne, in *An Interlude*, seems almost to anticipate T.S. Eliot with his lines:

And a bird overhead sang Follow,
  And a bird to the right sang Here;
And the arch of the leaves was hollow,
  And the meaning of May was clear.

The sensuous Swinburne brought his own skills as a poet to the interpretation he made of the work of the masterly François Villon. In *Translations from Villon – 'Complaint of the Fair Amouress'*, Swinburne conjures this image:

Sweet red splendid kissing mouth.

In his *A Match*, the poet brilliantly juxtaposes ideas, opposites, contrasts, and with brevity invokes striking images:

If you were thrall to sorrow,
And I were page to joy.
If you were April's lady,
And I were lord in May.

If you were queen of pleasure,
And I were king of pain.

Swinburne has the capacity of the true poet for thought at the deeper level:

As the deep dim soul of a star.

*

A little soul for a little bears up this
corpse which is man.
Hymn to Prosperine

With Swinburne's death in 1909 it seemed that the Post-Romantic era had run its course.

German Poetry – Influence in Europe

In connection with the Romantic Movement and its immediate aftermath some mention should be made of the German contribution. Through the writings of Goethe, world literature was made aware of German poetry, and when he died German literature included a body of poetry able to nourish subsequent generations, irrespective of 'Classical' or 'Romantic' inclination.

Goethe (1749-1832) is one of the supreme lyric poets; he was also a dramatist, writer of confessional and philosophical fiction and essayist. He was, in addition, a formidable botanist, antiquarian, and political agent. He was a leading figure in the Romantic Movement. His achievement, perhaps rather simplistically summarized, was a universal humanism of German origin rather than a German humanism of universal impact. He wrote passionately of love in the 'Charlotte' lyrics:

> For, since I have been absent from you,
> To me the noisy movement
> Of life at its swiftest
> Seems but a floating mist thro' which for ever
> As in the clouds I discern your form.

Goethe shared with Shakespeare the capacity to feel his identity as either masculine or feminine. Sexually metamorphic or undefinable figures are crucial to his imaginative creations – notably in *Faust II*.

Much of Goethe's large and benign wisdom appears in such a couplet as the following:

> Ever strive to be a whole, and if thou canst not
> become a whole thyself, to the service of a whole give thyself up.

He offers a definition to conjure with in *Spruche in Prosa* (1819), where he says enigmatically:

> Superstition is the poetry of life.

Goethe's verse was set to music by German composers – Reichardt, Zelter and Schubert. In fact, Schubert turned 70 of Goethe's poems into songs. His earlier lyrics have a pristine freshness and natural singing quality which inspired composers.

Goethe was and is (as Nietzsche remarked) not so much a great individual as a culture. His politics, developing as they did from an early arcadian radicalism to the later, sombre preference for 'order' over 'injustice', have a resonance with Plato and a timelessness which informs his writing. In summary, it could be said that there can be little understanding of Europe without a knowledge of and a delight in Goethe's work. He defined for his contemporaries, and imposed upon European intellectual and literary history, the notion of a 'classical norm'. His abundant life transcended his truism in *Iphigenie*: 'A useless life is an early death.' Finally, as a philosophic comment on Goethe's greatness, there is this, his own line from *Tasso*:

> Genius develops in quiet places,
> Character out in the full current of human life.

Schiller (1759-1805), the German poet and dramatist, produced in the 1790s a number of reflective and philosophical poems and also his most important essays on ethics, aesthetics, and education.

The last years of his life saw the appearance of that great series of blank-verse plays, from *Wallenstein* to *Wilhelm Tell*, which made him Germany's national dramatist. He referred to 'musical poetry' as that which is objectless but which (in common with music) produces only 'a certain emotional state'.

His work clearly appealed to composers: Schubert set 42 of Schiller's poems to music.

Schiller knew the sense of being lifted inwardly to a god-like level, while being reduced outwardly to nothingness:

> We willingly allow our imagination to find its master in the realm of phenomena; for after all, this is only one sensual power triumphing over another; but the absolutely great within us, nature in its boundlessness can never touch.

In *Das Gluck* (*Good Fortune*) Schiller writes:

> Be glad that the gift of song comes down from heaven, so the poet sings what the muse has taught him! Because the god inspires him he becomes a god to the listener; because *he* is fortunate you can be happy.

Heinrich **Heine** (1797-1856) was another German poet famous for his lyrics, his wit, and his irony. He wrote frequently in French as well as German and took a great interest in philosophy.

T.J. Reed, in a biographical note on Heine (1982), defined him paradoxically as a Romantic and a Realist. He went on to add that this German poet is 'a master of lyrical music and of ironic dissonance, a committed satirist and a doubter of all commitment – a deeply divided mind reflecting the complexity and conflict of his age.'

Heine's writing certainly bridges the divide between Romanticism and Realism, and in either mode his work carries an authentic ring.

> I know not why I am so sad; I cannot
> get out of my head a fairy-tale of olden times. *Die Lorelei*

Here is the confident cynicism of his irony:

> God will pardon me. It is His trade. *On His Deathbed*

Heine lived in Paris from 1831 until his death in 1856; there he enjoyed a high reputation with the leading figures in art, affairs, and intellectual life.

Schubert also set six of Heine's poems to song. The concentration and suggestive power of his lyrics made them favourite texts for German *Lied*-composers, including Richard Strauss.

Wo? (Where?)

> Where, when I am tired from my wanderings, will my last
> resting-place be? Under palms in the south? Under
> lime-trees on the Rhine?
>
> Will some stranger bury me somewhere in a desert? Or
> shall I rest in the sand beside an ocean coast?
>
> What does it matter? God's sky will be round me one way
> or the other, and above me the stars will hang down for
> funeral lamps at night.

Rainer Maria **Rilke** (1875-1926) was a German lyric poet, influenced by Baudelaire and the Romantics, known for his mysticism and his later use of a highly developed system of symbolism.

Here is a poem which catches one of the essential strands of Rilke's work – laudation.

Song of Love

Tell us, poet, what is it you do? – I praise. But the
deadly and monstrous things, how can you bear them, how
can you accept them? – I praise. But even what is
nameless, what is anonymous, how can you call upon it? –
I praise. What right have you to be true in every
disguise, beneath every mask? – I praise. And how is it
that both calm and violent things, like star and storm,
know you for their own? – Because I praise.

Rilke strove for unlimited objectivity. He wrote: 'Verses are not, as people imagine, simply feelings (we have these soon enough); they are experiences.' Such a simple statement does not bear out the general opinion that 'Rilke is untranslatable'. However, the aching sensibility, the sense of a poem being shaped and refined to the utmost transparency so that it expands into a commanding image or an entirely original idea is not usually caught by the translator.

In some of the *New Poems* published around 1908 Rilke succeeded in transmuting external phenomena into 'inwardness'. It had been his ambition for some years to express the 'thingness of things'; somehow to understand their spirit and to express that in poetry. The very first of the so-called *New Poems* was 'Panther', an animal he saw in Paris, in the Jardins des Plantes:

His gaze those bars keep passing is so misted
with tiredness, it can take in nothing more.

★

Just now and then the pupil's noiseless shutter
is lifted. – Then an image will indart,
down through the limbs' intensive stillness flutter,
and end its being in the heart.

Translated by J.B. Leishman

Here are some lines from a sequence of 55 *Sonnets to Orpheus* addressed ostensibly to the God of poetry – but also to the idealized Rilke:

I.9

Only he who has raised the lyre even among the shades
may sense and dispense the infinite praise.

Only he who ate of their poppy with the dead will never
lose even the softest note.

Though the reflection in the pond may often dissolve
before us – know the symbol!

Only in the double realm will voices be lasting and gentle.

Finally, in English translation, further lines from his *Sonnets to Orpheus*, II.150

> Whoever pours himself out like a spring,
> Knowing knows him and leads him
> Delighted through the tranquil creation that often
> ends at beginning and begins at ending.

Rilke had as much range and linguistic ability as any poet of his generation. To regard him principally as a thinker or mystic is a serious mistake, and although he transcends many of the theoretical aspects of the modern movement, he is important to an understanding of it.

Extremist Changes

In poetry many influences run concurrently at various times. Two tangential radical upheavals – *Symbolism* and *Imagism* – occurred in the infrastructure of poetry between about 1870 and 1917. For chronological reasons they are being mentioned briefly in passing now, but are dealt with more fully in another section of this volume.

The Symbolism movement in French literature, was at its height between 1870 and 1886. Its adherents were rebelling against realism and, influenced by the Pre-Raphaelite Brotherhood and the music of Wagner, sought to achieve in poetry the effects of music. Their basic approach was to employ clustered images and metaphors suggesting or symbolizing the fundamental idea or emotion of each poem (*see* Chapter 13 – Poetry's Figurative Element: Symbol and Symbolism).

This all went too far, and in 1913 a few poets, who came to be known as *Imagists*, were so disturbed by the current vagueness and conventionality of poetry that they adopted some radical principles of reform. Their movement was called *Imagism*. Imagist poetry was limited to an unambiguous rendering of visual experience and a few examples will show both the possibilities and the limitations of the form (*see* Chapter 13 – Poetry's Figurative Element: Image and Imagism). The radicalism of these dissidents pales before the work of a remarkable and outstanding poet; one whose work is said to have combined the rhythmic freedom of the Middle Ages, the religious intensity of the early 17th century, and the response to the natural world of the early 19th. Furthermore, he anticipated the 20th century by confronting the structural conventions of poetic form. This poet is Gerard Manley Hopkins.

Chronologically, it might be expected that Hopkins would be classified as a Victorian poet. However, a combination of circumstances delayed publication of his poems until 1918 – some 30 years after his death. This delay and his prescient stylistic innovations place him in a unique position among major poets.

The English poet Gerard Manley **Hopkins** (1844-89) was educated at Highgate School and Balliol College, Oxford, where he was a student of Walter Pater and Jowett. He was converted to Roman Catholicism in 1866 and inducted into the Jesuit Order in 1868, after which he became a follower of Cardinal Newman. The poet Robert Bridges was a life-long friend and later edited Hopkins' work, publishing a volume of *Poems* in 1918. At first the poetry was little appreciated, and then only by that minority of people who believed Hopkins to be a major poet. Gradually his reputation has grown, and now his work is regarded by many with veneration.

Hopkins the poet, reflecting his religious conditioning, speaks of poetry's process and its effects in his mind:

> Only what word
> Wisest my heart breeds dark heaven's baffling ban
> Bars or hell's spell thwarts. This to hoard unheard,
> Heard unheeded, leaves me a lonely began.
>
> *Poems*

This difficult poetry condenses meaning within a highly compressed syntax. The ear thrills to the effects of alliterative word pairings which echo and repeat as muscular verse. It succinctly reveals the poet's intense personal experience of God's mystery.

Hopkins is known for the power and striking originality of his lyrics, which deal with nature and religion and reveal the influence of the Metaphysical Poets – especially of George Herbert. He devoted much thought to theories of poetry and invented or coined words to enlarge understanding of his work:

Inscape	The essential quality of a thing which gives it its individuality, distinguishing it from other objects in the same class.
Instress	The force of these qualities upon the mind of an observer, determining the manner in which the observer is made aware of the object and the intensity of response.
Sprung rhythm	A system of scansion based on word stress rather than syllables.

In a letter Hopkins indicated that *inscape* meant 'design' or 'pattern' and added that this was what he aimed at above all in poetry. He also used the word as a verb meaning 'to recognize the single unifying principle of what he was observing'.

Devices occurring in Shakespeare find their parallel in Hopkins, an observation developed at length by F.R. Leavis in *New Bearings in English Poetry* (1932). Here are three fragments from Shakespeare:

> ... the world-without-end hour — Sonnet 57

> ... bloody, bawdy, villain!
> Remorseless, treacherous, lecherous, kindless villain! — *Hamlet*

> … what thou wouldst highly,
> That wouldst thou holily.
>
> *Macbeth*

Here are two examples from Hopkins' poems:

> O the mind, mind has mountains; cliffs of fall
> Frightful, sheer, no-man-fathomed. Hold them cheap
> May who ne'er hung there. Nor does long our small
> Durance deal with that steep or deep.
>
> Not, I'll not carrion comfort, Despair, not feast on thee;
> Not untwist – slack they may be – these last strands of man
> In me or, most weary, cry I can no more. I can;
> Can something, hope, wish day come, not choose not to be.
>
> *Carrion Comfort*

'Feeling, love in particular', wrote Hopkins, 'is the great moving power and spring of verse.' To express and release this energy he became an outstanding technical innovator who stretched poetic form beyond previous limits.

The essence of *sprung rhythm* is simple enough. Whereas a line of ordinary verse has a fixed number of stresses *and* a fixed number of syllables, a line of sprung rhythm has only a fixed number of stresses; the number of syllables can vary widely. This may seem strange but is in fact more familiar to us than we suppose. It is widespread in nursery rhymes. Hopkins gave the following example in his explanations:

	Stresses	*Syllables*
Díng dóng béll	3	3
Pússy's ín the wéll	3	5
Whó pút her ín	3	4
Líttle Jóhnny Thín	3	5

Hopkins wrote, 'I had long had haunting my ear the echo of a new rhythm which now I realized on paper … The effect of studying masterpieces is to make me admire and do otherwise. Perhaps more reading would only refine my singularity!' Hopkins' originality was radical and uncompromising.

This section from the 8th stanza of *The Wreck of the Deutschland* shows sprung rhythm in action. A combination of oral rhythm and literary style, it is to be read not 'with the eyes but with the ears'. The poet uses alliteration, internal rhymes and enjambment (continuation of a sentence beyond the second line of a couplet). With this he creates so rich a verbal texture that his poetry reads as if the torrential flow of inspiration can hardly be contained by technical means:

> How a lush-kept plush-capped sloe
>   Will, mouthed to flesh-burst,
> Gush! – flush the man, the being with it, sour or sweet

Brim, in a flash, full! – Hither then, last or first,
    To hero of Calvary, Christ's feet –
Never ask if meaning it, wanting it, warned of it – men go.

The Wreck of the Deutschland

The obstinate religious extremism, which twisted Hopkins as a person, became the seed of greatness in his poetry and drove his fervent originality. He created poems that expressed the utmost meaning from the English language.

Hopkins desired to bring into verse the energies of ordinary speech; the syllabic stresses in his lines are therefore syncopated, as they might be in conversation. He wrote to Robert Bridges in 1877: 'Why do I employ sprung rhythm at all? Because it is the nearest to … the native and natural rhythm of speech.'

His poetry, as well as being distinguished by the intricate pulse he called sprung rhythm, also employed an extremely individual technique of elliptical phrasing and compound metaphor, capable of great concentration of meaning. He is particularly skilful in the use of alliteration and sequences of coupled words; for example: 'fresh-firecoal, chestnut-falls'. In fact, his innovation, inventiveness, and originality are masterly.

Victorian poetry was, in its verse construction and syntax, stylistically conventional and familiar. This familiarity breaks down when we read the more difficult verse of Browning, but particularly so with Hopkins, whose work anticipates the formal obscurities and syntactical innovations of modernism.

Hopkins wrote his poetry mainly between 1875 and 1889, but it was not published until 1918. This fact lends his work a dimension of extra interest in the history of poetry because he presciently appears to anticipate certain later developments. As an early-20th-century poet, his interest in the Metaphysical Poets gives him an affinity with Eliot. Another interesting feature is that Hopkins, like his later imitator, DylanThomas, lets words tumble exuberantly into verse, each linking on to the next – sometimes conceptually, sometimes by sound. Here are some examples of Hopkins' wordplay from *Duns Scotus' Oxford*:

Towery city and branchy between towers
Cuckoo-echoing, bell-swarmed, lark-charmed,
    rook-racked, river rounded.

He produced some masterly alliteration and assonance:

What would the world be, once bereft
Of wet and wilderness? Let them be left,
O let them be left wildness and wet;
Long live the weeds and the wilderness yet.

Inversnaid

Some candle clear burns somewhere I came by.
I muse at how its being puts blissful back

> With yellowy moisture mild night's bear-all black,
> Or to-fro tender trambeams truckle at the eye.
>
> *The Candle Indoors*

> I caught this morning morning's minion, kingdom of
> daylight's dauphin, dapple-dawn-drawn Falcon.
>
> *The Windhover*

The Windhover is a sonnet. In the octave, the poet describes a falcon, expressing admiration for its consummate flight skills; in the sestet he perceives Christ's presence in the princely bird. The poem is written in sprung rhythm, five stresses per line, with *outrides*. (Outrides occur when one, two or three 'slack' syllables are added to a foot but do not count in the analysis of the rhythm.)

Hopkins himself said in a letter, 'No doubt my poetry errs on the side of oddness.' Certainly, obscurity has made his work inaccessible to many, but he enjoins us to read it with the ears 'as I always wish to be read, and my verse becomes all right'.

The care and particularity with which Hopkins, who was also a painter, discerned the things of the world of nature is almost unparalleled in English poetry. With his acuity of awareness, *this* cloud, bluebell, ash, is uniquely different from any other. With the master's universal eye he included what many would reject:

> All things counter, original, spare, strange;
> Whatever is fickle, freckled (who knows how?)
> With swift, slow; sweet, sour; adazzle, dim;
> He fathers-forth whose beauty is past change:
> Praise Him.
>
> *Pied Beauty*

Here, recorded in his journal notes of 1871, is a glimpsed insight of acute subtlety:

> Take a few primroses in a glass; the instress of brilliancy, sort of starriness (I have not the right word) that so simple a flower gives, is remarkable. It is, I think, due to the strong swell given by the deeper yellow middle.

This reluctant master poet resisted exercise of his talent on religious grounds. Fortunately for mankind, his spirit shone transparently through the inhibiting religiosity which others saw for what it was. Canon R.W. Dixon wrote to him in 1881: '… you have such gifts as have seldom been given by God to man.'

In 1889 Hopkins contracted typhoid fever and, after the onset of peritonitis, died on the 8 June. His last words were: 'I am so happy, so happy.'

Following discovery, Hopkins became almost at once the focus of a cult, leading to the usual mixture of overpraise and detracting criticism. F.R. Leavis (1932) pronounced him '… likely to prove for our time and the future, the only influential poet of the Victorian age …' There has been generally an academic acceptance of Hopkins, leading to his reincarnation as a 'modern' poet. The sheer size of his entry in the *New Cambridge Bibliography of English Literature* (1969) is one measure of his literary status.

So here is a master poet who by writing, some 30 years before being published, works as a *fin de siècle* poet, prepares us for the shock of Pound and Imagism. Hopkins, in this, is to some extent in unwitting synesis with W.B. Yeats who, beginning his career at the close of the Victorian era, became the 'last Romantic' and the first modernist of poetry.

9
A Fresh Lyricism

The Georgians

THE NAME *Georgian* came to be applied to a corpus of English poetry written, very broadly, between 1850 and 1950. The term was coined by Edward Marsh, a civil servant who, with Rupert Brooke, published a series of anthologies called *Georgian Poetry*, between 1912 and 1922. In retrospect, poets not included in the original collections are now seen also to have been writing in that genre, and in his *Georgian Poetry* (1962) James Reeves includes the following:

A.E. Housman	(1859-1936)
W.H. Davies	(1871-1940)
Walter de la Mare	(1873-1956)
John Masefield	(1878-1967)
Edward Thomas	(1878-1917)
Andrew Young	(1885-1971)
Siegfried Sassoon	(1886-1967)
Rupert Brooke	(1887-1915)
Victoria Sackville-West	(1892-1962)
Wilfred Owen	(1893-1918)
Robert Graves	(1895-1985)
Charles Sorley	(1895-1915)
Edmund Blunden	(1896-1974)

The description *Georgian* came, in due course, to be a term of disparagement, since the work of this time embodied the very elements that Symbolism and Imagism were setting out to countervail. The ordinary, unexceptional examples of Georgian verse were technically careless and loose, employing imprecise diction, facile rhythm, sentimentality and trivial or mundane themes, and showing a lack of direction. To this list, Edmund Blunden adds 'languor and studied homeliness of expression'. At their best the Georgian poets have a warmth, a strength, and a beauty; some poems have an ingenuous air of innocence which was never quite recaptured.

A.E. **Housman**, a Latin scholar and poet, produced a small output of lyrics showing the influence of traditional English ballads and classical verse, set against a background of the English countryside. His work is marked by economy, directness, and dramatic simplicity of style. One of Housman's models is Heine; another is *The Greek Anthology* – a collection of several thousands of poems, songs, epitaphs, and epigrams, the contents of which date from the 5th century BC to the 6th century AD.

Housman assigned his words their place with the precision he had learnt from Theocritus and Horace:

The weeping Pleiads wester,
And the moon is under seas;
From bourn to bourn of midnight
Far sighs the rainy breeze.

Echoes of Kipling's imperialistic sound occur frequently in Housman's poetry. Despite a certain triteness, he has also shown himself to be – at his best – an exquisite and moving poet. For years he was known only by his first book *A Shropshire Lad* (1896), from which this poem is taken:

II

Loveliest of trees, the cherry now
Is hung with bloom along the bough,
And stands about the woodland ride
Wearing white for Eastertide.

Now, of my threescore years and ten,
Twenty will not come again,
And take from seventy springs a score,
It only leaves me fifty more.

And since to look at things in bloom
Fifty springs are little room,
About the woodlands I will go
To see the cherry hung with snow.

In the next poem, the poet shows how 'the old wind in the old anger' has been blowing down the centuries; it disturbed the being of the earlier Roman invader, just as it does his now:

xxxi

On Wenlock Edge the wood's in trouble;
His forest fleece the Wrekin heaves;
The gale, it plies the saplings double,
And thick on Severn snow the leaves.

Housman often displays a spirit of irony and a certain sense of disillusionment and betrayal in love. With the descriptions of beauty come the recurring themes of patriotism and sin. It seems extraordinary in retrospect that, some 20 years before the event, Housman had anticipated the patriotism and anguished fatalism that was to be felt by so many young men sent to fight in the First World War. It was said that a copy of *A Shropshire Lad* could be found in every knapsack in the Flanders trenches. The descriptions of the English countryside alone would have been likely to recreate in the minds of the soldiers, their 'land of lost content':

XLII

Once in the wind of morning
  I ranged the thymy wold;
The world-wide air was azure
  And all the brooks ran gold.

★

Across the glittering pastures
  And empty upland still,
And solitude of shepherds
  High in the folded hill.

★

By blowing realms of woodland
  With sunstruck vanes afield,
And cloud-led shadows sailing
  About the windy weald.

The knapsack owner would have found the following lines more disquieting:

xxvii

'Is my team ploughing
  That I used to drive
And hear the harness jingle
  When I was man alive?'

Ay the horses trample,
  The harness jingles now;
No change though you lie under
  The land you used to plough.

★

'Is my girl happy,
  That I thought hard to leave,
And has she tired of weeping
  As she lies down at eve?'

Ay, she lies down lightly,
  She lies not down to weep:
Your girl is well contented.
  Be still, my lad, and sleep.

'Is my friend hearty,
  Now I am thin and pine,
And has he found to sleep in
  A better bed than mine?'

Yes, lad, I lie easy,
  I lie as lads would choose;
I cheer a dead man's sweetheart,
  Never ask me whose.

Many composers have been moved to set Housman's words. Vaughan Williams set the wry, epigrammic text *On Wenlock Edge* for piano quintet and later produced an orchestral version. George Butterworth's orchestral fantasy *A Shropshire Lad* is one of the finest miniatures in English music. Its nobility and tragedy pervade a composition of great harmonic richness; a work which acquires extra poignancy with the knowledge that Butterworth was killed on the Somme at the age of 31 – just three years after writing it. Here are some extracts from Housman's *Last Poems* (1922):

The troubles of our proud and angry dust
 Are from eternity, and shall not fail.
Bear them we can, and if we can we must.
 Shoulder the sky, my lad, and drink your ale.

Last Poems IX

The fairies break their dances
 And leave the printed lawn,
And up from India glances
 The silver sail of dawn.

The candles burn their sockets,
 The blinds let through the day,
The young man feels his pockets
 And wonders what's to pay.

ibid. XXI

See, in mid heaven the sun is mounted; hark,
 The belfries tingle to the noonday chime.
'Tis silent, and the subterranean dark
 Has crossed the nadir, and begins to climb.

ibid. XXXVI

Laurence **Housman** (1865-1959), the brother of A.E. Housman, was a novelist, dramatist, and illustrator. He was also a fine poet. Here are two examples from his collection of poems called *The Love Concealed* (1928); they give an indication of the spare lyric beauty of his verse:

Love and Life

I

Love's roof is sky; his bed the fruitful field;
And all the myriad mated lives concealed
By bud, and blade, and burrow, wood and hill –
His kindred, working the unchanging Will,
Of life the root. Minute to minute joins
Down the long ages; and from a million loins,
Each minute, changeful life at come and go
Faithful fulfilment makes; the sowers sow,
And womb's darkness becomes charged with light,
As from old worlds into new worlds goes sight.

The Drowned Lover

I

★

Stone-cold, starved, shivering land,
Where nothing wakes,
Gaunt, and gutted by storm: above in the gloom,
All one way come flying
Dim flakes of spume,
And menacing sea-mews, this way and that way crying,
Stretch their necks
And turn with a ghostly glide
Down to the gleaming hollows – wraiths to the tomb!
But here, in the door of my tent, a lamp stays lit;
And all night lonely I sit
By a shore that shakes,
Watching for wrecks,
With heart that aches and aches.

William Henry **Davies,** Welsh-born poet whose lyrics on nature and love are traditional in manner, wrote work known for its freshness, spontaneity, and simplicity. Until he was over 30 he was, by choice, a tramp and pedlar.

From his 6th volume of poems, *Foliage*, here is a piece daring in its simplicity, lyric in its word-music:

The lark that in heaven dim
  Can match a rainy hour
  With his own music's shower,
Can make me sing like him –
  Heigh ho! The rain!

Sing – when a Nightingale
  Pours forth her own sweet soul
  To hear dread thunder roll
Into a tearful tale –
  Heigh ho! The rain!

Sing – when a Sparrow's seen
  Trying to lie at rest
  By pressing his warm breast
To leaves so wet and green –
  Heigh ho! The rain!

The following utterly simple observations, too easily dismissed as trite, are emblematic of Davies' unsophisticated wisdom:

What is this life, if full of care,
We have no time to stand and stare? *Leisure*

The simple bird that thinks two notes a song.
April's Charms

Davies' originality is extraordinary and bold. Take, for instance, this image which explains how the month of May finds him, inexplicably, mute:

My lips, like gills in deep-sea homes,
Beat time, and still no music comes.

Finally, part of a poem called *This Night*, which expresses feeling and observation with a spareness that is the essence of simplicity:

This night, as I sit here alone,
And brood on what is dead and gone,
The owl that's in this Highgate Wood,
Has found his fellow in my mood
To every star as it doth rise –
Oh-o-o! Oh-o-o! he shivering cries.

Walter **de la Mare** is the author of sensitive, imaginative lyrics in traditional form, many expressing nostalgia for the past. He was an accomplished storyteller and essayist. The following verse begins what has been a favourite poem for generations of children:

The Listeners

'Is there anybody there?' said the Traveller,
Knocking on the moonlit door;
And his horse in the silence champed the grasses
Of the forest's ferny floor.
And a bird flew up out of the turret,
Above the Traveller's head:
And he smote upon the door a second time;
'Is there anybody there?' he said.

⋆

'Tell them I came, and no one answered,
That I kept my word,' he said.

⋆

Ay, they heard his foot upon the stirrup,
And the sound of iron on stone,
And how the silence surged softly backward,
When the plunging hoofs were gone.

This is a level of spirituality that children can appreciate!

Here is a dreamy poem about *Nod* the shepherd:

Softly along the road of evening,
  In a twilight dim with rose,
Wrinkled with age, and drenched with dew
  Old Nod, the shepherd, goes.

His drowsy flock streams on before him,
  Their fleeces charged with gold,
To where the sun's last beam leans low
  On Nod the shepherd's fold.

⋆

His are the quiet steps of dreamland,
  The waters of no-more pain;
His ram's bell rings 'neath an arch of stars,
  'Rest, rest and rest again.'

There is an echo of Browning's *Pied Piper* in these lines:

In Hans' old Mill his three black cats
Watch the bins for the thieving rats.
Whisker and claw, they crouch in the night,
Their five eyes smouldering green and bright ...

★

Jekkel and Jessup and one-eyed Jill. *Five Eyes*

Finally, a line that illustrates how a single word can 'make' a line of poetry:

Slowly, silently, now the moon
Walks the night in her silver shoon. *Silver*

John **Masefield**, poet, dramatist, novelist, and short-story writer is best-known for his poems and ballads dealing with the sea. He was made poet laureate in 1930. His work effectively combines the Romantic and the realistic. Here is an example from *Cargoes*:

Quinquireme of Nineveh from distant Ophir
Rowing home to haven in sunny Palestine,
With a cargo of ivory,
And apes and peacocks,
Sandalwood, cedarwood, and sweet white wine.

Dirty British coaster with a salt-caked smoke stack,
Butting through the Channel in the mad March days,
With a cargo of Tyne Coal,
Road-rail, pig-lead,
Firewood, iron-ware, and cheap tin trays.

At the age of 14 Masefield ran away from home and spent many years wandering about the world. Here is a line from *Beauty*:

Coming in solemn beauty like slow old tunes of Spain.

Masefield the wanderer says in a typical verse:

One road leads to London,
  One road leads to Wales,
My road leads me seawards
  To the white dipping sails.

Finally, some lines from his incomparable *Sea Fever*:

I must down to the seas again, to the
  lonely sea and the sky,
And all I ask is a tall ship and a star
  to steer her by,

And the wheel's kick and the wind's song
and the white sails shaking,
And a grey mist on the sea's face and
a grey dawn breaking.

★

I must down to the seas again, to the
vagrant gypsy life,
To the gull's way and the whale's way
Where the wind's like a whetted knife;
And all I ask is a merry yarn from a laughing
fellow-rover,
And quiet sleep and a sweet dream when
the long trick's over.

Edward **Thomas** was yet another English poet to die in 1917 during the First World War. He met Robert Frost in England and was much influenced by him. Walter de la Mare said of him, in the *Times Literary Supplement*, 18 October 1917: 'The word "England" meant for him its loveliness and oldness, its centuries of quiet labour, its villages and solitudes, its truest, simplest people.'

Thomas, apparently in an allusion to roads, by-lanes, field-paths, bridle-paths and rides, wrote:

They are lonely
While we sleep, lonelier
For lack of a traveller
Who is now a dream only ...

When Thomas moves from prose to verse the form is insubstantial, the metre merely hinted at:

The past is the only dead thing that smells sweet,
The only sweet thing that is not also fleet.
I'm bound away for ever,
Away somewhere, away for ever.

His evocative poem *Adlestrop* is quoted elsewhere in this volume (*see* Chapter 16 – The Nature of Poetry – Eternity).

As though prophetically anticipating solitude and oblivion, Thomas, one of so many sensitive men to go into the unknown in the Great War, wrote:

There is not any book
Nor face of dearest look
That I would not turn from now
To go into the unknown
I must enter and leave alone
I know not how.

The tall forest towers
Its cloudy foliage lowers

Ahead, shelf above shelf;
Its silence I hear and obey
That I may lose my way
And myself. *Lights Out*

Andrew **Young**, who was born in Elgin, Scotland, is a poet of the countryside. He had a specialist knowledge of wild flowers which had taken him to most parts of Britain. Young's nature poetry is acutely observed and, in addition, carries echoes of the English Metaphysical Poets of the 17th century. This gives his work a powerful realism combined with observation drawn from the realm beyond the physical. Here is his poet's view of a beech tree:

One elbow on the sloping earth it leans
  That steeply falls beneath
As though resting a century it means
  To take a moment's breath.

Examples of Young's verse are quoted in other sections of this volume. Here, in *A Prospect of Death*, he instructs us to anticipate the absence of life in a loved one:

If it should come to this
You cannot wake me with a kiss,
Think I but sleep too late
Or once again keep cold and angry state.
So now you have been told:
I or my breakfast may grow cold.

Encountering a rat, the poet, with some surprise, and bearing in mind past experience, writes:

Strange that you let me come so near
  And send no questing senses out
From eye's dull jelly, shell-pink ear,
  Fierce-whiskered snout.

He then realizes that the animal is dead:

... And as I leave you stiff and still
A death-like quietness has spread
  Across the hill.

In *A Shot Magpie* the poet says much in just seven lines:

Though on your long-tailed flight
You wore half-mourning of staid black and white,
So little did the thought of death
Enter your thievish head,
You never knew what choked your breath
When in a day turned night
You fell with feathers heavier than lead.

Speaking perhaps as the unsentimental priest-poet, Young can write:

> God, you've got so much to do,
> To think of, watch and listen to,
> That I will let all else go by
> And lending ear and eye
> Help you to watch.

Edmund **Blunden**, the English poet and critic, was awarded the Military Cross in World War I and made a Fellow of the Royal Society of Literature in 1930. He was principally a nature writer and, as Richard-Church said of him, 'I think no poet writing today has a closer association with the secret, shy self of England than has Edmund Blunden.'

In his poem *Forefathers*, those who preceded us are acknowledged for their worth and authenticity:

> These were men of pith and thew,
> Whom the city never called;
> Scarce could read or hold a quill
> Built the barn, the forge, the mill.

Here next is the poet, keenly observant but with compassionate understanding; it is from his *Almswomen*:

> All things they have in common being so poor,
> And their one fear, Death's shadow at the door.
> Each sundown makes them mournful, each sunrise
> Brings back the brightness in their failing eyes.

The sincerity and dignity of Blunden's lyrical poetry about the English countryside redeemed the diminished reputation of 'nature poetry'.

The poet looks forward and back, simultaneously combining the wonder of childhood with the serenity of maturity. Knowledge has not destroyed innocence; rather, simplicity has informed understanding. A man who survived the carnage of the 1914–18 War is at peace within himself:

> Deed and event of prouder stature
> Dare not always overshade
> The first fresh buddings of our nature;
> Their hidden colour does not fade.
>
> We well may quit our laboured action
> At some sweet call to early loves,
> And find the jewel of self-contraction
> Like saints in rocks and springs and groves.
>
> ★
>
> Return; how stands that man enchanted
> Who, after seas and mountains crossed,
> Finds his old threshold, so long scanted,
> With not a rose or robin lost!

The wise, from passion now retreating
To the hamlets of the mind,
In every glance have claimed the greeting
Of spirits infinitely kind.

Romanticism had represented a clear and deliberate break with the past, a severance generated by the artistic and literary world from within itself. Culturally, World War I sounded the death knell for the world of settled values. The battle carnage and the senseless destruction, in no small part the result of callous and incompetent military leadership, made a mockery of patriotic slogans, appeals to class, and the metaphysical unity of nations. A whole school of poets, many of whom did not survive the hostilities, gave vent to their hatred and disgust with this first modern war.

Wilfred **Owen**, with the poignancy and vividness of very effective poetry, makes clear the suffering of the men engaged in this pointless struggle. Sadly, the poet who was awarded the Military Cross in France, was killed while leading his men in an attack just one week before the Armistice:

Dulce et Decorum Est

Bent double, like old beggars under sacks,
Knock-kneed, coughing like hags, we cursed through sludge,
Till on the haunting flares we turned our backs
And towards our distant rest began to trudge.
Men marched asleep. Many had lost their boots
But limped on, blood-shod. All went lame; all blind;
Drunk with fatigue; deaf even to the hoots
Of tired, outstripped Five-Nines that dropped behind.

Gas! GAS! Quick, boys! – An ecstasy of fumbling,
Fitting the clumsy helmets just in time;
But someone still was yelling out and stumbling
And flound'ring like a man in fire or lime. –
Dim, through the misty panes and thick green light,
As under a green sea, I saw him drowning.
In all my dreams, before my helpless sight,
He plunges at me, guttering, choking, drowning.

If in some smothering dreams, you too could pace
Behind the wagon that we flung him in,
And watch the white eyes writhing in his face,
His hanging face, like a devil's sick of sin;
If you could hear, at every jolt, the blood
Come gargling from the froth-corrupted lungs,
Obscene as cancer, bitter as the cud
Of vile, incurable sores on innocent tongues, –
My friend, you would not tell with such high zest
To children ardent for some desperate glory,
The old Lie: *Dulce et decorum est*
Pro patria mori.

As Owen reminds us in his much-quoted gnomic statement: 'Above all I am not concerned with Poetry. My subject is War, and the pity of War. The Poetry is in the pity.'

Siegfried **Sassoon**, who was a friend of Wilfred Owen and encouraged him in his writing, won the Military Cross and Distinguished Service Cross for bravery in the First World War. He was twice wounded and hated war bitterly. His own poetry caught the pitiless suffering, horror, and waste of the war.

Sassoon wrote a poem called *Counter-Attack*, which he drafted in July 1916. It is included here to illustrate the power of poetry to convey the emotion and reality, the horrific circumstances of that particular war. The poet provides words and images – we supply from our experience of living, the tragedy and the poignancy of life and death presented in the poem:

We'd gained our first objective hours before
While dawn broke like a face with blinking eyes,
Pallid, unshaved and thirsty, blind with smoke.
Things seemed all right at first. We held their line,
With bombers posted, Lewis guns well placed,
And clink of shovels deepening the shallow trench.
 The place was rotten with dead; green clumsy legs
 High-booted, sprawled and grovelled along the saps
 And trunks, face downward, in the sucking mud,
 Wallowed like trodden sand-bags loosely filled;
  And naked sodden buttocks, mats of hair,
Bulged, clotted heads slept in the plastering slime.
And then the rain began, – the jolly old rain!

⋆

An officer came blundering down the trench:
'Stand-to and man the fire-step!' On he went …
Gasping and bawling, 'Fire-step … counter-attack!'

⋆

'O Christ, they're coming at us!' Bullets spat,
And he remembered his rifle … rapid fire …
And started blazing wildly … then a bang
Crumpled and spun him sideways, knocked him out
To grunt and wriggle: none heeded him; he choked
And fought the flapping veils of smothering gloom,
Lost in a blurred confusion of yells and groans …
Down, and down, and down, he sank and drowned,
Bleeding to death. The counter-attack had failed.

Sassoon, unlike Owen and Brooke, survived the War. Here is his poem of joy and release at the War's conclusion, *Everyone Sang*:

Everyone suddenly burst out singing;
And I was filled with such delight
As prisoned birds must find in freedom,

Winging wildly across the white
Orchards and dark-green fields; on-on-and out of sight.
Everyone's voice was suddenly lifted;
And beauty came like the setting sun:
My heart was shaken with tears; and horror
Drifted away ... O, but Everyone
was a bird; and the song was wordless; the
    singing will never be done.

In contrast to this sound of hope and optimism, it is curious how recurringly appropriate some lines of Rudyard Kipling (1865-1936) still seem:

A Dead Statesman

I could not dig; I dared not rob;
Therefore I lied to please the mob.
Now all my lies are proved untrue
And I must face the men I slew.
What tale shall serve me here among
The angry and defrauded young?

The cataclysm of the First World War changed everything. As A.C. Ward (1928) has put it, 'The old certainties were certainties no longer. Everything was held to be open to question; everything – from the nature of the Deity to the construction of verse-forms.'

Robert **Bridges** (1844-1930), the English poet and classical scholar appointed poet laureate in 1913, is best known for his work on metrics and his long philosophical work *The Testament of Beauty*. He was the chief correspondent and literary executor of the poet Gerard Manley Hopkins, who developed his poetic theories through the medium of their letters.

Here is the opening verse of *Nightingales*, which reflects his feeling for Keats:

Beautiful must be the mountains whence ye come,
And bright in the fruitful valleys the streams wherefrom
    Ye learn your song:
Where are those starry woods? O might I wander there,
  Among the flowers which in that heavenly air
    Bloom the year long!

A richly romantic spirit imbues the opening lines of his poem *A Passer-By*:

Whither, O splendid ship, thy white sails crowding,
  Leaning across the bosom of the urgent West,
That fearest not sea rising nor sky clouding,
  Whither away, fair rover, and what thy quest?

Walter de la Mare thought Bridges (like Edmund Spenser) very much a poet's poet. One can see what he means. As well as being a consummate artist, Bridges' work was a reflection of his quality of mind. As a scholar, Bridges ranged over a wide field of interests but his work was unerringly and essentially directed to poetry:

> Think not that thou canst all things know, nor deem
> Such knowledge happiness ...
> but what 'tis joy to learn
> Or use to know, that may'st thou ask of right ...

On accepting this:

> O soul be patient: thou shalt find
> A little matter mend all this;
> Some strain of music to thy mind,
> Some praise for skill not spent amiss. *Dejection*

With brevity and an almost austere lyricism Bridges writes a hymn-like avowal:

> I love all beauteous things,
> I seek and adore them;
> God hath no better praise,
> And man in his hasty* days
> Is honoured for them.
>
> I too will something make
> And joy in the making;
> Although tomorrow it seem
> Like empty words of a dream
> Remembered on waking. *I Love All Beauteous Things*

Writers in the Romantic tradition had become increasingly detached from the experience of life and were persisting with a depleted poetic idiom. As T.S. Pearce (1967) put it, 'The vein of poetry first cut into by Wordsworth had been worked out.' An excursion into sensationalism had been made by the Pre-Raphaelites, but certain other poets at the beginning of the 20th century were undergoing a re-evaluation as good minor poets. After the earlier denigration of the Georgian poets, some of them, such as John Masefield, W.H. Davies, Edward Thomas, and Walter de la Mare, were being positively reappraised.

William Butler **Yeats** (1865-1939), an Irish poet and dramatist, was leader of the Irish Renaissance. Many themes and influences bore upon the work of this remarkable lyric poet. In his early verse there are echoes of Shelley and Spenser. His later work reflects his fascination with Irish folk-tales and legends; with themes from Blake and other mystics. By the turn of the century the poetry expressed the powerful effects of the Symbolist poets. From here it developed to the more direct style of his later maturity. Ireland's troubled history and the major upheavals of the new century profoundly influenced and shaped the creative work of this outstanding man of letters. The Irish scene at this time is made, in his poetry,

* *Hasty* means 'passing quickly'.

to symbolize the dilemma of the human race. Yeats' mastery as a poet and his command over the lyric use of language has given him a unique place in Western poetry. Many consider him to be a master poet. He was influenced by the Pre-Raphaelites, Blake, Shelley, Maeterlinck, French Symbolism and Hindu philosophy. He is celebrated for poems and plays, mystic and Celtic legendary themes, and for the highly developed symbolism of his later poetry. He was the son of John Butler Yeats, a well-known Irish landscape painter, and he himself studied painting for three years. Yeats was honoured widely as one of the most important poets of the 20th century. He was elected a Senator of the Irish Free State in 1922 and a year later was awarded the Nobel Prize for Literature.

He spent his boyhood between school in London and his mother's native county of Sligo, a wild and beautiful region in north-Western Ireland which is a background to much of his poetry.

His early poems, for example *The Wind among the Reeds* (1899), sprang from late-19th-century aestheticism and were languorous and mannered. They were distinguishable from other verse of the period by their use of Celtic mythology, and carried Yeats' sense of identity with the culture of his native land which was a permanent feature of his writing – and was always a strength. He was constantly remaking traditional lyric forms. Two major processes are discernible in his work:

1 The development of an individual mythology based on elements of spiritualism, classical lore, astrology, and Eastern philosophy. These provided basic symbols leading to the rich, oblique, almost rhetorical sounding verse of, for instance, *Byzantium*.
2 A movement towards a bare, direct utterance, sinewy yet musical, and having the simplicity of folk poetry. This direction produced some of his most moving poetry, helped by his sympathies for the Irish Nationalist cause.

His poetic development begins with Romantic themes borne on hypnotic rhythms; for example *The Lake of Innisfree*, which is dated 1893:

I will arise and go now, and go to Innisfree,
And a small cabin build there, of clay and wattles made:
Nine bean-rows will I have there, a hive for the honey-bee,
And live alone in the bee-loud glade.

And I shall have some peace there, for peace comes dropping slow,
Dropping from the veils of the morning to where the cricket sings;
There midnight's all a-glimmer, and noon a purple glow,
And evening full of the linnet's wings.

I will arise and go now, for always night and day
I hear lake water lapping with low sounds by the shore;
While I stand on the roadway, or on the pavements gray
I hear it in the deep heart's core.

Here are two verses of 'A Song' from *The Wild Swans at Coole* (1919), showing Yeats' superb use of a refrain:

I thought no more was needed
Youth to prolong
Than dumb-bell and foil
To keep the body young.
O who could have foretold
That the heart grows old?

Though I have many words,
What woman's satisfied,
I am no longer faint
Because at her side?
O who could have foretold
That the heart grows old?

Here is another example, 'The Long-Legged Fly', but this is much later, from *Last Poems* (1939):

That civilisation may not sink
Its great battle lost,
Quiet the dog, tether the pony
To a distant post;
Our master Caesar is in the tent
Where the maps are spread,
His eyes fixed upon nothing,
A hand under his head.
Like a long-legged fly upon the stream
His mind moves upon silence.

⋆

The girls at puberty may find
The first Adam in their thoughts,
Shut the door of the Pope's chapel,
Keep those children out.
There on the scaffolding reclines
Michel Angelo
With no more sound than the mice make
His hand moves to and fro.
Like a long-legged fly upon the stream
His mind moves upon silence.

During the years 1889-1909 Yeats was a leading member of the Aesthetic Movement in London, which grew out of Pre-Raphaelitism and owed much to the influence of Walter Pater. In his poem, *The Wanderings of Oisin*, written during this time, there is this tender statement:

When you are old and grey and full of sleep,
And nodding by the fire, take down this book,
And slowly read, and dream of the soft look

> Your eyes had once, and of their shadows deep;
> How many loved your moments of glad grace,
> And loved your beauty with love false or true.

At this time he was contributing to the public voice of the Aesthetic Movement, the *Yellow Book*, in which he offered prose and verse-plays. One of these, *The Countess Cathleen*, contains these typical Yeatsian black images and despair:

> The years like great black oxen tread the world,
> And God the herdsman goads them on behind,
> And I am broken by their passing feet.

As he said on another occasion, 'We begin to live when we have conceived life as tragedy.' With poignancy in brevity he wrote in *The Pity of Love*:

> A pity beyond all telling
> Is hid in the heart of love.

In 1899 Yeats, with the help of Lady Gregory and others, built up the Irish National Theatre, which found a home in the Abbey Theatre, Dublin. He was its manager until 1909. In many ways it was a disillusioning period but a formative one for him as a poet. Even so, he produced only one volume of verse during these ten years: *In the Seven Woods* (1903). During the years 1910 to 1918 he met Ezra Pound and T.S. Eliot. At this time his mood is harsher and he has lost some of his faith. However, he continued to search for symbols which could yield meaning to history and life.

> I balanced all, brought all to mind,
> The years to come seemed waste of breath,
> A waste of breath the years behind
> In balance with this life, this death.
>
> *An Irish Airman Foresees His Death*

> For the elemental creatures go
> About my table to and fro
>
> *To Ireland in the Coming Times*

It was during the years 1919 to 1939 that Yeats grew in stature and was acknowledged one of the major poets of the 20th century. In his work at this time he evolves a system of symbolic mythology, flawed as a system but serving as a vehicle in which he could express poetically human experience deeply and extensively. During this period his writing includes:

The Wild Swans at Coole	(1919)
Michael Robartes and the Dancer	(1921)
The Tower	(1928)
The Winding Stair	(1933)

These works are marked by strong rhythms, by stanza and rhyme patterns which compel thought and hold attention. His style employs severe diction, with few adjectives and a range of symbols, each constituting the nucleus of a cluster of meanings.

Yeats read Plato, Berkeley, Kant, Hegel, and Croce, but what he derived from them was often quite fantastic. Nevertheless, he imbibed the philosophy and it influenced his poems. For Yeats, philosophy descended in two great streams of thought: *will* and *knowledge*. Of these 'two paths to reality' (as he terms them) knowledge proved the most attractive. Poetry yields a special kind of knowledge. Through poetry man comes to know himself in relation to reality and thus attains wisdom.

When Yeats' health was in decline in 1936 he went to Palma, Majorca, for rest with Shankar Grajanan Purohit – later known to his disciples as Shree Purohit Swami. Together they translated some *Upanishads* (ancient Indian teachings) and the *Yoga-Sutra* (*Aphorisms of Yoga*) by the celebrated author, Patanjali. Here is an example; it is the opening of the *Eesha Upanishad*:

> That is perfect. This is perfect. Perfect comes from perfect.
> Take perfect from perfect, the remainder is perfect.
> May peace and peace and peace be everywhere.
>
> ⋆
>
> Whatever lives is full of the Lord. Claim nothing; enjoy, do not covet His property.
>
> Then hope for a hundred years of life doing your duty. No other way can prevent deeds from clinging, proud as you are of your human life.

This *Upanishad*, belonging to the pre-Christian era, contains a beautiful description of the Absolute principle of the created world, referred to as 'the Self':

> The Self is one. Unmoving, it moves faster than the mind. The senses lag, but Self runs ahead. Unmoving, it outruns pursuit. Out of Self comes the breath that is the life of all things.
>
> Unmoving, it moves, is far away, yet near; within all, outside all.

Yeats continued to the end of his life writing plays and improving his dramatic idiom, partly under the influence of the Japanese *Noh* drama. Many consider his best play (nearly his last) to be *Purgatory* (1939).

In the final verse of *The Circus Animals' Desertion* (a poem about being unable to find the theme for a poem) Yeats uses a starkness of image that foreshadows the shock which such bluntness would later arouse in Eliot's *The Waste Land*:

Those masterful images because complete
Grew in pure mind, but out of what began?
A mound of refuse or the sweepings of a street,
Old kettles, old bottles, and a broken can,
Old iron, old bones, old rags, that raving slut
Who keeps the till. Now that my ladder's gone,
I must lie down where all the ladders start,
In the foul rag-and-bone shop of the heart.

The Circus Animals' Desertion

Yeats considered poetry generally to be lofty and aristocratic but also in touch with the people; his work was, like Homer's, both aristocratic and popularly rooted. It conspicuously is not middle-class intellectual art – as, for example, is Eliot's *The Waste Land*. Yeats believed that image was of the eternal and the ideal, but that its origin was in the common and transitory. He was a superb craftsman, working hard at the art that conceals art:

A line will take us hours may be;
Yet if it does not seem a moment's thought,
Our stitching and unstitching has been naught.

Adam's Curse

Yeats described what he strove for: 'I desire a mysterious art, always reminding and half-reminding those who understand it of dearly loved things, doing its work by suggestion, not by direct statement, a complexity of rhythm, colour, gesture, not space-pervading like the intellect but a memory and a prophecy …'

With the demise of Yeats the era of Romanticism was at an end. He had been a colourful and innovative figure on its stage but, prophetically, had much earlier anticipated the changing world that was coming.

10
New Approaches

Modern Poetry

THE DISRUPTION produced by World War I between the years 1914–18 might not, of itself, have brought an end to Romanticism, which had prevailed (in literature and the general conduct of life) since the closing years of the 18th century. But the post-war economic depression, coupled with a deepening spiritual dejection, brought a fundamental shift which unseated Romanticism. The seeds of change had been sown earlier.

At the end of the 1914–18 War, W.B. Yeats, profoundly moved by unrest in his own country (particularly the Easter Rebellion of 1916) and the rising militarism on the Continent, wrote a beautiful and prophetic poem, *The Second Coming*. The title is fatefully ironic, since it refers not to the promised return of the Saviour of the World but to an ominously inferred happening only hinted at in this prescient poem (the extract given seems strikingly relevant to the present era, following the fall of Communism):

> Things fall apart; the centre cannot hold;
> Mere anarchy is loosed upon the world,
> The blood-dimmed tide is loosed, and everywhere
> The ceremony of innocence is drowned;
> The best lack all conviction, while the worst
> Are full of passionate intensity.
>
> *The Second Coming*

The year 1922 was significant for literary modernism, for at that time T.S. Eliot published his poem *The Waste Land* and James Joyce his novel *Ulysses*. In their respective works Eliot and Joyce manifest some of the primary characteristics of what is now considered to be the modernist tendency in literature. There is fragmentation of line and image, abandonment of traditional forms and an overwhelming sense of alienation and 'homelessness' (both authors were self-imposed exiles). In these circumstances there was an ambivalence towards the prevailing culture and an intense desire to find an anchoring connection in the past – a past drifting out of reach. There is in these two writers a lessening distinction between the reality of the world 'out there' and subjective experience. In their writing there is an extension and widening of language, to derive new meanings and modes of expression for a world now seen as exhausted.

For Joyce there was the conviction that only art could yield a new view of the world, one which would furnish meaning. Eliot, in resonance with this, felt that if civilization were to survive there must be a recovery of the sense of cultural continuity with the artistic and religious tradition of the past.

Thomas Stearns **Eliot** (1888-1965) was born in St Louis, Missouri, the seventh and youngest child of a New England family. He was educated at Harvard, The Sorbonne and Merton College, Oxford. He settled in London in 1915 and married an Englishwoman. After schoolmastering for a year, in 1917 he entered the Foreign and Colonial Department of Lloyds Bank, where he stayed until 1925. Two years later he became a naturalized British citizen and steadily developed the persona of an English gentleman with High Anglican and royalist leanings.

As the years advanced, his stature grew until, in 1948, his position in literature was acknowledged with both the Order of Merit and the Nobel Prize for Literature. In 1955 he received the Hanseatic Goethe Prize and is now widely acknowledged to be one of the century's major international literary figures.

Volumes of poetry include:

1917	*Prufrock, and Other Observations*
1920	*Poems*
1922	*The Waste Land*
1925	*The Hollow Men*
1909-25	*Poems*
1930	*Ash Wednesday*
1932	*Sweeney Agonistes: Fragments of an Aristophanic Melodrama*
1942	*Four Quartets*

Poetic dramas and plays:

1934	*The Rock*
1935	*Murder in the Cathedral*
1939	*The Family Reunion*
1950	*The Cocktail Party*
1954	*The Confidential Clerk*
1959	*The Elder Statesman*

Prose:

1920	*The Sacred Wood: Essays on Poetry and Criticism.*

Other works of literary criticism include:

Dante
The Use of Poetry and the Use of Criticism

	Notes toward a Definition of Culture
1957	*On Poets and Poetry*

Eliot became the most influential poet and spokesman of his generation, especially for the younger writers disillusioned by World War I and frustrated in their search for culture, particularly in the United States of America. His reputation as this point of focus was based on the way he expressed the disillusionment, despair, and repugnance of that time towards the industrial and materialistic civilization of the 20th century in his poems *The Love Song of J. Alfred Prufrock*, *The Waste Land* and *The Hollow Men*.

The poetry of Eliot reveals the influence of the Elizabethans, the Metaphysical Poets and the French Symbolists, and is distinguished by its irony, trenchancy of phrasing, dramatic use of symbols and wide learning. It often includes the abstraction of whole passages from an earlier source for incorporation into a current poem.

Eliot had the strong conviction that, if culture were to endure, there had to be a sense of continuity with former cultural and spiritual tradition. This may explain why his poems contain so many allusions to works of art, classical literature, and elements of Christian ritual. Sometimes these are merely echoes and resonances; at other times there is direct resemblance, for example:

> The beginning and the end are common … Heraclitus
>
> In my end is my beginning … Eliot, *East Coker*

In his essay on *The Metaphysical Poets* (1921) Eliot coins the phrase 'dissociation of sensibility', which is connected with the idea of 'felt thought'. As Eliot puts it, 'A thought to Donne was an experience; it modified his sensibility.' But it must be said that, whereas Donne's imagination was invariably passionate and consuming, Eliot's was often anaemic and chill – particularly in the early poetry. As Helen Gardner, in *The Art of T.S. Eliot*, so objectively expressed it: 'Certain limitations of temperament in the earlier poetry revealed themselves in certain limitations of imagery and style…' However, poets (other than those of the Chivalric Age), do not ask us to be passive listeners to their woes, perplexities, and unrequited loves, but rather to hear their poetry and, by this means, move beyond the ordinary to a higher level of reality.

Bertrand Russell, Eliot's philosophy tutor and an admirer of his intellect, described him as 'altogether impeccable in his taste but has no vigour of life – or enthusiasm'. He married in June 1915 for what Russell described as 'stimulation', but the anguish evident in the early poetry was due in part to the fact that this first marriage caused Eliot considerable discomfiture. His bride, Vivienne Haigh-Wood, had a vitality and lack of inhibition which must have been challenging for the 26-year-old don who had lived an intensely intellectual life and had been brought up in a puritanical household. In a line of his poetry at this time, Eliot wrote, 'It is terrible to be alone with another person'.

In his tribute to John Davidson, Eliot said it was necessary for a poet to 'free himself completely from the poetic diction of English verse of his time …' Eliot himself achieved this and demonstrates it superbly in *The Love Song of J. Alfred Prufrock*. This, like its successors, exemplifies Eliot's technical excellence – particularly the superb control of tone, but also the matter-of-fact juxtaposition of colloquial speech and literary allusion. B.C. Southam, in *A Student's Guide to the Selected Poems of T.S. Eliot* (1968), believes that the opening lines of *Prufrock* 'take their point from the Dante epigraph' and that *Prufrock* 'is conducting us through the realm of a 20th-century *Inferno* and *Purgatory*':

> Let us go then, you and I,
> When the evening is spread out against the sky
> Like a patient etherised upon a table;
> Let us go, through certain half-deserted streets,
> The muttering retreats
> Of restless nights in one-night cheap hotels
> And sawdust restaurants with oyster-shells:
> Streets that follow like a tedious argument
> Of insidious intent
> To lead you to an overwhelming question …
> Oh, do not ask, 'What is it?'
> Let us go and make our visit.
>
> In the room the women come and go
> Talking of Michelangelo.

Eliot's friend Ezra Pound, long settled in London and a leading literary figure, championed his cause and became his mentor. The 1914-18 War kept Eliot in England, where, committed to literature, he was intensively searching for some form of spiritual truth. His conviction that man's nature was corrupt dogged him, and poverty and overwork, first as a schoolmaster, then as a bank official, affected him to the point where he sought professional help in Switzerland. He returned from Lausanne via Paris, where he presented Ezra Pound with the first drafts of what was to become *The Waste Land*. Eliot recalled in 1946 that the 'sprawling, chaotic poem' left Pound's hands 'reduced to about half its size'. It was to Pound that Eliot dedicated the completed poem.

The Waste Land

When *The Waste Land* first appeared, its critics saw in it nothing but chaos and its author as no more than the producer of chaos. Here was another example of the urge to attack the messenger rather than intelligently to interpret his tidings. If Eliot was perceived as the poet of disorder, it was not least because he wrote from a clear view of the order from which the present situation had departed. Conditioning by tradition left his critics unable to share Eliot's vision. Moreover, because Eliot juxtaposes apparently disconnected passages, the reader has to supply whatever logical or emotional connections are available to him.

Eliot himself deprecatingly referred to *The Waste Land* as 'just a piece of rhythmical grumbling', but it is much more than this. The poem is not merely a description of life in the early 1920s and how it came to be like that. Rather, it is a meditation on spiritual experience centred on a continuity of the tradition linking the past with the modern world. It was composed in scraps between 1912 and 1921, by which time a first draft was complete. It was ruthlessly cut by Pound, and it is widely thought that this version is preferable to the original, restored by Eliot's widow after his death and published in 1971. The first readers of *The Waste Land* were unsettled by the absence of any narrative links within the poem. This effect was accentuated by Pound's many excisions from the original version. On the whole, critics have regarded these deletions of Pound's to be judicious; the omitted passages certainly are poetically inferior. But the effect was to make the poem, when it finally appeared in 1922, perhaps too much like an Imagist poem. Despite his debt to Pound, Eliot was not really an Imagist, neither does he appear in any Imagist anthologies of that period.

C.H. Sisson (1914-2003), writing of his early enthusiasm for Eliot, makes clear what it was like 'to catch a first glimpse of names which over the years would become significant ... and above all to understand how far-reaching, both in subject and country of origin, were the intellectual interests from which the severe mind of the master drew sustenance. Greek, Latin, French, German, Italian and Sanskrit: it seemed that one had to have the gift of tongues and to have read everything.' Sisson perhaps speaks for many of the young, even in our own day, coming freshly to Eliot.

The principal sources and allusions in *The Waste Land* are ably explored by Stephen Coote (1985). They include Frazer's *The Golden Bough*, J.L. Weston's *From Ritual to Romance*, Tarot Cards, the *Bible*, the *Upanishads*, Buddhism, Shakespeare, Greek poet-playwrights, Latin writers, St Augustine, Baudelaire, Dante, Spenser, Herman Hesse and Richard Wagner's *Tristan and Isolde*.

The Waste Land is a long poem in five sections, to which are added the Author's Notes:

I The Burial of the Dead
II A Game of Chess
III The Fire Sermon
IV Death by Water
V What the Thunder Said

It is a highly personal poem, capable of being interpreted on different levels. For many, this work encapsulated the mood of disillusionment which characterized those years immediately following World War I.

Others see it as a record of a sensitive and sexually defeated man adrift in a civilization he loathes. The poem resonates perfectly with its era, yet the individuality and strength of Eliot's writing lift the poetry clear of any limiting period in time. As poetry, the work is characterized by its use of ellipsis, an elegantly rendered satirical negativity, and a richness of literary allusion.

The following example of ellipsis is from Part III where the prevailing theme is apathy; Eliot excises words, leaving the reader to augment the minimalist spareness:

The river sweats
Oil and tar
The barges drift
With the turning tide
Red sails
Wide
To leeward, swing on the heavy spar.
The barges wash
Drifting logs
Down Greenwich reach
Past the Isle of Dogs.

Once having come to terms with the technique, it is by no means the most difficult of Eliot's poems. It has a fairly obvious development and the images, with a few exceptions, are not difficult to interpret. However, for I.A. Richards its unity lies in 'emotional effects' rather than 'an intellectual scheme that analysis must work out'.

In Part I, 'The Burial of the Dead', Eliot makes an impact by contrasting his opening statement with the stirring excitement of Chaucer's first lines in the Prologue to *The Canterbury Tales* (*see* Chaucer, page 71).

April is the cruellest month, breeding
Lilacs out of the dead land, mixing
Memory and desire, stirring
Dull roots with spring rain.

In Part II, 'A Game of Chess', there are lines which carry the authentic sound of biographical experience. Eliot's wife's health had deteriorated, and in later years she became mentally ill:

'My nerves are bad tonight. Yes, bad. Stay with me.
Speak to me. Why do you never speak? Speak.
What are you thinking of? What thinking? What?
I never know what you are thinking. Think.'

I think we are in rat's alley
Where the dead men lost their bones.
'What is that noise?'
The wind under the door.
'What is that noise now? What is the wind doing?'
Nothing again nothing.

Such passages as these indicate the potential verse-dramatist in Eliot, and we remark the virtuosity in the counterpointing of the hesitating rhythm, the agitated tones of the speaking voice and the intricate syntax.

In Part III, 'The Fire Sermon', Eliot describes with deadly dismissiveness one of the lower orders of society:

> He, the young man carbuncular, arrives,
> A small house agent's clerk, with one bold stare,
> One of the low on whom assurance sits
> As a silk hat on a Bradford millionaire.

Eliot then describes, with consummate mastery, one of the most empty and perfunctory sexual encounters in English poetry:

> The time is now propitious, as he guesses,
> The meal is ended, she is bored and tired,
> Endeavours to engage her in caresses
> Which still are unreproved, if undesired.
> Flushed and decided, he assaults at once;
> Exploring hands encounter no defence;
> His vanity requires no response,
> And makes a welcome of indifference.
> (And I Tiresias have foresuffered all
> Enacted on this same divan or bed;
> I who have sat by Thebes below the wall
> And walked among the lowest of the dead.)
> Bestows one final patronising kiss,
> And gropes his way, finding the stairs unlit …
>   She turns and looks a moment in the glass,
> Hardly aware of her departed lover;
> Her brain allows one half-formed thought to pass:
> 'Well now that's done: and I'm glad it's over.'
> When lovely woman stoops to folly and
> Paces about her room again, alone,
> She smoothes her hair with automatic hand,
> And puts a record on the gramophone.

In Part IV, 'Death by Water', which has only ten lines of poetry, Eliot achieves scathing succinctness:

> Phlebas the Phoenician, a fortnight dead,
> Forgot the cry of gulls, and the deep sea swell
> And the profit and loss.

In Part V, 'What the Thunder Said', the poet conveys the total aridity of the absence of water, water that gives life to all beings and symbolizes the uniting bond of love:

> Here is no water but only rock
> Rock and no water and the sandy road
> The road winding above among the mountains

Which are mountains of rock without water
If there were water we should stop and drink
Amongst the rock one cannot stop or think
Sweat is dry and feet are in the sand
If there were only water amongst the rock
Dead mountain mouth of carious teeth that cannot spit
Here one can neither stand nor lie nor sit
There is not even silence in the mountains
But dry sterile thunder without rain

Eliot's writing with its absence of punctuation rolls remorselessly, endlessly, inexorably, on and on. Circling thoughts turn in the mind, a strange sense of reasoning underlying the plodding delirium. Then the rhythm changes, and there is peremptory, terse image-making:

If there were water
And no rock
If there were rock
And also water
And water
A spring
A pool among the rock
If there were the sound of water only
Not the cicada
And dry grass singing
But sound of water over a rock
Where the hermit-thrush sings in the pine trees
Drip drop drip drop drop drop drop
But there is no water

Later in the poem, two lines seem, stylistically, to anticipate the chorus of *Murder in the Cathedral*:

What is that sound high in the air
Murmur of maternal lamentation

Eliot brings his poem to a close with the three-fold Sanskrit reiteration:

Shantih, shantih, shantih.

Yeats, just a few years before, had put this Sanskrit into the expanded form:

May peace and peace and peace be everywhere.

Four Quartets

Another World War was raging as Eliot brought to completion his *Four Quartets*. These poems articulated Eliot's mature affirmation of the Christian faith as a bulwark against the ravages of modern culture. A careful parallel reading of *The Waste Land* and *Four Quartets* reveals how one sensitive mind moves from chaos to stability during the disturbing period between the two World Wars.

The title *Four Quartets* indicates that this is not four poems together making a quartet, but four quartets together making a whole. Perhaps something of a musical inference could be drawn from the use of the concept 'quartet', since each one contains five movements or sections, each with its own rhythm and mood.

The *Quartets* with their associations are:

	Title	*Derivation*
1936	*Burnt Norton*	Village in Gloucestershire
1940	*East Coker*	Village in Somerset from which Eliot's 17th-century ancestors emigrated
1941	*The Dry Salvages*	Three rocks with a beacon off Massachusetts, USA (Salvages rhymes with assuages)
1942	*Little Gidding*	Village in Huntingdonshire

If some detractor had wanted to parody Eliot, the master of paradox, he might have fortuitously penned this statement from *The Dry Salvages*:

> And the way up is the way down, the way forward is the way back.

But no disparager would be likely to create the following lines, based as they are upon a knowledge of Eastern philosophy:

> There are three conditions which often look alike
> Yet differ completely, flourish in the same hedgerow;
> Attachment to self and to things and to persons, detachment
> From self and from things and from persons; and, growing between them, indifference
> Which resembles the others as death resembles life. *Little Gidding*

A major theme and its implications for man in the *Four Quartets* is 'time':

Theme	*Expansion*
Time	What is time? How is it experienced? What is past, present, future, and what-might-have-been?
Time and eternity	Can be imagined but not described. Eternity is not time in perpetuity.
Place of man in the scheme of things	Man's unique understanding of why things happen, while not knowing his own imperfections.
Man's response	Acceptance, endurance, relief, release, detachment, indifference, purification.

In the two following quotations Eliot neatly contrasts apparently trivial detail (which is, in reality, far from trivial) with the conventionally large-scale:

> … there is a time for building
> And a time for living and for generation
> And a time for the wind to break the loosened pane
> And to shake the wainscot where the field-mouse trots
> And to shake the tattered arras woven with a silent motto.
>
> *East Coker*

> Time present and time past
> Are both perhaps present in time future
> And time future contained in time past. *Burnt Norton*

This statement summates the Buddhist teaching on Samsāra, which in different words is expressed in the old adage:

> If today was like yesterday, tomorrow will be like today.

Somewhat chillingly, Eliot reaches into the past and diminishes what remains of its significance:

> It seems, as one becomes older,
> That the past has another pattern, and ceases
> to be a mere
> sequence –
> Or even development *The Dry Salvages*

On a somewhat different tack, Eliot succinctly makes a profound point constantly reiterated in Indian philosophy:

> Desire itself is movement
> Not in itself desirable;
> Love is itself unmoving … *Burnt Norton*

There is a perceptible positive lift from the nadir of cultural despair in *The Waste Land*, which moves inexorably onward through his later poems, *The Hollow Men* (1925), *Ash Wednesday* (1930) and culminates in *Four Quartets*, even though the Second World War was still at its height. The subtlety of the poetry of *Four Quartets* may be the result of seeking to articulate extreme refinements of fleeting experience. At the end of the poems, Eliot expresses his belief that the ultimate simplicity of a total response to the calling of love will result in a condition of unity:

> And all shall be well and
> All manner of thing shall be well …

Murder in the Cathedral

Eliot's verse-play, *Murder in the Cathedral*, which was first seen in 1935, is still regarded by many as the finest poetic drama of the 20th century.

Thomas à Becket, minor cleric and companion of King Henry II, is elevated by him to the Archbishopric of Canterbury. He develops, almost unwillingly, a devotion to a higher purpose which sets him in conflict with the King; later this turns into a bitter power struggle between Church and State. After seven years of self-imposed exile in France, Becket returns to England, knowing that this is likely to bring about his death. In December 1170 he is murdered by four knights in accordance, it must be supposed, with the King's wishes. After his martyrdom a great cult-following develops, centred on Becket's tomb, which becomes a major focus of pilgrimage in England.

Eliot, perhaps with the benefit of hindsight, considers in the play whether or not Becket deliberately chose martyrdom. Intriguingly, the word *martyr* (*martur*) originally meant 'witness'. The question is, whether Becket (like many modern politicians) had enough detachment and a broad enough view of history to be able to knowingly predestinate his place in the history books. In record time, little more than two years, he was canonized.

In a sense, Becket runs with the hare and the hounds. He is delinquent first and godly afterwards, a typical progression, but this switch frustrates the King. There is no consistency in Becket. The Archbishop is now becoming a nuisance: excommunicating officials, exiling himself to France, now back in England. What is he up to here?

As to the state of his mind, was he sated with worldly affairs and now deliberately electing to champion spiritual values? Was he the subject of a Saul-like conversion? Furthermore, did the martyrdom take place through a misreading by the knights of the King's true wishes? Or did the King originally intend Becket's death, then afterwards change his mind and for reasons of expediency make a show of regret? There are dramatic precedents for such politic afterthoughts. In Shakespeare's *Richard II*, Bolingbroke, after the King's murder, claims that he, similarly, was taken too literally. Having spoken fateful words and now wearing the murdered King's crown, he rounds on the knight who did the deed (Sir Pierce of Exton) and berates and exiles him. The relevant exchanges are:

EXTON: Didst thou not mark the king, what words he spake?
'Have I no friend will rid me of this living fear?'

SERVANT: Those were his very words. Act V, Scene iii

Exton responds by slaying Richard. Later, at Windsor, the slain Richard lies on his bier, and Exton addresses Bolingbroke:

EXTON: Great king, within this coffin I present
Thy buried fear …

BOLINGBROKE: Exton I thank thee not; for thou hast wrought
A deed of slander with thy fatal hand
Upon my head and all this famous land.

EXTON: From your own mouth, my lord, did I this deed.

BOLINGBROKE: They love not poison that do poison need,
Nor do I thee: though I did wish him dead,
I hate the murderer, love him murdered.

Richard II, Act V, Scene iv

It is interesting to speculate on the reasons for the slaying of Becket on the steps of a cathedral altar, when a paid assassin could have knifed him in less provocative circumstances. Such questions would intrigue an intellect like Eliot's, and his fascinating play both prompts these questions and explores their implications.

The play opens with Becket's return to his cathedral, mindful of his destiny and motivation. With dramatic poetic skill, Eliot sets this circumstance against a background chorus of priests and women of Canterbury. Despite its apparently unprepossessing dramatic potential, Becket's predicament gains dramatic force through the authenticity of the poetry and the vivid imagery of the language.

At one point in the play, Becket is contending with his inner temptations and the outer enemy, his erstwhile boon-companion, King Henry II. The following passage articulates the Archbishop's thoughts in themes perhaps personal to Eliot: the burden of guilt, the sense of outrage, the impossibility of communication and the rejection of love.

TEMPTER: Your thoughts have more power than kings to compel you.
You have also thought, sometimes at your prayers,
Sometimes hesitating at the angles of stairs,
And between sleep and waking, early in the morning,
When the bird cries, have thought of further scorning.

*

That nothing lasts, but the wheel turns,
The nest is rifled, and the bird mourns …

*

THOMAS: But what is there to do? What is left to be done?
Is there no enduring crown to be won?

TEMPTER: Yes, Thomas, yes; you have thought of that too.

In the course of his sermon on Christmas morning, Becket explains: a Christian martyrdom is never an accident … it is never the design of man; for the true martyr is he who has become the instrument of God, who has lost his will in the will of God, and who no longer desires anything for himself, not even the glory of being a martyr. However, he goes on to say:

… because dear children, I do not think I shall ever
preach to you again; and because it is possible that in
a short time you may have yet another martyr …

Later, he tells his fellow clerics:

... we have fought the beast
And have conquered. We have only to conquer
Now by suffering. This is the easier victory.

When the knights arrive, he could be said to behave in a provocative manner, as if determined to impel matters to the completion he now desires.

An irony which emerges from Eliot's play (written in 1935 at the height of Fascism), and strengthened when viewed from the vantage point of the post-Communist era, is that ordinary people are destined to be plagued either by political autocrats or by priestly ones. Becket insists that Church is above State. His error is, as it has always been, the failure to understand that it is not the Church, but what it stands for, that is higher than the State. Quotations from the play appear elsewhere in this volume, but if one rhyming couplet catches the spirit and the ultimate question concerning Becket's murder it is perhaps this:

The last temptation is the greatest treason:
To do the right deed for the wrong reason.

Eliot and Valéry

All eminent men have their detractors, and Eliot has been attacked consistently since the 1930s, when he was assailed by sociological critics for his religious and academic leanings. Others accused him of pedantry, eclecticism for effect, and elitism. This assessment is reinforced by the fact that Paul Valéry (1871-1945) is Eliot's proclaimed master of our time. Valéry, the French poet and critic, was at first influenced by the school of Symbolism, but his interest later turned to philosophy, mathematics, science, and economics. He later professed himself to be attracted to poetry only as a mental exercise. He is known for his emphasis on the importance of the intellectual classes in shaping and controlling society. His poetry is distinguished by its precision, extreme contraction, and abstruseness of theme. Declaring that he was a businessman rather than a bohemian, Valéry made a point of keeping his works inaccessible in order to increase their value, insisting that they be published only in limited and distinctive editions.

In what amounts to a defence of the somewhat trivial content of much of Valéry's poetry, Eliot says somewhat archly: 'He remains a poet, because the translation of the content of any of his poems into conceptual terms converts it into something else – and *something else of less value*.' Valéry's poetry repays slow and careful savouring. With all the risks of translation into metre (rather than literal translation with its even graver risks), here is a taste of Valéry. This, with other French verse, has been superbly rendered into English by Alan Conder in *Cassell's Anthology of French Poetry* (1950):

The Bee

However fine and mortal be
Thy subtle sting, O golden bee,
My tender pollen-basket is
But hid 'neath dreamy traceries.

Then prick the fair gourd of the breast,
Where Love doth die or drowse, at rest,
That something of me, red and fresh,
May stain the round and rebel flesh!

Rather a torment keen and brief
That quickly ends and brings relief
Than pain that sleeps quiescently.

With that elfin gold alarm then be
My kindled sense, or let Love lie
And on my bosom sleep or die.

And these opening lines from Valéry's poem *Pomegranates*:

Hard pomegranate wide-open now
Yielding to your seeds' excess,
I seem to see a sovran brow
Burst by its discoveries!

Here, finally, is one verse from Valéry's long poem *The Graveyard by the Sea*:

And you, great soul, hope for an illusion
That will not have these colours of delusion
Spun here for eyes of flesh by gold and wave?
Will you still sing when you are air? *All* dies;
Athwart our porous being filters even
The holy urge bestowed on us by heaven.

Even from these brief extracts it is clear why Eliot spoke of Valéry as 'a writer for whom I have considerable respect'.

The Final Years

After his earlier unhappiness it gives pleasure to note that on 10 January 1957, Eliot and Valerie Fletcher, his devoted secretary for several years, were married. Robert Giroux retrospectively reported that the most striking single aspect of nearly 20 years of knowing Eliot as a friend was the contrast between the rather sad and lonely aura of the earlier period and the happiness he radiated in the later one. In the last eight or so years of his life, and of course his marriage, he was heard to mutter more than once, 'I'm the luckiest man in the world.' In his new happiness he wrote these sensuous lines in *Dedication to My Wife*:

To whom I owe the leaping delight
That quickens my senses in our wakingtime
And the rhythm that governs the repose of our sleepingtime,

> The breathing in unison
> Of lovers whose bodies smell of each other
> Who think the same thoughts without need of speech
> And babble the same speech without need of meaning.

As a poet, Eliot has a very individual voice. In his work he uses or discards metre and rhyme innovatively; he leavens serious poems with satiric humour; expresses everyday matters in haunting imagery; describes wonders in simple, ordinary language. His work is sinewy, powerful and beautiful, but because the writing can be simultaneously allusive, elliptical, and condensed there are occasions when meaning can be inferred only by its organizational context.

The range and diversity of Yeats have caused many to consider him the greatest poet of our age, but Eliot the more influential and significant. Eliot set the scene and defined the tenor of the poetic landscape in the 1920s, and his is the dominant mind in poetry until the early 1950s.

To the art of poetry Eliot contributed discipline of form and new rhythms, but as well as the classical control of his verse forms, there is his reservation about emotion. In his poetry, an emotive romantic phrase or image is usually followed by a countering idea as though a corrective were needed. His use of erudite allusion and pitiless analysis of the moral depravity and purposelessness of a spiritually arid civilization in *The Waste Land* is masterly. Although Eliot's poetic technique may have ceased to have any direct influence, his criticism is as vital a force as ever.

Eliot, the stooping mandarin of poetry, was variously described as 'the mysterious, the elusive Eliot', 'the invisible poet' etc, but by virtue of his position as a director of the publishing house which is now Faber & Faber, and by his practical encouragement of poets, he exercised a shaping influence on the course of modern poetry.

The Social Poets

The so-called *Social Poets* – W.H. Auden, Stephen Spender, Cecil Day-Lewis and Louis MacNeice – received the largest share of attention among the poets of the Thirties. Some of their work, with that of numerous others, is offered in two representative anthologies of the period: *New Signatures* (1932) and *The Faber Book of Modern Verse* (1936).

W.H. **Auden** (1907-73) was the best-known of a group of poets all of whom at that time adhered strongly to radically left-wing views. The revolutionary movement of ideas afforded a measure of self-definition for poets emerging from the shadow of Yeats and Eliot, but during World War II Auden's socialist preoccupations gave way to a growing interest in Protestant Christianity – as in *New Year Letter* (1941).

Eliot was enthusiastic about Auden's early poetry, which showed great promise, and published his *Poems* (1930), followed by *The Orators* (1932). In his early satirical poetry Auden parodied the style of numerous traditional English poets, but the poems echoing Wordsworth carry the sound of isolation and disappointment. Occasionally, he brilliantly and succinctly catches the essence of a thing. In his poem *On this Island* he speaks of the White Cliffs:

> Here at the small field's ending pause
> When the chalk wall falls to the foam and its tall ledges
> Oppose the pluck
> And knock of the tide,
> And the shingle scrambles after the sucking surf,
> And the gull lodges
> A moment on its sheer side.

Auden's early poems examined the contemporary scene using imagery which combined the farcical and the tragic. His style, with its unusual rhythms, seemed exciting at the time, and some of the early poems are still considered to be among his best. His bold phrases and images, the topical cogency and air of intellectual commitment, courted critical attention. He was copious, facile, fluent, versatile, inconsistent. Moreover, Auden constantly revised and rejected his poems – an activity which exasperated many critics. Indeed, it must be said that Auden failed to develop his potential – to the disappointment of many. The acerbic F.R. Leavis, in *Scrutiny* (1936), said of Auden: 'His talent was indubitable; one has waited for him to do something with it … He has no organization.' Leavis goes on to complain that, although Auden is a satirist, his irony is self-indulgent, and that too much of his poetry is made out of his private neuroses and memories. He scathingly accuses him of being adolescent. R.G. Lienhardt (1945) criticized his 'determination to write on a grand scale with the mental equipment of only a minor poet'. Even so, his final long poem, *The Age of Anxiety* (New York, 1947; London, 1948), an elaborate work reminiscent of Joyce, won the 1948 Pulitzer Prize.

In contrast to these derogatory assessments, others insist that the more one reads Auden (especially the later work) the more impressive he becomes. He is a problematic poet to assess and evaluate. Altogether, his collaborations and editorships constitute a formidable list and he was the recipient of many poetry awards and honours.

Auden's own view was that poetry was 'a game of knowledge'. He experimented with many forms including the Japanese haiku and tanka. He collaborated on the libretto of Stravinsky's opera *The Rake's Progress*. A series of anti-Romantic lectures, *The Enchafèd Flood* (1950) and *The Dyer's Hand* (1963), are critical prose works.

Auden married Thomas Mann's daughter Erika (an anti-Nazi) in 1938 so that she could obtain British citizenship; Auden himself was homosexual. Poetry, always a prime vehicle for expressing heterosexual love, is no less effective in revealing emotion in same-sex relationships. From him we learn of the anguish arising from betrayal, as young men towards whom he was attracted exercised the inherent male propensity for transient liaisons. It has been observed that Auden carried the conviction for a long time that he was separated from personal love by his sexuality and his intellect. In *Our Hunting Fathers* (in which he seemed directly to be paraphrasing Lenin) he penned the lines:

> ... Guessed Love by nature suited to
> The intricate ways of guilt ...

Auden, like many poets of his generation, had learned much from Eliot; David Daiches (Lecturer in English at Cambridge) considered that Auden's lines:

> Lay your sleeping head, my love,
> Human on my faithless arm ...

were a moving counterpart to the 'young man carbuncular' and his unfortunate typist in Eliot's *The Waste Land*.

Auden emigrated to the United States in 1939, and later became an American citizen. After the Second World War he lived for much of the time in Italy and Austria. Auden seemed constantly to be looking for a fresh start or 'chapter', or a new turning point. He moved around the world, re-converted to Christianity, took up various kinds of employment; he even served with the Strategic Bombing Survey of the US Army in Germany during World War II. He taught in an English school and in both English and American universities. In 1956 he became professor of poetry at Oxford, but he was an increasingly isolated figure. He died of a heart attack in Austria in 1973.

Curiously, in the late 1990s, more than 20 years after his death, a resurgence of interest in Auden occurred, largely on the strength of the appearance in a popular film of his poem about bereavement, *Stop All the Clocks*, written in April 1936.

Robert Lowell (1967) wrote that John Crowe Ransom (the American educator and poet) had expressed to him the view that 'we had made an even exchange, when we lost Eliot to England, and later gained Auden'. (There is comparison with Eliot again.) The last word here will be that of Nicholas Jenkins (Oxford, 1994), who speaks of Auden's 'encyclopaedic intellectual scope, his polyglot linguistic inclusiveness, and his insistence that all forms and subjects are still available to the contemporary poet'. Jenkins concludes that this is the very dynamic of poetry manifesting itself through W.H. Auden.

Louis **MacNeice** (1907-63) wrote poetry permeated by a greater preoccupation with psychological problems than that of his associates. His work contained skilful manipulations of the symbols of everyday 20th-century life – rather in the manner of Auden. Occasionally, his poetry suggests the influence of his studies in Latin and Greek classical literature.

In his poem *Wessex Guidebook* he begins each seven-line verse with a double rhythm which is the very stuff of poetry:

Hayfoot; strawfoot; the illiterate seasons
Still clump their way through Somerset and Dorset …

★

Flake-tool; core tool; in the small museum
Rare butterflies, green coins of Caracalla …

★

And thatchpoll numskull rows of limestone houses,
Dead from the navel down in plate glass windows …

★

But hindmost, topmost, those illiterate seasons
Still smoke their pipes in swallow-hole and hide-out.

Here, in a series of 'Nature Notes', is *The Sea*:

Incorrigible, ruthless,
It rattled the shingly beach of my childhood,
Subtle, the opposite of earth,
And, unlike earth, capable
Any time at all of proclaiming eternity
Like something or someone to whom
We have to surrender, finding
Through that surrender, life.

The poetry of Stephen **Spender** (1909-95) is regarded by critics as more personal, lyrical, and romantic in tone than that of the other members of his immediate group. It deals with his own emotional reactions as he contemplates unemployment, poverty, suffering or injustice, and he visualizes the amelioration of these by a Socialist state. The imagery and ideas are often those relevant to a mechanistic industrial civilization. Here is an example:

In railway halls, on pavements near the traffic,
They beg, their eyes made big by empty staring
And only measuring Time, like the blank clock.
No, I shall weave no tracery of pen ornament
To make them birds upon my singing tree:
Time merely drives these lives which do not live
As tides push rotten stuff along the shore.

In Railway Halls

From My Diary

'She was', my father said (in an aside),
'A great beauty, forty years ago.'

★

I only saw her being seventy,
I could not see the girl my father saw.

★

Faces we've once loved
Fit into their seven ages as Russian dolls

Into one another. My memory
Penetrates through successive layers
Back to the face which first I saw. So when the last
Exterior image is laid under its lid,
Your first face seen will shine through all.

In his poem *Ultima Ratio Regum*, Spender remarks the death of a young man, setting it in timeless social comment on the waste of youthful lives in war:

The guns spell money's ultimate reason
In letters of lead on the Spring hillside.
But the boy lying dead under the olive trees
Was too young and too silly
To have been notable to their important eye.
He was a better target for a kiss.

Cecil **Day-Lewis** (1904-72) used traditional lyric forms in the 1930s to comment upon the decadence of the bourgeois English society of his time and to extol the benefits of a Socialist community. His work is chiefly didactic, using the social and industrial symbols of the 20th century. Critics say that his poetry has neither the virtuosity and satirical brilliance of Auden's, nor the emotional intensity of Spender's. Day-Lewis makes a wistful and wry observation in his short poem:

Where are the War Poets?

It is the logic of our times,
No subject for immortal verse –
That we who lived by honest dreams
Defend the bad against the worse.

Day-Lewis's failures, it is said, are verbal; his successes rhythmical. Here are some lines from *The Poet*:

For me there is no dismay
Though ills enough impend,
I have learned to count each day
Minute by breathing minute –
Birds that lightly begin it,
Shadows muting its end –
As lovers count for luck
Their own heart-beats and believe
In the forest of time they pluck
Eternity's single leaf.

When Cecil Day-Lewis died in May 1972 he was poet laureate.

Christopher **Isherwood** (1904-86) was a long-time friend of Auden and Stephen Spender. He wrote some celebrated fiction during the 1930s and for a time, early on, Auden collaborated with Isherwood in verse plays: *The Dog Beneath the Skin* (1936), *The Ascent of F6* (1937), and *On the Frontier* (1939).

The English Thirties Movement faded under the pressure of the Second World War, but a vigorous new group of poets was ready to carry poetry forward into the turmoil that lay ahead.

John **Betjeman** (1906-84) is not included among the so-called Social Poets, although his writing is full of social comment on his times. Poet and critic of architecture (he published some 20 books on the subject), he was made poet laureate in 1972. As if he were a poetic social historian, Betjeman wrote about children's parties, handsome tennis-girls, the arrest of Oscar Wilde, parish churches and church furnishings, Victorian railway stations and the Metropolitan Railway, which he evokes with a strange nostalgic fervour and an ingenious verbal artistry. His language is simple, his rhymes clearly marked, his rhythms 'catchy' and persuasive.

Rumbling under blackened girders, Midland bound for Cricklewood,
Puffed its sulphur to the sunset where that Land of Laundries stood.
Rumble under, thunder over, train and tram alternate go,
Shake the floor and smudge the ledger, Charrington, Sells, Dale and Co…

Interspersed with a wide range of subjects were fragments of autobiography, and personal statements about death, lust, love and remorse. He was noted for his anti-modernist approach and for his wit, pastiche, and parody. He admired poets with the ability 'to catch the atmosphere of places and times' – a skill which was one of his own chief characteristics. Here are lines from his poem *The Wykehamist*:

Broad of church and 'broad of mind',
Broad before and broad behind,
A keen ecclesiologist,
A rather dirty Wykehamist.
'Tis not for us to wonder why
He wears that curious knitted tie;
We should not cast reflections on
The very slightest kind of don.

⋆

And 'six o'clock' St Mary calls
Above the mellow college walls.
The evening stretches arms to twist
And captivate her Wykehamist.
But not for him those autumn days,
He shuts them out with heavy baize;
He gives his Ovaltine a stir
And nibbles at a 'petit beurre',
And, satisfying fleshly wants,
He settles down to Norman fonts.

His work always carried a feeling of simple sincerity; the language had vivacity and a precise aptness. These lines are addressed to God in Westminster Abbey:

Now I feel a little better,
   What a treat to hear Thy Word,
Where the bones of leading statesmen,
   Have so often been interr'd.
And now, dear Lord, I cannot wait
   Because I have a luncheon date.

Betjeman's poetry was not always admired by literary critics. It is too easy to dismiss much of his work as over-facile, but the apparently naive simplicity often conceals a careful craftsmanship.

At the time of evening when cars run sweetly,
   Syringas blossom by Oxford gates.
In her evening velvet with a rose pinned neatly
   By the distant bus-stop a don's wife waits.

Another verse about the Oxford experience:

Shall we ever, my staunch Myfanwy,
   Bicycle down to North Parade?

Kant on the handle-bars, Marx in the saddle-bag,
   Light my touch on your shoulder-blade.

The scene shifts to London:

From the geyser ventilators
   Autumn winds are blowing down
On a thousand business women
   Having baths in Camden Town.

Waste pipes chuckle into runnels,
   Steam's escaping here and there,
Morning trains through Camden cutting
   Shake the Crescent and the Square.

His struggle to preserve old values, coupled with a dash of misanthropy, are plain in this celebrated poem:

Come, friendly bombs, and fall on Slough
It isn't fit for humans now …

*

And get that man with double chin
Who'll always cheat and always win,
Who washes his repulsive skin
      In women's tears.

Betjeman's poetry was liked by the middle classes, of whom he wrote with both affection and irony:

Gaily into Ruislip Gardens
   Runs the red electric train,
With a thousand 'Ta s' and 'Pardon s'

Daintily alights Elaine;
Hurries down the concrete station
With a frown of concentration,
Out into the outskirt's edges
Where a few surviving hedges
Keep alive our lost Elysium – rural Middlesex again.

New Apocalypse

In 1939 a group of young writers calling themselves the New Apocalypse took for their model the poetry of Dylan Thomas. They rejected what they described as the self-conscious and over-intellectualized manner of Auden and his immediate group. Instead, they wanted to become intoxicated with words, to create myths and indulge themselves with Gothic effects. For their part, some of the Thirties poets adopted religious overtones, perhaps to counter their rejection of the adequacy of a social interpretation of reality. As Arthur Koestler put it, Auden had moved from the commissar to the yogi end of the spectrum.

In the 1940s Robert Conquest was concerned that poetry lacked a major component – intelligence. Kenneth Allott, in his *English Poetry 1918-60* (1961), wrote that anyone who studies the poetry of the Fifties is impressed less by the 'emphasis on intelligence, welcome as this is,' than by the fact that 'the poetic revolution has a mainly literary motivation'. In explaining this he points out that the Social Poets of the Thirties wrote differently from Eliot because they thought their important social message would lose by being dressed in his 'complexity'. This rather implies that poets can offer what they have to say either simply, directly, and unambiguously, or intentionally clothe it in recondite and abstruse words with a seasoning of classical allusions and references.

An intelligent poet valued for his directness and down-to-earth reality is Alun **Lewis** (1915-44). It has been said of his writing that it shines with a most attractive honesty and unpretentiousness. 'My longing,' said Lewis, 'is more and more for one thing only, integrity, and I discount the other qualities in people far too ruthlessly if they lack that fundamental sincerity and wholeness.' The following extract is from his poem *The Mahratta Ghats*, based on his experience serving with the army as a lieutenant in India:

Will she who burns and withers on the plain
Leave, ere too late, her scraggy herds of pain,
The cow-dung fire and the trembling beasts,
The little wicked gods, the grinning priests,
And climb, before a thousand years have fled,
High as the eagle to her mountain bed
Whose soil is fine as flour and blood-red?
But no! She cannot move. Each arid patch
Owns the lean folk who plough and scythe and thatch
Its grudging yield and scratch its stubborn stones.
The small gods suck the marrow from their bones.

Who is it climbs the summit of the road?
Only the beggar bumming his dark load.
Who was it cried to see the falling star?
Only the landless soldier lost in war.
And did a thousand years go by in vain?
And does another thousand start again?

*Ha! Ha! Among the Trumpets** (1944)

Hal **Summers** (1911-2005) sketches with deft touches a figure who had grown into his occupation:

His eyes are cold blue daylight,
His face is roughened and red;
Set on bridge of shoulders
The wheelhouse of his head.
He walks the bucking coaster
Like a wheel set in a groove,
But lurches on the dry land
As though the earth did move.

Sea-Captain

R.S. **Thomas** (1913-2000) contrasts the blackbird's appearance with its song:

It seems wrong that out of this bird,
Black, bold, a suggestion of dark
Places about it, there yet should come
Such rich music, as though the notes'
Ore were changed to a rare metal
At one touch of that bright bill.

A Blackbird Singing

D.J. **Enright** (1920-2000) muses and lets his thoughts flow reflectively...

Dreaming in the Shanghai Restaurant

I would like to be that elderly Chinese gentleman.
He wears a gold watch with a gold bracelet,
But a shirt without sleeves or tie.
He has good luck moles on his face, but is not disfigured
with fortune.
His wife resembles him, but is still a handsome woman,
She has never bound her feet or her belly.
Some of the party are his children, it seems,
And some his grandchildren;
No generation appears to intimidate another.
He is interested in people, without wanting to convert them
or pervert them.
He eats with gusto, but not with lust;
And he drinks, but is not drunk.

* This curious title derives from the description of the war-horse in the Book of Job: 'He saith among the trumpets Ha! Ha!, and he smelleth the battle afar off.'

He is content with his age, which has always suited him.
When he discusses a dish with the pretty waitress,
It is the dish he discusses, not the waitress.
The table-cloth is not so clean as to show indifference,
Not so dirty as to signify lack of manners.
He proposes to pay the bill but knows he will not be
allowed to.
He walks to the door, like a man who doesn't fret about
being respected, since he is;
A daughter or grand-daughter opens the door for him,
And he thanks her.
It has been a satisfying evening. Tomorrow
Will be a satisfying morning. In between he will sleep
satisfactorily.

Stewart **Conn** (b1936) in *Family Visit* begins his poem by evoking the slow pace of the activity he depicts, together with the jerkiness of the movement:

Laying linoleum, my father spends hours
With his tape-measure.
Littering the floor
As he checks his figures, gets
The angle right; then cuts
Carefully, to the music
Of a slow logic. In despair
I conjure up a room where
A boy sits and plays with coloured bricks

Poetry of the First World War expressed feelings of rage, disgust, pity; occasionally, the best poets spoke with prophetic utterance. The poems written during the Second World War had a matter-of-fact realism which can be particularly chilling; this especially because the poet often sees (in parallel with the present danger), glimpses of ordinariness which the war is passing by. A single example makes the point well; it is by the Scottish poet, Edwin **Muir** (1887-1959):

The Interrogation

We could have crossed the road but hesitated,
And then came the patrol:
The leader conscientious and intent,
The men surly, indifferent.
While we stood by and waited
The interrogation began. He says the whole
Must come out now, who, what we are,
Where we have come from, with what purpose, whose
Country or camp we plot for or betray.
Question on question.
We have stood and answered through the standing day
And watched across the road beyond the hedge

The careless lovers in pairs go by,
Hand linked in hand, wandering another star,
So near we could shout to them. We cannot choose
Answer or action here,
Though still the careless lovers saunter by
And the thoughtless field is near.
We are on the very edge,
Endurance almost done,
And still the interrogation is going on.

Seamus **Heaney** (b1939), who was awarded the Nobel Prize for Literature in 1995, vividly describes the reversal that the passage of time wreaks on father and son:

Follower

My father worked with a horse-plough,
His shoulders globed like a full sail strung
Between the shafts and the furrow.
The horses strained at his clicking tongue.

An expert. He would set the wing
And fit the bright steel-pointed sock.
The sod rolled over without breaking.
At the headrig, with a single-pluck

Of reins, the sweating team turned round
And back into the land. His eye
Narrowed and angled at the ground,
Mapping the furrow exactly.

I stumbled in his hob-nailed wake,
Fell sometimes on the polished sod;
Sometimes he rode me on his back
Dipping and rising to his plod.

I wanted to grow up and plough,
To close one eye, stiffen my arm,
All I ever did was follow
In his broad shadow round the farm.

I was a nuisance, tripping, falling,
Yapping always. But today
It is my father who keeps stumbling
Behind me, and will not go away.

Seamus Heaney, as a child (the eldest of eight) born into a family of farmers of Co. Derry, was part of what in his own words was an 'old traditional community which has since disappeared'. His poetry is a vehicle for humour, tolerance, and tragedy: childhood memories, the beauty of nature, and hauntingly moving poems on death, as well as verse expressing his response to the Troubles and the IRA ceasefire of 1994. The collections *Door into the Dark* (1969) and *Wintering Out* (1972) allow us to connect with the early Heaney. Here is the quality of his observation, from 'Digging':

> Under my window, the spade sinks into gravelly ground:
> My father digging. I look down till his straining rump
> among the flower beds bends low, comes up twenty years away
> Stooping in rhythm through potato drills where he was
> digging.
> 'By God, the old man could handle a spade,
> just like his old man.'

Something of the Celtic feeling of the early Heaney had been expressed by the Welsh poet Dylan **Thomas** (1914-53). But the work of Thomas (who was an imitator of Gerard Manley Hopkins) precipitated a fierce reaction from those who were to carry poetry forward into the Sixties.

Although Dylan Thomas's early poetry had original things to say and the rhetoric to make what was said memorable, later the rhetoric rolled on but the meaning had become elusive. Unfortunately his imitators waived meaning altogether, caring only that the verse sounded impressive, and during these years it seemed that intelligence had disappeared from poetry.

It has been said by Kenneth Allott (1950) of Dylan Thomas that he married the *Old Testament* to Freud, and moreover it was Freud perceived through the thinking of D.H. Lawrence. With the death of Thomas in 1953, voices of revulsion were heard describing him as a powerful but evil influence on poetry. The vituperation appeared to focus and attach itself to those who belonged to what was called The Movement (a term apparently coined by a journalist on the *Spectator*). From The Movement there came a reaction against wild, loose emotion. As A. Alvarez has pointed out in *The New Poetry* (1962), of the nine poets to appear in Robert Conquest's *New Lines*, six were university teachers, two were librarians and one was a civil servant. The verse was intelligent, knowledgeable, efficient, polished, and conventionally structured, but the pieties of The Movement were as predictable as the politics of the Thirties' poets.

Philip **Larkin** in *Church-going* speaks in the 'plain-man' stance typical of this period:

> Hatless, I take off
> My cycle-clips in awkward reverence

Certain British poets prominent in the Fifties (Philip Larkin, Kingsley Amis, John Wain, and others with similar attitudes), were intelligent and lively but distrustful of the high-flown romanticism so recently in fashion. This resulted in a more cautious use of imagery, a preference for a poetically even tone, and a socially neutral attitude.

Robert Conquest's anthology *New Lines* began appearing in 1956; the poets who appeared in these collections were:

Robert Conquest
D.J. Enright
Elizabeth Jennings
Kingsley Amis
John Holloway
Thom Gunn
Philip Larkin
John Wain
Donald Davie

After what has been presented in the name of modern poetry it is reassuring to know that Robert Conquest, the editor of *New Lines I and II*, says of his own poetry:

> I suppose my main theme is the poet's relationship to the phenomenal universe – in particular to landscape, women, art and war. Forms usually, though not always, traditional. Sometimes straight lyric, more often with development of a train of thought; an attempt to master, or transmit, a presented reality in intellectual and emotive terms simultaneously. The vocabulary often runs to words – not specialist ones – drawn from the technical, scientific and philosophical spheres and mediatised into the ordinary language.
>
> Since all this is in principle a complex and difficult process, a strong effort goes into keeping it as comprehensible as possible, avoidance of forced obscurities, and provision of a rigorous guidance of sound and structure.

Perhaps the two most widely known post-Dylan-Thomas poets in Britain are Ted Hughes and Philip Larkin. A. Alvares called Ted **Hughes** 'a poet of the first importance'. Others must have thought so too as he was made poet laureate in 1984.

For many, the violence in Hughes is repellent, but there is in his natural images the sudden, sharp feeling of truth. Human sentiment, given sway, would soon dislocate the natural world, rendering it disorganized and chaotic. In his poem *The Pike* Hughes catches the ominousness of the unreasoning, superstitious fears that lurk in the depths of the imagination:

The pond I fished, fifty yards across,
Whose lilies and muscular tench
Had outlasted every visible stone
Of the monastery that planted them –

Stilled legendry depth:
It was as deep as England. It held
Pike too immense to stir, so immense and old
That past nightfall I dared not cast

But silently cast and fished
With the hair frozen on my head
For what might move, for what eye might move.
The still splashes on the dark pond,

Owls hushing the floating woods
Frail on my ear against the dream
Darkness beneath night's darkness had freed,
That rose slowly towards me, watching.

In a radio programme Larkin spoke of the releasing freedom and sense of direction which he received from reading another poet:

> When I came to Hardy it was with the sense of relief that I didn't have to try and jack myself up to a concept of poetry that lay outside my own life ... One could simply relapse back into one's own life and write from it.

Here, in summary, are some of the features that characterize four decades of contemporary poetry:

1930s The Social Poets espousing strong left-wing views; parody of traditional styles.

1940s Second World War. New Apocalypse (neo-Romantics, nurturing and protecting individuality against totalitarian oppression).

1950s Intellect re-enters poetry; suspicion of highly figurative language; influence of The Movement; anti-Dylan-Thomas bias; Graves and Empson offered as models.

1960s Some poets returning to conventional rhyme and rhythm patterns, for example Philip Larkin; ordinary life in poetry: no system of culture into which poetry must fit.

In the welter of verse emerging from all sides it is not easy to discern a focus or centre that offers a generic term for the poetry of the Seventies or Eighties (although A. Alvarez has coined the questionable term 'new depth poetry'). He imagines a serious poetry where the openness to experience, the psychological insight and integrity of D.H. Lawrence would combine with the technical skill and formal intelligence of T.S. Eliot. If this were to happen, says Alvarez optimistically, we would have contemporary work which, like Coleridge's faculty of imagination, would reconcile 'a more than usual state of emotion with more than usual order'.

What comes to mind here is the dictum, 'If you would protect the future, reflect the past.' Perhaps Thomas Hardy had this in view when, in the 1920s, he remarked to Robert Graves, 'All we can do is to write on the old themes in the old styles, but try to do a little better than those who went before us.'

Experimentation has always extended further than innovations of technique. The incessant action and reaction in poetry brings excesses at both extremes, but within the median stratum where developing poetry has its life, growth continues unharmed.

As the Fifties gave way to the Sixties, a number of poets decided to subject their work regularly to each other's scrutiny in a series of poetry workshops. They formed what became known as The Group. Poets usually associated with this grouping are:

Philip Hobsbaum	George MacBeth	Peter Redgrove
Martin Bell	Edward Lucie-Smith	
Peter Porter	David Wevill	

Examples of their work appear in Edward Lucie-Smith's anthology for Penguin, *British Poetry Since 1945* (1970). The generally modernist poetry of the Sixties and Seventies has proceeded largely without critical recognition and evaluation. This has probably been for two reasons:

1 The tendency for today's poets to reject the academic world and academic criticism.

2 The new movements in poetry have found their focus, not in London but in various provincial cities such as Birmingham, Liverpool, Newcastle, and Belfast.

The Sixties produced in England what came to be called *pop* poetry. It combined with both the new pop music cults and radical protest among students; this provided heady entertainment when performed live before mass audiences. What has come to be dubbed *pop protest poetry* rose on a tide of euphoria which encouraged in certain poets an anti-elitist bias. This has been thought by some to have led to the literary dead-end of trying to appeal to a 'non-literary audience' and the phenomena of *performance poets* and *bar poets*.

However, there are poets who seem quietly to have taken stock of the merits of transiently fashionable unpretentiousness, without losing sight of literary values. These poets have focused intelligently on subjects of personal or public concern without recourse either to cheap declamatory rhetoric or to verbal clowning.

An example of the use of traditional metrics and quality is Jon **Stallworthy**'s poem 'The Almond Tree' from *Root and Branch* (1969), in which a father copes with the birth of his Down's Syndrome son:

At seven-thirty
the visitor's bell
scissored the calm
of the corridors.
The doctor walked with me
to the slicing doors.

His hand upon my arm,
his voice – *I have to tell*
you – set another bell
beating in my head:
your son is a mongol
the doctor said.

How easily the word went in –
clean as a bullet
leaving no mark on the skin,
stopping the heart within it.

Another impressive and careful craftsman is Peter **Scupham** (b1933), whose sequence of sonnets in *The Hinterland* (1977) weighs the significance and cost of two World Wars. A later, equally well-written, collection is called *Winter Quarters* (1983). Here are some lines from his more recent poetry:

Wind

The trees push their loose heads about,
Dark hair angry with bee-voices,
The sob and growl of the unwelcome dead.
Fingers to fingers, feeling the world slide,
We call again 'Have you a message for us?

★

These oracles are bare of priestcraft.
Only the deep-drawn sigh, the gusty breath
That there is no disputing.
We die into and across your voices,
The light fading, and ambivalent.

Out Late (1986)

His poem *Dead Wood* opens with these lines:

Not a breath of wind to set the grasses talking,
But rain, unsteady, thin,
Which promised something more than a mere soaking
To more than skin,
And the wood crumbling through its own fingers.

A child's view of the adult world is evocatively recalled in *At the Stairhead*:

Your feet could not get colder than this,
Your head hung over the stairwell, the carpet-rods
Pure slips of gold gone into powdery dark.
The shining of things goes down, and always down;
The bed is marooned by acres of crackling board.

★

Voices chinking tipsily in their cups
Or lipping softly down the corridor,
Growling in dullness, rising, slipping, falling:
Kennelled things. Your ears sing with blood,
Alert as if the stars could make frost music.

★

The voices too are making a bad song
Where light might live behind the closing of doors.
There is nothing here for you, just the white cold
Pressing itself on flesh, on the gold slips
Which travel down and down to the powdery dark,
To the nothings of velvet, the stupid voices
In a long house of thin glass and throaty curtains.

The Air Show (1988)

Here are some lines from his poignant poem *Visitor*:

'Please ma'am,
It's the man with the darkness, come to put the candles out.'

Our table-talk ran out in shifts and corners;
I saw the patch on her grey worsted stockings,
Such homely things, down to their last mending,
And a face tired out by years of resignation
To its own image, wrinkling as she cleaned
The stain of living from our host of surfaces.

⋆

Meanwhile she stood there with her usual patience
Laid out before us like a supper-tray.

Out Late (1986)

In a lighter vein, an excess of adjectives and progress-slowing asides are parodied in this poem by George **MacBeth** written 'just to annoy people and, perhaps, also to amuse children – small children'. It is called *The Red Herring*:

There was once a high wall, a bare wall. And
against this wall, there was a ladder,
a long ladder. And on the ground,
under the ladder, there was a red
herring. A dry red herring.

And then a man came along. And in his hands
(they were dirty hands) this man had
a heavy hammer, a long nail
(it was also a sharp nail) and
a ball of string. A thick ball of string.

Five more verses explain precisely what this Lewis-Carroll-style figure does before he comes to a stop. A full stop.

Thus far, this survey has taken a long glance at 4,000 years of poetry, from the *Epic of Gilgamesh* to the poetry of Peter Scupham. In spite of some fluctuations of quality throughout its history, there appears to be no reason to doubt that poetry continues to flourish.

Michael **Thwaites**, the Australian poet born in 1915, tells us what he steers by:

> Most of my poems originate in personal experience, but seek to relate themselves to the situation of mankind. I have searched for, but not strained after, new idioms and movements of verse, but springing from, and not independent of traditional structures of English verse. I look to poetry as a communication between men, and not only between poets, or among the few.

Such statements are an encouraging sign of the continuing good health of poetry. Even when the art seems to be reflecting only some lowest common denominator of reduced standards, there are always diligent and able craftsmen carefully transforming thought and feeling into poetry of a universally acceptable standard.

As a badly wrought ornament made of gold continues to be gold, so poetry – however indifferent its quality – is still poetry and in truth cannot be denied its identity. There are no assayers of poetry as there are of gold and silver. That which, in absolute terms, *is* poetry is not harmed by poets, readers, or critics. Poetry *itself* is a continuum. It is *all* poetry taken together as one – plus something else. The mysterious 'something else' is the subject of the remaining sections of this book.

11
Differences Within Universality

Oriental Poetry

THE POETRY of any civilization inevitably employs the chief and obvious characteristics of the language from which it has arisen and reflects the discernments, faiths, and arts of the civilization it serves. In any culture we are likely to find:

1 mystical or metaphysical poetry,
2 verse that reflects the natural world,
3 love poetry.

Rather than an introductory essay at this point, drawing out distinctive features of language, sociology, and psychology in the Orient, examples of poetry will show that past and present people in the East have more in common with us than difference. The universality of mankind is revealed as cogently in poetry as in any other art form.

INDIA

The art and poetry of India stem from a majestic civilization extending with but few intervals from 3000 BC to the present day. Much Indian poetry reflects the fundamental harmony that exists between human beings and nature, a resonance which people everywhere are now seeking to re-establish with a new sense of spiritual urgency.

The oldest evidence of Indian literature is an extensive Vedic text anthology – one of four – called the *Rigveda* ('the knowledge [*veda*] laid down in verse [*rig*]'). The work is thought to have been compiled some time between 1200 BC and 800 BC. It contains some 1,028 hymns (a total of 10,580 verses) which are arranged in ten 'song cycles' (*mandalas*). Most of the hymns are addressed to personifications of natural forces, glorified as divinities, for example, *Agni* (Fire). The overall conception is magnificent; the Universe produces itself by itself and the divine is in all. Here, as an example, is *The Hymn of Creation* based on a prose rendering from the ancient Sanskrit by V. Raghavan:

> At that time there was neither non-existence nor existence; neither the worlds nor the sky; nor anything that is beyond; what covered everything,

> and where, and for whose enjoyment? Was there water unfathomable and deep? Death was not, nor was immortality there; no knowing of night or day; that One breathed without air, by its own strength; besides that, nothing existed.
>
> Darkness there was, veiled by darkness; undifferentiated, all this was one water; the incipient covered by void, that One became creative by the power of its own heat (concentration).

The texts are written in an archaic form of Sanskrit, extremely difficult to interpret. In spite of this the *Rigveda* is one of the most important linguistic, mythological-religious, literary, and cultural documents of humanity. This is archetypal poetry fulfilling a core requirement, the human need to express the ineffable.

Of central importance in Indian poetry is the *Bhagavad-Gītā* ('Song of the Lord'). This philosophical didactic poetry constitutes the sixth book of the epic poem *Mahābhārata* (which was composed somewhere between 500 BC and 200 BC). In essence, it is a fundamental teaching set within the context of a great 18-day battle. As such, it symbolizes the sometimes bitter conflicts experienced within each human being:

1 between the forces of good and evil in human nature;
2 between the ego and one's higher nature.

Here are just four verses from a vast work containing crucial dialogue between Prince Arjuna and his master, the Lord Krishna:

> I do not find any remedy for the grief that parches my senses – even were I to gain unrivalled and prosperous monarchy on earth, or sovereignty over the celestials. II.8
>
> Man does not gain actionlessness by abstaining from activity, nor does he rise to perfection by mere renunciation. III.4
>
> Verily, there is no purifier in this world like knowledge. He that is perfected in yoga realizes this in his own heart in due time. IV.38
>
> My delusion is destroyed. I have regained my memory through Your grace, O Achyuta.* I am firm; I am free from doubt. I shall act according to Your word. XVIII.73
>
> Translation by Swami Chidbhavananda

The *Upanishads*

The word *Upanishad* means 'to sit down near to' the feet of the *guru* (teacher) to hear the definitive tuition of sages articulating the Vedic revelation. Traditionally there are said to be 108 *Upanishads*. The earliest (*Bṛihadāranyaka*) dates from about 800 BC; the most recent from about 200 years ago. They were composed, within an oral tradition, to be chanted and memorized; many are repetitive and incantatory – their

* *Achyuta* is 'He who does not deviate from His Supreme State.'

power is enhanced when sounded aloud. They have several of the characteristics of poetry (for examples see Yeats, page 197).

Vidyapati (c1352-c1448) was born in north Bihar. A love poet who wrote songs in Maithili (the language spoken in the towns and villages of Mithila), his songs are included in the UNESCO collection of *Representative Works of India*, and merit major emphasis. Here, we have room for just one song:

A dark day
The cloud broke,
Rain fell.
I dressed for my love,
Believing it was night.
My deed of daring
Brought us to our goal.
The cloud
Kept other eyes away.
O friend,
How can I tell you what I felt?
To steal an elephant in broad daylight ...*

Translated by Deben Bhattacharya

Kālidāsa is generally considered to be the greatest poet writing in classical Sanskrit, and among the most eminent poet-dramatists in world literature. Of his works that survive there are three plays, three long poems, and an incomplete epic. His most famous compositions are the play *Shakuntalā* and the long poem *Meghadūtam* (*The Cloud Messenger*).

Little is known of Kālidāsa's personal history. All that has been related of him is that he lived at Ujjayini or Oujein (in Madhya Pradesh), and that he was 'one of the nine jewels of the court of Vikramāditya'. However, as there were several Vikramādityas at Ujjayini, it makes the floreat of the great poet as uncertain as that of any figure in the ancient history of India. Probable dates have ranged from 'towards the end of the 1st millennium BC' to 'the middle of the 6th century'.

Kālidāsa's work reflects his response to the sensuous beauty in woman and the natural world. He describes superbly the influence of nature upon the minds of lovers, subtly blending the eroticism and spirituality that characterizes mythology surrounding the worship of Śiva. Here is Goethe's oft-quoted four lines on Kālidāsa's place in Indian dramatic writing:

Could all spring blossom and all fruit of year's decline,
And all by which the charmed, enraptured soul is fed –
Yea very Earth and Heaven – in one name combine;
But speak Shakuntalā and all in one is said!

Based on a translation by E.B. Eastwick

* For a girl to meet her lover by day and not be seen or caught is as difficult as stealing an elephant in the full light of day.

Shakuntalā, India's most celebrated drama, was translated by Monier-Williams (Routledge, 1855), and more recently by Chandra Rajan (Penguin, 1989). This drama exerted considerable influence on the Romantic Movement of the early 19th century.

The play is based in 'another world' – a world of deep and dark forests – in which lives the heroine, Shakuntalā, a 'Child of Nature'. She is the daughter of the sage Viśwāmitra and Menakā, a water nymph; she is brought up by a hermit. One day King Dushyanta comes to the hermitage during a hunt, and persuades her to marry him; later, giving her a ring, he returns to his throne. In due course a son is born, and Shakuntalā sets out with the boy to find his father. During the journey, while bathing, she loses the ring. Without the ring (and because the King is under an enchantment), he does not recognize her. Subsequently the ring is found by a fisherman inside a fish he has caught. Now the King recognizes his wife and publicly proclaims her his Queen. Bharata, his son and heir, becomes the founder of the glorious race of the Bharatas.

The opening of Act IV is thought by many to be especially fine. A pupil of the hermit Kanwa has been asked to ascertain if it is yet dawn; he exclaims in wonder at the scene outside the hermitage:

> Ah! it is daybreak already.
> Here in this quarter, the Moon,
> Lord of the herbs and nightly flowers, is
> Descending to his bed beyond the western hills;
> While there in the east, preceded by Dawn
> His blushing charioteer, the glorious Sun
> Begins his course – and far into the gloom
> Casts the first radiance of his orient beams.
> Hail! you co-eternal orbs that rise to set
> Only to rise again; symbols divine
> Of man's reverses and life's vicissitudes.

And now,

> As the Moon withdraws his light
> Beneath the western sky, the open flower
> Of the pool's moon-lotus (sorrowing his loss)
> Is but a sweet memory of loveliness
> To my bereft sight – even as the bride
> Disconsolately mourns her absent lord,
> Yielding her heart a prey to anxious grief.

Based on the translation by Monier-Williams

Kashyapa was a sage, the son of Marichi, the son of Brahma, and one of the Prajapatis or progenitors of created things. In the drama of *Shakuntalā*, the King finds himself in the sacred grove of the holy Kashyapa:

King

As I look I am filled with awe and wonder.
In such a place as this do saints of earth
Desire to act out their penance; here,
Beneath the shades of everlasting trees
Transplanted from the groves of Paradise,
Inhaling the balm of this air, they need
No other nourishment; here they bathe
In fountains sparkling with golden pollen
Of lilies; here on inlaid slabs of marble,
Deep in their meditation they sit – merged.

The final words of the play are given to the King, who expresses this wish:

May kings reign only for their subjects' weal;
May the divine Saraswatī, the source
Of speech, and goddess of dramatic art,
Be ever honoured by the great and wise;
And may the purple self-existent god
Whose vital Energy pervades all space,
From future transmigrations save my soul.

Based on a translation by Monier-Williams

Bhartṛihari was a Sanskrit poet and grammarian who seems to have lived around the beginnning of the Christian era. He wrote a grammatical treatise, but his *Vākya Pradīya* or *Metrical Maxims on the Philosophy of Syntax*, are better known. They are often cited under the name *Harikarica* and carry an authority second only to the precepts of Pānini. However, it is as a poet that Bhartṛihari has a place in this volume; his *Śataka*, or centuries of verses, are much admired. It should be emphasized that it is tradition that ascribes authorship of all these works to Bhartṛihari but, as with the *Odyssey* and the 'Homer question', it is the work itself that really matters.

The poetry of Bhartṛihari was translated into Dutch in 1651 and into German in 1663; various English translations appeared from the 19th century onwards. An important version, *The Epigrams Attributed to Bhartṛihari* (Bombay, 1948) was based on the collection called *Śatakatrayam*, critically edited by D.D. Kosambi.

Translations and versions differ greatly but, remarkably, the impression left in the mind of the reader by any of them is broadly the same. Even when he is experiencing extreme passion, the poet is somehow detached in his being, witnessing events without losing his philosophic awareness of the pain ever-present beneath the ephemeral pleasure of desire.

In his erotic poetry Bhartṛihari expresses an emotion which transcends the multiplicity of sensuous experience – scents, sounds, colours. He achieves a compression of the various qualities and their rich profusion, into a *rasa* ('flavour, taste'). He so controls language that he conjures the erotic emotion (which is present as magic) in the natural world as well as in women's eyes. He evokes the fragrance of fresh flowers, the scent of breezes laden with sandalwood and nourishing rain; the sound of peacocks and cuckoos. Yet, when he is moralizing, his lines carry the stern sound of the priest-philosopher. Together, they constitute a rich collection of Sanskrit lyric and gnomic poetry. The couplets fully express the conflict experienced by the poet between the profound attraction to sensual beauty and a yearning for liberation from it.

The Sanskrit language, so perfect for spiritual discourse, also offers a magnificent richness to the poet. Bhartṛihari employs elaborate ornamentation (*alamkara*) to achieve superb compression and distillation. He uses figurative devices – punning, metaphor (implied and direct), simile, allegory, synecdoche, antithesis, hyperbole, irony.

Like many poets (and here Donne comes to mind), Bhartṛihari's work divides into three sections, each dealing with a different aspect of the writer's life:

Nīti Śataka:	Worldly concerns and ideals.
Sringāra Śataka:	Erotic moods and analysis of the nature of passion.
Vairāgya Śataka:	Disillusionment with the world.

Here are some verses showing the poet's work under the three headings:

Nīti Śataka

The poet indicates the ideal to which his aspiration is directed:

> Salutation to the deity not definable in time or space;
> Infinite; pure intelligence in incarnate form;
> Who is peace and glory; whose sole essence is self-knowledge.

Caught in the cross-fire of human affections, the poet has had enough:

> The woman there is attracted by another man
> she whom I supposed to be always devoted to me!
> To her another man is attached; meanwhile a
> certain other woman takes pleasure in my doings.
> Fie on her and on him, on the god of
> love, on that woman – and on myself!

★

> When I knew but a little, I was blinded
> by pride – as an elephant is blinded by passion;
> My mind was exalted, and in my
> arrogance I thought I knew all things.
> Then I came into the presence of the wise
> who really know and my pride left me like a departing fever.

★

> Be well disposed towards relatives, liberal
> to inferiors; always hate evil, love
> the good, be obedient to princes,
> honour the wise.

★

Be firm towards enemies, be respectful
to venerable men, deal shrewdly with
women; live after these precepts –
prosper in the world.

Based on a translation by B.H. Wortham (1886)

Sringāra Śataka

Kama, why trouble your hand with the string of your bow?
Cuckoo, you utter your tender notes in vain;
Damsels! no more of your glances, so
Affectionate, artful, arousing desire.
My thought is intent on meditation's nectar,
Tasted at the feet of moon-crested Śiva.

★

Having passed half the night in exhausting
embraces of passionate sport,
Now, on a secluded verandah he
indulges his insatiable thirst with
intoxicating draughts, poured from
a jug held by the languid arm
of his love-wearied mistress.
That man is cursed, who never drinks
this cool water, its crystal stream
scintillating in moonlight!

★

If her breasts are full, her hips
roundly voluptuous, her face
exquisite, why my heart do
you pine in despair?
Earn merit if you covet her –
the longed-for luxuries are
denied a man who has no merit.

★

When the darkness of passion wove
Its web of ignorance about me,
To my mind, a woman seemingly
Entirely filled the expansive world.
But now, blessed with the salve
Of enlightened discernment,
My tranquil sight sees only Brahman
Everywhere pervading the world.

Based on a translation by B.S. Miller (1966)

★

As long as the temple of the body is
well and strong, as long as old age
is far off, as long as the senses are
unimpaired, as long as there is no
diminution of life – so long will

the wise man make great efforts to
gain immortality for himself.
What is the use of digging a well
when the house is already on fire?

Based on a translation by B.H. Wortham (1886)

Vairāgya Śataka

Delightful are the rays of the moon,
delightful the grassy places of the forest;
delightful the society of beloved friends,
delightful the tales of the poets;
delightful the face of one's beloved sparkling
with the tear-drops of anger.
But who cares any more for these delights
when his mind reflects on their uncertainty.

Based on a translation by B.H. Wortham

Vālmīki is the author of the famous Sanskrit epic poem *Rāmāyana*. He is generally considered to be the first poet of India to be known by name. He was not the sole composer of the *Rāmāyana*, but he undoubtedly devised the characteristic metre (*shloka*) used in Indian epics – his own as well as most of the *Mahābhārata*. Good translations of these works abound. Vālmīki is also credited with another epic work, *Yoga-Vasishtha*.

Not surprisingly, much of the poetry of India is an expression of that civilization's powerful philosophical substratum. Here is a stanza by Civārakkiyar (writing just prior to the 10th century AD) a poet of Tamil India:

Within the Five Realized Sounds*
there is the Universe and the Unlimited One;
Within the Five Realized Sounds
there are the Three Primaeval Ones.†

Tulsīdās or Tulasīdās (1532-1623), was the greatest Indian poet of his time. His Hindi version of Vālmīki's *Rāmāyana* is still, today, the most beloved and influential book of North and Central India. His *Rāmcharit-Mānas* (*The Holy Sea of Rāma's Deeds*) has shaped the moral and spiritual life of millions of Hindus. Of the 37 works ascribed to Tulsīdās, only 12 are known with certainty to have been composed by him. His second great work, the *Vinaya-Patrikā* (*The Petition*) reveals in its moving hymns a man whose heart is full of devotion.

Modern Poetry

After the declaration of independence (at midnight on 14/15 August 1947), it was decided that the Constitution would officially recognize 15

* Five syllables constituting the very sacred *mantra śivāyanama* (obeisance to Śiva).

† These are Brahmā the Creator, Viṣṇu the Preserver, and Śiva the Destructor, who form the Hindu Trinity.

languages. Now each state has its own regional language. Hindi (based on Sanskrit and with echoes in many European languages), is the official national language of India. However, English continues to be used in conjunction with Hindi for official purposes. Much modern Indian poetry, perhaps because it is written in English rather than the mother tongue, is sadly uninspired and the English education which brought great benefit to so many is tending to choke the Indian genius.

An exception is **Kamala Das**, a lady born in Malabar, South India, in 1934. Her poetry (she also writes short stories using the pseudonym 'Madhavikutty'), has spontaneity and freshness. In it she reflects her unhappiness with present Indian society. Her poems, while having no formal structure, are impelled by an inner urgency that makes them moving and relevant. The following lines exemplify her realism:

> When I asked for love, not knowing what else to ask
> For, he drew a youth of sixteen into the
> Bedroom and closed the door.

CHINA

The Chinese majority are people of the mainland. In thought, as in the life of their civilization, they did not set out on questing adventures to discover new continents; but they belonged to an ancient civilization which discovered how to make paper, and invented printing. Their strength as human beings lay in their tolerance and rationality. They had a potency in their reflective analysis that revealed deep levels of human emotion, close reasoning, and philosophic subtlety.

For the European poet the relationship between man and woman is of supreme importance and mystery. For the Chinese it is something commonplace and obvious, prompted by the need of the body; it is not for the satisfaction of the emotion, which is achieved by and reserved for friendship. Culture is essentially a product of the metropolitan and contains a strong element of the Confucian insistence on public service.

The oldest Chinese poetry anthology, the *Book of Odes*, is so full of difficulty as a text that the Chinese themselves have not read the originals without the aid of glosses and commentaries down the centuries. Poetry later grew more simple, but rich in simile and metaphor. Eventually, the later Chinese poetry was diminished and devalued by a great weight of classical allusion and artificiality. Poets were recommended to use figures which became ever more extravagant, for example, moon was 'silver dish', sun was 'lantern dragon'.

The poetry of any civilization inevitably uses the chief and obvious characteristics of the language in which it occurs. For instance, English poetry is largely based on rhyme-accentuation (stress) and alliteration, whereas in Chinese poetry before the 6th century much use was made of rhyme and length of line as structural features. An important element of the Chinese language, which assumed increasing importance in poetry after the 5th century, is *tone*. There are four tones which derive from two distinctive operations applied to the sound of the syllables:

The Four Tones of Classical Chinese

1 Voice remains level
2 Voice rises
3 Voice falls
4 Voice is abruptly arrested

For centuries, China closed its doors and windows to the outside world and, as a result, its civilization was based on one of the most remarkable mental outlooks ever to express itself. It might be termed the 'Chinese mind'. Because the Western world with its Renaissance, science, and medicine were rigorously excluded, the resulting Chinese view of the world seems almost impenetrable to the Western mind.

The Chinese language and script were codified under the First Universal Emperor. Essential features of the Chinese mind are:

1 A synthetic and concrete (almost feminine) apprehension of reality.
2 A strong distaste for analytical, inductive and deductive reasoning.
3 An aversion for abstraction and a consequent non-attunement to generalities.
4 Attunement to the 'singular' and the unusual.

An indication of the subtlety of Chinese as a language may be gained from the fact that there is no concept of, or term for, 'old person' generally. Instead, a variety of expressions differentiate the detail found in life. For instance, the word *k'i* designates an undernourished old man; *k'ao* the asthmatic, *lao* the over seventy, etc.

The emotion expressed by the Chinese in their poetry is timeless and relevant to any civilization:

Li Fu-Jen

The sound of her silk skirt has stopped;
On the marble pavement dust grows;
Her empty room is cold and still;
Fallen leaves are piled against the doors;
Longing for that lovely lady
How can I bring my aching heart to rest?

Wu-ti (157-87 BC), 6th Emperor of the Han dynasty

That poem was written by Wu-ti after the death of his beloved mistress, Li Fu-Jen. So unbearable was his grief that he summoned wizards from all parts of China, in the hope that they could put him in touch with her spirit. Here is a further poem by Wu-ti:

People hide their love

Who says
That it's by my desire,
This separation, this living so far from you?
My dress still smells of the lavender you gave:
My hand still holds the letter you sent.
Round my waist I wear a double sash:
I dream that it binds us both with a same-heart knot.
Did not you know that people hide their love,
Like a flower that seems too precious to be picked?

Li Po (or **Li T'ai-Po**) (AD 701-62) was born well to the west of China, which brought him under the influence of central Asian languages and cultures. Morally he was of dubious character, but those who met him were fascinated by his personality and instantly felt themselves to be in the presence of an extraordinary genius. His contemporaries considered his talent to have been bestowed from some supernatural origin, but to us (in translation) his poetry speaks with a direct, simple voice. A poem well known by the world's many widely dispersed Chinese expatriates is this account of night thoughts:

Before my bed
there is bright moonlight
So that it seems
like frost on the ground:

Lifting my head
I watch the bright moon;
Lowering my head
I dream that I'm home.

Translated by Arthur Cooper

Tu Fu (AD 712-70) came of a family distinguished for its service to the State. He was born at Shao-ling, not far from the capital of Shensi, a mountainous province of central China. He was friendly with Li Po and together they are traditionally regarded as the greatest poets of China.

The more popular poet is Tu Fu. He wrote directly from his experience of civil war with compassion and realism; excellent translations are available of these poems. As with most Chinese, his powers of observation of the natural world were clear and acute. Here, from *Nine Short Songs*, is an exquisite word-picture:

The catkins line the lanes,
making white carpets,
And leaves on lotus streams
spread like green money:

Pheasants root bamboo shoots,
 nobody looking,
While ducklings on the sands
 sleep by their mothers.

Translated by Arthur Cooper

The following poem shows that the separation of those who are in love, and their discretion in concealment, is timeless:

P'u-P'u Sa Man

Glimmer of flowers, a shrouded moon and shallow mist for cover;
A perfect moment this to steal away and join her lover.

Down scented paths in stockinged feet she goes,
Clasped in her hands her gold-embroidered shoes.

The south side of the painted hall their tryst;
She leans one instant quivering on his breast:
'So seldom can I come to you, my love,
That all the love you ask of me, I give!'

Li Yu (AD 937-978)

Exquisite descriptions enhance the tenderness of this next poem:

P'u-Shao Nien Yu

Knife from Ping as bright as water,
 Salt from Wu surpassing snow,
An orange rare her slender fingers tear.
 Newly warmed embroidered curtains,
 Incense from the dragon burner;
Playing the sheng they face each other there.

 Her low voice softly asks
 'Where are you going to spend the night?
They've called the third watch from the city wall.
 Your horse will slip, the frost's so thick;

 You'd do much better not to go;
There's hardly anyone about at all.'

Chou Pang Yen (AD 1057-1121)

Here is a description of shyness from another age:

A glimpse into a courtyard

A green bird
With a grape in its beak
Alights
On the metal well-edge.
A pretty maiden,

Startled,
Runs indoors,

And does not even dare
to lift her curtain
And look out!

P'Eng Chien P'u

A succinct, evocative simplicity is the essence of this poem:

Nightfall

The night comes on;
The river grows dark.
The peasants come in slowly
From the fields.
In a hut hid deep
Amid the towering trees
Glows a tiny flame
To guide a husband home.

T'ang Dynasty (AD 618-905)

The heaviness of time hanging over the sick person is beautifully expressed in this next poem:

Illness

Sad, sad – lean with long illness;
Monotonous, monotonous – day and nights pass.
The summer trees have clad themselves in shade;
The autumn tree-lichen already houses the dew.
The eggs that lay in nest when I took to bed
Have changed to birds and flown away.
The larva hidden in its hole
Has hatched into a cricket, sitting on the tree.
The Four Seasons go on for ever and ever:
In all Nature nothing stops to rest
Even for a moment. Only the sick man's heart
Deep down still aches as of old!

Po Chu-i (AD 772-846)

The poignancy of separation is timelessly expressed in this poem:

Winter Night

My bed is so empty that I keep waking up:
As the cold increases, the night-wind begins to blow.
It rustles the curtains, making a noise like the sea:
Oh that those were waves which could carry me back to you!

The following lines show acute observation of human behaviour under stress:

The Rejected Wife

Entering the Hall, she meets the new wife:
Leaving the gate, she encounters her husband.
Words demur: she does not manage to say anything:

She presses her hands together and hesitates.
Agitates moon-like fan – sheds tears like pearls –
Realizes she loves him as much as ever:
That her present pain will never have an end.

Yuan-ti (AD 508-554)

Here are two delightful pieces written by the poetess, **Tzu Yeh** of the Chin Dynasty (AD 265-419):

To him I love

Do you not see
That you and I
Are as the branches
Of one tree?
With your rejoicing
Comes my laughter;
With your sadness
Start my tears.
Love,
Could life be otherwise
With you and me?

*

Through your window

I watched your red lips move
In song,
And your jade-like fingers pluck
The stringed lute.

Love urged me on –
To enter,
Take you in my arms,
Make you my own.

But I blushed, I trembled,
I dared not move –
And now
It is too late!

JAPAN

In the early period (about AD 2 to 5) poetry tended to be concerned with: the four seasons; the affections; allegorical and occasional poems. Down the centuries, Japanese poetry displays certain recurring characteristics:

- a gentle melancholy;
- unrequited or waning love;
- sad lessons of transience found in nature;
- the quiet pleasures of solitude.

Japanese poetry differs very largely from anything we are used to in the West; it has no rhyme or alliteration, and – as we understand it – little, if any, rhythm. For many years the only form of verse known to the Japanese was the tanka. *Tanka* verse has 5 lines and 31 syllables, arranged in the measures:

5 – 7 – 5 – 7 – 7

One of the most popular anthologies of Japanese classical poetry is *A Hundred Verses from Old Japan* (Hyakunin Isshu). Collected during the Kamakura era in the 13th century, it contains love poems and so-called 'picture poems' which describe scenes from the natural world in tanka form. These poems are widely known by the people of Japan today. The translations offered here are based on the work of Heihachiro Honda (1956).

> Of all the seasons of the year (here in the mountain hamlets) it is winter which is so bare, so forlorn, so drear – because men and grass have become rare …
>
> Minamoto-no Mune-Yuki (died AD 940)

★

> On this brilliant sunlit spring day, the cherry blossoms
> are the cause of pain.
> Why do they not remain longer on the boughs in May?
> But no – as usual – the showers of petals descend
> like rain …
>
> Ki-no Tomonori (died AD 864)

★

> Here deep in the forest, rich with its red autumn
> colouring,
> I can hear the plaintive cries of deer
> wandering on the soft carpet of fallen leaves
> – and the autumn seems very sad …
>
> Saru Maru, a Shinto Official

★

> From here where I sit, I view the sight of Mount
> Fuji's sublime summit, above the clouds,
> All covered with the white snow that is falling there,
> now …
>
> Yamabe-no-Akahito (lived about AD 700)

The Emperor Tenchi reigned from AD 668 to 671. His capital was Otsu, not far from Kyoto, and he is chiefly remembered for his kindness and benevolence.

> The sleeves of my robe are wet with the dew of night
> Because I have to sleep in this badly thatched cottage;
> I sleep, guarding the fields of grain bright with their
> ripe autumn colour –
> So that they can be reaped by the farmers!
>
> Tenchi Tenno

★

O friendly fisher man, tell my dear folks at
home that it is for them that I set out alone
across the vast sea
To a group of islands very, very far from here.

Takamura, Privy Councillor

★

How the people of the village will greet me I know not;
But from this old and well-loved plum tree,
the fragrant flowers greet me
Graciously, as they have always done – all
down the years!

Kino Tsura-Yuki (AD 884-946)

★

You cannot imagine how it has irked me
To be lying awake in bed thinking, unable to sleep
For the whole of this night – which seems as
long as the tail of one of those mountain-pheasants
in the wood!

Kaki-no-Moto (?- AD 737)

The writer was a foundling, adopted by Abaye. He was picked up at the foot of a persimmon tree (*Kaki* in Japanese), from which he got his name. After his death he was deified as a God of Poetry.

Just as the cascading stream descends ever downwards
across the face of Mount Tsukuba, where it falls into
deep pools – there to be held fast,
So profound love is holding me securely in its thrall …

The Retired Emperor Yozei (died AD 949)

★

She promised me she would come to me here – soon;
I eagerly and impatiently await her
Yet all that has arrived so far, is the silvery moon;
No sight of her at all.

The Priest Sosei (born AD 850)

The writer's real name was Sadakata Fujiwara; he died AD 932.

O my dear, if you knew how much I love you
You would not fail to come to me.
Is there *no* prayer of mine which could move you
To come and meet me here – secretly.

Sanjo Udaijin

★

You might well learn to imitate the cockerel's cry,
To fool the watchman so that you can pass the
barriers before sunrise,
But then – how to reach *me* across the palace
barrier-gate; what power of yours can such a
result devise?

Sei Sho-nagon

The Lady Sei (Sho-nagon being merely a title) was the authoress of *Makura-no-Soshi* ('a story book to keep under one's pillow'). She was a lady-in-waiting at court, until she retired to a convent in the year AD 1000.

Let him forget me if he so pleases,
But he did utter a vow before the gods.
It is *their* anger he now has to appease,
And it is for that (on his behalf) I am worrying now.

The Lady Ukon

★

If man and woman did not contrive to meet in the first place,
Sorrow would not be so all-pervasive!
Why do we always think the love-tryst so very sweet
When it causes so much grief to all and sundry?

Chunagon Asatada (died in AD 961)

The lady who wrote the following poem was the daughter of Masamine Oye and the wife of Michidasa Tachibana, Governor of the Province of Izumi – hence her name. The verse was addressed to her husband or lover just before her death.

My sands of life are running low
So grant me now, this sole request,
To see you once before I leave,
That by you I will be remembered,
When all alone I take my rest.

The Lady Izumi Shikibu

During the Muromachi Period (1335-1573), although no great poets appeared it was the era when *renga* (long poems composed by several persons) became extremely popular. The practice grew of holding poetry parties at which amateur poets shared in the making of these long poems.

The Yedo Period (1603-1868) saw a renaissance of national literature and the emergence of the greatest haiku poets. *Haiku* are poems of 17 syllables (14 syllables shorter than the ordinary tanka poems); they are set out in three lines containing 5, 7 and 5 syllables respectively. The earliest writer of these poems is said to have been Yamazaki Sokan (1445-1534), but until the advent of Matsuo **Bashō** (1643-94), haiku had not been considered comparable with tanka. Bashō demonstrated its potential and, moreover, unlike the tanka for which a preparatory training was required, almost anyone with a smattering of education could compose poems that resembled haiku. It is said that even farmers had their poetry parties.

Bashō made pilgrimages all over the country as a wandering priest (he had served a Zen Buddhist master), and it was during these journeys that he composed some of his finest poems.

Here is a haiku demonstrating one of Bashō's glimpses of man's mystical oneness with nature.

Amidst the grassland
Sings a skylark
Free and disengaged from all things.

Here is a winter haiku:

How cold –
Freshly washed
White leeks. Bashō

A leading poet of the late 18th century, Yosa Buson (1716-84), was also a celebrated painter. Here are two haiku, which demonstrate his pictorial and lyrical skills, and his delicate sensitivity:

Grasses are misty,
The waters silent –
A tranquil evening.

★

Butterfly in my hand –
As if it were a spirit
Unearthly, insubstantial. Buson

Naito Joso (1662-1704), who was first a samurai, then a priest, joined Bashō's group in 1689 and, after the master's death, mourned him for three years.

The sleet falls
As if coming through the bottom
of loneliness. Joso

Kobayashi Issa (1763-1827) was the first son of a farmer in Shinano (now Niigata prefecture). When he was 14 years of age he went to Edo (Tokyo) where he studied haiku. His natural images are full of down-to-earth simple realism:

Sparrows
Playing hide-and-seek
Among the tea blossoms.

★

Sleeping, waking,
And then giving a great yawn,
The cat goes out for lovemaking.

Issa

Having contracted tuberculosis in his youth and become an invalid, Masaoka Shiki (1867-1902) devoted his life to literature – essays, haiku, and tanka. He initiated a major reform of haiku by advocating the writing of *shasei* (sketches from life). He began the celebrated haiku magazine *Hototogisu* ('cuckoo').

A spring day –
A long line of footprints
On the sandy beach. Shiki

Born in China, where his father was in the diplomatic corps, Nakamura Kusatao (1901-83) became a contributor to the journal *Hototogisu*, founded by Masaoka Shiki. He later established his own magazine, *Banryoku*.

On the winter sea
Seagulls float
Like fallen leaves. Kusatao

Senryu, a humorous version of haiku, also attained great popularity during this period. The form was originated by Karai Hachiemon (1718-90). Two typical examples are:

Dancing girls
Are always
Nineteen years old.

★

Crockery cupboard
Empty, sink completely full –
His wife is away!

The translations in this section are by Yuzuru Miura (1991).

For fuller background information relating to haiku and senryu, *see* the author's *Breathing With The Mind* and *Awareness Beyond Mind* (details in Bibliography).

RUSSIA

Aleksandr Sergeyevich **Pushkin** (1799-1837) is Russia's greatest poet; his standing in his own country is equivalent to Shakespeare's in England. In addition he was a dramatist, novelist, and short-story writer who almost single-handedly created a classical literary heritage for Russian writers, producing the first good examples of work in almost every major genre.

Pushkin was descended in his father's line from an ancient noble family. On his mother's side he was a great-great-grandson of an Abyssinian Negro, Gannibal, who served under Peter the Great. Born in Moscow, he graduated from the Lyceum in 1817 and entered the Ministry of Foreign Affairs. His *Ode to Liberty* (1820) resulted in his exile to southern Russia, although he continued to hold office. He was finally dismissed from public service for his liberality of views. Later he was mortally wounded in a duel.

Among his works are *Ruslan and Ludmilla* (1820), *Boris Godunov* (published in 1831), *Eugene Onegin* (1832), *The Queen of Spades* (1834), and *The Captain's Daughter* (1836). Several of his works inspired operas by major Russian composers – Glinka, Moussorgsky and Tchaikovsky.

It is said, even by Russian-speakers, that Pushkin's lines sound 'flat' and uninteresting in translation, but in the Russian even quite simple lines carry nobility and power. Pushkin seems to exhibit a determination to be Byronic, Horation, Romantic – even to be 'French'. These stylistic threads in his manner and expression, together with the economy and agility of his thought, coalesce in literature which is as sophisticated as any work in European literature. In reputation Puskin's poetry *is* language; it essentializes Russia the nation. The following lines carry something of the indigenous Russian fatalism:

I've lived to bury my desires,
And see my dreams corrode with rust;
Now all that's left are fruitless fires
That burn my empty heart to dust.

Struck by the storms of cruel Fate
My crown of summer bloom is sere;
Alone and sad I watch and wait,
And wonder if the end is near.

As conquered by the last cold air,
When winter whistles in the wind,
Alone upon a branch that's bare
A trembling leaf is left behind.

Translated by Maurice Baring

These lines are among those that were set as the celebrated 'Letter Scene' in Tchaikovsky's opera *Eugene Onegin*:

Tatyana's Letter

That I am writing you this letter
Will tell you all; and you are free
Now to despise me; and how better,
I wonder, could you punish me?

★

Why came you? why to us? alone,
In this forgotten hamlet hidden,
I never should have known you, known
This bitterness of pangs unbidden.
And these emotions would have slept,
My soul its quiet ignorance kept:
– So, in due season, might I find,
Who knows? a husband to my mind;
Have been a true wife – to another,
A pious honourable Mother.

★

No more of this; I dread to read it;
Yet though I sink with fear and shame,
Your honour keeps me safe; I plead it,
And to it boldly put my name.

Translated by Oliver Elton

These verses by Alexey **Tolstoy** (1817-75) deftly catch the essence of Mother Russia for its many exiles:

Land of mine, where I was bred,
  Horses wildly flying,
Eagles screeching overhead,
  On the fields wolves crying!

Hail, dear land of my delight,
  Pinewoods thickly growing,
Nightingales that sing at night,
  Steppe and cloud and blowing!

Translated by C.M. Bowra

With characteristic compassion and the poet's eye for detail, Tolstoy writes six stanzas on the indomitable spirit of some passing shackled prisoners; here are the first and final verses:

The Convicts

The sun on the steppes is sinking,
And gold is the distant grass.
The convict's fetters are clinking
On the dusty road as they pass.

★

Of freedom and steppes they are singing;
They sing of an untamed will.
The day grows darker, and ringing
On the road the fetters clink still.

Translated by C.M. Bowra

Boris **Pasternak** (1890-1960), Russian poet and novelist, was awarded the Nobel Prize for Literature in 1958. He renounced it following the acrimonious reaction aroused by the award in the USSR, where critics and political leaders rightly perceived the direct connection between the prize and the publication in Italy (1957) of his 'traitorous' novel *Doctor Zhivago*. His work has a robustness of spirit, a resilience, and a sharp freshness that will ensure his survival as a world writer. Here are some lines of his poetry:

This winter season of the year
I live near Moscow. Foul or fair
The day – in frost or snow – I go
By train to deal with my affairs.

★

Disposed in every sort of posture,
In little knots, in quiet nooks,
The children and the young sit still,
Engrossed, like experts, reading books.

The poem continues until the passengers emerge from the Moscow underground station into the silver-grey mist of the city:

And crowding to the exits, going
Their way, our youth and future spread
The freshness of wild cherry soap
And the smell of honeyed gingerbread.

On Early Trains (1941), translated by E.M. Kayden

Here from *Doctor Zhivago's Poetry*:

The plaudits die. I come on stage
Again. Leaning against the doorpost,
I strain to see afar in time
The fate that awaits our present age.

★

I love Thy large design, and I
Would gladly act this role of woe.
But there's another play on stage;
Then spare me now, and let me go.

Hamlet, Translated by E.M. Kayden

Having survived the trauma of the Second World War and the post-Stalinist thaw of 1954-56, Pasternak ends his poem *Hail All Things Glad* (1957) with a vigorous optimism:

O World, O Life, immortal Time!
I will now in secret adoration
Live, trembling, faithful in thy service
With tears of joy and exaltation.

Translated by E.M. Kayden

Among the best-known poets of the younger generation is Evgeny **Yevtushenko** (b1933). After early success, he is now considered by some critics to have been wildly over-praised. His work might be termed middlebrow poetry, fresh but not strikingly innovatory. Yevtushenko was born in a remote town called Zima on the trans-Siberian railway. He was of mixed Ukranian, Russian, and Tartar blood, and grew up amid the impressions of a peasant family. He begins a long autobiographical poem called *Zima Junction* with this verse:

As we get older we get honester,
that's something.
And these objective changes correspond
like a language to me and my mutations.
If the way I see you now is not the way
in which we saw you once, if in you
what I see now is new
it was by self-discovery I found it.
I realize that my twenty years might be

less than mature: but for a reassessment:
what I said and ought not to have said,
and ought to have said and was silent.

The poet concludes this lengthy revealing and reflective poem with these lines:

Walk with a cold pride.
Utterly ahead
wild attentive eyes
head flicked by the rain-wet
green needles of the pine,
eyelashes that shine
with tears and with thunders.
Love people.
Love entertains its own discrimination.
Have me in mind, I shall be watching.
You can return to me.
Now go.

In this next poem, Yevtushenko catches the unheeding exuberance and breathlessness of young lovers meeting:

Waiting

My love will come
will fling open her arms and fold me in them,
will understand my fears, observe my changes.
In from the pouring dark, from the pitch night
without stopping to bang the taxi door
she'll run upstairs through the decaying porch
burning with love and love's happiness,
she'll run dripping upstairs, she won't knock,
will take my head in her hands,
and when she drops her overcoat on a chair,
it will slide to the floor in a blue heap!

Irina **Ratushinskaya** (b1954) is a poet who spent three years in a Gulag 'strict regime' labour camp at Barashevo in Mordovia. A Soviet judge called her 'a danger to the State' and in March 1983, one day before her 29th birthday, she was sentenced to seven years' hard labour, to be followed by five years of internal exile. Her crime – writing poetry. Many of her prison-camp poems were first written with burnt matchsticks on bars of soap, then memorized. (It was a moving experience to hear the poet reciting some of these deeply remembered poems in London on 23 April 1991.)

Irina was born in Odessa where she gained a degree in physics in 1976. Although a scientist by profession, she had written poetry from childhood. Despite an atheist upbringing, she joined the Russian Orthodox Church. She married the human rights activist Igor Geraschenko in 1979.

Here are the opening lines from her poem *Passer-by*:

Passer-by, don't drink the water in this town –
Its savour, with the taste of summer,
Will make you fall mortally in love!
Don't lay your head down – the years will stop.
You have not completed the Path –
Remember that.

From a poem written after the first arrest:

The Sparrows of Butyrki

Now even the snow has grown sad –
Let your overwhelmed reason go,
And let's smoke our cigarettes through the air-vent,
Let's at least set the smoke free.
A sparrow flies up –
And looks at us with searching eye:
'Share your crust with me!'
And in honourable fashion you share it with him.
The sparrows know
Whom to ask for bread.

From the long poignant poem *I will Live and Survive*:

I will live and survive and be asked:
How they slammed my head against a trestle,
How I had to freeze at nights,
How my hair started to turn grey ...
And brush away the encroaching shadow.

★

And I'll be asked: 'Doesn't it hurt you to remember?'
Not being deceived by my outward flippancy.

★

And I will tell of the best people in all the earth,
The most tender, but also the most invincible,
How they said farewell, how they went to be tortured,
How they waited for letters from their loved ones.
And I'll be asked: what helped us to live
When there were neither letters nor any news – only walls,
And the cold of the cell, and the blather of official lies,
And the sickening promises made in exchange for betrayal.
And I will tell of the first beauty
I saw in captivity.
A frost-covered window!

★

A cast pattern – none more beautiful could be dreamt!

★

Such a gift can only be received once,
And perhaps it is only needed once.

30 November 1983

Sufi Poetry

The adherents of Islamic Sufism (Islamic mysticism) were, originally, interested chiefly in ascetic practices and moral discipline. Later, there were other followers whose principal aim was to attain experiences of ecstasy. The word *suf* refers to the coarse wool worn by ascetics. The Sufis believed that by annihilation of their egos they could make a place for God and (by a transformational process) could, in a sense, *become one with* God. Their ascetic training and mystical contemplation aspired towards a purification of consciousness which would dissolve the dualism of me (subject) and God – or the world (object). They therefore often refer in their writing to 'union with God' and even being 'merged with or becoming God'.

Sufi poetry reflected the mystical union of form and substance, in language of elegant lyrical expression identical in style with temporal love poetry. By employing imagery of this nature, Sufis were more able to express poetically the Divine Unity; they presented a symbolic portrait of the Beloved object which constituted the goal of the wayfarer's quest.

Such images and metaphors more readily penetrated and impressed the heart than abstract philosophical terms. This gave to the Sufi a profound and more immediate sense of the Attributes and Powers of God. By using love allusions and metaphors, Sufis have effectively conveyed their spiritual states to others.

These metaphors have the further advantage of allowing Sufis to protect the secrets of their inward journey from falling into the hands of the uninitiated. This ensures that only adepts with experience of spiritual states – in practice – can fully comprehend what is being expressed in symbolic terms.

Dispel all doubts
and you'll be a seer
If within everything
you contemplate God's Visage. Hāfiz

In this state the adept sees only God – everywhere:

There's but one Essence
amongst all these essences
but one Name exists
under all these names. Maghrebi

The world is but form of
the Beloved – its Reality.
Look to the Reality,
and *everything* is the Beloved. Sirus Izadi

'What is ecstasy?' the Sufi master was asked. He replied, 'It is the illumination of one's innermost consciousness by an influx of inspiration, which the spirit absorbs; its fragrance reaches the heart.'

The poet Hāfiz expresses the Sufi's approach to others:

> Where's the openhanded man of magnanimity
> Who from his banquet of ecstasy would bestow
> A draught upon one betided by grief,
> and slake an ever-languishing thirst for wine?
>
> Hāfiz

The Sufi was drunk with Love of the Divine. Not for him the epithet, 'God is Love'; but rather, 'Love is God!'

Poetry's Infrastructure

This brief survey of Oriental poetry has indicated that themes are universal because mankind is the universal human being writ large. Poetry, is by its nature, an expression of universals.

The infrastructure of poetry is revealed by an investigation of substance and form and it is this that is addressed in the next section.

12
Substance and Form

> Not by wisdom do poets make what they compose, but by a gift of nature and an inspiration similar to that of the diviners and the oracles.
>
> Plato's *Apology*, 4th Century BC

Aristotle's Treatise on Poetry

POETRY WAS under scrutiny by evaluative analysts from the earliest times. One of the first great minds to interpret the role of poetry and consider its nature was Aristotle (384-322 BC), who was born at Stagira in northern Greece, the son of a physician attending the King of Macedonia. At the age of 18 he went to Athens, where he studied under Plato for some 20 years. After this he was tutor to Alexander the Great, a position he held for seven years. In the year 335, then aged 50, he returned to Athens and founded a school which met outside the city, in the Lyceum.

Aristotle's treatise on poetry, known as *Poetics*, was fundamental in giving direction to the formal, structural organization of literature and has always been highly influential. It is descriptive rather than prescriptive, since he is mainly concerned with the methods and work of acknowledged masters such as Homer and Sophocles. Aristotle distinguishes tragedy, epic, and comedy as the chief kinds of poetry. He discerns the origin of poetry in the instinctive love of imitation, and traces the special origins and development of tragedy and comedy. The *Poetics*, in its fragmentary state, resembles notes for lectures rather than a treatise prepared for publication. Its authoritative dominance in European thought from the 16th to the 18th centuries seems to have two causes:

- its importance to such Roman writers as Horace;
- the fact that its rediscovery at the end of the 15th century (when the Renaissance was at its height) lent further emphasis to the feeling that the spirit of Greek and Roman writers was the essence of civilization.

Aristotle brought to the masterpieces of Greek literature an analytical acumen, possibly unsurpassed in the history of literary criticism. His dispassionate analysis of the best examples of Greek art, above all Greek poetry, resulted in his principal idea that the good work of art is a unity of interdependent interacting parts, existing for the sake of the whole. For Aristotle, poetry 'imitates in a universal fashion'. Art is not nature, because art makes connections between things; and the concern of poetry (as with philosophy) is not with things but with meanings. Poetry lets things speak for themselves.

The *Poetics* remains one of the most outstanding works of European thought. Critics still use Aristotle's terminology in classifying poetic forms; his theory of art as imitation (different from Plato's) is still the starting point of much aesthetic discussion; such terms as *harmatia* for the element in human nature which makes it vulnerable to tragedy, *peripeteia* for the reversal of fortunes common in tragic narrative, and *katharsis* for the effect of tragedy on the mind of the audience, continue to serve us well in their succinct aptness.

The Structure of Poetry

All art forms have an inherent structure, however minimal. Music has its integrated notation; painting its composition. To enjoy these things superficially it is not necessary to understand composition, but for fuller appreciation some knowledge of compositional structure is essential. In poetry grammatical structure is sometimes deliberately manipulated to give an unusual pattern to the line or to achieve a rhyme. At least three levels of structure inform a poem:

- sounds and syllables,
- formal construction,
- contrived configuration of language and special effects.

The structure of poetry proceeds from the formal arrangement of its words and the development of its theme in images, figures of speech and, in short, every conceivable legitimate variation that ingenious minds can wrest from language. A question that must be addressed is: Does structure in poetry matter? Since much contemporary poetry has dubious poetic structure, it might be instructive to consult a modern expert.

George **MacBeth** (b1932), who obtained First Class Honours in Classical Greats at New College, Oxford and was joint winner of the first Geoffrey Faber Memorial Award for poetry in 1964, was a producer of programmes about literature and the arts for BBC radio, a poet, an editor of anthologies, and much more. Mr MacBeth, in *Poetry For Today* (1984), says in his introductory section 'How to Write a Poem':

> The most important thing to say about writing
> a poem is that it doesn't need to be a poem.

He goes on: 'The easiest way to turn a piece of prose into a poem is simply to take something already written and arrange the ends of the line and the spaces between the lines in a new way. It can be any way you like.' He continues with two suggestions:

The most important thing to
Say about writing a poem
is that is doesn't need
to be a poem. Write

what you want to write
and then make it a
poem later. It may even
be a poem already.

MacBeth then offers an alternative layout:

The most important
thing to
say about
writing a
poem
is that it
doesn't
need to be
a poem. Write
what you
want to
write, and
then make
it …

The question is, does our expert's sentence rearrangement really turn prose into poetry? This approach, carried to extremes, can make 'poetry' look like the following American example:

2

But there could be just so much
heat if he were himself
a
system
just so much loss of
heat a certain maximum
death as if his entropic increase
were the fictive need of a fictive past
imagined
movement in his standing
still
something
affixing itself
in a precise measure
to the available niche
of a quantized
orbit as if a man weeping
could not
hear

himself
  above the howl of wind   the rattling
        window pane
  but knew the sound
      was there
        a steady static
      posited ...

Curve Away from Stillness, John Allman

In these 'poems', published in the 1980s, Allman dispenses with punctuation and soon fills a book with his zigzags of descending broken lines. It is reminiscent of Dodgson's more restrained and witty use of the device, as Alice contemplates the Mouse's tale (tail) in *Alice in Wonderland*.

If visual arrangement alone seems insufficient to assure us that we are addressing poetry, what else should we look for? Dylan Thomas, writing in *The Adelphi* (1934), reminds us that a poem is more than appearance:

> Too much poetry today is flat on the page, a black and white thing of words created by intelligences that no longer think it necessary for a poem to be read and understood by anything but the eyes.

Poetry is a powerful medium in which to give utterance to ideas. The composition will be memorable if the language used is expressive and the images clear, systematically arranged and well articulated. That is, the speech sounds and words must be put together in a properly connected way. When this is done well, meaning should not be obscured by the form, structure or arrangement of the poem. With these points in mind, here is an example from the work of Dylan Thomas:

I, in my intricate image

1

I, in my intricate image, stride on two levels,
Forged in man's minerals, the brassy orator
Laying my ghost in metal,
The scales of this twin world tread on the double,
My half ghost in armour hold hard in death's corridor,
To my man-iron sidle.

Beginning with doom in the bulb, the spring unravels,
Bright as her spinning-wheels, the colic season
Worked on a world of petals;
She threads off the sap and needles, blood and bubble
Casts to the pine roots, raising man like a mountain
Out of the naked entrail.

Beginning with doom in the ghost, and the springing marvels,
Image of images, my metal phantom
Forcing forth through the harebell,

My man of leaves and the bronze root, mortal, unmortal,
I, in my fusion of rose and male motion,
Create this twin miracle.

In responding to some of Thomas's poetry we have to seek his argument and message beneath the torrent of words. Moreover, we are required to *contribute* meaning to the piece; or to supply at least a connotation, even though wholeness of meaning appears to be absent from the poem itself. Yet, with Thomas's work, as with that of many modern poets, a kind of meaning hovers tantalizingly close. Sometimes it seems that poets sacrifice clarity of meaning for seductive word combinations. The delicious ambiguity in poetry that teases our intellect, but awakens insight, is quite another matter.

Prose in a Verse-Play

It is perhaps relevant at this point to consider what determines the playwright's decision to use verse or prose in a particular application. In Elizabethan poetic drama, major and well-born characters tend to be given verse to speak, whereas the minor or lowly born are likely to be given prose lines. But there is enough inconsistency in this for it not to be regarded as a rule, particularly in Shakespeare.

It is significant that Falstaff (in *Henry IV, Part 2*), although crucial to the play, speaks no verse; nor does Prince Hal when in his company. Styan (1965) has suggested that this is intended to be an indication of *convention* and *feeling* in a particular scene. Prose brings the hearer down to earth and the audience was expected to make the connection with these changes of nuance and theme.

Here is an example of rhyme, spoken by Capulet in *Romeo and Juliet*. In an earlier scene he had acknowledged his reluctance to lose his only child to marriage; he is resolved, finally, to respect her own wishes:

But woo her, gentle Paris, get her heart,
My will to her consent is but a part;
An she agree, within her scope of choice
Lies my consent and fair according voice.

Romeo and Juliet, Act I, Scene ii

Rhyming is not always the most effective way to achieve an effect. For example, when Hamlet harangues the visiting players, he achieves maximum contrast with the old actor's later speech by addressing them in prose:

... with this special observance, that you o'erstep not the modesty of nature; for anything so overdone is from the purpose of playing, whose end, both at the first and now, was and is, to hold, as 'twere, the mirror up to nature.

Hamlet, Act III, Scene ii

In *Murder in the Cathedral* T.S. Eliot created a choreutic language mode for the Women of Canterbury, using 20th-century rhythms of speaking. His development of a verse-form, able to accommodate both rhetorical and colloquial idioms, is flexible and dramatically relevant. An example occurs when, after the murder, we hear the concluding words of the chorus:

> Clear the air! clean the sky! wash the wind! take the stone from the stone,
> take the skin from the arm, take the muscle from the bone, wash the brain,
> wash the soul, wash them wash them!

The almost boundless ingenuity of the poet's use of language stems from the versatility of words, but words must be precisely ordered if they are to be obedient to the poet's will. Dylan Thomas, in his exuberance, sometimes brings expression perilously close to verbal anarchy; a closer examination of word order will show why.

Words In Their Place

It is all too easy to forget the primacy of the *word* and the fact that words are not merely the names of things. A single word is an extension of human perception and has the power to organize how we think and feel about something. Key words can dominate a whole sentence, leaping out of the page and subordinating the rest. Conversely, a person may inadvertently fail to read a significant word and the overall meaning is changed. The Greek word *logos* is defined as 'word, idea or speech'; it thus combines and unites elements to give the very essence of the word. A precisely selected word does three things: generates a sound; condenses perception; and symbolizes experience.

The linear successive order which characterizes much language is known as discursiveness and can seem a limitation on writing and speech. The Imagists sought to counter this by using little or no punctuation and by eliminating prepositions. Symbolism affects us first through associations deep in our memory, for example: 'light', 'water', 'autumn'. A sentence is a happening or process and, in purist terms, 'expresses a complete thought'. The way a writer structures sentences is fundamental to style. Moreover, as Eliot says, 'Not only every great poet, but every genuine though lesser poet, fulfils once for all some possibility of the language, leaving one possibility less for his successors.'

Word

The word bites like a fish.
Shall I throw it back, free
Arrowing to that sea
Where thoughts lash tail and fin?
Or shall I put it in
To rhyme upon a dish?

Stephen Spender

There is no place in poetry for the despotic style of intellectual rhetoric; no place for the finite, quantitative terms of the science academic. The best poetry is a highly intelligent statement of structured language, charged with thought and feeling. The manner in which words are arranged structurally and contextually is fundamental to the substance of poetry. Planned configuration, and other special effects, occur in prose, but it is the way they are employed in poetry that produces the felicity and grace of good verse. A simple way to obtain a rhyme or a special effect is to alter the word order. For instance, the convention of having an adjective *precede* the noun it describes was waived by Milton many times in *Paradise Lost* to facilitate rhyming, for example:

> Of dulcet symphonies and voices sweet

In such an instance style must be balanced with meaning if ambiguity is to be avoided.

The use of superfluous words to strengthen expression or prolong a dwelling on the theme is called *pleonasm*.

> That time of year thou mayst in me behold
> When yellow leaves, or none, or few, do hang
> Upon those boughs which shake against the cold …
>
> Shakespeare: Sonnet 73

Order and context produce the matrix of words alluded to in Eliot's description from *Little Gidding*:

> … where every word is at home
> Taking its place to support the others

The tauter the poem's structure, the greater the importance of word order and context. Eliot uses repetition rhetorically to stress and explore the meaning of key words:

> We had the experience but missed the meaning,
> And approach to the meaning restores the experience.

Another minor but important feature of word order in poetry is that it can render words self-punctuating.

In a lecture called *Scylla and Charybdis* Eliot spoke of the poet's unending pursuit of *the right word*. He says: 'To take the problem first in its simplest form. The word which is the right word in the one respect may be the wrong word in another. The *poetic* value, the poetic *meaning* I may say, of a passage of verse, depends upon three things:

- the literal meaning of the word
- the association of the word
- the sound of the word

If the word makes the wrong sound the surface of the poem is defaced; if it has the wrong meaning the poem will not stand examination. In neither case, is the result poetry.' As for the *association* of the word, Eliot goes on at length about the ill effect which will result if the associations of a word are too lightly regarded.

Poets invent words and manipulate them creatively to produce special effects. Dylan Thomas often made adjectives from nouns:

> And the mussel-pooled and the heron
> Priested shore
>
> *Poem in October*
>
> ... starfish sands
> With their fishwife cross
> Gulls ...
>
> Author's Prologue to his collected *Poems*

In the same prologue, Dylan Thomas plays with words in a riotous exuberance:

> In my seashaken house
> On a breakneck of rocks
> Tangled with chirrup and fruit,
> Froth, flute, fin and quill
> At a wood's dancing hoof,
> By scummed, starfish sands.

Structural Analysis

When extra vocal force is given to syllables or words in speaking, that accent (emphasis or stress) is what produces rhythm. To scan a series of words or syllables in poetry to determine rhythm pattern is called scansion or close-reading. Most children are no longer taught to dissect verse into its metrical components, but although some will not mourn its passing, this process offered a valuable understanding of the fabric of poetry. Such an appreciation enables the reader to participate vicariously in the act of creation; just as in reading his work, we taste the poet's mind and share his emotional perception.

Metre and Rhythm

> Poetry is the rhythmical creation of beauty
> whose purpose is to elevate the soul.
>
> Edgar Allen Poe

No special knowledge is required to enjoy rhythm in poetry; the metrical beat of verse rhythm arises directly from the syllabic structure of words. But a knowledge of metrics is important for the effective reading of poetry. Both prose and verse have inherent rhythms; well composed prose is constructed with varied rhythm to avoid monotony or sameness. Poetry is written within a matrix of regular rhythms, but its composition finds variety within this framework. We can feel the strong sense of movement engendered by Eliot in *The Love Song of J. Alfred Prufrock* with his reprise line:

> In the room the women come and go
> Talking of Michelangelo.

In English, some two-syllable words carry stress on the first, others on the second:

Stressed *first* syllable: com.pound, hap.pen
Stressed *second* syllable: e.nough, be.yond

But note the difference in stress between de.fect (verb) and de.fect (noun).

A syllable in English does not conform to a definite rule. For example, the word *ser.ious* has two syllables but, strictly, is spoken with three, although the central one is only lightly touched: *ser.i.ous*. The word *medicine* is often pronounced *med.sin*. The next section shows how rhythm is produced by stresses.

The Metrical Foot

A metrical *foot* (or unit of rhythm) consists of a group of combined stressed and unstressed syllables. The name 'foot' was used by the Greeks for that group of beats measured by the single rise and fall of the foot in dancing. The lifting beat (*arsis*) and the descending beat (*thesis*) give shape to the metrical patterns which commonly occur in English verse. For example, the word *quality* constitutes a foot: qua.li.ty. It has one *thesis* down beat (syllable) and two *arsis* lifting beats (syllables).

In English verse, the major combinations of two or three stressed and unstressed syllables occur in four patterns, shown below with their Greek names. Examples of principal metres in English verse:

Iambic (foot: the iamb)
The cuck.oo's dou.ble note

Trochaic (foot: the trochee)
Home art *gone* and ta'en thy wag.es

Anapestic (foot: the anapest)
I am mon.arch of all I sur.vey

Dactyllic (foot: the dactyl)
Half-a-league, half-a-league,
half-a-league on.ward

In the last example, the word *onward* is a spondee, that is, a metrical foot of two stressed syllables.

In his poem *From a Railway Carriage*, Robert Louis Stevenson achieves the 'beat' of the train bogie-wheels rhythmically passing the joins in the rails:

Faster than fairies, faster than witches,
Bridges and houses, hedges and ditches;
And charging along like troops in battle,
All through the meadows the horses and cattle …

★

Here is a child who clambers and scrambles,
All by himself and gathering brambles …

★

And here is a mill, and there is a river:
Each a glimpse and gone for ever!

Here with his whimsical rhyme is Hilaire Belloc:

Physicians of the utmost fame
Were called at once, but when they came
They answered as they took their fees,
'There is no cure for this disease.'

A familiar pattern of metrical rhythm is the *iambic pentameter*, which occurs in Shakespeare's plays. As its name implies, the line of ten syllables consists of five iambuses. Blank verse is continuous verse with no rhyme-scheme. Here is an example of iambic pentameter:

Was <u>this</u>\the <u>face</u>\that <u>launched</u>\a <u>thou</u>.sand\<u>ships</u>? Marlowe's *Faustus*

Variety is introduced when a poet achieves a rhythm by counting the number of stressed syllables to a line, regardless of the the number of unstressed syllables. The recurring pattern of stressed syllables is selected at the whim of the poet. A nice judgement is required to achieve natural sounding statements with the desired rhythmic effect. Robert Frost said, 'It is painful to watch our sprung-rhythmists straining to the point of omitting one short from a foot for relief from monotony. I have a publisher who insists on maintaining *the flow*, that is, *the monotony* by rigidly adhering to his liking for unvarying arsis and thesis to the detriment of many sounds.'

In these next two lines, note how Coleridge scrambles through at the end with the words 'of its clan'.

There is not wind enough to twirl
The one red leaf, the last of its clan. *Christabel*

Even in a marching song with a stress expected on each footfall, variety makes the piece more memorable:

Keep right on to the end of the road,
Keep right on to the end.
Though the way be long let your heart be strong,
Keep right on round the bend.

Song of the 1914-18 War

It is generally accepted that lines of up to eight feet are possible, but the hearer would be likely to perceive shorter lengths. A deliberate choice of metre may be made by the poet to achieve a desired effect:

> The cur.few tolls the knell of par.ting day
>
> Gray's *Elegy* ...

For the reader, one test of a poem is its 'rightness'. Metrical monotony may occasionally be used deliberately for effect, but departure from the metrical pattern is essential if mechanicalness is to be avoided. As in dance and music, variation is attractive.

Sometimes the stress of a metre falls coincidentally with the stress of natural speech. This is called *sprung rhythm* and it tends to produce abrupt and unrhythmical lines:

> Old King Cole was a merry old soul ...

In the following verse Shakespeare combines song-like rhythm, proverbial wisdom, a knowledge of behavioural psychology, and idiomatic use of language:

> Jog on, jog on, the footpath way,
> And merrily hent* the stile-a:
> A merry heart goes all the day,
> Your sad tires in a mile-a.
>
> *Winter's Tale*, Act IV, Scene ii

Sound and Rhyme

Onomatopoeia

The formation of words by imitation of natural sounds associated with the object named is *onomatopoeia*, from the Greek *onomat-(os)*, 'name', and *poiein*, 'to make'. Examples are: 'splash', 'buzz', 'cuckoo'.

This can be quite subtle in poetry. In his *Ode to Autumn*, Keats intensifies the feeling of drowsy warmth and timelessness in the line which images wetness and the soaked filters of the cider-press, by his use of onomatopoeic sibilants:

> Or by a cider-press, with patient look,
> Thou watchest the last oozings, hours by hours.

The sound inherent in words is significant, not least because it offers reinforcement of their literal meaning. The dramatic effect is increased by the power of sound they carry and the quality of the tone.

Assonance

A form employed to provide or intensify rhythm, and sometimes as a substitute for end-rhyme, is *assonance*. It is near rhyme, or similarity of

* *Hent* means 'to take, seize'.

sound without actual rhyme. These examples of assonance are from Spenser's *The Fairie Queene*:

Her angel's face
As the great eye of heaven shined bright,
And made a sunshine in the shady place;
Did never mortal eye behold such heavenly grace.

★

Her godly eyes like sapphires shining bright.

As in music, words can make a discord acoustically through dissimilarity in sonority, the effect called *dissonance*. In poetry this is achieved by the use of an occasional non-rhyming word among rhymed lines.

Alliteration

The repetition of both vowel and consonant sounds, either with the same spelling or independently of spelling, is called *alliteration*:

Apt alliteration's artful aid. Winston Churchill

So long as men can breathe or eyes can see,
So long lives this and this gives life to thee.
Shakespeare: Sonnet 18

Note the menace and quiet venom of the alliterative 'f' sounds and the staccato guttural effect of this curse from *King Lear*:

… infect her beauty,
You fen-suck'd fogs

In *Othello*, Shakespeare conveys the finality of death with a terrible and terminal alliteration. Here is the doomed and almost delirious Othello, at the end of the play:

It is the cause, it is the cause, my soul …

★

Put out the light, and then put out the light …

★

O Desdemona! Desdemona! dead!
Oh! Oh!

★

O fool! fool! fool!

Consonance

If the consonants of stressed syllables are in accord but the vowels differ, the device is called *consonance*. The sounds of language and their functional effect occur in abundance in Dylan Thomas's play for voices, *Under Milk Wood*. In the opening narration the sea is described as:

the sloeblack, slow, black, crowblack,
fishing boat-bobbing sea.

In his poem *And death shall have no dominion*, Dylan Thomas indicates the importance of sound in the sonorous continuum that constitutes this three-verse piece:

And death shall have no dominion.
Dead men naked they shall be one
With the man in the wind and the west moon;
When their bones are picked clean and the clean bones gone,
They shall have star at elbow and foot;
Though they go mad they shall be sane,
Though they sink through the sea they shall rise again;
Though lovers be lost love shall not;
And death shall have no dominion.
And death shall have no dominion.
Under the windings of the sea
They lying long shall not die windily;
Twisting on racks when sinews give way,
Strapped to a wheel, yet they shall not break.

Music in Poetry

In poetry, words are not chosen for their sound alone or exclusively for their meaning. Sense, intellect, and feeling are all satisfied if that 'miraculous instinct for selection' (as James Reeves calls it) occurs, as it does in the best poetry. In effective verse there is no obvious separation of ear and mind. In Greece, elegiac poetry and iambic verse were both in their earliest days lyric, that is, were wholly or partly sung to music. However, by the 5th century BC their connection with music was relaxed or lost.

Sometimes vague references are made to 'music' in poetry and 'the music of words'. The longstanding association between poetry and the legendary Muse, together with the fact that music is 'a composition of rhythmical, melodic, harmonic sounds or tones', has brought confused allusions to the 'sound-qualities' of language. The speaking of verse in public performance has contributed to a development of verse speaking in which tone and sound quality are considered important, particularly by academies of Music and Dramatic Art. But this is not to say that there is notional music in poetry; nor does poetry need another art form to reveal its felicities. Rather, it has itself been used to evaluate creatively other kinds of art. For instance, a critic of ballet wrote: 'It was visual poetry – and the line was perfect.' However, music has been applied analogously to the sounds and word-patterns of poetry for centuries. Eliot maintained that 'in a poem of any length there must be transitions between passages of greater and lesser intensity, to give rhythm of fluctuating emotion essential to the musical structure of the whole.' The poet Kathleen Raine (1908-2003), commenting upon Eliot's *Ash Wednesday*, said that, for her, the desolation was in the music of the free verse.

The 'music of the spheres' is a metaphysical and uncanny 'sound' that down the ages has represented the ultimate in harmony. Sir Philip Sidney insisted that, 'You cannot hear the planet-like music of poetry.' However, we do hear musical attributes such as rhythm, cadence, harmony, etc. Many people insist that musical nuances of feeling arise during a reading of Coleridge's *Kubla Khan*:

In Xanadu did Kubla Khan
A stately pleasure-dome decree:
Where Alph, the sacred river, ran
Through caverns measureless to man
  Down to a sunless sea.
So twice five miles of fertile ground
With walls and towers were gilded round:
And here were gardens bright with sinuous rills,
Where blossomed many an incense-bearing tree;
And here were forests ancient as the hills,
Enfolding sunny spots of greenery.

But oh! that deep romantic chasm which slanted
Down the green hill athwart a cedarn cover!
A savage place! as holy and enchanted
As e'er beneath a waning moon was haunted
By woman wailing for her demon-lover!

As for music itself, of 37 plays of Shakespeare, 32 contain references to music and musical matters in the text itself. These occur mostly in the comedies and are generally the occasion of word-quibbling and witticisms. Besides the songs most commonly known, some by earlier authors, there are many allusions to different kinds of vocal music and scraps (with actual words of old songs).

How sweet the moonlight sleeps upon this bank!
Here will we sit, and let the sounds of music
Creep in our ears.

★

There's not the smallest orb which thou behold'st
But in his motion like an angel sings,
Still quiring to the young-ey'd cherubins.
Such harmony is in immortal souls;
But, whilst this muddy vesture of decay
Doth grossly close it in, we cannot hear it.

Merchant of Venice, Act V, Scene i

13
Poetry's Figurative Element

Defining Poetry

IT IS SOMETIMES held that poets are born, not made; and moreover, that such births are comparatively rare. If this is true, it is also noticeable that vast numbers of people have an innate response to poetry. In ancient times the bard, the Seer, was one who saw more deeply into the human condition than his fellows. What is more, he could interpret and present to an audience what he had seen. The master poet is always a seer, which perhaps indicates that the poet's experience of being himself is deeper and richer than for many ordinary people, and more real.

Poetry appeals to the ear. Its mere sound, the melodious use of words, rhythm, rhyme, has much to do with the same elements of enjoyment that come with music. But its principal appeal is to the intellect through memories, feelings, emotions – in short, our existing experience. By this route, poetry reveals many different aspects of truth and beauty.

As a form for addressing and gaining access to truth and natural beauty, poetry sometimes approaches perfection. It resonates with our imagination, experience and memory so that it connects with what *lives* in our being. Poetry has the capacity to lift what is observed from the commonplace into beauty. The transforming effect of poetry works because it connects with what is already there – truth itself.

It has been said that more poetry is being written today, but less is being read. Much of this so-called poetry is rough, inartistic, jingling verse, with careless and irregular rhyming, or none at all. In short, it is either doggerel or poetically arranged prose. There is often a tendency for people to eschew rules which have not been learned, but to ignore rules competently (as experts sometimes do for effect) it is first necessary to acquire the discipline.

So it seems that at this time an unusually large number of people feel impelled to give utterance to their ideas and feelings – in poetry. Some of these expressions *are* poetry and others are word arrangements that barely merit the description 'poetry'. A question arises: Why attempt to claim these lesser outpourings as poetry at all? Two answers suggest themselves:

- Poetry has an ageless attraction for mankind because the infrastructure of this art form embodies substance, emotion, intelligence, beauty, spirit.
- Many writers seek to superimpose a false vitality upon thoughts and feelings otherwise lacking a life of their own.

Poetry *itself* needs no protection from unworthy practitioners; the universal is never realistically in danger from the relative. But the *reputation* of poetry could suffer and this could deprive young newcomers from embarking on a voyage of beauty and significance which many believe to be the birthright of each new human being.

If the experience of good poetry is once lodged within the psyche, it promotes appreciation of the real thing and the rejection of inept imitations. So what constitutes good verse? *Verse*, 'a metrical composition of lines', is now interchangeable, as a term, with *poetry*. However, in older poetry it was considered to be the equivalent of a line and defined as a succession of feet in one line. The more general term, *poetry*, would seem to have no all-inclusive definition. Although T.S. Eliot loftily asks, 'What is man to decide what poetry is?', another poet, Santayana, helpfully offers, 'Poetry is metrical discourse.' The process of defining (from Latin *definire*, 'to limit, set bounds to') is to apply meaning from the outside. Because conventional definition is necessarily a limitation, it may prove more instructive to explore further elements of poetry – and allow poetry to define itself.

Rhyme

Why is intelligent rhyming shunned by so many contemporary poets? (Rhyming is a correspondence or agreement in the terminating sounds of two or more words; rhyme differs from assonance, but often includes it.) It would seem that too many modern poets do not have the energy, application or discipline to use rhyme effectively. This is disappointing, because it is often the rhyming scheme that contributes to a poem's memorability:

Elected Silence, sing to me
And beat upon my whorled ear,
Pipe me to pastures still and be
The music that I care to hear.

The Habit of Perfection, Gerard Manley Hopkins

This couplet occurs in Byron's *Don Juan*:

O ye lords of ladies intellectual
Inform us truly, have they not henpecked you all?

Ronald Arbuthnott **Knox** (1888-1957) wrote his well-known, witty verse to point up the tendency of people to think that something exists solely because the human mind has been brought to bear upon it:

There was once a man who said 'God
Must think it exceedingly odd
If he finds that this tree
Continues to be
When there's no one about in the Quad.'

Knox's rhyming satire illustrates the power of rhyme to make something, even an obscure philosophic point, more likely to lodge in the memory.

A Sonnet Within a Play

During the vital first exchange between Romeo and Juliet in his play of that name, Shakespeare brings rhyme into his blank verse when he gives the lovers lines of engaging wit and gentle repartee in near-sonnet form. The elevated and exceptional verse enhances this initial encounter of natural and spontaneous love. Juliet's beauty and radiance has produced in Romeo an almost immediate maturity. This sharpens his wit and Juliet matches it – until the nurse interrupts them:

ROMEO: If I profane with my unworthiest hand
This holy shrine, the gentle sin is this;
My lips, two blushing pilgrims, ready stand
To smooth that rough touch with a tender kiss.

JULIET: Good pilgrim, you do wrong your hand too much,
Which mannerly devotion shows in this;
For saints have hands that pilgrims' hands do touch,
And palm to palm is holy palmers' kiss.

ROMEO: Have not saints lips, and holy palmers too?

JULIET: Ay, pilgrim, lips that they must use in prayer.

ROMEO: O! then, dear saint, let lips do what hands do;
They pray, grant thou, lest faith turn to despair.

JULIET: Saints do not move, though grant for prayers' sake.

ROMEO: Then move not, while my prayer's effect I take.

Needing a few more lines for completion at this point, Shakespeare extends the sonnet form with some extra lines:

Thus from my lips, by thine, my sin is purg'd.
(Kissing her)

JULIET: Then have my lips the sin that they have took.

ROMEO: Sin from my lips? O trespass sweetly urg'd!
Give me my sin again.

JULIET: You kiss by the book.

Romeo and Juliet, Act I, Scene v

The poet arranges for the last line to be shared by both lovers as though to symbolize the unity of their love.

Figurative Language

Words arranged in their conventional order and carrying their usual meaning tend to produce unambiguous but unremarkable communication. The deliberate departure from the normal order, construction, and meaning of language enables the writer to convey his intentions in a fresh and powerful way. This figurative language uses a number of devices which bring impact and effectiveness to a statement, making it unusual – perhaps memorable. These figures of speech are the 'special effects' of language.

Poetic inspiration and imagination are expressed in figurative language. Examples: language carrying a symbolical or metaphorical meaning; and language expressing an idea by means of a symbol or emblem. A.E. Housman, as have many before him, claims that metaphor and simile are 'things inessential to poetry; accessories, merely helpful in making sense clearer or conception more vivid.' He goes on to say that such devices are used by the poet 'for ornament' because, even without them, the image possesses an 'independent power to please'.

Here is a poem by Robert Graves in which symbol and metaphor are vivid with implication and significance:

The Door

When she came suddenly in
It seemed the door could never close again,
Nor even did she close it – she, – she –
The room lay open to a visiting sea
Which no door could restrain.

Yet when at last she smiled, tilting her head
To take her leave of me,
Where she had smiled, instead
There was a dark door closing endlessly,
The waves receded.

In his earlier work Shakespeare employs images, similes, and metaphors to adorn his verse, but with his development in power as a poet, mere ornament is transcended. Metaphor goes on to constitute the very substance of what is portrayed. In this, like Aeschylus, he is a master. An exemplary passage occurs in *Macbeth*, where there is a supremely creative use of imagery:

To-morrow, and to-morrow, and to-morrow,
Creeps in this petty pace from day to day,
To the last syllable of recorded time;
And all our yesterdays have lighted fools
The way to dusty death. Out, out, brief candle!
Life's but a walking shadow, a poor player
That struts and frets his hour upon the stage,
And then is heard no more; it is a tale

Told by an idiot, full of sound and fury,
Signifying nothing.
Macbeth, Act V, Scene v

Far from being merely decorative, the images form the very sinew of the theme. We may categorize them under three headings:

Visual images	*Auditory images*	*Motor images*
lighted	syllable	creeps
brief candle	heard no more	walking shadow
shadow	sound and fury	struts and frets

Note too, in the same play, how, as Macbeth's enemies draw near to Dunsinane, one of them describes his deeds in a way that suggests blood congealing without mentioning it by name:

Now does he feel
His secret murders sticking on his hands.

But turning to a more pleasant example of genius in the use of metaphor, we find Cleopatra saying of Antony:

his delights
Were dolphin-like, they show'd his back above
The element they liv'd in …

The most successful figurative language may incur the penalty of becoming a cliché, although this need not daunt the more able poet who, wanting to use a specific image, can undo the cliché. For example, in Andrew Young's *A Dead Mole*:

Strong-shouldered mole,
That so much lived below the ground,
Dug, fought and loved, hunted and fed,
For you to raise a mound
Was as for us to make a hole;
What wonder now that being dead
Your body lies here stout and square
Buried within the blue vault of the air?

The last line, by re-creating the worn phrase 'vault of heaven', bestows fresh and unusual meaning on an over-familiar form. Many a cliché was once yesterday's daring metaphor, a figure of speech which is the very essence of poetry.

Metaphor

Each 'thing' in creation is unique, individual and, in a sense, separate. Mankind tends to make comparisons and draw distinctions. Comparison can, for effect, be made with anything: for example, the 'dawn of civilization'. This is the realm of figurative language. It introduces a departure from what users of a language deem to be the standard meaning of words. Such *figures* have for long been considered ornaments to language, but in fact they are integral to its function and indispensable in poetry and many kinds of discourse.

Quintilian, the Roman rhetorician of the 1st century AD, was probably the earliest writer to divide figurative language into two classes, as given in his *Institutes of Oratory*:

- 'Figures of thought' or *tropes* (turns, conversations) in which words or phrases are used in such a way that a radical change in their standard meaning is presented. This emphasizes the spirit rather than the letter of the meaning. Tropes include metaphor, simile, hyperbole, metonymy, synecdoche, and irony.

This use can be enlarged to affect a whole expression, as in this modern example of irony:

As one door shuts another closes. Anthony Burgess

The standard or literal meaning is contrasted with the *tropic* meaning.

- 'Figures of speech', 'rhetorical figures' or *schemes* (from the Greek word for 'form') where departure from standard meaning occurs primarily in the order of words.

Before Abraham was I am. John 8:58

The substance of poetry is language; its essence is metaphor. What is metaphor? In his *Poetics* Aristotle said simply: 'Metaphor consists in giving the thing a name that belongs to something else.' The Welsh poet R.S. Thomas said of it that it gives 'direct access to meaning and eternity'.

The word *metaphor* derives from the Greek *metaphora* meaning 'transference; a carrying'. The metaphor is a figure of speech in which a word or phrase is used to denote or describe something entirely different from the object, idea, action, or quality which it primarily and usually expresses, thereby suggesting a resemblance or analogy: for example, 'the curtain of night'. A metaphor may employ a word or expression to denote a thing or action applied illustratively to another thing or action without asserting a comparison.

I.A. Richards (1893-1979), the English literary critic, psychologist, and aesthetician, made a useful contribution to penetrating the subtlety of metaphor. He distinguishes two elements:

1 *Tenor*: The subject to which the metaphor is applied.
But, soft! What light through yonder window breaks?
It is the East, and Juliet is the sun!

2 *Vehicle*: The metaphorical image itself.
It is the East, and Juliet is the sun!

Romeo and Juliet, Act II, Scene ii

In an *implicit metaphor* the tenor is not itself specifically stated but only implied. The following metaphor alludes to the death of a human being, by implication:

> ... a reed too frail to withstand
> the storm of its own sorrows.

Usually, nouns are used as the metaphoric terms. The following example uses a noun in a complex metaphor:

> Eye gazelle, delicate wanderer,
> Drinker of horizon's fluid line. Stephen Spender

Here is an example in which a verb is used:

> How sweet the moonlight sleeps upon this bank!
> *Merchant of Venice*, Act V, Scene i

Next, an adjective as metaphor component:

> Annihilating all that's made
> To a green thought in a green shade ...
> *The Garden*, Andrew Marvell

Mixed metaphor combines two or more diverse metaphoric vehicles. When used inadvertently, or without sensitivity to the possible incongruity of the vehicles, the effect can be ludicrous:

> Seeking re-election, the chairman took the bull by
> the horns and tossed his hat into the ring.

Intensely figurative poets like Shakespeare often mix metaphors in a functional way without detrimental effect.

> to take arms against a sea of troubles,
> And by opposing end them?
> *Hamlet*, Act III, Scene i

A *dead metaphor* is an expression like 'the heart of the matter', which is so commonly employed that its vehicle and tenor have been blended by use.

A subtle shift occurs in the figure called *metonymy* (Greek for 'change of name'). In this, the term for one thing is applied to another with which it is closely associated, in such a way that it becomes almost a substitute, for example, the crown for the monarchy or the turf for racing with horses. Typical attire may signify the male and female:

> doublet and hose ought to show itself
> courageous to petticoat.
> *As You Like It*, Act II, Scene iv

In *synecdoche* (Greek for 'taking together') a part of something is taken to represent the whole: for example, 'All hands on deck!' uses 'hands' to represent crew members. To be clear, a good *synecdoche* must be based on an important part of the whole and that part selected to represent the whole should be directly associated with the subject under discussion.

The hearts
That spaniel'd me at heels, to whom I gave
Their wishes …

Antony and Cleopatra, Act IV, Scene x

Another figure related to metaphor is *personification*, or in the Greek term *prosopopeia*, in which either an inanimate object or an abstract concept is as though endowed with life, human attributes or feelings:

Shall I believe
That unsubstantial Death is amorous,
And that the lean abhorred monster keeps
Thee here in dark to be his paramour?

Romeo and Juliet, Act V, Scene iii

In Old English poems like *Beowulf* the ordinary name for a thing is replaced by a *kenning*. This is a type of *periphrasis* (Greek 'roundabout speech') often used as a stereotyped expression in the highly formulaic poetry of the various old Germanic tongues. Some kennings are metonymy, for example, 'the whale-road' (sea); 'the ring-giver' (king). Other kennings are synecdoche, for example, 'the ringed prow' (ship). In Homer's great epic, *Odyssey*, he uses a similar figurative device, referring over and over again to the 'wine-dark sea' and 'bright-eyed Athene'.

The *simile* enables direct comparison to be expressed between two distinct things (using 'like' or 'as'). For example:

How like a winter hath my absence been …

Shakespeare: Sonnet 97

O my love's like a red, red rose
That's newly sprung in June:
O, my love's like the melody
That's sweetly played in tune …

Robert Burns

An extension of this figurative form is the *epic simile*. This is a structured and sustained simile in which the secondary subject (vehicle) is developed well beyond an obvious parallel with the primary subject (tenor). For example in *Paradise Lost* Milton uses nine lines to elaborate a simile comparing the thronging of fallen angels with swarming bees.

This use of 'tenor' is consonant with its dictionary meaning: 'course, general direction followed, career':

… the noiseless tenor of their way

Gray

It also means: 'general hearing, meaning, drift (of a statement, speech, document).'

Imagination is the poetic energy which informs the language of simile and metaphor. These two figures of speech are quite distinct and are used differently. When the poet uses *simile*, we are explicitly invited to observe the similarities and difference of two referents. In Shakespeare's *Henry VIII*, as the disgraced Wolsey reviews his mistakes in the speech beginning, 'Farewell! a long farewell, to all my greatness!', he uses a series of metaphors to rationalize his predicament. In the midst of these comes a simile, one which is quite unexpected from such a highly placed prelate:

> … I have ventur'd,
> Like little wanton boys that swim on bladders,
> This many summers in a sea of glory,
> But far beyond my depth …
>
> *Henry VIII*, Act III, Scene ii

When *metaphor* is used, a word is drawn from a quite different context to suggest a resemblance or analogy. Examples are: the *lion* of England, the *ocean* of life. In essence, the metaphor is a representation; the simile offers a comparison.

Walter **de la Mare** (1873-1956) said of metaphor: 'When the fusion of image and what it reveals is absolute, the metaphor is as much one with that it colours, enriches, illuminates, as is the rainbow in a drop of dew.'

The metaphor is often considered unsuitable for imparting scientific and technical information, but its central role in poetry is undisputed. Unlike religion, where certain statements cannot be verified and metaphor is, as it were, a substitute for fact, in poetry metaphor *is* the reality. In metaphysical poetry, where the import may be more disturbing and far-reaching than the most exact paraphrase in prose, this effect will almost certainly have been achieved by the use of metaphor.

In his *Poetics*, Aristotle says that, 'The most important thing in style is to have a command of metaphor.' The poet's imagination soars as it ascends first into the ample air of simile, then into the divine aether of metaphor. The metaphor carries an image of reality mirrored in intellect. In the mind's eye reality is as an essence, revealed, distilled from the substantiality conveyed by the senses. The poet proclaims visual imagery in written word vividly alive with illumination. Indeed, poetry activates and squeezes the word to its utmost, using the pressure of contextual significance to release its richest potential.

> This outward-sainted deputy,
> Whose settled visage and deliberate word
> Nips youth i' the head, and follies doth enmew
> As falcon doth the fowl, is yet a devil …
>
> *Measure for Measure*, Act III, Scene i

In the opening two lines of *Richard III* Shakespeare uses a seasonal metaphor to set the scene of mood-change for a nation:

Now is the winter of our discontent
Made glorious summer by this sun of York …

Act I, Scene i

In four lines, by use of a simple metaphor, Shakespeare provides Prince Hal's own positive gloss on his association with Falstaff, in *Henry IV, Part 1*:

And like bright metal on a sullen ground,
My reformation, glittering o'er my fault,
Shall show more goodly and attract more eyes
Than that which hath no foil to set it off.

Act I, Scene ii

Proverbs embody their wisdom in a metaphor with the stark brevity of a Zen poem:

A rolling stone gathers no moss.

Many such metaphors undergo a change in semantic meaning during their wide circulation, and may justify lexical entries in dictionaries, for example, from *The Shorter Oxford English Dictionary*:

To cry wolf: raise a false alarm;
a wolf in sheep's clothing: a person of mild appearance and manners but of a sinister and malevolent nature;
to keep the wolf from the door: to stave off want or destitution;
to have the wolf by the ears: to be in a dangerous dilemma.

Metaphor is such a powerful device that it can be employed to reveal levels of incredible subtlety and beauty. Its power is in the fact that the conceptual meaning on both sides of the metaphor equation is already known. Here is a quatrain from Omar Khayyám's *Rubáiyát*:

'Awake! for Morning in the Bowl of Night
Has flung the Stone* that puts the Stars to Flight;
And lo! the Hunter of the East has caught
The Sultan's Turret in a Noose of Light.'

Roland Barthes (1915-80) constantly argued against the notion of subtle depth; against the idea that the most real is latent, submerged. But Susan Sontag, who edited and introduced a selection of his work, found an inconsistency in this. She commented that, 'The aesthete's posture alternates between *never* being satisfied and *always* finding a way of being satisfied, being pleased with virtually everything.' The metaphor helps to resolve this apparent uncertainty. Metaphor in poetry offers a metaphysical bridge, profound in its simplicity and inviting in its familiarity. It permits a very subtle transference of meaning which does not jar the intellect. In the passage from *Macbeth* which we considered earlier, Shakespeare used a homely metaphor, the domestic candle, to allude to the light of human life-experience. Here he uses it again in a different context:

* The sound of a stone flung into a large metal bowl signalled the start of a horse race.

> ... There's husbandry in heaven;
> Their candles are all out ...
>
> *Macbeth*, Act II, Scene i

Image is the essence of metaphor. If truth is not to be the first casualty of image, the metaphor must avoid distortion and misrepresentation. To this end it should be a carefully selected, resonating parallel, exactly expressing the original concept.

The metaphor is unlimited in scope. Dylan Thomas, in his poem *If I were tickled by the rub of love*, says powerfully and simply, 'Man be my metaphor'. R.S. Thomas, whose apprehension had become razor-sharp by dwelling in utter simplicity, regards the Universe as one gigantic metaphor. He speaks in his poetry of 'drawing nearer to That ubiquity by remaining still' and thus being able to address 'the silence we call God'. From the unlimited metaphor, to a figure of speech proportioned and measured to suit the situation – *analogy*.

Analogy

An *analogue* (from the Greek *analogon*, 'according to due ratio or proportion') means that which corresponds to, or is compared with, something else. An *analogy* (from the Greek *analogia*, 'proportion') means a theoretical comparison or point-by-point correspondence between particulars of different things, rather than a categorical likeness; resemblance in certain parallels; logical inference that, if two things are alike in some respects, they will be alike in others. An example might be the similarity between a *chairman* and the *Speaker of the House of Commons*.

As a literary term it also denotes a story with parallel examples in other languages and literatures. A well-known example is Chaucer's *The Pardoner's Tale*, the theme and basic plot of which were found over much of Europe in the Middle Ages. The original idea for the tale is thought by J.A. Cuddon to emanate from a 3rd-century Buddhist text known as the *Jatakas*.

Figures of speech are variations on the essence of conceptual and verbal meaning. A powerful concentration of significance resides in *symbol*.

Symbol

The word *symbol* comes from the Greek *sumbolon* and means 'mark, token, ticket, watchword, outward sign, covenant'. In essence, a symbol is something which represents or typifies another thing, quality, etc. In an earlier section it was seen that the metaphor also is a representation; it works by correspondences and similarities which allow one image to appear for something else. The symbol differs from metaphor in that it is 'a formal and authorative representation', for example, the Cross as a symbol of Christianity.

Here is a reference to symbol; it is Iago's exaggeration of the effects of Desdemona's persuasive power over Othello:

… And then for her
To win the Moor, were't to renounce his baptism,
All seals and symbols of redeemed sin …

Othello, Act II, Scene iii

In the 19th century the simple device of symbol was so expanded and extrapolated that it became the creative process underlying a movement in literature bearing the name *Symbolism*.

Symbolism

Symbolism was a movement in French literature, reaching the height of its importance between the years 1870 and 1886. Rebelling against realism, and influenced by the English Pre-Raphaelite Brotherhood and the music of Wagner, the new movement sought to achieve in poetry the effects of music. It made use of clustered images and metaphors, suggesting or symbolizing the basic idea or emotion of each poem. Precursors of Symbolism were Verlaine, Rimbaud and Baudelaire, all of whom had an important influence on the movement; its leader and theorist was Stephane Mallarmé (1842-98). W.B. Yeats was strongly influenced by Symbolism in his early years; T.S. Eliot and James Joyce are considered to have made adaptations of the Symbolist technique in the development of their individual styles.

Paul **Verlaine** (1844-96) is usually regarded as an immediate forerunner of Symbolism, yet he expressed the ideas of the Symbolists better than any other French poets of his period. However, for him it seems to have been only a passing phase. Here are some lines from his *Celestial Hour*:

Glassed in the deep
And tranquil mere,
Black shadows sleep
Of willows where
The breezes sough …

'Tis dream-time now.
A tender peace
From Heaven's shore
Descends on us:
The evening star
Is like a flower …

Celestial hour!

Translated by Alan Conder

As for Stephane **Mallarmé**, he was a French poet and teacher as well as leader of the School of Symbolism and a formulator of its aesthetic theories. His poetry is distinguished by elliptical phrases, unusual syntax and condensed figures – each poem being built about a central symbol, idea, or metaphor and employing subordinate images that illustrate and assist in developing the principal idea.

Mallarmé used to receive his friends on Tuesday evenings in a small flat in the Rue de Rome in Paris and talk to them. To them he *was* poetry; a master of never fully comprehended mysteries. No one who went ever forgot the experience. He taught English in Provence, at Tournon, and for seven years at Avignon.

Provençal poetry is mysterious to the French, being closer to instinctive feeling than other French poetry. The tradition of France emphasized eloquence rather than poetry and a certain sterility predominated by 1870 – which Mallarmé dispelled. When Mallarmé's spirited flashes of imagery are compared with all but the best poets of the Romantic period, the work of that time seems tawdry and heavy. Certainly Blake's poetry, in quality and quantity, outshone the work of the French poets.

In the opinion of Denis Saurat, Professor of French Languages and Literature at the University of London, Kings College:

> Mallarmé's great handicap is that he cannot write, either in prose or in poetry: he is a thinker and a talker, not a writer; this fatal fault has also descended to many of his disciples, in whom only the talker survived. Therefore Mallarmé has to be explained …

This comes as a relief to many who strive to discern what Eliot saw in his poetry that was so seminal. If it is Mallarmé's thought, ideas, imagery, and vision that matter, then the struggle to evaluate his poetic mastery can subside and a different view can be taken. We can contemplate Mallarmé purveying the higher ideal of poetic imagination, by the hour, from the height of his mantelpiece yet quite unable to give it expression in verse.

Mallarmé reminds us that it is by giving up meaning that we penetrate into the eternal world; by giving up 'ourselves' we reach God. Here are some examples of his verse:

In Thought

What silks endured with time's own balms,
Where the coiled Chimera faints, compare
With the curling, cloudlike native charms
You draw out of your mirror there!

★

Royalty

I triumphed, fleeing gorgeous suicide
In a glow of glory, gold, storm, blood afoam!
O jest! if so bedrape my empty tomb
They spread a pall down there of purple pride!

★

Miss Mallarmé's Fan to Its Owner

Dreamer, to let my wing dive deep
In pure and pathless ecstasy,
Feign subtly I am free, yet keep
Me still held in captivity.

A twilight freshness comes from me
To you with every pinioned beat,
That delicately, constantly,
Persuades the skyline to retreat.

Bewilderment! space is athrill
Like a vast and dizzy kiss that's born
For no one, that can not be still
Nor soar, – that's blissful, yet forlorn.

Translations by Alan Conder

Denis Saurat writes, in *Modern French Literature, 1870-1940*:

> Poetry is by its very essence a failure; from each poet a few lines survive as successful, as a true echo from a higher world, produced in the poet no one knows how. The writing of poetry is practically impossible.

He does, however, except Shakespeare from this comprehensive judgement. Saurat goes on:

> Mallarmé and his band, besides producing a few specimens of good poetry, taught all their successors that some things, until then thought to be first-rate, were not literature; and also in what direction good literature lay; and all writers ever since have been in a little doubt about themselves, which is good for writers, and yet not too good. But after 1900 or so, all honest writers wondered what Mallarmé would have thought of them.

Debussy was inspired by Mallarmé's poem *L'Apres-midi d'un faune* to produce his evocative orchestral piece of the same name. The Symbolist Movement also had an important influence on *Imagism*

Image and Imagism

Image

The concept *image*, which is very much a preoccupation of the advertising, commercial, and industrial world of modern times, has a key role in poetry and literature. Image in advertising is designed to build product-appeal around a positive or prestigious image (for example by association with success, vitality or romance) rather than by describing the product's specific qualities and attributes. The word *image* proceeds from the Latin *imago*: 'a representation, portrait, statue; a likeness, an appearance, pretence; mental representation, idea. Figurative expression; simile, metaphor; *to speak in images*.'

Dylan Thomas said on this subject: 'Images *are* what they say, not what they stand for.' Whether or not they stand for anything, it is clear that they imply purpose, effect and inter-relationship. *Image* can be spiritual, mental, or physical. Here is a series of examples of the word's use in the *Bible* and Shakespeare:

> 'Shew me the tribute money' – and they brought unto him a penny. And he saith unto them, 'Whose is this *image* and superscription?' *Matthew* 22:20

And God said, 'Let us make man in our *image*, after our likeness.' *Genesis* 1:26

And as we have borne the *image* of the earthy, we shall also bear the *image* of the heavenly. *1 Corinthians* 15:49

Who being the brightness of his glory, and the express *image* of his person … *Hebrews* 1:3

You mistake, sir: I am sure no man hath any quarrel to me: my remembrance is very free from any *image* of offence done to any man. *Twelfth Night*, Act III, Scene iv

… to show virtue her own feature, scorn her own *image*, and the very age and body of the time his form and pressure. *Hamlet*, Act III, Scene ii

The power and immediacy of images conveyed by words is evident in these lines from *Pastures* by Herbert Read:

We scurry over the pastures
 chasing the windstrewn oak-leaves.
We kiss
 the fresh petals of cowslips and primroses.
We discover frog-spawns in the wet ditch.

In literature, the term *image* means a literal and concrete representation of something perceived through the senses. The image is a distinctive element of the 'language of art'. It is of the essence of meaning in literary work, not merely a decoration. *Imagery* is the systematic use of *images*.

In the 18th century it was believed that *imagination* was a faculty of visualization and that literature was a medium prompting visual responses from the reader, that is, that it generated images. Descriptive poetry flourished in this atmosphere. In due course figurative language such as metaphors, similes, and symbols was imprecisely regarded as imagery. Such a broadening into generalization so that one word, *image*, becomes a symbolic utterance, blurs and debases its meaning.

Finally, *New Critical* poetics (developed in the 1920s) encouraged the view that poems are concrete artefacts and that the whole poem is an image. This brings to a focus the question: Is verbal texture incidental ornament or the integral structure of the piece? The effect of over-reliance on the word *image* is to encourage a view of literature which makes syntax, argument, and plot, together with temporal and relational structures, recede into invisibility, while descriptive and figurative language advances into prominence to a distorted degree. The whole is imagined as a 'cluster' of *images* and what began as a gesture of respect for the texture becomes the importation of an over-structure. It can lead to a rejection of the work's inherent order, as mere abstraction, while the search goes on for some more esoteric 'hidden' pattern. Thus *image* has, for many, become associated with a mysterious additional requirement: that is to respect what is 'there' in the work.

As I.A. Richards (1936) has pointed out, this connotation of *image* blurs the verbal facts about metaphor by obscuring the *relationship* between tenor and vehicle. This implies that the real context of *image* is a group of assumptions which 'place' poetry in relation to some 'deeper' structure, for example, depth psychology – all of which might at first seem to dignify and deepen literature but in the end improverishes it. In place of the diversity and fluidity of the literary medium, it substitutes a shadow-play of images whose resolution lies elsewhere.

Imagism

Imagism was a poetic vogue promulgated by a group of poets who flourished immediately before the First World War. The best known English and American writers were T.E. Hulme, Ezra Pound, Amy Lowell, Richard Aldington and his wife 'HD' (Hilda Doolittle). An imagist poem was *designed* using common, everyday language; it had a hard, clear image, had no rhyme scheme, and rendered the subject precisely and tersely. Here are 'the rules':

- To write in the language of common speech, using the exact word rather than a merely decorative word.
- To create new rhythms as the expression of new moods.
- To allow for the fuller expression of the poet's individuality by using free verse instead of conventional forms.
- To allow total freedom in the choice of subject.
- To present an image of particular exactness, avoiding generalities.
- To produce poetry which is 'hard' and 'clear', never blurred or indefinite.
- To show that concentration is the very essence of poetry.

The reaction against the traditional values in poetry might have been less vehement had it been a revolt from within Europe. It may be relevant to note that the poets who first held these views were American by birth. One very radical writer, Laura Riding, considered poetry to be the ultimate residuum of significance in language, free from extrinsic decoration, superficial contemporaneity and didactic bias. Soon, a number of 'Imagist' anthologies appeared, edited by Ezra Pound.

The Imagists were influenced by the Symbolists in France, but the precise distinction between the two seminal concepts did not always appear to be clear to the Imagists themselves, who sometimes confused the two:

Image: The clear evocation of a material thing.
Symbol: The word which stirs subconscious memories.

Ezra Pound favoured classical Greek and Roman poetry, as well as the poetry of China and Japan and the French Symbolists, as models for new work. A celebrated example shows the concentration of image he sought:

In a Station of the Metro

The apparition of these faces in the crowd
Petals on a wet, black bough.

This poem, like many Imagist pieces, was influenced by the Eastern dictum, 'Less is more,' and by the Japanese haiku verse-form. (A haiku is strictly a 17-syllable verse, recording the poet's impression of a natural object or scene viewed at a particular season or month.)

Imagism advocated the use of free verse (*vers libre*), new rhythmic effects, colloquial language, a greater freedom than ever before in the choice of subject-matter, and the creation of precise, concentrated, sharply delineated images. All this was designed to evoke a unified impression in which the *emotion or association represented* and *the object in itself* are balanced equally in importance. In his writings about *vers libre*, Eliot was careful to validate it against 'traditional' metres. He would not have allowed, as poetry, lines of 'chopped-up prose'. Imagism was to embody the following principal characteristics:

- Direct treatment of the subject.
- Economy of word use.
- Innovative, preferably new, rhythms.
- Word exactness (no cliches, etc).

The new poetry was to comprise 'small dry things' evoked by concrete visual metaphor. It rejected infinity, mystery, and indulgence in emotion. Pound himself considered exemplary a poem by Hilda **Doolittle** (1886-1961), who by general consent was regarded as representative of the genre:

Oread

Whirl up, sea –
whirl your pointed pines,
splash your great pines
on our rocks
hurl your green over us,
cover us with your pools of fir.

This style conveys the impression that sculpture is entering speech with attendant concrete discomfort. T.S. Eliot felt that its benefit to verse was 'critical rather than creative, and as criticism very important'. This view was echoed by F.R. Leavis (1895-1978), who thought that 'in itself it amounted to little more than a recognition that something was wrong with poetry'. It insisted on the functional rather than the merely ornamental. Stephen Spender (1909-95) suggested that Imagism 'isolated the basic unit of the modern poem'. Its detractors say its very starkness is, in the end, self-limiting and, as ever with extremes, its effect was salutary but not enduring. Its supporters say it laid the foundation for modern poetry.

Pound's *Doctrine of the Image* centres in his successive definitions, which need to be taken in relationship with each other:

> ... an 'Image' is that which presents an intellectual and emotional complex in an instant of time. The Image is the poet's 'primary pigment' and with the Image (the 'word beyond formulated language') the poet has the medium which is specifically his. In the 'hard' writing of Imagist poetry 'one idea is set on another' to bring about language's 'point of maximum energy'. Such an approach is powerful and astringent.

Leavis, in his *New Bearings in English Poetry* (1932), felt that, with one exception, Pound's books reflected 'The contemporary plight – the lack of form, grammar, principle and direction', and that to rescue significant art from that plight 'needed the seriousness, the spiritual and moral intensity, and the resolute intelligence' that are behind *The Waste Land* of T.S. Eliot.

After the cerebral aridity of Imagism it is refreshing to return to the ordinary world of people and things. In the next section we explore the figurative language of *epigrams* and *proverbs*.

Epigram

The word *epigram* comes from the Greek *epigramma*, 'an inscription; brief pointed sentence in prose or verse expressing a witty, often satirical idea, tersely and compactly'.

An epigram is a succinct form of verse, popular in ancient times. As its etymology implies, it was originally simply an inscription such as might be found on a statue, monument, or triumphal arch. It has since come to mean a short poem, recording something the writer thought noteworthy. Defining what would constitute a good example, Professor Mackail (1859-1945) said it should have compression and conciseness, and, notwithstanding its brevity, should be simple, lucid, balanced, and well wrought. An anonymous Latin *distich* (couplet) defines the epigram neatly:

> Three things must epigrams, like bees, have all,
> A sting, and honey, and a body small.

Earlier we considered the man who is perhaps the best known exponent of the form, Marcus Valerius Martialis, more simply known as Martial. Here is the famous epitaph he wrote for the diminutive slave Erotion:

> Lie lightly on her, turf and dew;
> She put so little weight on you.
>
> Translated by James Michie

Another epigram, astringently voicing a sentiment felt by many:

> Philo never dines at home
> Behaviour he'll repeat;
> The truth is, if he cannot cadge,
> Our Philo does not eat! Martial

Seven wealthy towns contend for Homer dead,
Through which the living Homer begged his bread.

Dryden

When a saying is very brief it begins to veer towards *proverb*. For instance, it is not clear if the following examples are epigrams or proverbs:

When firmness is sufficient, rashness is unnecessary.

Napoleon

On the fall of an oak, every man gathers wood.

Menander

Proverb

The word *proverb* comes from the Latin *proverbium*. It is a traditional, occasionally trite saying, embodying commonplace experience or an obvious truism, in a brief (often inelegant) form of words. The dictionary defines it as: 'Something well-known and familiar; a byword; a traditional saying which expresses advice or reveals a moral in a short and pithy manner.' Paradoxically, many phrases called 'proverbial' are not proverbs as we now understand the term. Before the 18th century the term *proverb* also covered metaphorical phrases, similes, and descriptive epithets, and was used far more loosely than it is today. Nowadays we expect a proverb to be cast in the form of a sentence.

Proverbs tend to be found in three forms:

- Abstract statements expressing general truths:
  Nature abhors a vacuum.
- Everyday experience making a general point:
  It's no use crying over spilt milk.
- Sayings applying to specific applications (for example, weather) from traditional wisdom and folklore:
  Red sky at night, shepherds' delight.

The compression in proverbs is amazing. Here is an example expressing an aspect of the law of diminishing returns (from Economics) in six words:

Too many cooks spoil the broth.

Common metaphorical phrases are only notionally proverbs. 'A stitch in time saves nine' is a plain statement of fact relating to the prudence of repairing something before the damage gets worse. A modern example relating to computers is 'garbage in; garbage out'. Here are some Japanese proverbs:

Don't waste your prayers in the horse's ear.
Don't test every stone bridge with your stick.

A fool at forty, a fool for ever.
Sooner or later you act out what you really think.

The following proverb is Turkish:

If you speak the truth have a foot in the stirrup.

As Aldous Huxley said in *Jesting Pilate* (1926), 'Proverbs are always platitudes until you have personally experienced the truth of them.'

Emblems and Ensigns

Emblem

The word *emblem* comes from the Greek *emblema(-at-)*, the noun formed from the verb *emballo*, 'throw in, insert', but an emblem is neither as 'full' nor as concentrated as a symbol, although full of significance.

She had all the royal makings of a queen;
As holy oil, Edward Confessor's crown,
The rod, and bird of peace, and all such emblems.

Shakespeare's *Henry VIII*, Act IV, Scene i

Ensign

The word *ensign* comes from the Old French *enseigne* and Spanish *insignia*, meaning 'battle-cry, watchword; sign, token, badge; banner'. Here is an example of its use:

So, now dismiss your army when ye please;
Hang up your ensigns, let your drums be still,
For here we entertain a solemn peace.

Shakespeare's *Henry VI Part I*, Act V, Scene iv

Allegory

The word *allegory* derives from the Greek *allegoria*, 'speaking otherwise'. An allegory is an exposition or figurative representation with a double meaning; one primary and on the surface; the other secondary, implied beneath the surface. In some allegories, three or even four levels of meaning can be interpreted.

Structurally, an allegory is a large-scale piece of symbolism in which matters are conceptualized, analysed, examined, and expressed. It is distinguishable from metaphor by being more extensively sustained and more fully detailed. Also, unlike the metaphor, allegory does not assert that one thing *is* another. It was Emerson's view that 'good writing and brilliant discourse are perpetual allegories'. Fables and parables are short allegories with a single main moral; allegories are parables which embody the very nature of poetry.

The term *personification allegory* is sometimes used for allegorical poems in which abstract qualities are accorded human attributes in order to expand the story. In the *Romance of the Rose*, the experience of falling in love is abstracted from the specifically human process and extrapolated into personified faculties, for example, Reason, Shame, Jealousy, who meet and hinder or help the lover in his search for the rose of love.

The allegory flourishes still in satire, underground literature, and science fiction. George Orwell's *Animal Farm* (1945) is a modern example of allegorical satire. *Animal Farm* has an intentionally colourless style – it is after all an account of revolution in the guise of a fairy tale. Parts of the work are over-sensationalized, but on the whole it wears its irony with a grim melancholy. Irony is not easily defined, but its usual characteristics are a surface appearance covering an underlying reality and a detachment masquerading as unawareness (real or simulated).

We continue with an exploration of a linguistic study which interprets poetry's infrastructure as an information system – indeed, as the 'system of systems'.

Semiotics

The significance of poetry is its universality and its relevance, even in what might be termed the Scientific Age. In their *Guesses at Truth*, J.C. and A.W. Hare write, 'Science sees signs; poetry is that which is signified.' Poetry does not always yield its secrets readily. Perception of a poem's grammatical structure may heighten awareness of its meaning, but the days are gone when it was enough to thrill to the beauty of imagery. The study of *semiotics*, *structural analysis*, and *structural linguistics*, has brought an added dimension of literary criticism to language. The first matter to be resolved is terminology.

The prefix *semeio-* derives from the Greek *semeion*, meaning 'sign'. It is linked with the Greek *semantikos*, 'significant meaning', and hence *semantics*. *Semeiology* (from the Greek, meaning 'sign language') is the general, if tentative, science of signs. Now generally known as *semiology*, it deals with systems of significance, for example, means by which human beings, individually or in groups, communicate or attempt to communicate by *signal*. This may include words, graffiti, slogans, morse code, smoke signals (as in a papal election), ritual, symbol, gestures. An essential distinction needs to be made here. For the hunter in pursuit, the *sign* will be: spoor (a footprint or pawmark), a broken twig, pressed grass, a nibbled herb, droppings, etc. Essentially, the *sign* is inadvertent; the *signal* is intentional.

Ferdinand de Saussure (1857-1913), the Swiss Indo-European scholar and teacher often credited with the founding of modern linguistics, insisted that *meaning* be studied in the context of the triple relationship: mind, world, and language.

European *semiology* developed into cultural *semiotics*, an area of study with a different focus from that of past periods. Taking the modern term *semiotic* (used as a noun), we note that this study has a long and continuous history that dates back to the debates between the Stoics and Epicureans over the status of the sign as an object of interpretation.

Heraclitus (c540-c475 BC), seeming to anticipate semiotics, said of the Delphic Oracle:

> The lord whose oracle is in Delphi neither
> declares nor conceals, but gives a sign.

A leading Soviet semiotician, Yuri Lotman, developed a process of poetry analysis which he set out in *The Structure of the Artistic Text* (1970) and *The Analysis of the Poetic Text* (1972). Lotman views the poetic text as a stratified system in which meaning exists only contextually and is determined by sets of similarities and oppositions. He contends that poetic text is 'semantically saturated', that is, condensing more information than any other statement. This is so, because in good poetry there is a minimum of redundancy and the structure develops a richer set of images than any other expression of language. Lotman's emphasis on compression of meaning certainly applies to the haiku:

> In the morning dew,
> Covered in dirt, but quite fresh,
> A muddy melon. Bashō
>
> Spiders in corners,
> Don't worry yourselves; I shall
> Not be cleaning them. Issa

The King in *Hamlet*, ruefully praying, says:

> My stronger guilt defeats my strong intent;
> And, like a man to double business bound,
> I stand in pause where I shall first begin,
> And both neglect. Act III, Scene iii

Lotman believes that 'information is beauty', and he castigates poetry which carries insufficient information. He contends that every literary text comprises a number of systems – lexical, metrical, phonological, grammatical, contextual. For Lotman the poetic text is a 'system of systems', a relation of relations; a complex form of discourse condensing and resolving tensions, parallels, oppositions, and syntheses.

Roland Barthes (1915-80), the French writer and critic who inherited Jean-Paul Sartre's mantle as intellectual guru of the Paris Left Bank, developed and popularized the application of *semiological* analysis to cultural processes. Barthes, who was professor of literary semiology at the College de France until his death, used techniques similar to linguists who regard language as a contingent system of signs and symbols. He said in 1968: 'Language … is at the same time a social institution and a system of values … The individual cannot by himself either create or modify it; it is essentially a collective contract which one must accept in its entirety if one wishes to communicate. Moreover, this social product is autonomous, like a game with its own rules.'

It seems odd that Barthes, although speaking in (and perhaps for) the 20th century, should so totally disregard the achievement of an individual like William Shakespeare and his contribution to the shaping, development, and enrichment of the English language. In the vagueness of generalization he discounts the universality of such outstanding men.

There are difficulties in trying to account, in philosophical terms, for the relationship between words and the objects to which they refer. This is particularly so when the theory is extended to words which have no concrete referent, for example, 'honesty'. Often, a distinction is drawn between literal (*cognitive*) meaning and associative meaning. Many linguists contend that the meanings of words may be analysed into such constituents as those used by Noam Chomsky to derive the *surface structure* of sentences from their *deep structure*. Some linguistic philosophers (such as Wittgenstein in his later period and J.L. Austin) view word meaning, not in terms of logical structure, but rather in accordance with the speaker's *intention* in using a particular word or utterance. However, logical analysis is widely accepted as explaining that aspect of meaning which is a function of grammatical structure, that is, sentence meaning is a matter of internal relationships among the *words*, '*word particles*', and *phrases* involved.

In his book *In Search of Semiotics* (1986), David Sless has re-examined the ideas of the originators. He believes that Saussure, the main European founder of semiotics, and Pierce, who made such a substantial contribution to the study, both 'generated a wealth of debate but with only a superficial understanding of the underlying issues.' David Sless, near the end of his book, says: 'Semiosis is a truly ubiquitous phenomenon and we need to understand our engagement with it directly, so that we can transform our world to suit our own interests.' Under the heading 'Semiotics as Metaphysics' he goes on to say that, 'In the final analysis, semiotics is a way of thinking – an intellectual *position* from which to try to understand the universe.' This seems like the full turn of a circle in which study (of semiotics and language) has produced much cerebration but little insight. David Sless insists that a knowledge of semiosis would enable us to alter 'our world' to suit 'our own interests'. Ironically, this would have greater validity if by 'our world' Sless means our interior reflection of the exterior world. This would alter our response to the language of Shakespeare's poetry and of the *King James Bible*, ie instead of *projecting* comprehension, we would allow the language *to speak to us*.

14
The Poet and His Faculties

Poetry lifts the veil from the hidden beauty of the world.
Shelley

The Poet

A question that often arises is: Are poets born or made? But in the modern world, with our intense interest in technique and infrastructure, it is without doubt now believed that poets are born *and* made – a product of nature and nurture.

In turning to the East first for a view of the role of the poet, we at once see the universality of poetry in great civilizations:

The Poet

Taking a position at the centre, the poet contemplates the mystery of the universe.
He feeds emotions and mind on the great works of the past.
Gazing at the myriad objects he considers the complexity of the world;
Moving with the four seasons, he sighs at the passing of time,
And notes with sadness the falling leaves in boisterous autumn;
He feels awe when the heart experiences chill;
He joys in the delicate buds of the fragrant spring;
With solemnity of spirit he turns his gaze to the clouds.
He acclaims the work of his predecessors, breathing the clean fragrance of past masters;
He ranges in the verdant groves of literature and praises the symmetry of great art.
Moved, he pushes away his books, takes up the writing brush and prepares to express himself in letters.

★

We poets struggle with Non-being to force it to yield Being;
We knock upon silence for an answering music.
We enclose boundless space in a square foot of paper;
We pour out a deluge from the inch space of the heart.

Lu Chi (? – AD 303), based on a translation by Achilles Fang

Thus, in the 3rd century, the poet indicates the range of his contemplation, the scope and perspective of his thought, his task and his achievement. Shakespeare, with tongue in cheek, sought our pardon for attempting to ... 'cram Within this wooden O the very casques / That did affright the air at Agincourt.'

Lu Chi assertively tells us that poets enclose boundless space within a square foot of paper; R.S. Thomas sees the whole cosmos as a gigantic metaphor. The poet has vision and perspective, he commands language, and has what Shakespeare has called the 'divine frenzy'. The muse sits at his shoulder because of it.

The Elizabethans use *frenzy* to mean a sort of madness, akin to *ecstasy* (from the Latin *ecstasis* and the Greek *ekstasis*, 'removal from the proper place; distraction of mind; astonishment; trance'), a state of extreme emotional exaltation. The Greek etymology suggests 'standing beside oneself', and this, the condition of detached observer, seems to be exactly the role of the poet, 'being out of oneself; standing aside'.

The frenzy alluded to by Shakespeare is not the simple 'loss of mental balance or control' defined by the dictionary. It is rather a freedom from those confining limitations of mind that inhibit creativity in the generality of mankind. In the past, such a condition was considered to be 'divine madness'.

Marsilio **Ficino** (1433-99), the great Renaissance philosopher and leader of the Florentine Academy, distinguished four kinds of divine madness:

Type and Connection	*Source*
Poetic madness	The Muses
Connected with the mysteries	Dionysus
Associated with prophecy	Apollo
Arising from love	Venus

Ficino declares that these divine madnesses 'raise the soul'. Of the four, the most powerful and noble is the amatory madness, because the others depend upon it. The poetic, the religious, and the prophetic madnesses entail the exercise of zeal, piety, and worship. Ficino insists that these attributes amount to no less than love itself and asserts that Anacreon, Sappho, and Socrates were all seized powerfully with the amatory madness. It is, says Ficino, love which enables the soul to rise above mind into unity.

Philosophy in Poetry

Poets, the first instructors of mankind.

Horace, *Ars Poetica*

Few philosophers are poets, but in most poets there is something of the philosopher. The philosopher ('lover of wisdom') is 'one versed in philosophy or engaged in its study'. The word *wis* and the Old English *wissian* mean 'to make (a thing) known'. Wisdom is defined as 'the practical application of knowledge'. It is the knowledge of truth expressed in simple language. This is how the poet speaks. These attributes are central to the poet's function and his view of the universe; he tells us 'how things are'. For example:

> Exquisite roadside
> Flower – nonchalantly
> Eaten by my horse! Bashō

This statement is packed with Stoic philosophy.

Here are two verses from Thom Gunn's (b1929) poem *Human Condition*, in which his evening walk through enveloping fog prompts a philosophical reflection on the separation and isolation we experience with the concepts 'I', 'me', and 'mine':

> The street lamps, visible,
> Drop no light on the ground,
> But press beams painfully
> In a yard of fog around.
> I am condemned to be
> An individual.
>
> ★
>
> Much is unknowable.
> No problem shall be faced
> Until the problem is;
> I, born to fog, to waste,
> Walk through hypothesis,
> An individual.

As if anticipating Shakespeare, Sophocles describes the life of man as dream-like:

> I see we're nothing else, just as we are,
> But dreams; our life is but a fleeting shadow.

Towards the end of *The Tempest*, Shakespeare speaks of the temporal illusion which this world presents to the witnessing awareness of the human being:

> You do look, my son, in a mov'd sort,
> As if you were dismay'd: be cheerful, sir:
> Our revels now are ended. These our actors,
> As I foretold you, were all spirits and
> Are melted into air, into thin air:
> And, like the baseless fabric of this vision,
> The cloud-capp'd towers, the gorgeous palaces,
> The solemn temples, the great globe itself,
> Yea, all which it inherit, shall dissolve
> And, like this insubstantial pageant faded,
> Leave not a rack behind. We are such stuff
> As dreams are made on, and our little life
> Is rounded with a sleep.
>
> *The Tempest*, Act IV, Scene i

In Prospero's deeply moving Epilogue he appeals for the human aid that mankind's individuals can give, each to the other:

> Now my charms are all o'erthrown,
> And what strength I have's mine own;
> Which is most faint... Now I want
> Spirits to enforce, art to enchant;
> And my ending is despair,
> Unless I be reliev'd by prayer, ...
> As you from crimes would pardon'd be,
> Let your indulgence set me free.
>
> *The Tempest*, Act V, Scene i

Shakespeare distinguished his view of philosophers from the subject *philosophy*. Of the practitioner he wrote:

> For there was never yet philosopher
> That could endure the toothache patiently;
> However they have writ the style of gods
> And made a push at chance and sufferance.
>
> *Much Ado About Nothing*, Act V, Scene i

The irony of having to suffer the pronouncements of professional stoics and sages was not lost on Shakespeare, the philosopher poet. He was not, however, unremittingly jaundiced:

> TOUCHSTONE: Art thou wise?
>
> WILLIAM: Ay, sir, I have a pretty wit.
>
> TOUCHSTONE: Why, thou sayest well. I do now remember a saying, 'The fool doth think he is wise, but the wise man knows himself to be a fool.' The heathen philosopher, when he had a desire to eat a grape, would open his lips when he put it into his mouth ...
>
> *As You Like It*, Act V, Scene i

The Chinese philosopher Lao-Tzu (the name means, literally, 'Old Master') is traditionally considered to be the author of the *Tao-Teh Ching*, and is thought to have been a contemporary of Confucius (6th century BC). One of his highly compressed paradoxes tells us:

> Those who know do not speak; those who speak do not know.
> When the realized man is hungry he just eats.

It is not unusual to find that Shakespeare, who is less severe, has given words of profound philosophy to minor characters in his plays. In *As You Like It* the Duke expounds his simple distinction between the haunts of men and the woodlands:

> DUKE: Are not these woods
> More free from peril than the envious court?
> Here we feel but the penalty of Adam,

The seasons' difference: as, the icy fang
And churlish chiding of the winter's wind,
Which, when it bites and blows upon my body,
Even till I shrink with cold, I smile and say
'This is no flattery: these are counsellors
That feelingly persuade me what I am.'

★

And this our life exempt from public haunt,
Finds tongues in trees, books in the running brooks,
Sermons in stones, and good in every thing.

As You Like It, Act II, Scene i

Poetry, like an impartial third eye, is able to illuminate our values as we observe the natural world. Blake, in a poem we met earlier, notices the seeming waste of beauty in the parasitic consuming of one creature by another.

O Rose, thou art sick.
The invisible worm
That flies in the night,
In the howling storm,

Has found out thy bed
Of crimson joy,
And his dark secret love
Does thy life destroy.

There is a parallel in the dark side of human behaviour – consuming, instead of giving, in the name of love. From here it is but a sliding step into the malignity of jealousy, at its consuming worst in Shakespeare's *Othello*. We watch helplessly as Desdemona asks of her predator:

O good Iago,
What shall I do to win my lord again? Act IV, Scene ii

The poignant essence of tragedy lies in the poet's choice of words and what they touch in us, the hearers. Stephen Spender describes dramatically the debt mankind owes to those who promote the flowering of the spirit:

I think continually of those who were truly great,
Who, from the womb, remembered the soul's history
Through corridors of light where the hours are suns,
Endless and singing. Whose lovely ambition
Was that their lips, still touched with fire,
Should tell of the spirit, clothed from head to foot in song.

What is precious is never to forget …
Never to allow gradually the traffic to smother
With noise and fog the flowering of the spirit.

The perceptive Alexander **Pope** (1688-1744), in *An Essay on Man*, expressed his philosophy using *anaphora's* repetition to achieve penetration:

All nature is but art unknown to thee,
All chance, direction which thou canst not see;
All discord, harmony not understood;
All partial evil, universal good;
And, spite of pride, in erring reason's spite,
One truth is clear, whatever is, is right.

He went on:

Know then thyself, presume not God to scan,
The proper study of mankind is man.

And later:

The learn'd is happy nature to explore
The fool is happy that he knows no more.

The American poet Walt **Whitman** (1819-92) wrote a collection of verse called *Leaves of Grass*, the first poem of which was 'Song of Myself'. This uneven, ungainly book is monumental and very much of its time. Uttering the word 'democratic, the word en-masse', the poet sings – seemingly of his individual self as a symbol of a continent, which, in turn, is representing the cosmos:

Of life immense in passion, pulse and power,
Cheerful, for freest action, formed under the laws divine:
The Modern Man I sing.

Whitman said of this work:

> I have allowed the stress of my poems from beginning to end to bear upon American individuality and assist it – not only because that is a great lesson in nature, amid all her generalizing laws, but as counterpoise to the levelling tendencies of Democracy.

Many perceptive readers, penetrating beyond the philosophic shallowness, may well conclude that *Leaves of Grass* is an uncannily accurate title from a writer whose driving force was 'identity with my body'.

Another American poet, writing some 100 years later, left a no less powerful an impression, but the focus has shifted dramatically. Although seemingly more personal, the verse nevertheless has an uncanny reach.

Sylvia **Plath** (1932-63) was brought up in the USA. Her reputation was established, after her suicide, with the publication of her poetry collection *Ariel* (1965). Her poems contain bold imagery and original rhythms, constrained by a strenuous artistic control. Here she writes of a mother's response to the new-born child:

One cry, and I stumble from bed, cow-heavy and floral
In my Victorian nightgown.
Your mouth opens clean as a cat's.
...   And now you try
Your handful of notes;
The clear vowels rise like balloons.

Her later work is a subject for psychopathology; the themes of her poems describe states of a mind in extremity. In a recording for the British Council she insisted that, 'One should be able to control and manipulate experiences, even the most terrifying ... with an informed and intelligent mind.'

Here is a poem which illustrates her finely forged, sparse style. It expresses an almost orgiastic satisfaction, an adolescent curiosity and a sense of guilt at the flux of blood after severing her thumb during a household chore:

Cut

What a thrill –
My thumb instead of an onion.
The top quite gone
Except for a sort of hinge.
Of skin like a hat,
Dead white then the red plush.

How you jump –
Trepanned veteran,
Dirty girl,
Thumb stump.

This poem, like much of Plath's work, is a 'now' incident, with pointed observation, detached reporting, intelligent description. After a mere 31 years her young life was over – graphic, terse, tragic, Sylvia ... who demonstrated how mind and poetry together constitute a mirror which reflects back the world's face.

Poetry the Mirror of Images

No, Cassius; for the eye sees not itself,
But by reflection, by some other things.

Julius Caesar, Act I, Scene ii

In the Dark Ages, until the time of Alfred the Great (AD 849-899), the Old English poet was a man with a public function. He was the voice and memory of the tribe and, when the lord called upon him for a lay, everyone listened. As Michael Alexander (1966) reminds us, in poetry of such rich imagery and narrative thrust as *Beowulf* the poet becomes invisible.

In *A Defence of Poetry*, Shelley wrote, 'A poem is the very image of life, expressed in its eternal truth.' As if to confirm that the creator of something so intangible would have mysterious powers, Wallace Stevens (1879-1955) was to write in a later age, 'The poet is the priest of the invisible.' The poet interprets and represents what others 'saw' but did not *see*; he sharpens the indistinct shafts of imagination that pattern the musings of common men, articulating their sighs and murmurings.

In the theatre of his mind Shakespeare was the only producer, creating the play of words with all their freshness, intimacy, and immediacy.

Hamlet, counselling the itinerant players, essentializes the function of the play:

> ... to hold, as 'twere, the mirror up to nature. *Hamlet*, Act III, Scene ii

Shakespeare's allusion to 'the mirror' is subtly relevant. A mirror has two sides. The back shows nothing; the glass reflects what is looking into it. The poet confirms what we can see without his aid, but the mirror of his words focuses the image where we can see it. Thus he reveals to his hearers what they knew without realizing it.

Poetry may convey factual information, express philosophy, or disclose emotion. A poem is a linguistic artefact and is as much an artistic creation as a painting, a sculpture, or a piece of ceramics. A piece of poetry does something more than communicate ideas or emotional feeling. In this next piece Robert **Herrick** (1591-1674) conveys both and, in addition, creates one of the most delightful poems in the English language:

Upon Julia's Clothes

Whenas in silks my Julia goes,
Then, then, methinks, how sweetly flows
The liquefaction of her clothes.
Next when I cast mine eyes, and see
That brave vibration each way free,
O, how that glittering taketh me!

Such a poem is a reminder of the simple statement of Somerset Maugham: 'Art is for delight.'

The mercurial activity of sounds and words in poetry conjures into being an impression of the whole range and sweep of the human spirit, its relationships and conflicts. Poetry both reflects experience and is, in itself, an experience. T.S. Eliot, writing in *What Dante Means to Me*, explains that it is the poet's function to furnish words with which to express hitherto unarticulated feelings, to join his visionary perception and ordinary understanding:

> *The Divine Comedy* is a constant reminder to the poet, of the obligation to explore, to find words for the inarticulate, to capture those feelings which people can hardly even feel, because they have no words for them; and at the same time, a reminder that the explorer beyond the frontiers of ordinary consciousness will only be able to return and report to his fellow-citizens, if he has a firm grasp upon the realities with which they are already acquainted.

It is the view of Eliot that, of the very few poets of similar stature to Dante, none – not even Virgil – has been more attentive to the *art* of poetry, or more scrupulous, painstaking and *conscious* a practitioner of the *craft*. Eliot also believes that no English poet other than Shakespeare can be compared with him in this respect. The more striving craftsmen (and here Eliot is thinking primarily of Milton) were somewhat limited as poets in their craft. Eliot goes on to say that the poet should be the servant of language, rather than master of it. He considers Dante (like Shakespeare) to be one that gives developmental substance to the soul of language, discerning its latent possibilities.

Robert **Herrick**, the 17th-century English poet, lived throughout the period of Puritan rule and into the Restoration of Charles II. After the constraints and bleakness of the Commonwealth period, he wrote a poem which commended a certain disorder, ostensibly of dress, but by implication of manners and morals. This is seen by many as a clear statement of anti-Puritan criticism and, as such, demonstrates how poetry implies more than it says.

Delight in Disorder

A sweet disorder in the dress
Kindles in clothes a wantonness.
A lawn about the shoulders thrown
Into a fine distraction;
An erring lace, which here and there
Enthrals the crimson stomacher;
A cuff neglectful, and thereby
Ribbands to flow confusedly;
A winning wave, deserving note,
In the tempestuous petticoat;
A careless shoestring, in whose tie
I see a wild civility;
Do more bewitch me, than when art
Is too precise in every part.

Because this piece of writing is poetry, it opens the reader's receptivity to multiple meanings. In it Herrick demonstrates how well poetry can set up resonances and implications, enabling the poet to write simultaneously about clothing, ladies' behaviour – and morality.

Poetry may provide personal emotion with a public expression because, as a medium, it transcends mere individuality. In the church of Saint John the Baptist, Burford, Oxfordshire is the monument to Sir Lawrence Tanfield, who died in 1625. He was a lawyer of the Elizabethan and Stuart age who rose to be Lord Chief Baron of His Majesty's Court of Exchequer. When he died, his widow composed some poetry which was engraved on the family monument:

Here shadowe lie,
  Whilst life is sadd.
Still hopes to die,
  To him she hadd.
In bliss is he
  Whom I lov'd best;
Thrice happy shee
  With him to rest.

★

So shall I be
    With him I loved;
And hee with mee
    And both us blessed.
Love made me Poet,
    And this I writt;
My harte did doe yt
    And not my witt.

Mulk Raj Anand in *Contemporary Novelists* (1976) wrote:

> The highest aim of poetry and art is to integrate the individual into inner growth and outer adjustment. The broken bundle of mirrors which constitute the human personality in our time can only become the enchanted mirror if the sensibility is touched in its utmost pain, sheer pleasure, and tenderest moments.

The mirror of poetry is highly reflective and, in good hands, presents a true likeness. Distorting mirrors at the fairground show how disastrously and grotesquely normality can be contorted if the mirror does not reflect truly what is before it. Master poets like Shakespeare offer a still, clear reflection – moreover, it is multi-dimensional.

15
Creativity

Making Poetry

> The crown of literature is poetry.
> It is its end and aim; it
> is the sublimest activity of
> the human mind.
>
> W. Somerset Maugham

THE WORD *poem* derives from the Greek *poiema*, 'something made, created', and hence a work of art. A poem is a metrical composition, a work of verse, which may be in rhyme, blank verse, or a combination of the two. Its innate structure might require a fixed number of syllables, as does the sonnet (which has 14 lines, each containing 10 syllables) or the Japanese haiku (which has 17 syllables).

W.H. Auden (1907-73) suggests that, 'In poetry you have a form looking for a subject and a subject looking for a form. When they come together successfully you have a poem.' T.S. Eliot, in *The Use of Poetry and the Use of Criticism* (1933), asserts that 'no generation is interested in Art in quite the same way as any other; each generation, like each individual, brings to the contemplation of art its own categories of appreciation, makes its own demands upon art, and has its own uses of art.' Poetry is an art form and as such its composition may be considered in two parts: *what* is expressed and *how* it has been achieved. In general, art is created in a sequential process which takes the conception forward from inception to completion:

- Inspiration
- Selection of subject matter
- Arrangement
- Articulation into form

That which makes a poem different from other forms of word-composition is what J.A. Cuddon has called 'a species of magic'. In poetry, words are so structured that their juxtaposition, one with another, strikes resonances, produces echoes, rhythms, assonances, and other subtle effects. This amounts to a felicity yielded by no other word pattern, which is certainly beyond the expressive ability of prose.

Summarizing much of what has been said earlier, poetry is distinguished from prose by the deliberate employment of metre, rhythm, rhyme, sound, and figurative language. Poetry, as a form of language distinct from ordinary speech, probably originated in religious ritual and was an earlier development than prose. The earliest poetic landmarks in Western literature are Homer's *Odyssey* and *Iliad*, which evolved from a primitive oral tradition (which included song), and later became models for the epic poems of Virgil and other poets. A tradition of didactic verse, extending back to Hesiod, employed metre or rhyme to assist the expression of ideas.

Poetry is the art of thinking in images. It avoids the verbal logic of philosophy but gains the strength of verbal imagery from metaphysics. This accounts for the mysterious quality of reality in certain poems. In *Burnt Norton*, Eliot attempts to describe entry into the timeless moment while remaining in a moving world. He gains effect by borrowing the resonance of an image from Eastern art:

> Words after speech, reach
> Into the silence. Only by form, the pattern,
> Can words or music reach
> The stillness, as a Chinese jar still
> Moves perpetually in its stillness.

Poetry achieves its effects by rhythm, sound patterns, and imagery. Characteristically, the poetic form evokes emotional response, conveys a loftiness of tone, and fires ideas with further energy.

Eliot lets us enter the mind of the poet in his revelation that, 'In a poem, one does not altogether know what it is that one has to say, until one has said it; for what one intends to say is altered in the course of making poetry of it.' He speaks characteristically on the endlessly discussed problem of form and content and on what is called 'engagement' or commitment. Should we regard poetry as a vehicle for the expression of our ideas, beliefs, emotions, observations, and experiences, or should we regard these phenomena as the material from which to make a poem?

Eliot considers bad verse to be a deception, leading some readers into believing either that an idea has been transmuted into poetry or that a melodious arrangement of words contains an idea. He is scathing of those he considers to have nothing to say but who have, in poetically expressing their vacuity, merely made use of verse, exploiting its resources and drawing down upon the medium opprobrium.

The poet, free of the strict criteria governing scientific definitions and declarations, is able to connect more directly with the faculty of insight. In this freedom, connections may be made within experience over a greater range and with finer delicacy. As Dylan Thomas reminds us, 'A good poem is a contribution to reality.' In the following poem he recalls his 1920s boyhood when he stayed at his aunt's dairy farm near Llangain in Carmarthen.

Fernhill

Now as I was young and easy under the apple boughs
About the lilting house and happy as the grass was green,
    The night above the dingle starry,
        Time let me hail and climb
    Golden in the heydays of his eyes,
And honoured among wagons I was prince of the apple towns
And once below a time I lordly had the trees and leaves
        Trail with daisies and barley
    Down the rivers of the windfall light.

All the sun long it was running, it was lovely, the hay
Fields as high as the house, the tunes from the chimneys, it was air
    And playing, lovely and watery
        And fire green as grass.
    And nightly under the simple stars
As I rode to sleep the owls were bearing the farm away,
All the moon long I heard, blessed among stables, the nightjars
    Flying with the ricks, and the horses
        Flashing into the dark.

Shakespeare's capacity to see what lay about him is, in the words of Dr Johnson, 'in the highest degree curious and attentive, proceeding from vigilance of observation.' Such powers, wedded to creativity, are evident when Ulysses says of the wanton Cressida:

There's language in her eye, her cheek, her lip,
Nay, her foot speaks.

Troilus and Cressida, Act IV, Scene v

Poetry can depict and represent dream or reality, moving easily between the two. When the truth, or ordinariness, is represented by the poet it may delight, either because it is newly seen and marvellously clear, or because it becomes so under the poet's hand. Intellect and imagination merge effectively to produce a cogent felicity, unique to poetry.

John Dennis (1657-1734) asserted that poetry is an imitation of nature and that passion is more necessary to it than harmony. He said that this was because 'harmony only distinguishes its instrument from that of prose but passion distinguishes its very nature and character. Poetry is poetry because it is more passionate and sensual than prose ... so it must be the best and the nobler Art.'

Strong feeling and intense emotion are not the only attributes elevating poetry to its pinnacle in the arts. But, as Lodovico Antonio Muratori indicated in *The Perfection of Italian Poetry* (1706), poetry delights our understanding and pleases the sense of hearing by the harmony and music of the verse. He says, 'But such beauty is superficial ornament, necessary indeed to beautiful poetry, but not able to make it truly and intrinsically beautiful ... The beauty by which its sweetness delights and moves the human understanding is nothing else than an illuminating and resplendent aspect of the truth.' He goes on to say that, apart from its other attributes, this illumination consists in brevity or clarity. Although in practice these two characteristics are not always compatible, an exception occurs in haiku, in which the succinctness pares away experience to reveal an impression of startling directness and clarity:

On a withered bough
A solitary crow sits –
Autumn evening. Bashō (1644-99)

One Western master poet who has the ability to present poetry with the clarity and brevity so praised by Muratori is Eliot. But the simple words, clear in themselves, sometimes give rise to a delicious ambiguity. In the opening lines of *Burnt Norton* there occurs an example:

Time past and time future
What might have been and what has been
Point to one end, which is always present.

The word *end* obviously carries meaning beyond 'termination', but the question is: What is Eliot implying? What he does not say is itself full of meaning.

'Poetry and art are, intrinsically, mediators between the immaterial and the concrete,' said Sri Aurobindo (1872-1950), and it is this crucial vantage point which gives poetry its special opportunity. Truth and goodness are said to be the two ultimate ends to which the desires of our intellect and our will always and naturally tend. They are not found in the dream but are always in the ever-present *now*. As Eliot in the last lines of *Burnt Norton* says, somewhat unpoetically,

Quick now, here, now, always –
A condition of complete simplicity …

But for everyman in the dream of everyday living, the moment *now* goes by unheeded:

For most of us, there is only the unattended
Moment, the moment in and out of time …
The Dry Salvages

The celebrated axiom, 'Man is the measure of all things,' leads to a question. Is the spirit of poetry simply another way of describing the spirit of man writing poetry? The poet is sometimes a silent listener; at other times a voice that asks questions. But when the poet asks questions he asks on behalf of all mankind. The poet searching for truth is completely devoted to totality of experience in a state of aesthetic contemplation. When this occurs, subject and object are one:

… music heard so deeply
That it is not heard at all, but you are the music
While the music lasts. *The Dry Salvages*

Poetic truth is a function of a realized insight and Eliot's verse has the extraordinary power to set up echoes in the reader's mind, as though he knows about us and our journey:

> If you came this way,
> Taking the route you would be likely to take
> From the place you would be likely to come from.
>
> *Little Gidding*

The voice of a man coming from his predetermined source to his inevitable destination is likely to be muted. Poetry can amplify the indeterminate sound and shape its articulation. King Lear had to be reduced to beggary before he discovered the authenticity of his own voice: 'The weight of this sad time we must obey, speak what we feel, not what we ought to say.' Lear is involved in a gigantic struggle with his own nature, his pride, and above all, his immense ego:

> Which of you shall we say doth love us most?
>
> *King Lear*, Act I, Scene i

Man has discovered what he truly is, and inwardly hears the authentic universal voice, only when the obscuring ego is reduced in intensity. This process is often achieved by one or other of the meditation techniques available over the centuries. Here is Tennyson describing just such a process:

> More than once when I
> Sat all alone, revolving in myself
> The word that is the symbol of myself,
> The mortal limit of the Self was loosed,
> And passed into the nameless, as a cloud
> Melts into heaven.
>
> *The Ancient Sage*

Two sonnets by the author, Kenneth Verity (b1931), describe the effect and experience of such a system of meditation:

> Seated and still – within myself the guest,
> Both hemispheres of mind in equipoise;
> Reason and intellect are now at rest
> As no event discernment's eye employs.
> No inner voice speaks words and sentences
> In commentary on what the sense has caught;
> That which I felt I was, no longer is;
> Such dreamed existence was a toy of thought.
> Life is perceived to be a pulsing stream –
> Phenomena, of passing movement spun.
> All that was sensed before now seems a dream;
> Plurality has been absorbed in one.
> Spirit, untrammelled by creation's thrall
> Is, in this timelessness, acknowledged All.

★

I sit in silence, disengaged from quest,
Life's energies are cooled to heatless fire;
With balance now restored, and deep in rest,
The consciousness is emptied of desire.
All that was once imagined has dissolved
As merging integrates the separateness;
Apparent difference has been resolved
And urgent passing time hangs motionless.
No voluntary action gains support –
The body image held in mind has gone;
There is no need to shape or frame a thought,
When naught remains to seek comparison.
  In spacious stillness, yielding all reserve;
  As the eternal witness, I observe.

The *self* or *spirit* referred to by poets as a presence is drawn into experience by their words. Here is a description of this presence and its effect in *Lines Composed A Few Miles Above Tintern Abbey* by Wordsworth:

… And I have felt
A presence that disturbs me with the joy
Of elevated thoughts; a sense sublime
Of something far more deeply interfused,
Whose dwelling is the light of setting suns,
And the round ocean and the living air,
And the blue sky, and in the mind of man;
A motion and a spirit, that impels
All thinking things, all objects of all thought,
And rolls through all things.

The *Spirit presence* mentioned by Wordsworth is synonymous with the *self* alluded to by Tennyson. The spirit of poetry *is* the self or, put another way, it is the Spirit pervading all creation. A concluding word on this vast subject is given by W.B. Yeats who, in collaboration with Sri Purohit Swami, put into English an Indian spiritual teaching, the *Eesha Upanishad*:

> The Self is everywhere, without a body, without a shape, whole, wise, all knowing, far shining, self-depending, all transcending.

In the continuum which is poetry, words are always available to express what has been vouchsafed to the poet in the mirror of *imagination*.

Imagination

In the formation of a poem, two contributory processes are at work:

- contemplative imagination
- creative imagination

Ananda K. Coomaraswamy (1877-1947) considered the poem, like the icon, to be a support for contemplation, linked to the inner life of the person. The poet objectifies and discloses his feeling, allowing it to be shared by others.

It is of the essence of poetry to question by what process the external becomes the agent's expression. Attempting to define visual imagination, Eliot cites *Macbeth*, observing that it offers not only 'something to the eye, but, so to speak, to the common sense':

> Light thickens, and the crow
> Makes wing to the rooky wood.
>
> Act III, Scene ii

The liberating genius of the poet's language reveals beauty in the substance of forms. A good poet summons the archetypal from the common experience, being able to visualize the subtler reality hidden in things. He has the faculty of externalizing the inmost truth in words.

Imagination is more than a visualization in the head, although that is the place where the activity occurs – 'In my mind's eye, Horatio,' says Hamlet. The simplicity of Shakespeare's view is enlarged by Joubert (1754-1824), who said, 'Imagination is the eye of the soul.' John Davidson (1857-1909), the Scottish poet and playwright, indicates a high level of function for imagination:

> That minister of ministers,
> Imagination, gathers up
> The undiscovered Universe.

In his *Leviathan* Thomas Hobbes (1588-1679), a forerunner of associational psychology and a leader of modern rationalism, notes that: 'Imagination and memory are but one thing.' This helps to explain why imagination is one of the most powerful faculties of the human being. For anyone who thinks that imagination is simply a Romantic's dream imagery, Albert Einstein (1879-1955), propounder of the theory of relativity, set a high perspective by saying that, 'Imagination is more important than knowledge.' There is a further step in the creative process before image can be transmuted from imagination into poetry – it must first be *interpreted*.

Interpretation

Because we see and perceive everything from a 'point of view', we therefore feel individual and believe ourselves to be separate observers. Once this concept of separation has been established and the idea of 'person' derived, there follows 'my view of things' and 'my interpretation'.

Brain and mind process the data available to 'our perception'. With this, we do the best we can to make sense of what we see around us. We learn how others have responded previously to similar impressions; we formulate questions; we seek answers. Many turn to religion, philosophy – and poetry – for responses to these questions.

That which poetry represents, it expresses in language. In skilled hands, an impression – even hard fact – may be conveyed distinctively by figurative language. A simple fact may be designated in scientific writings by an unembellished noun, but in poetry directness and clarity are not enough. By use of a metaphor or a figure of speech the same fact is alluded to with grace and feeling. But what is this 'fact' upon which so much literary ability may be lavished?

Nietzsche (1844–1900) believed (many would think rightly) that, 'There are no facts, only interpretation.' Turning from observed things to the inner world: 'All thinking is interpretation,' wrote Susan Sontag (1989). So if the 'facts' of our everyday world are an interpretation of our sensations, and if thinking about those facts is more interpretation, are we not erecting one intellectual meaning upon another? It is perhaps for this reason that poetry (which can carry reason, insight, and feeling) seems to go straight to the essential meaning of things.

The verb *interpret* comes from the Latin *interpretari*, 'to explain, expound; translate'. It is thought to have originally meant 'to act as agent between two parties in a bargain'. There are other meanings:

- To translate into a foreign language as interpreter.
- To represent objectively so as to bring out meaning and character – as a musician interprets the music of a composer.
- To understand in a specific way, or construe a meaning – as when a person's silence is interpreted unfavourably.

A psychologist might define *interpretation* as 'an activity in which a physical or psychological datum is related to a conceptual model which assigns place and significance to the datum'. In other words, what is 'out there' – the world – is related to what is 'in here' – the head. Interpretation is a way of understanding, a view of a set of facts from a certain perspective. Some argue that it is the interpretation that matters rather than the facts themselves.

To take a simple everyday example: hardly a look or gesture passes between two human beings without it being interpreted for significance and meaning. You will remember the exchanges between the servants of the two rival houses in *Romeo and Juliet*:

ABRAHAM: Do you bite your thumb at us, sir?
SAMPSON: I do bite my thumb, sir.
ABRAHAM: Do you bite your thumb at us, sir?
SAMPSON (Aside to Gregory): Is the law of our side if I say ay?
GREGORY (Aside to Sampson): No.
SAMPSON: No, sir, I do not bite my thumb at you, sir; but I bite my thumb, sir.

Act I, Scene i

Each of us in our daily exchanges with others has to interpret and evaluate frowns, smiles, words, etc. We construe for meaning, significance, or implication.

Several possible meanings can be inferred from a piece of poetry, and only the writer can definitely pronounce upon the validity of the reader's interpretation. For example, here is Kathleen Raine's poem, *Shadow*:

> Because I see these mountains they are brought low,
> Because I drink these waters they are bitter,
> Because I tread these black rocks they are barren,
> Because I have found these islands they are lost;
> Upon seal and seabird dreaming their innocent world
> My shadow has fallen.

A poem like this raises many questions, such as:

1 Is this a poem about the bitter doctrine of original sin?
2 Is it a statement of the bleak nihilist view that nothing has real existence?
3 Is it saying that the human race blights everything it touches?
4 Is its meaning that the human mind diminishes the grandeur and fineness of anything it conceptualizes?
5 Is it expressing the sadness of the loss of innocence that occurred in the mythical Garden of Eden?
6 Is it a modern way of saying what Wordsworth said: 'It is not now as it hath been of yore'?
7 Has the poet's individuality reduced the universality of these natural created things?
8 Has the recognition of the transience of these ephemera reduced them in the poet's heightened awareness?
9 Is my 'shadow' my ego, or my mortality, my limitation of conscious light, my projected deconstructing analysis?

The questions must stop; only Miss Raine can tell us what she glimpsed, knew, felt. So much for interpretation!

Susan Sontag (*Against Interpretation*) speaks of the innocence that disappeared when art was considered to have 'content'. This entailed the perennial, never to be consummated, project of *interpretation*. She goes on to say that, 'Interpretation makes art manageable, comfortable,' but complains that, 'The world, our world, is depleted, impoverished enough. Away with all duplicates of it, until we again experience more immediately what we have.' She reminds us that we have all suffered a steady diminution of sharpness in our sensory experience and concludes by saying:

> The function of criticism should be to show *how* it is what it is, even *that* it is what it is, rather than to show what it *means*.

This raises further questions. The reader has to interpret, but is the poet also an interpreter? Answers to such questions are not as simple as they may at first appear. Two quatrains from the *Rubáiyát* of Omar Khayyám are relevant here:

> I saw a potter in the bazaar yesterday,
> He was violently pounding some fresh clay,
> And that clay said to him in mystic language,
> 'I was once like thee – so treat me well.'
>
> ⋆
>
> There was the door to which I found no key;
> There was the veil through which I might not see:
> Some little talk awhile of me and thee
> There was – and then no more of thee and me.

These translations of the *Rubáiyát* of Omar Khayyám are from original Persian sources by E. Heron-Allen, published by Bernard Quaritch (1899). The verses carry implications arising from mysticism, philosophy, religion, and psychology. Shakespeare and Eliot are no less perceptive and articulate. It would seem that the poet is indeed an interpreter *par excellence*. Critics and specialists make a vital contribution to understanding, but ultimately the poet's words speak for themselves, and we draw from them what we can.

In *The Music of Poetry* (1942) Eliot reminds us that it is a commonplace to observe that the meaning of a poem may be something larger than its author's conscious purpose. A reader's interpretation of a poem may differ from the author's and be equally valid; indeed, it may be even better. This would seem to be something to do with the nature of poetry itself: as if poetry has a manifest end product, but is also full of unmanifest resonances. The problem of interpretation is compounded if *translation* is also required.

Translation

The Venerable Bede, speaking of an attempt to render the sense of Caedmon's lay, said:

> This is the sense but not the order of the words as he sang them in his sleep; for verses, though never so well composed, cannot be literally translated out of one language into another without loss of their beauty and loftiness.

A similarly fundamental weighing of loss arises when considering whether or not contemporary works should be translated into a different style of language from classics; for example, should the English for a Latin translation be made to sound 'harder and more bronze-like'. Certainly, the 'feeling' of the translation should respect the spirit of the other culture – as closely as that can be accommodated.

Dryden suggested an emphasis on imitation rather than translation:

> I take imitation of an author … to be an endeavour of a later poet to write like one which has written before him on the same subject; that is, not to

> translate his words, or to be confined to his sense, but only to set as a pattern, what he supposes that author would have done, had he lived in our age, and in our country.

That said, an English translation has to be appropriately worded and to sound 'right' to English readers. It seems sensible that some liberties be taken with a text – totally literal translation rarely suits poetry. But there are limits. Vladimir Nabokov avers that 'the clumsiest literal translation is a thousand times more useful than the prettiest paraphrase'.

Pierre Emanuel asserts the seemingly obvious – that a translator who does not know the original cannot really translate. He merely 'mimics in his own rhythm, and sometimes with his own twists of language, something which remains alien to him'. A useful approach adopted by some translators of Chinese is to work in pairs, one partner having a good understanding of Chinese, the other a high competence in English. As we saw earlier, this collaborative process worked well when W.B. Yeats and Purohit Swami presented certain *Upanishads* in English from originals in Sankrit.

How much more of a towering achievement was the work of William Tyndale (1492?-1536) who, alone, translated into English the *New Testament* from the Greek, and the larger part of the *Old Testament* from the Hebrew. When, in 1604, the revisers commenced work on the Authorized Version they had before them not only the work of Tyndale, but all translations that had appeared during the 70 years following his death. Yet when the English *Bible* of 1611 left their hands, the felicitous and inspired work of Tyndale remained largely undisturbed.

In the extract from Tyndale's translation which follows, note particularly how references to 'that worde' are without gender. It was Jesus, incarnation of the Universal Creative Principle, who carried maleness – an inevitable consequence of His embodiment.

THE GOSPELL OF SAINCTE IOHN

> In the beginnynge was that worde, and that worde was with god: and god was thatt worde. The same was in the beginnynge wyth god. Allthynges were made by it, and with out it, was made noo thinge, that made was. In it was lyfe, And lyfe was the light of men, And the light shyneth in darcknes, and darcknes comprehended it not.

Usually a choice has to be made from three types of rendition:

- *Literal translation*, word-for-word, conveying the intellectual meaning at the expense of the original language's structure, rhythms, stresses – and, probably, feeling.
- *A close but inexact rendition* which connects with meaning in the other language *and* transfers some poetic sensibility.
- *A less sharply focused translation* making no undue attempt to catch the poetic feeling of the other language, but creating a new piece of poetry in the second language, based on the original.

Elizabeth Radice (scholar and translator) deprecated what she called a 'lack of responsible relationship to the original'. Among the perennial questions which inevitably arise are: How can one be scholarly without being pedantic? How can one *represent* faithfully what the originator wrote? Is it essential to be a poet to translate poetry well? Can *style* be transmitted in another language with a different tradition? Can the necessary light touch be retained while transferring the originator's strong effect? Can good contemporary prose or a seemingly apposite rhyme-scheme be relevant without being ephemeral or dated? Is it always a good idea to insert a word to save a footnote? So the questions go on. What does seem inescapable, is that truly great translations arise from a combination of factors: scholarship without pedantry, careful research, fortuitous association, a touch of reason, personal courage, and – inspiration. Translation is often an approximation; sometimes it transcends the original.

The Breath of Creativity

> The essence of all inspiration is the lyrical moment. Tchaikovsky

In a sense the poet is disengaged from what is described, as if observing from outside or beyond the subject matter. This implies the presence of a directing 'spirit' or muse within the agent who is in-spired. It is a misuse of the concept *inspiration* to apply it to an external connection (with rain or a woman's beauty, for example) and attribute to it no more than the function of stimulus.

It was Cicero (106-43 BC) who asserted that, 'No man was ever great without some portion of divine inspiration.' Our word *inspire* comes from the Latin *inspir-(are)*, which means 'to breathe into, blow upon; to excite, inflame; to arouse by divine influence'.

Closely associated with inspiration is the legend of the Muses – *muse* from the Latin *musa* and Greek *mousa*, meaning 'music'. From its mythological origins, it has come to mean poetical inspiration or *genius*. The English noun *genius* comes from the Latin *genius*, 'tutelary deity: inclination, natural taste'. Originally, perhaps, it meant the personification of reproductive power. When this meaning is attributed personally to an individual that person is described as having 'extraordinary and exceptional intellectual and imaginative endowment, power, faculty' – particularly of a creative, inventive, originative kind. When Jonson alluded to '*gentle* Shakespeare' it was to a genius who acknowledged his debt to his muse.

Poetic inspiration cannot be commanded. The archaic verb *muse* meant to engage in 'profound meditation; rapt thought'. Such a state prepared the creative artist to receive a visit from his muse. It was necessary to be receptively available in a state of non-volitional waiting, with the mind still and the heart open.

The Muses were the nine daughters of Zeus and Mnemosyne. They were originally goddesses of memory only, but then became the Greek deities of poetry, literature, music, and dance; later also of astronomy, philosophy, and all intellectual pursuits. Throughout antiquity the prevailing conception of the Muses follows Hesiod, who is responsible for the canonical number of nine, together with their traditional names.

Calliope	First in rank, the Muse of Epic Poetry and Eloquence
Erato	Muse of Love Poetry
Terpsichore	Muse of Lyric Poetry and of Dance
Melpomene	Muse of Tragedy
Thalia	Muse of Comedy
Euterpe	Muse of Music
Polyhymnia	Muse of Mimic Art and Sacred Song
Urania	Muse of Astronomy
Clio	Muse of History

The Muses were for long merged in an indissoluble choir which presided over music and poetry in general; it was only later that a special province was assigned to each. The cult of the Muses originated in Thrace (Pieria), as their oldest sanctuary testifies. At Thespiae, festivals in honour of the Muses were celebrated every five years and included poetic contests.

As Virgil writes in his *Georgics*, Book II, in the translation by C. Day-Lewis:

> Since Poetry for me comes first – my goddess and chief delight
> Whose devotee I am, with a master-passion adoring –
> I wish above all she accept me.

In Sonnet 100, Shakespeare speaks directly to the Muse:

> Return forgetful Muse, and straight redeem
> In gentle numbers time so idly spent.
> Sing to the ear that doth thy lays esteem
> And gives thy pen both skill and argument.

Shakespeare in Sonnet 78, metaphorically addresses his beloved as his muse; in the final couplet he writes with deferential acknowledgement:

> But thou art all my art, and dost advance
> As high as learning my rude ignorance.

Inspiration, it seems, can include both the idea and the enhancement given to that idea's expression. An example of the latter is found in *Romeo and Juliet*. An outstanding passage occurs in the concluding tragic meeting of the two lovers in the Capulets' monument. The idea, as George Steevens (1736-1800) has shown, comes from some lines by Samuel Daniel (c1562-1619) in *The Complaint of Rosamond* (1592):

And nought respecting death (the last of paines)
Plac'd his pale colours (th' ensign of his might)
Upon his new-got spoil.

Using this image of the victor's standard, Shakespeare writes:

O my love! my wife!
Death, that hath suck'd the honey of thy breath,
Hath had no power yet upon thy beauty:
Thou art not conquer'd; beauty's ensign yet
Is crimson in thy lips and in thy cheeks,
And death's pale flag is not advancèd there.

Romeo and Juliet, Act V, Scene iii

Shakespeare's development of the idea gives his lines a compelling power.

Sometimes the mysterious quality of reality in a poem arises from something seen, physically or in the mind's eye. On other occasions, a fanciful thought will occur to the poet as he observes an ordinary incident of life:

Where was the shepherd's wife,
Who left those flapping clothes to dry,
Taking no thought for her family?
For, as they bellied out
And limbs took shape and waved about,
I thought, she little knows
That ghosts are trying on her children's clothes.

Andrew Young

Paul Valéry (1871-1945), speaking of the creative process, referred to the *ligne donnée* of a poem: one line is given to the poet by God or by nature – the rest he has to provide for himself.

The intense energy of the process of composition is described by Tchaikovsky (1840-93) in a letter written from Florence in 1878:

> Generally speaking, the germ of a composition comes suddenly and unexpectedly. If the soil is ready – that is to say, if the disposition for work is there – it takes root with extraordinary force and rapidity, shoots up through the earth, puts forth branches, leaves and, finally, blossoms. I cannot define the creative process in any other way than by this simile. The great difficulty is that the germ must appear at a favourable moment, the rest of itself.

Later, in the same letter, he referred directly to inspiration and the potency of that exhilarating inhalation:

> If that condition of mind and soul, which we call *inspiration*, lasted long without intermission, no artist could survive it. The strings would break and the instrument be shattered into fragments. It is already a wonderful thing if just the main ideas and general outline of a work come without the racking of brains, through that supernatural and inexplicable force we call inspiration.

In his essay on *The Name and Nature of Poetry*, A.E. Housman (1933) spoke of the process of creativity:

> As I went along, thinking of nothing in particular, only looking at things around me and following the progress of the seasons, there would flow into my mind, with sudden and unaccountable emotion, sometimes a line or two of verse, sometimes of a whole stanza at once, accompanied, not preceded, by a vague notion of the poem which they were destined to form part of. Then there would usually be a lull of an hour or so, then perhaps the spring would bubble up again.

Robert **Frost** (1874–1963) described how, during one evening, he went outside in the snowy darkness for some air and into his mind came the whole of the poem *Stopping by Woods on a Snowy Evening*. As he wrote the series of verses its pattern of rhymes was so continuous that, in order to bring the poem to a close, it was necessary to break the rhythm in the final quatrain.

Whose woods these are I think I know,
His house is in the village though;
He will not see me stopping here
To watch his woods fill up with snow.

My little horse must think it queer
To stop without a farmhouse near
Between the woods and frozen lake
The darkest evening of the year.

He gives his harness bells a shake
To ask if there is some mistake.
The only other sound's the sweep
Of easy wind and downy flake.

The woods are lovely, dark and deep,
But I have promises to keep,
And miles to go before I sleep,
And miles to go before I sleep.

In a well-known letter attributed to Wolfgang Amadeus Mozart, written in or about the year 1789, he describes his experience of the creative process:

> When I am, as it were, completely myself, entirely alone, and of good cheer – say, travelling in a carriage, or walking after a good meal, or during the night when I cannot sleep; it is on such occasions that my ideas flow best and most abundantly. *Whence* and *how* they come, I know not; nor can I force them. Those pleasures that please me I retain in memory, and am accustomed, as I have been told, to hum them to myself. If I continue in this way, it soon occurs to me how I may turn this or that morsel to account, so as to make a good dish of it, that is to say, agreeably to the rules of counterpoint, to the peculiarities of the various instruments, etc.

All this fires my soul, and, provided I am not disturbed, my subject enlarges itself, becomes methodized and defined, and the whole, though it be long, stands almost complete and finished in my mind, so that I can survey it, like a fine picture or a beautiful statue, at a glance. Nor do I hear in my imagination the parts *successively*, but I hear them, as it were, all at once [*gleich alles zusammen*]. What a delight this is I cannot tell! All this inventing, this producing, takes place in a pleasing lively dream. Still the actual hearing of the *tout ensemble* is after all the best. What has been thus produced I do not easily forget, and this is perhaps the best gift I have my Divine Maker to thank for.

When I proceed to write down my ideas, I take out of the bag of my memory, if I may use that phrase, what has been previously collected into it in the way I have mentioned. For this reason the committing to paper is done quickly enough, for everything is, as I have said before, already finished; and it rarely differs on paper from what it was in my imagination. At this occupation I can therefore suffer myself to be disturbed; for whatever may be going on around me, I write, and even talk, but only of fowls and geese, or of Gretel or Barbel, or some such matters. But why my productions take from my hand that particular form and style that makes them 'Mozartish', and different from the works of other composers, is probably owing to the same cause which renders my nose so large or so aquiline, or, in short, makes it Mozart's, and different from those of other people. For I really do not study or aim at any originality.

There exists a mysterious process by which inchoate inspiration is transformed into the structured creativity of the mature artist. This felicitous operation – be it an act of grace or a biological phenomenon – draws a divine energy into the poet, by whom, as insight, it is given expression:

Poetry is the breath and finer spirit of all knowledge; it is the impassioned expression which is the countenance of all science.

Wordsworth

16
The Nature of Poetry

Aesthetics

> Genuine works of art carry their own aesthetic theory implicit within them and suggest the standards according to which they are to be judged. Goethe, letter, 1808

THE ABILITY to see objects as representations of other things is a sublimation of visual perception, an ability and benefit of the human condition. By extension we may similarly 'see' beyond the metaphor in poetry. With this faculty we may penetrate the surface of things to the core of existence – the centre which is everywhere. The *image* becomes more transparent as the view moves 'in' from the individual state to the universal.

It is held by many that an 'aesthetic distance' should be maintained to avoid emotional involvement, a pre-requisite for the 'aesthetic attitude'. A question arises: What is *aesthetics*? Our word *aesthetics* derives from the Greek *aisthetikos*: 'one who is perceptive of things through sensations, feelings and intuitions'. The word *aisthesis* means 'primary, rudimentary sensation'. At first sight there is nothing here to suggest the great tracts of theory and philosophy associated with Aesthetics.

Pure aesthetic experience is theirs in whom the knowledge of ideal beauty is innate; it is known intuitively at the highest level of conscious being, in intellectual ecstasy – without the accompaniment of idea formation. It is a transformation, not merely of feeling (as implied by the word *aesthesis*), but equally of understanding. Aesthetic experience is available to the spectator, hearer, and listener only by virtue of their own innate capacity to respond.

Craig **Raine** (born at Shildon, County Durham, in 1944) shows, evocatively, how words can catch at dissolving ephemera – for example, scented air from which a woman has just departed:

Perfume

She left behind
a fragrant ghost:

the idea of down
on the ear lobes,

a naked wrist,
another wrist,

caressing each other
like delicate lovers,

and scent the shape
of her collar bones,

leaving the air
alive with herself.

Beauty

Rules may obviate faults, but can never confer beauties.
Dr Johnson, *The Idler* (1758)

The word *aesthetics* was first used by Baumgarten (about 1750) for that science of sensuous knowledge concerned with beauty, in contradistinction to logic concerned with truth. Immanuel Kant (1724-1804) used the term *transcendental aesthetics* in alluding to the *a priori* principles of sensible experience. Georg Wilhelm Friedrick Hegel (1770-1831) in the 1820s established the word in its present sense in his writings on art under the title *Aesthetik*. Recent aesthetics, while not abandoning interest in beauty and evaluation in art, adopts a descriptive, factual approach to art and aesthetic experience. Writings under the heading 'aesthetics' now often include much detailed, empirical study of particular phenomena rather than abstract dissertations on the meaning of beauty and the sublime (and their subjective, or objective value). Some argue that this approach, with its departure from discussion of the usual relationship to pleasure, moral goodness, the purpose of art, and the nature of aesthetic value, hardly deserves the name *aesthetics*.

Conventional aesthetic theory explores three main aspects:

- imitation
- expression
- form

Some of the difficulties that arise from considering these concepts, particularly Plato's *imitation* (*mimetikos*), can be resolved by re-interpreting the customary concepts as:

- resonance
- style
- composition

It also seems helpful to distinguish the *afferent aesthetic effect* on the observer and the *efferent aesthetic response*.

Imitation
Plato placed emphasis on *imitation*. The usual inference is that he was suggesting that art, like nature, was an imitative representation of an Ideal Form which inspired it. The difficulty is finding an Ideal Form behind every natural object, then distinguishing Nature from Art. May we not, rather, interpret Plato's imitation as a resonance which expresses one essential reality behind all appearance? If every thing has an appearance (as an object) but is an aspect of the one Reality (which provides the being and unity of the created multiplicity) then there is a sense in which Plato's imitation of an Ideal Form can be realized.

Expression
The second conventional aspect of aesthetics is *expression*, implying a distinction between what is represented and its spiritual or emotional content. In turn this discrepancy diminishes the aesthetic value. If expression is re-interpreted as *style*, and we accept that 'style is the man', then intrinsically the emotional and spiritual content of the artist's vision is externalized by his unique style.

Leonardo da Vinci's style differs from that of Botticelli, but their work seems to be breathed through by inspiration from the same source. One way to articulate the inspiration which lies within a Phidias sculpture, a Rembrandt painting or a Mozart string quartet is to describe it as a resonance with reality. The ontological nature of that Reality is something each person has to discover individually. It takes many years to surrender early conditioning to the extent that enables an individual to resonate with it naturally and easily.

Form
The third component of aesthetics, conventionally considered, is *form*. The Latin *forma* meaning 'shape' seems a somewhat limited concept to be considered as a major aspect of the aesthetic effect. It is more comprehensive to look towards *composition* as the third aspect, that is, 'the combination of the parts or elements of the whole, a synthesis of forces, the manner in which a thing is composed, its construction, the product as a whole'.

The *critical process* has a place in aesthetics in its twin forms of *interpretation* and *evaluation*. These occur as a simultaneous discernment during the aesthetic response to a fine object or a significant event. An acknowledgement occurs which is like an affirmation of being, accompanied by a fine resonance of spirit, a clear and open mind and a still, alert body. There is recognition that the underlying one Reality is being reflected by the aesthetically satisfying object or event.

In ancient India, at a time when poetry had to some extent become an end in itself, a debate took place as to whether or not *ornaments* represented the essence of poetry. The consensus emerged that poetry differed from prose (that is, the poetic from the prosaic, not verse from prose) by its *sapidity* or *flavour* (*rasa* in Sanskrit, corresponding to the Latin *sapientia* 'wisdom').

The Sanskrit word for poetry, *kavya*, can be taken in the general sense to mean 'art'. Essential meanings in the root *ku* include 'wisdom' and 'skill'. In the tradition of Indian art, *fine art* is an expression or statement 'informed by the ideal of beauty'. The statement is the *body* of the work; its *rasa* (savour) is beauty, the *soul* of the work.

The Asian view, which accords with Plato's, contends that there are two Beauties: the one absolute or ideal; the other relative and more appropriately termed 'loveliness' because determined by human affections. These two concepts are clearly distinguished in Indian aesthetics, which asserts that Beauty subsists in the *experience* of beauty. The poet represents and facilitates participation in that experience.

Much of Western awareness and reflection upon art has been founded upon the Greek theory of art as *mimesis* or representation. With this there has arisen an intellectual distinction between *form* and *content*. There seems to be a powerful insistence that a work of art *is* its content; that a work of art is, by definition, saying something.

Even if the work of art is in the form of language – a poem – we need not read it as necessarily 'saying something'. Might it not rather be indicating, signalling or pointing to – reality; beyond words, behind representation; on to the invisible but very real presence of that immanent, other *something* beyond the obvious – indicated by sense, emotion, or *spirit*?

The sense of beauty arises when the difference between subject and object has been dissolved, when the subject termed 'I' and the object called 'it' have both disappeared into the realm of non-dual Entirety, that is, the total unity of everything. This is when there is no longer anybody to transfer, or anything to be transferred. Put another way, there is no one to interpret and nothing to express. For the free play of intuition, there needs to be no thing between *self* and *object*. In Zen Buddhist terms, this is the sphere of non-duality, the liberation resulting from 'no-mind'.

There seems to be a natural aesthetic which corresponds to a universal order, consonant with absolute Beauty. At this level, individual subjectivity falls away and stylistic features arising from time and culture are irrelevant. Awareness transcends individuality and rests in the reality existing apart from perception. It is as though reality exists inherently within the thing itself, as an essence more actual than the appearance. This Reality is beyond the form but simultaneously present with it. In the observer there arises a transparency which dissolves any sense of inner or outer, this or other. Only that which has reality of existence *is*; I myself, in my deepest identity, am not different from it. Distinction between the aesthetic effect and the aesthetic response dissolves in unity.

Attitudes to Form

The nature of a thing is expressed in and revealed by its form; the structure of the form discovers its maker.

> The structure of prose is, in the widest sense of the word, *logical* ... The structure of poetry, on the other hand, is ultimately determined by its technique. The part ... played by logic in prose falls in poetry to the metre, the rhyme, the alliterations and the associative values of the words.
>
> F.W. Bateson, *English Poetry and the English Language* (Oxford, 1934)

> There is also the question of how to read those modern poets who have abandoned metres altogether and write free verse. If the authority of the measured rhythms is played out for them, I suggest that their prose-poetry is Delphic in character, or sibylline, it is cryptic, metaphorical, portentous, prophetic; for against prose norms which have been so carefully worked out, it is demonstrably elliptic, distorted, over-emphatic and sometimes not easily intelligible.
>
> John Crowe Ransom, *The Strange Music of English Verse* (1956)

Ransom also reminds us that the old measures were ritualistic in their tendency to make prose sound solemn, pious, or quaint, to those unable to connect with its spirit.

In a sense people apply the term *poetry* TO writing, as a projection – as though calling it poetry *made* it poetry. A question arises: Can poetry be tested against criteria which enable poetry to be distinguishable from other arrangements of words?

'A poem is the very image of life expressed in its eternal truth,' said Shelley in *A Defence of Poetry* (1821). Dr Johnson asserted that 'poetry is the art of uniting pleasure with truth, by calling imagination to the help of reason'. The Oxford English Dictionary defines poetry as 'composition in verse or metrical language, or in some equivalent patterned arrangement of language'. But what does 'equivalent' mean in this context? If the uncertainty of equivalence has to do with the distinction between good prose and well written poetry, no less an authority than Wordsworth makes an important point. He said, 'It may be safely affirmed, that there neither is, nor can be, any essential difference between the language of prose and metrical composition ...'

In *The Times* (5 May 1995), 'Nature Notes' contained the following two sentences:

> On the hawthorns, the small spherical flowerbuds are turning into sheets of white blossom with a powerful scent. Cow parsley is starting to form misty white ribbons along the sides of the lanes.

Wordsworth's point is valid; the *language* of poetry and well-written prose is not different. Turning to another aspect of the vital distinction, Edwin Morgan, in *The Times Literary Supplement* (28 January 1965), wrote:

> Can prose become poetry through typographical rearrangement? I rather think it can.

This, of course, does not hold good with just any old words (*see* Chapter 12 – The Structure of Poetry).

On 7 May 1995, in the *Independent on Sunday*, Allison Pearson highlighted a phrase from one of Churchill's wartime speeches as an illustration of the war leader's visual sense. After Alamein he said: 'A bright gleam has caught the helmets of our soldiers.' As the critic remarked, they might have been Homer's words in a reference to events at Troy.

It is said that in the very idea of poetry we infer the metrical form; furthermore, that words arranged in a metrical pattern with end-rhymes constitute poetry. Somewhat sardonically, and to make a point, Jonathan Swift (1710) meets these criteria:

> Sweepings from butchers' stalls, dung, guts and blood,
> Drowned puppies, stinking sprats, all drenched in mud,
> Dead cats and turnip-tops, come tumbling down the flood.

This illustration strengthens the validity of the view, held by many, that a known poetic form produces expectations in the reader. The structure in itself, has implications for tone, voice, emotion, and mood. Poetry is a vehicle with special resources for influencing meaning that are not available in other media. It is language that is highly organized and thus well charged with meaning.

In one sense, *poetry* is the sum of all that has been written in its name; in another, poetry is an absolute, independent of the billions of poetically organized words. If there *is* an independent 'something else' we should be able to discuss and analyse it. When an entity is 'more than the sum of its component parts' we look beyond the expression to a principle, a process, or an energy flow. Scale is a useful indication of significance. Bishop Richard Hurd, in his *Discourse on Poetical Imitation* (1751), said that 'Poetry ... is indeed the noblest and most extensive of the mimetic [imitative] arts, having all creation for its object and ranging over the entire circuit of universal being.' Reason suggests that there are not two worlds – a world of poetry and the world of reality. In fact, for Shakespeare and for the Zen haiku poets, reality *is* the world of poetry. This view enlarges a limiting perception of poetry – that it comprises beautiful ideas or elevated thought, coupled with imagination and feeling, embodied in language specially adapted to stir the imagination and the emotions.

Eliot considered that, when what is ordinarily apprehensible only by thought is brought within the grasp of feeling, or when what is ordinarily only felt is transformed into thought without ceasing to be feeling, *then* we enter the realm of metaphysical poetry. Since metaphysics means simply '*beyond* physics', this is not anything vague or unworldly; thought and feeling experienced simultaneously is an everyday occurrence.

I.A. Richards (1893-1979), the English critic whose approach to poetry was philosophic, linguistic, and psychological, addresses several important questions in relation to poetry. He discusses what kind of truth constitutes the subject-matter of poetry, and the place of poetry in the context of life; and he investigates the critical judgement of poetry. He worked to his conclusion along what might be considered Benthamite Utilitarian lines; for instance, by asking, 'What is the use of poetry?' Ultimately, he concludes, as have many before him (Matthew Arnold, Pound, Wyndham Lewis, Eliot, Leavis), that poetry's function in the modern world is that dimension which was formerly the province of religion – to provide a 'touchstone' of evaluation and hence, even if only indirectly, a guide to living. Poets are as persuasive as priests when they examine for us the transience and impermanence of life. Through the poet we can contemplate the essence, but we witness the existence.

Temporality

> Wherever anything lives, there is, open somewhere,
> a register in which time is being inscribed.
>
> Henri Bergson, *Creative Evolution*

Time, the elapsing of existence, is often regarded as 'the enemy' and whoever thinks thus will have his or her reasons for this view. Sophocles (in his *Electra*) said, 'Time is a gentle deity'. Centuries later Shakespeare, in *The Two Gentlemen of Verona*, insisted that, 'Time is the nurse and breeder of all good.' That life 'elapses' cannot be denied. Its passing is perceived as a dimension or a flow and, once either percept has been abstracted, the poet can work upon it – and he does. Time has always been a major preoccupation of the human race:

- *How long* will things last?
- *How much time* will be allotted to me or those I love?
- *When* will life end?
- What is *eternity*?

At first these might seem to be questions for the theologian or the philosopher, but instead, like the Greeks, we might seek provocative, stimulating answers from the poet, who *is* philosopher in understanding, insight, and vision.

Francis Bacon, in his *Advancement of Learning* (1605), indicates this direction by alluding to, 'Time which is the author of authors.' The dictionary indicates the origin and meaning of *time* (Old English *tima*): 'time, date; proper time; period of time; lifetime; season of the year.' But there is more to time than this. The fundamental sense of the origin and base of the word *time* is 'to divide; division'. The Sanskrit word *day*, means 'to divide, allot' (Monier-Williams). *Genesis* I tells us that, 'God divided the light from the darkness … and called the light Day'. This suggests the primary division of time. From the notion *time* come such ideas as 'before and after; past, present, and future; beginning, and end; duration'.

Like proverbs which sometimes contradict each other but are nevertheless true of a specific situation, poetry brings out different views of time. For Juvenal (c60-c140), in *Satires*:

> The noiseless foot of Time steals swiftly by,
> And, ere we dream of manhood, age is nigh!

In contrast to such stealth, Andrew Marvell, addressing *His Coy Mistress*, introduces a sense of urgency:

> But at my back I always hear
> Time's wingèd chariot hurrying near.

Not always so fleet of foot,

> Time goes on crutches till love hath all his rites.
>
> *Much Ado About Nothing*, Act II, Scene i

Reassuringly, John Florio (c1553-1626) writes in *First Fruits*: 'Who hath time hath life,' but as Horace reminds us, 'Even while we speak, envious time has fled.' Many writers have commented on the silent, insidious nature of time's passing:

> Time is a file that wears and makes no noise.
>
> English proverb

Tennyson succinctly defines aspects of time in lines which have about them an aphoristic brevity:

> In time there is no present,
> In eternity no future,
> In eternity no past.

A prose statement by Richard Jeffries (1848-87) has in it the felicity of poetry:

> It is eternity now. I am in the midst of it. It is about me in the sunshine; I am in it as the butterfly in the laden air. Nothing has to come; it is now. Now is eternity; now is the immortal life.

That humans should not attach too much importance to time has been a contention of philosophers for centuries. Here is a more recent pronouncement:

> To realise the unimportance of time is the gate of wisdom.
>
> Bertrand Russell, *Mysticism and Logic* (1917)

Sometimes we would have the passing moment stay; on other occasions we are grateful that, inevitably, events will pass.

> Time is that in which all things pass away …
>
> Schopenhauer, *The Vanity of Existence*

Come what come may,
Time and the hour runs through the roughest day.

Macbeth, Act I, Scene iii

Our experience of time is both the intuition of the moment and the knowledge that we are perpetually perishing.

J.B. Leishman (1961) distinguishes four aspects of the phenomenon *time* and considers the manner in which the poet addresses this inescapable feature of existence:

Time Characteristic	*Poet*
Devouring time	Horace, Ovid, Pindar
Brief time-span of a human life	Horace, Sestius, Shakespeare
The fleeting brevity of youth and beauty	Shakespeare
Time defied and transcended by love	Shakespeare

Horace seems almost despairing with his, 'Life's short span forbids us to set out after far-reaching hopes,' and confirms this view with, 'Snatch at today and trust as little as you can in tomorrow.' Ovid, in his *Metamorphoses*, is uncompromising: 'Time the devourer of all things.'

The promise of immortality through verse is a commonplace of classical and Renaissance poetry. Shakespeare shares with Horace the powerful conviction that it is in and through poetry alone that anything of ourselves will survive impermanence. This *self*, the etymology of which is unknown although it occurs in Old English, means 'the essential quality, character, genius, quintessence, inmost nature of anything'. The self is for Shakespeare that 'better part'. In Sonnet 39 his reference to the object of his love is, 'When thou art all the better part of me'. He goes on, 'And what is't but mine own when I praise thee?' In Sonnet 74 he confirms this assertion: 'My spirit is thine, the better part of me.' In Sonnet 18 he defies time as he says of the beloved:

When in eternal lines to time thou grow'st;
So long as men can breathe, or eyes can see,
So long lives this, and this gives life to thee.

In an earlier age, a love poet would have been unlikely to declare that his love would outlast the beauty of his mistress. As Leishman puts it, 'we seem to hear no longer merely the poet, but love itself defying time.' The essence of Shakespeare's approach is that love is the vanquisher of time. There is to be no compromise, no fraternizing, no placating the enemy:

Love's not Time's fool, though rosy lips and cheeks
Within his bending sickle's compass come.

Sonnet 116

Shakespeare recognizes that the self of the beloved transcends corporeality and must be addressed metaphysically:

> What is your substance, whereof are you made,
> That millions of strange shadows on you tend?
>
> Sonnet 53

> What's in the brain, that ink may character,
> Which hath not figur'd to thee my true spirity
>
> Sonnet 108

The poet Valéry in *Mauvaises pensées et autres* (1942) continues the questioning, 'Are you not the future of all the memories stored within you? The future of a past?' Shakespeare indicates strongly that the prisoner of time can attain release. Eternity is freedom, poetry reveals its direction.

Eternity

> Thou, silent form, dost tease us
> out of thought as doth eternity.
>
> Keats, *Ode on a Grecian Urn*

Time is a measure of the serial lapse of existence and this temporality is usually contrasted with eternity. *Eternity* is not simply 'never-ending time'. The *eternal* from the Latin *aetern-(us)*, 'everlasting', has additional meanings: 'without beginning or end; of infinite duration; without intermission, unceasing'.

> Reversion to destiny is called eternity …
>
> Lao-Tzu, *The Character of Tao* (6 BC)

> The One remains, the many change and pass …
>
> Shelley, *Adonais* (1821)

Elizabeth Barrett Browning emphasizes in a sonnet that the unique beloved is loved, not for what is received, not under the compulsion of dependency, but for love itself:

> But love me for love's sake, that evermore
> Thou mayst love on, through love's eternity.
>
> *Sonnets from the Portuguese*

Time is something of which we are all too aware in the 21st century. Eliot's *J. Alfred Prufrock* may have claimed, 'I have measured out my life with coffee spoons', but most people would acknowledge that their life is measured in 'breaths' or moments. Poetry has the capacity to catch the fleeting moment and enlarge it – or, more accurately, reveal its seeming timelessness. In the second verse of his poem *Adlestrop*, Edward Thomas (1878-1917) captures a moment that reveals the stillness which is always present, beyond time:

Adlestrop

Yes, I remember Adlestrop –
The name, because one afternoon
Of heat the express-train drew up there
Unwontedly. It was late June.

The steam hissed. Someone cleared his throat
No one left and no one came
On the bare platform. What I saw
Was Adlestrop – only the name

And willows, willow-herb, and grass,
And meadows sweet, and haycocks dry,
No whit less still and lonely fair
Than the high cloudlets in the sky.

And for that minute a blackbird sang
Close by, and round him, mistier,
Farther and farther, all the birds
Of Oxfordshire and Gloucestershire.

When time seemingly stands still, its eternal quality can make the moment seem endless. In the following extract from a poem by Rupert Brooke (1887-1915) he reports what he saw when time appeared to be at rest.

Dining-room Tea

I watched the quivering lamplight fall
On plate and flowers and pouring tea
And cup and cloth; and they and we
Flung all the dancing moments by
With jest and glitter. Lip and eye
Flashed on the glory, shone and cried,
Improvident, unmemoried;
And fitfully and like a flame
The light of laughter went and came.
Proud in their careless transience moved
The changing faces that I loved.

Till suddenly, and otherwhence,
I looked upon your innocence
For lifted clear and still and strange
From the dark woven flow of change
Under a vast and starless sky
I saw the immortal moment lie.
One instant I, an instant, knew
As God knows all. And it and you
I, above Time, oh, blind! could see
In witless immortality.

I saw the marble cup; the tea,
Hung on the air, an amber stream;

I saw the fire's unglittering gleam,
The painted flame, the frozen smoke.
No more the flooding lamplight broke
On flying eyes and lips and hair;
But lay, but slept unbroken there,
On stiller flesh, and body breathless,
And lips and laughter stayed and deathless,
And words on which no silence grew.
Light was more alive than you.

For suddenly, and otherwhence,
I looked on your magnificence.
I saw the stillness and the light,
And you, august, immortal, white,
Holy and strange; and every glint
Posture and jest and thought and tint
Freed from the mask of transiency,
Triumphant in eternity,
Immote, immortal.

Dazed at length
Human eyes grew, mortal strength
Wearied; and Time began to creep.
Change closed about me like a sleep.
Light glinted on the eyes I loved.
The cup was filled. The bodies moved.
The drifting petal came to ground.
The laughter chimed its perfect round.
The broken syllable was ended.

Robert Browning wrote, 'I count life just a stuff to try the soul's strength on'. Coleridge in *Youth and Age* says simply: 'Life is but thought.' The transience, relativity, and unreality of life is emphasized by poets and spiritual philosophers alike. Robert Burns in a *Lament* wrote that, 'Life and love are all a dream.' Those inclining towards the spirit would not agree with Burns that love is a dream – rather that love is universal and absolute.

Richard III, as Shakespeare portrays him, feels that he has nothing to lose by trying his fortune and, like a gambler, taking what he wants from life:

… I have set my life upon a cast,
And I will stand the hazard of the die.

Act V, Scene iv

Tennyson believes that we are like marionettes, manipulated helplessly. The question is who or what is pulling the strings:

We are puppets, Man in his pride, and Beauty fair in her flower;
Do we move ourselves, or are we moved by an unseen hand at a game
That ever pushes us off from the board, and others ever succeed?

Maud

With poetic realism the philosopher ruler Marcus Aurelius (121-180), in his *Meditations*, prompts us to, 'Remember that man's life lies all within this present, as 'twere but a hair's breadth of time; as for the rest, the past is gone, the future may never be. Short, therefore, is man's life, and narrow is the corner of the earth wherein he dwells.'

The insecurity of life is remarked by Shakespeare in *Timon of Athens* as, 'Life's uncertain voyage'. Another poet, Cowper (1731-1800), in his poem *Hope*, observed shrewdly that:

> Men deal with life as children with their play,
> Who first misuse, then cast their toys away.

The eternal world of possibility, of potential, is the direction of the individual under the impelling force of destiny. All experience is limited and temporal. The master poet sees this and its transience but, because he is the *seer*, he can look beyond the passing to the ever-present eternal. In this stillness, where there is no movement, time ceases. Past and future merge in the moment *now*. The Irish poet Thomas Moore (1779-1852), with the admirable succinctness of the poet-philosopher, writes in *Lalla Rookh: The Veiled Prophet of Khorassan* (1817):

> The past, the future, two eternities!

The poet has indicated that eternity is reached in either direction; poetry constitutes a 4,000 year history of the human mind coming to terms with this insight.

Master Poets

Through the medium of history, people in the present attempt to understand the past. Poetry is a vital strand of the history of the human race. It is also a critical and sympathetic interpretative commentary on the ways and beliefs of mankind. History is not merely a record of events. It is, inherently:

- a selection,
- an interpretation,
- an evaluative assessment,
- a moral, political and socialistic appraisement.

Poetry is all of these. The nature of poetry is evolving continuously. It pulsates with the movement of life, of which it is an expression and interpretation. There could be said to be four levels of poetry. Here they are presented in a descending order of spiritual and literary excellence:

1 Inspired master poetry, produced seemingly without effort; the unlaboured expression of the poet's perfect harmony. Since the poet has the necessary technical ability, its production is, as it were, inevitable and executed with the art that conceals art.

2 Profoundly mysterious poetry which admits the reader or hearer to a glimpse of the true reality.
3 Poetry which is no more than merely clever.
4 Finally, poetry revealing only what the highest level of the art assumes as a minimum – a technical competence in the craft.

Eliot, commenting on the state of poetry as he saw it in his own times, wrote, 'Samuel Johnson could accept as poetry, much which seems to us merely competent and correct; we, on the other hand, are too ready to accept as poetry what is neither competent nor correct.'

Quite evidently, personality may spoil poetry. John Keats said, 'A poet has no identity.' Certainly the finest poetry confirms not only that identity transcends individuality, but also that it dissolves towards the universal. Eliot spoke of the transparency of the author within an important genus of poetry, the religious or 'devotional'.

I entered in, I know not where,
And I remained, though knowing naught,
Transcending knowledge with my thought.

Poems of St John of the Cross, IV
Translation by Roy Campbell

Referring to St John of the Cross, Eliot speaks of the emotion being so directly *the consequence of the idea* that the personality of the author is, somehow, annihilated. In experiencing the poem, 'we seem to be in direct relation with what he saw, without mediation through the personality of the author himself'. For this reason, the highest and best poetry can communicate – even before it is understood.

Every poet reflects his beliefs and philosophy through his art. The reputation of the great poet is not dependent upon genius alone, but also upon his actual and cultural surroundings – all of which affect his position as a poet in his time and literary context. To use a *gestalt* term, the *figure* (the poet) and the *ground* (context) are mutually interacting; Shakespeare is, perhaps, the supreme example of this influential mutual exchange which is one of the defining characteristics of the master poet.

The master poet, although a person, is not a personality; his personal idiosyncrasy is at the most a part of his equipment – never the occasion of his art. Throughout the history of Western literature there have been major and minor poets, but a few of the best were such superlative writers that they may be distinguished as master poets. The group listed in this volume is the author's selection, but it accords with the wider evaluation and acknowledgement of many generations of readers.

Homer	Petrarch	Shakespeare	Eliot
Hesiod	Dante	Hopkins	
Virgil	Chaucer	Yeats	

Hopkins, Yeats, and Eliot may, for some, seem debatable choices, but the other poets, having attracted general high estimation down the centuries, would appear on most listings. All ten of these men wrote exemplary verse and were the authentic voice of their age. As though speaking presciently of the master poet, Lucretius (in *De Rerum Natura*, i, 72-4) described the perspective of such a human being:

> The lively power of his mind prevailed and he journeyed far out beyond the flaming walls of the world, and traversed infinity in his intellect and imagination.

Even among master poets, one stands above all; that man was William Shakespeare:

> The man who of all modern, and perhaps ancient poets, had the largest and most comprehensive soul.
>
> Dryden

The standard established by the master poets has been accepted by successive generations as a measure of excellence in literature. The master poet is open-minded, with an abundant enthusiasm – a cool, impartial seeker after truth. Throughout this volume, as the work of each master poet has been examined and evaluated, specific characteristics have been discerned and defined:

- universality, permanence,
- wholeness, genius,
- comprehensiveness, supremacy.

The master poet is aware of the relationships constituting the integrated totality of the created world. From their vantage point in history master poets contribute to the development of their own phase of civilization. But more than this, with their insight and imagination, they may be said to interpret for the human race. How do they achieve this?

Coleridge, writing in the *Biographia Literaria*, says that the poet 'brings the whole soul of man into activity … This power reveals itself in … a more than usual state of emotion with more than usual order.'

Plato contended, in the dialogue *Ion*, that all good poets write beautiful poems not to create works of art, but because they are inspired and possessed. This *possession* is the combination of fine skill and an insight which compels the poet to write.

The poet's intellect distils experience and expresses the innermost truth of things. His is an ability to visualize the subtler image; to reveal the extraordinary hidden within the commonplace. For the American poet Carl Sandburg (1878-1967), 'Poetry is the opening and closing of a door.' That the glimpses afforded to the poet might be other than rational seems to have been in the mind of Christopher Morley, who asserted that, 'The courage of the poet is to keep ajar the door that leads into madness.' Shakespeare touched on this with his usual eloquence:

> The poet's eye, in a fine frenzy rolling,
> Doth glance from heaven to earth, from earth to heaven;
> And, as imagination bodies forth
> The forms of things unknown, the poet's pen
> Turns them to shapes, and gives to airy nothing
> A local habitation and a name.
>
> *A Midsummer-Night's Dream*, Act V, Scene i

In a letter, Oscar Wilde insisted that the 'mystery of the world is the visible, not the invisible'. If the visible *is* mysterious, and few reflective minds would dissent from this, what then of the invisible – for example, daylight or the space in silence? As J.R. Lowell put it, 'To make the common marvellous ... is the test of genius.' The poet, through earth's veiling mist, marks the gleam of dawn that others are unable to discern. The poet's vision begins to emerge more clearly as we examine his work and discover how the invisible is made visible. As Eliot expressed it, 'Poetry is not the assertion of truth, but the making of that truth more fully real to us.' This territory is traversed with assuredness by the poet but there are special difficulties, resolved only by clarity of thought and competence in the use of language.

Ambiguity

Since the poet is totally responsible for his text, a question arises over vagueness, obscurity, and difficulty in understanding the poet's intentions. Heraclitus (c540-c475 BC) said:

> Eyes and ears are poor witnesses for men if their souls do not understand the language.

There is irony in this, because he himself wrote in such a cryptic style that he has been subject, over time, to very different interpretations.

William Empson (1906-84), the British literary critic and poet, suggested that the greatness of a poem might inhere in its multiplicities of meanings, of which some might be unintentional. He argued that the ambiguities involved in poetic statements establish the very tension that produces the dramatic richness of poetry. In essence, he says that without ambiguity there would be no poetry.

Ambiguity should not be confused with complexity. A sad smile is complex but not ambiguous. The great works of mankind often combine a high degree of order with complexity (although beauty and elegance are likely to stem from simplicity). Neither need be ambiguous. Sheer quantity can sometimes give an impression of complexity, ambiguity even, but the impression is misleading. In examples of ordinary things, like a daisy's petals or tiles on a roof, order and simplicity underlie the apparent complexity, the ambiguous mass effect.

Of concern here is the difference between an ambiguity of subject competently expressed, and an uncertainty of intention or execution, caused by the poet's vagueness of thought, incoherence, or inarticulation.

In *Seven Types of Ambiguity* (1930) Empson distinguishes and analyses the effects arising from deliberate or inadvertent employment of ambiguity in poetry. The concepts he explores may be summarized:

1 A detail is presented in several different ways simultaneously.
2 Two or more possible meanings are effectively resolved into a unity.
3 Two seemingly unconnected meanings are presented together.
4 Meanings combine, thus clarifying a complexity in the author's mind.
5 A fortunate fusion which enables the author to find clarification in the act of writing.
6 Contradictory or irrelevant presentations which compel the reader to invent interpretations.
7 Complete contradiction revealing divison in the author's mind.

In Eliot's hands ambiguity becomes an aspect of the integrity and strength of the piece:

And the children in the apple-tree
Not known, because not looked for
But heard, half-heard, in the stillness
Between two waves of the sea.
Quick now, here, now, always –
A condition of complete simplicity
(Costing not less than everything)
And all shall be well and
All manner of things shall be well
When the tongues of flames are in-folded
Into the crowned knot of fire
And the fire and the rose are one.

Little Gidding

The true poet strives to keep his expression poised on a tense miraculous line between an acceptable ambiguity and obscurity. Penetrating ambiguity is one of the functions of the critic.

The Critic

A man's mind is hidden in his writings; criticism brings it to light.

Solomon Ibn Gabirol, *The Choice of Pearls* (c1050)

Modern critics sometimes encourage the examination of poetry for aspects of meaning not intended by the poet. Some poets appear to build in vagueness or unclear meaning deliberately to give their work 'depth'. The virtue of deliberate ambiguity is dubious. Superficially, access to the poet's understanding seems a simple enough process:

- read the text,
- follow the images,
- enter the poet's mind.

Much will depend upon the clarity of the poet's own perception and the transparency of the writing. In poetry we find imagery, feeling, and intelligence expressed through language. Language *is* what it *does*, although the significance of this seemingly obvious comment may not be immediately apparent. The poet interprets and presents what all may see but many do not, and is sometimes criticized for obscurity. It was said, even of Eliot, that his words, are attractive but contain no 'real' meaning. But to this, George Masri (1991) has responded, 'Why doubt; if he has made an impression, is that not enough?' Expression, at the deeper levels of understanding, will inevitably carry obscurity. 'Real' meaning is in the direction away from the concrete, the physical. An example is that the *idea* 'table' is held to be more real and more enduring than the object 'a wooden table', which has a finite physical existence. This may seem to run counter to logic. In fact, as Eliot himself made clear: the pre-logical mentality persists in civilized man, but becomes available only to or through the poet. Moreover, poetry makes that truth more evident to us.

As to the lucidity of poetry, E.B. White assures us that, 'A poet dares to be just so clear and no clearer ... He unzips the veil from beauty, but does not remove it. A poet utterly clear is a trifle glaring.' This would be more convincing if all poets were able to regulate their obscurity. Some poetry is shallow and there is little to hide; some is deep but the poet's unclear vision or poor technique leads to inadvertent ambiguity. This was addressed by a critic reviewing the poetry of A.E. Housman:

> A feature that has perhaps not endeared him to critics is that at his most beautiful, there is not a great deal to say about him.

And of a particular piece:

> By its transparent inevitability, the poem puts the critic out of work.

The critic has not been without influence on the nature of poetry. Poets, not surprisingly, are sensitive to the vagaries of critics and especially of uninformed criticism. The Elizabethan poet Sir Henry Wotton spoke for generations of writers when he said, 'The critics are like brushers of noblemen's clothes', making an evaluation that at worst viewed them as parasitic, at best as in the second category in the axiom, 'Those who can, do; those who can't, teach.'

T.S. Eliot, writing in *The Use of Poetry and the Use of Criticism* (1933), makes some pointed comments on the role of the critic and his *modus operandi*:

> The majority of critics can be expected only to parrot the opinions of the last master of criticism; among more independent minds a period of destruction, of preposterous over-estimation, and of successive fashions takes place, until a new authority comes to introduce some order. And it is not merely the passage of time and accumulation of new artistic experience, nor the ineradicable tendency of the great majority of men to repeat the opinions of those few who have taken the trouble to think, nor the tendency of a nimble but myopic majority of men to progenerate heterodoxies, that makes new assessments necessary. It is that no generation is interested in Art in quite the same way as any other; each generation, like each individual, brings to the contemplation of art its own categories of appreciation, makes its own demands upon art, and has its own uses of art.

Anatole France (1844-1924) emphasizes the critic's perceived subjectivity in his tribute: 'The good critic is he who relates the adventures of his soul among masterpieces.' Perhaps we should not press too hard for objectivity in the critic until it is more developed in ourselves. What we may welcome from the critic is to be directed to something in a work of art not seen before, and for the piece to be related to its context.

A critic who also wrote poetry was Wallace Stevens (1879-1955). Here, from his poem *The Blue Guitar*, are four lines of sheer poetry which yield a philosophic meaning commensurate with the reader's level of being:

> They said, 'You have a blue guitar,
> You do not play things as they are.'
> The man replied, 'Things as they are
> Are changed upon the blue guitar.'

Charles **Baudelaire** (1821-67) was another poet who wrote important articles of aesthetic criticism and achieved rare and strange beauty in his word music. He held that the great poet was inevitably a critic; otherwise he would be incomplete as an artist, a mere romantic inspired by instinct and personal feeling. The poet, said Baudelaire, translates experience into sounds, rhythms, and images; the critic translates experience into meditation on the nature of that experience and reflects on the process of artistic distillation and crystallization. The poet reaches beyond the subjective perception to full understanding of art, beauty, and truth. It is considered by many that Baudelaire's criticism is the key to his poetry, while his poetry extends and fulfils his aesthetic doctrine.

Believing that every object in this world expresses its spiritual source, Baudelaire considered that only poets who had reached a high degree of spirituality were capable of understanding and interpreting these mysteries. Beauty is essentially a spiritual reality; the search for beauty and the attraction of the underlying spirit are one and the same. He insisted that it is beauty that gives spirit its radiance, claiming that, in the context of this spirit, the poet could distil beauty from ugliness. He loftily sought the art in which all artistic languages would, as one, express the spiritual experience. In his poetry he endeavoured to employ the idioms of other arts which, in his verse, would glide imperceptibly from one to the other. He wanted to render colour by means of harmony, sound by colour and line. It was in this spirit that he wrote the evocative poems which are perhaps his highest achievement – *L'Invitation au Voyage*, *Harmonie du Soir*, *La Vie anterieure*. Perhaps his magnificent poem *Le Voyage* is the pinnacle of his achievement; in it, he remarks:

> O bitter is the knowledge that one draws from the voyage!

His poem *Correspondences*, with its concept of *le symbole*, became the origin of the new school of poetry, Symbolism. His poem describes these 'symbols':

> Nature is a shrine whose living pillars
> Sometimes emanate confused words;
> Man comes having traversed forests of symbols
> Observing him with familiar regard.
>
> ★
>
> There are perfumes fresh as children's flesh,
> Soft as oboes, green as meadows,
> And others – tainted, rich and triumphant.
>
> Expanding into diffusion of infinite things,
> Like amber, musk, incense and aromatic resin,
> The ecstatic song of spirit and senses.
>
> *Correspondences*, based on the translation by G.A. Wagner

Baudelaire had an octoroon mistress, the celebrated (and infamous) Jeanne Duval. Here are two verses from *Sed Non Satiata*:

> Strange deity, brown as nights,
> With the perfumes of musk and Havanah
> Magical creation, Faust of the savanna,
> Sorceress with the ebony thighs, child of black midnights,
>
> ★
>
> From those two great black eyes, chimmeys of your spirit,
> O pitiless demon, throw out less flame at me …
>
> Translated by G.A. Wagner

We leave this poet with the final verse of his *Morning Twilight*:

> Dawn chattering with cold in its red and green robe,
> Advanced slowly along the deserted Seine,
> And grey Paris rubbing its eyes,
> Reached for its tools, like an assiduous old man.

Baudelaire pushed back the limits of the world, giving his readers glimpses of hitherto unexplored realms of man's inner self. In the best tradition of his art, he is a poet and critic of great evocative and suggestive power, but at the same time a poet of realism, aware of the commonplace and the ordinary.

Conclusion

So we are reaching the end of this survey covering 4,000 years of the work of poets. There are no interruptions in the continuum of poetry; this is well understood by its practitioners. James Elroy Flecker (1884-1915), an English poet and playwright who died young, addresses a poet of 'a thousand years hence':

> O friend unseen, unborn, unknown,
>   Student of our sweet English tongue,
> Read out my words at night, alone:
>   I was a poet, I was young.
> Since I can never see your face
>   And never shake you by the hand,
> I send my soul through time and space
>   To greet you. You will understand.

The human spirit is an unchanging and everlasting principle. Whoever embodies that spirit is endowed with the power of understanding all that pertains to it without limitation of time or place.

The poet expresses the relationship between dream and reality; he interprets the reality for those who can only dream, because he glimpses it directly. This insight brings redemption to the world, held as it is in thrall to dream and illusion. The nihilistic rejection of reality comes not only from the apish tricks of the ego's quest for instantaneous gratification, but also from the apathy of dream, and from intellectual feebleness. As the poet sifts his understanding of words, he painstakingly distils meaning from the glimpsed shapes within shadowy mystery. The poet's devotion to words is as fundamental as the potter's to clay.

To change the metaphor, poetry is wondrous alchemy. It is action, passion, and power, generating and carrying the innovation that exceeds boundaries of custom and tradition. Love is its centre, and its place is everywhere. It elevates and expands the understanding of what is, by expressing it.

The British critic F.W. Bateson, in *Contemporary Literary Critics* (1977), put poetry into its master-poet context when he said:

> Poetry is … the point of maximum consciousness, the synthesis of a particular social order, in which that society achieves its most significant self-expression, and ultimately its historical meaning.

What of the future? The Indian poet Sri Aurobindo indicates the scale of the requirement:

> The poetry of the future has to solve … a problem new to the art of poetic speech; an utterance of the deepest soul of man and of the universal spirit

in things – not only with another and a more complete vision, but in the very inmost language of the self-experience of the soul and the sight of the spiritual mind ... the poets of whatever tongue and race who most completely see with this vision and speak with the inspiration of its utterance are those who shall be the creators of the poetry of the future.

Glossary

Accent: emphasis; stress. Extra voice power on certain syllables to make rhythm or to form measure.

Aesthetics: the science which attempts to determine the canons of taste upon which criticism of the arts is based.

Alexandrine: an iambic hexapody, that is, 6 iambic feet in each line; a total of 12 syllables. Spenser used it in *The Fairie Queene*, for example: 'Still did he wake, and still did watch for morning light.'

Allegory: a description or narrative conveyed by another account, differing from it, but resembling it sufficiently to representatively suggest it. A figurative story with levels of meaning, often designed to convey a moral teaching.

Alliteration: beginning adjacent or closely connected words with the same sound or letter.

Allusion: a reference *to*, in speech or writing: direct, indirect, and covert.

Analogy: partial resemblance or agreement between two things – particularly points of agreement upon which a comparison between two things is based.

Anapest: a three-syllable foot or group of three syllables – two unaccented followed by one accented. The reverse of a dactyl.

Anaphora: Greek 'carrying upwards' the deliberate repetition in rhetoric of a word or phrase at the beginning of several successive verses, clauses, or paragraphs.

Antithesis: two contrary ideas brought into apposition:

> The prodigal deprives his heir,
> The miser deprives himself.

Antithetical parallelism: an idea expressed in one line is contrasted in a succeeding line.

Apostrophe: a figure in which a speaker or writer suddenly stops in discourse and addresses pointedly some person or thing, present or absent.

Assonance: a device used to provide or intensify rhythm. A substitute for an end rhyme. Pairs of words with assonance are:

(1) rate and came, (2) penitent and reticence.

In the following example the words *blackness* and *dances*; *roaming* and *floating* have assonance:

> Maiden crowned with glossy blackness,
> Lithe as panther forest roaming
> Long-armed naead when she dances
> In the stream of aether floating.
>
> Eliot's *Spanish Gypsy*

Blank verse: a description deriving from the fact that lines do not have end rhymes, that is, they are 'blank'. Used extensively in dramatic verse as *iambic pentameters* which are unrhymed. As a verse form it is close to the natural rhythms of English speech and constitutes the lines of five iambic feet used by Shakespeare in his plays.

Caesura or cesura: a 'cutting'; a light but definite break or pause in verse or line. It usually coincides with the natural rhythm in reading.

Canzone: a variety of lyric poetry derived from the Italian, which consists of a series of verses in stanza form but without a refrain. Although the term itself is Provençal (*canso* – meaning song) it was in Italian poetry that the form was utilized in a literary sense.

Consonance: Sounds in words in which the consonants of the stressed syllables agree, but the vowels differ. For example, *dissolute* and *resolute*.

Couplet: two consecutive lines which are end-rhymed.

Dactyl: Greek 'joints of the finger': a metrical foot consisting of one accented and two unaccented syllables.

Dissonance: unrhymed lines in a group of rhymed lines where the acoustic effect is achieved by a difference of sonorous elements.

Ellipsis: word omission leaving the construction incomplete but the context intact.

What! All my pretty chickens, and their dam –
at one fell swoop?

Macbeth, Act IV, Scene iii

Elision: omission of a word or the slurring of pronunciation to achieve a designed result. For example, *o'er* for *over* to reduce the number of syllables.

End-stopped: line ends in full pause, usually indicated by some mark of punctuation.

Enjambment: placing a word or words into a subsequent line to complete the sense. With enjambment, verse endings are neglected during reading so that there is no interference with the meaning which has been carried over into the next line or stanza. For example:

You do not know how much they mean to me, my friends,
And how, how rare and strange it is, to find
In a life composed so much, so much of odds and ends ....

Eliot's *Portrait of a Lady*

Epithet: from the Latin *epitheton* and the Greek *epi tithenai*, 'to put'. A word or phrase adjectival in force which characterizes or denotes some quality or attribute of the person or thing to which it refers. An additional or descriptive name expressing an attribute of the person or thing referred to for example:

Jack the Giant Killer; the wily Ulysses ...

In poetry, an aspect of metonymy is referred to as *transferred epithet*, a device of emphasis used to attribute a characteristic of one thing to something else closely associated:

And drowsy tinklings* lull the distant folds ...

Thomas Gray (1716-71)

* The drowsiness of the sheep at dusk is transferred to their bells.

Epode: last portion of an ode; a refrain. This is the third part of an ode, following the strophe and anti-strophe. An aspect of the lyric poem invented by Archilocus in which a long line is followed by a shorter one in non-elegiac metre. The best known examples are in the *Odes of Horace*.

Figure of speech: an unusual, essentially metaphorical mode of expression, used for effect in speech and writing: intended to clarify or deepen meaning by suggesting similitudes which provoke thought. Hamlet, preparing to confront his mother says:

> I will speak daggers to her, but use none.

Foot: a metrical unit of poetry. A group of syllables, one of which is accented or stressed more than the others. The word *foot* was used by the Greeks to designate the group of beats equivalent to the rise and fall (once) of the foot in dancing, or the hand beating time.

Free verse, *vers libre*: a verse form disregarding traditional features such as rhyme, form and metre solely to achieve cadences. It does use assonance and alliteration.

Haiku: a Japanese verse form comprising three lines of 5, 7, 5 syllables respectively, unrhymed and likely to contain reference to one of the four seasons.

Hemistich: a half line or section of verse; sometimes used to name a line of less than the usual length.

Humanism: is a term of varying emphasis. It has been used generally to indicate a system of practice with man at its centre. In the humanism of the Italian Renaissance, theoretical speculation about God was of less significance than the study of the works of man as revealed in history, literature, and art. There was also an emphasis on human nature, for instance, the educational prominence given to the Humanities rather than the Natural Sciences. Also, in British Pragmatism, the slogan adopted was taken from the thesis of Protagoras that, 'Man is the measure of all things.' Under this emphasis beliefs, logic and aspects of language were seen as human instruments in the service of conduct; not as reflections of the independent nature of things.

Hyperbole: a figure of speech consisting of exaggerated statement. Used to express strong feeling or produce a strong impression and not intended to be taken literally.

Iamb, iambus: from the Latin *iambus* and Greek *iambos*, a metrical foot consisting of an unaccented syllable followed by an accented syllable.

Iambic: pertaining to, containing or composed of iambuses.

Implied metaphor (*see* Metaphor): this figure is quite subtle. Not only does a metaphor link two unrelated things but they are also linked by attribute. Moreover, implication has been incorporated.

> Life, like a dome of many-coloured glass,
> Stains the white radiance of Eternity.

In the second of these two lines by Shelley it is assumed and implied that Eternity is radiant light.

Irony: from the Greek meaning 'assumed or feigned ignorance; dissembler'. Use of words, with humorous or sarcastic intention, so that the meaning is the opposite of what is actually said. Socratic irony: assumption of ignorance for the purpose of confounding an opponent in dispute.

Measure: a foot in prosody; a group of syllables.

Metaphor: Greek *metaphora*: 'transference, a carrying'. Figure of speech in which a word or phrase is used to denote or describe something entirely different from the object, idea, action or quality which it primarily and usually expresses, thus suggesting a resemblance or analogy, for example, 'the curtain of night'. Distinction between metaphor and simile: metaphor carries the sense in a direct comparison:

Love is a babe; then might I not say so
To give full growth to that which still doth grow?
Shakespeare: Sonnet 115

Simile says it is like:

O, my love is like a red, red rose. Robert Burns
So are you to my thoughts as food to life. Shakespeare: Sonnet 75

Metonymy: a figure of speech in which the name of an attribute or adjunct is substituted for the thing meant, for example: 'sceptre' for 'authority'.

Molossus: a foot of three long (stressed) syllables, found mainly in Latin prosody.

Negative metaphor: the two things connected by the metaphor are related negatively:

If hairs be wires, black wires grow on her head. Shakespeare: Sonnet 130

Negative simile: a simile connecting two things negatively:

My mistress' eyes are nothing like the Sun.

Ode: originally a lyric poem intended to be sung or chanted (from the Greek verb 'to sing'). The ode usually deals with a single dignified or exalted subject, and is produced for a specific purpose.

Onomatopoeic: Onomatopoeic words like 'splash' and 'cuckoo' are not always universally obvious. Many people would think it almost self-evident that the word *woof* represents the sound made by a dog. But in the Mandarin dialect of Chinese, the word for the utterance of dogs is not *woof* but *wang*.

Paean: Greek *paiein*, 'to strike'. A song (hymn) of exultation, thanksgiving or praise; originally used in hymns to Apollo the Striker – who strikes blows to heal mankind. Gerard Manley Hopkins experimented with it successfully – see his poem *The Windhover: to Christ Our Lord*, just one of many examples.

Parabasis: from the Greek meaning 'going aside, stepping forward'. Near the end of a performance in Greek Old Comedy, the Chorus (without masks) came forward and addressed the audience directly in a speech expressing the personal views of the author on some religious or political topical matter. T.S. Eliot's *Murder in the Cathedral* is a modern example of an effective use of parabasis.

Paradox: statement or tenet contrary to received opinion or expectation. (Can be with favourable or unfavourable connotation.)

Pathetic fallacy: the ascribing of human traits and feelings to inanimate objects of nature, or the use of anthropomorphic images or metaphors.

Pentameter: consisting of five measures or feet.

Pentasyllabic: of five syllables.

Personification: to conceive and represent as a person; to endow with or regard as possessing, personal attributes.

Pleonasm: the use of superfluous words to reinforce the expression or to maintain attention on the subject.

Poesy: poetic works; poetry collectively or generally.

Prosody: the science or art of versification; theory and principles of rhythm and metre.

Prosopopeia: a figure by means of which an imaginary or absent person is represented as speaking.

Prosthesis: the prefixing of an expletive syllable to a word, for example, be̲moan.

Pun: etymology unknown. A play upon words, a humorous use of words having the same or nearly the same sound with different meanings.

Quatrain: from the Latin *quattuor*, 'four'. A four-line stanza.

Rhyme: within or at the ends of two or more lines, word-endings having the same vowel sound and successive consonants.

Rhythm: recurrence – in poetry, stresses and pauses. From the Greek *rhuthmos*, 'measured motion, time, rhythm; proportion, symmetry; temper, disposition'. Movement characterized by regular recurrence and intermission, or by increase or decrease at regular intervals.

Run-on: line not ending in punctuation. The running on into the next line of its sense and thought is called *enjambment*.

Scansion: the action or art of scanning verse. The division of verse into metrical feet; an instance of this construction.

Scop: the bard who sang at Anglo-Saxon feasts.

Semantics: From the Latin *philologia*, 'study of literature; linguistic science'. In broad terms, semantics is the branch of philology concerned with the study of the relationship between words and meanings.

Semeiotics (modern spelling *semiotics*): from the Greek *semeion*, 'sign'. The study of signs and their relationships to the things or concepts that they signify. Semiology, has application in mathematical logic and in the philosophy of language.

Sestet: from the Latin *sextus*, 'sixth'. The last six lines of a sonnet.

Sign: from the Latin *signum*, 'mark, token, sign'. Anything which conveys a meaning to the mind; indication, evidence, symptom.

Simile: Latin *similis*, 'like', resembling, having certain qualities in common. Rhetorical figure and a poetic ornament by means of which one thing is compared to another by means of a connective, for example: like, as, etc. An imaginative comparison (*see* Metaphor). Example of a simile:

> Like as the waves make towards the pebbled shore,
> So do our minutes hasten to their end.
>
> Shakespeare: Sonnet 60

Soliloquy: Latin *solus*, 'alone'. Declamation by a character in a play, in which he utters his thoughts when alone on the stage.

Sonnet: a piece of verse (properly expressive of one main idea) consisting of 14 decasyllable lines, with rhymes arranged according to one or other of certain rhyme-schemes and line groupings.

Spondee: Late Middle English: 'a metrical foot consisting of two accented syllables'.

Sprung rhythm: a poetic metre approximating to speech rhythm associated particularly with Gerard Manley Hopkins. A system based on word stress rather than syllables.

Stanza: a group of lines in a poem arranged in orderly fashion, generally with a rhyme-scheme.

Stress: emphasis on a word or phrase in speaking; accent on a syllable in verse.

Syllable: a vocal sound or set of sounds uttered with a single effort of articulation and forming a word or element of a word. The least portion or detail of speech or writing.

Symbol: Latin *symbola*, Greek *sumbolon*, 'token; pledge; covenant'. Something which represents or typifies another thing, quality, etc. A graphic character (letter or figure), sign, used to express a sound, a mathematical quantity etc.

Synecdoche: a figure by which a more comprehensive term is used for one that is less comprehensive (and vice versa), for example: 'all hands on deck'.

Tone: in the context of spoken poetry it would be defined as 'musical sound'. It is involved in many examples of *synaesthesia*, the close association of a mental image perceived by one of the senses with an image perceived by another sense.

Trochee: opposite of iambus, that is, one accented syllable followed by an unaccentuated syllable.

Verse: from the Latin *versus*, 'a furrow; a line, row; a line of poetry, verse'; also *vertere*, 'to turn'. A metrical line containing a certain number of feet or accented syllables arranged according to a definite metrical rule. Metrical composition or structure; division of a poem consisting of several lines and forming in itself a unity.

Bibliography

1 – The Ancient World

Lloyd, S., *The Art of the Ancient Near East*, Thames & Hudson, London, 1961
Murray, M.A., *Egyptian Religious Poetry*, John Murray, London, 1949
Roux, G., *Ancient Iraq*, Allen & Unwin, London, 1964
Temizsoy, Director, *Anatolian Civilizations* (Museum Catalogue), 1990

2 – The Greeks

Barnard, Mary, *Sappho*, University of California Press, 1958
Davenport, G., *Carmina Archilochi, The Fragments of Archilochos*, University of California Press, 1964
Davenport, G., *Sappho, Poems and Fragments*, University of Michigan, 1965
Furness, R.A., *Poems of Callimachus*, Jonathan Cape, London, 1931
Garman, D.M., *A Literary History of Greece*, Elek Books, London, 1964
Glover, T.R., *Herodotus*, University of California Press, 1924
Hallard, J.H., *The Idylls of Theocritus with the Poems of Bion and Moschus*, Routledge, London, 1924
Jay, P., *The Greek Anthology*, Penguin Books, 1973
Lang, A., *Homeric Hymns*, George Allen, London, 1899
Lattimore, R., *Greek Lyrics* (2nd edn), University of Chicago, 1960
Lattimore, R., *Hesiod*, University of Michigan Press, 1959
Lattimore, R., *The Iliad of Homer*, University of Chicago Press, 1951
Lattimore, R., *The Odes of Pindar*, University of Chicago Press, 1947
Lattimore, R., *The Odyssey of Homer*, Harper & Row, London, 1965
Lyne, R.O.A.M., *The Latin Love Poets*, Oxford University Press, 1980
Myers, E., *The Extant Odes of Pindar*, Macmillan, London, 1888
Petracos, B.C., Director, Museum, Delphi, museum catalogue
Powell, J., *Sappho, a Garland*, HarperCollins, Canada, 1993
Kahn, C.H., *The Art and Thought of Heraclitus*, Cambridge University Press, 1979
Reid, F., *Poems from the Greek Anthology*, Faber & Faber, 1943
Sinclair, A., *The Greek Anthology*, Weidenfeld & Nicolson, 1967
Symonds, J.A., *Studies of the Greek Poets*, Vols 1 & 2, Adam & Charles Black, 1893
Whibley, Leonard, *A Companion to Greek Studies*, Cambridge, 1916
Willcock, M.M., *A Companion to the Iliad*, University of Chicago Press, 1976

3 – The Romans

Bennett, C.E., *Horace, The Odes and Epodes*, Loeb Classical Library, William Heinemann, London, 1914
Bradshaw, W., *The Ten Tragedies of Seneca*, Swan Sonnenschein, London, 1902
Campbell, R.A., *Seneca, Letters from a Stoic*, Penguin, London, 1969
Carrier, C., *The Poems of Propertius*, Indiana University Press, 1963

Clarke, M.L., *Rhetoric at Rome, A Historical Survey*, Cohen & West, London, 1953
Cornish, F.W., *The Poems of Gaius Valerius Catullus*, William Heinemann, London, 1912
Day-Lewis, C., *The Georgics of Virgil*, Jonathan Cape, London, 1943
Edmonds, C.R., *Cicero's Three Books of Offices or Moral Duties ...*, G. Bell, London, 1916
Glover, T.R., *Studies in Virgil*, Edward Arnold, London, 1904
Handford, S.A., *Fables of Aesop*, Penguin, 1954
Henze, H.R., *The Odes of Horace*, University of Oklahoma Press, 1961
Humphries, R., *Martial, Selected Epigrams*, Indiana University Press, 1963
Humphries, R., *Ovid, The Art of Love*, Indiana University Press, 1957
Humphries, R., *Ovid, Metamorphoses*, Indiana University Press, 1961
Lonsdale, J. & Lee, S., *The Works of Virgil*, Macmillan, London, 1894
Innes, M.M., *The Metamorphoses of Ovid*, Penguin, 1955
Ker, W.C.A., *Martial, Epigrams* (2 vols), Loeb Classical Library, William Heinemann, London, 1919 & 1927
Ker, W.C.A., *Cicero, Phillippics*, Loeb Classical Library, William Heinemann, London, 1926
Mackail, J.W., *An Introduction to Virgil's Aeneid*, The Virgil Society, 1946
McKay, A.G., *Vergil's Italy*, Adams & Dart, Somerset, 1971
Michie, J., *The Odes of Horace*, Rupert Hart-Davis, London, 1964
Michie, J., *The Poems of Catullus*, Rupert Hart-Davis, London, 1969
Radice, B., *Terence, The Brothers and Other Plays*, Penguin, London, 1965
Rose, J.B., *Comedies of Terence*, Dorrell, London, 1870
Rouse, W.H.D., *Lucretius, de Rerum Natura*, Loeb Classical Library, William Heinemann, London, 1924
Sandys, Sir John E., *A Companion to Latin Studies*, Cambridge, 1925
Showerman, G., *Ovid, Heroides and Amores*, Loeb Classical Library, William Heinemann, London, 1921
Sisson, C.H., *Catullus*, MacGibbon & Kee, London, 1966
Swanson, R.A., *The Complete Poetry of Catullus*, The Liberal Arts Press, Indianapolis, 1959
Watts, A.E., *The Poems of Sextus Propertius*, Centaur Press, Sussex, 1961
Wheeler, L., *Catullus and the Traditions of Ancient Poetry*, University of California Press, 1964

4 – Poetry in the Shadows

Atkinson, Geoffrey, *The Works of François Villon*, Eric Partridge Ltd at the Scholartis Press, London, 1930
Burrow, J.A. (ed), *Sir Gawain and the Green Knight*, Penguin English Poets
Clark Hall, J.R., *Beowulf*, Swan Sonnenschein, London, 1911
Coghill, Nevill, *Geoffrey Chaucer, The Canterbury Tales*, Penguin Books, London, 1951
Davis, N. (ed), *A Chaucer Glossary*, Oxford, 1979
Skeat, Rev. Walter W., *The Complete Works of Geoffrey Chaucer*, The Clarendon Press, Oxford, 1901
Stone, B., *Sir Gawain and the Green Knight*, Penguin Classics, 1959
Thorndike, L., *Medieval Europe*, Harrap, London, 1920

Warren, K.M., *Old English Literature 7th to 11th Century*, Constable, London, 1908
Wyndham Lewis, D.B., *François Villon, A Documented Survey*, Sheed & Ward, London, 1945

5 – Humanism and Spirituality

Collinson, Diane, *Fifty Major Philosophers*, Routledge, London, 1987
Durling, R.M., *Petrarch's Lyric Poems*, Harvard University Press, 1976
Edwards, P. & Pap, A., *A Modern Introduction to Philosophy*, Macmillan, USA
Enright, D.J., *Man in an Onion*, Chatto & Windus, 1972
Jayne, Sears, *John Colet and Marsilio Ficino*, Oxford University Press, 1963
Musa, M., *Petrarch, Selections from the Canzoniere and Other Works*, Oxford, 1985
Reed, Jeremy, *Madness, the Price of Poetry*, Peter Owen, London, 1989
Salzman, L.F., *English Life in the Middle Ages*, Oxford, 1926
Shapiro, H. (ed), *Medieval Philosophy*, Random House, USA, 1964
Thorndike, Lynn, *Medieval Europe*, George Harrap, London, 1920
Williamson, M., *Saphho's Immortal Daughters*, Harvard University Press, 1995

6 – The Renaissance Enters England

Abbot, E.A., *A Shakespearian Grammar*, Dover Publications, New York, 1966
Bate, J., *Shakespeare and Ovid*, Oxford, 1993
Boswell-Stone, W.G., *Shakespeare's Holinshed, The Chronicle and the Plays Compared*, Dover Publications, USA, 1968
Bullough, G. (ed) *Narrative and Dramatic Sources of Shakespeare* (4 vols), Routledge & Kegan Paul, London, 1960
Bush, D., *English Literature in the Earlier Seventeenth Century, 1600-1669*, Clarendon Press, Oxford, 1962
Gervinus, G.G., *Shakespeare Commentaries*, Smith, Elder, London, 1875
Gittings, R., *Shakespeare's Rival*, William Heinemann, 1960
Greg, W.W., *The Shakespeare First Folio, Its Bibliographical and Textual History*, Oxford University Press, 1955
Holinshed, R., *Holinshed's Chronicles of England, Scotland and Ireland* (6 vols), privately printed, London, 1807
Lindsay, J., *The Troubadours and Their World*, Frederick Muller, London, 1976
Muir, K., *Shakespeare's Sonnets*, George Allen & Unwin, London, 1982
Schmidt, A., *Shakespeare Lexicon and Quotation Dictionary* (2 vols), Dover Publications, New York, 1971
Schoenbaum, Samuel, *William Shakespeare, A Documentary Life*, Oxford, in association with The Scolar Press, 1975
Schoenbaum, Samuel, *Shakespeare, The Globe and the World*, Folger Shakespeare Library & Oxford, 1979
Spurgeon, Caroline F.E., *Shakespeare's Imagery and What It Tells Us*, Cambridge University Press, 1935
Staunton, H. *(In Exact Facsimile) The First Folio, 1620 of William Shakespeare*, Day & Son, Lithographers, London, 1866
Thomson, P., *Shakespeare's Professional Career*, Cambridge University Press, 1992
Thomson, P., *Wyatt, The Critical Heritage*, Routledge & Kegan Paul, 1974
Williams, C., *A Short Life of Shakespeare*, Oxford, 1933

7 – Metaphysical Poetry
Bennett, J., *Five Metaphysical Poets*, Cambridge University Press, 1964
Smith, A.J., *John Donne, The Complete English Poems*, Penguin Books, 1971
Winney, J., *A Preface to Donne*, Longman, 1970

8 – Ideals and Dreams
Bowra, Maurice, *The Romantic Imagination*, Harvard University Press, 1950
Herford, C.H., *Goethe*, T.C. & E.C. Jack, London, 1913
Hollingdale, R.J., *Elective Affinities*, Penguin Classics, 1971

9 – A Fresh Lyricism
De la Mare, W., *The Burning Glass*, Faber & Faber, 1945
De la Mare, W., *Private View*, Faber & Faber 1953
Foss, M., *Poetry of the World Wars*, Michael O'Mara Books, London, 1990
Housman, A.E., *The Name and Nature of Poetry*, Cambridge University Press, 1940

10 – New Approaches
Agenda, Vol. 23, Nos 1-2, 'T.S. Eliot', London, 1985
Eliot, T.S., *Collected Poems 1909-62*, Faber & Faber, London, 1963
Eliot, T.S., *The Complete Poems and Plays*, 1909-50, Harcourt, Brace & World, New York, 1971
Morrison, B., *The Movement*, Oxford University Press, 1980
Press, John, *A Map of Modern English Verse*, Oxford University Press, 1969
Williamson, G., *A Reader's Guide to T.S. Eliot* (2nd edn), Thames & Hudson, London, 1967

11 – Difference Within Universality
Avery, P. & Heath-Stubbs, J., *The Rubáiyát of Omar Khayyám*, Book Club Associates, London, 1979
Ayling, Alan & Mackintosh, Duncan, *A Collection of Chinese Lyrics*, Routledge & Kegan Paul, 1965
Ayling, Alan & Mackintosh, Duncan, *A Further Collection of Chinese Lyrics*, Routledge & Kegan Paul, 1969
Arberry, A.J., *Discourses of Rumi*, John Murray, London, 1961
Arberry, A.J., *The Rubáiyát of Jalal Al-din Rumi*, Emery Walker Ltd, London, 1949
Bhattacharya, D., *Love Songs of Chandidas*, George Allen & Unwin, 1967
Bhattacharya, D., *Love Songs of Vidyapati*, George Allen & Unwin, 1963
Bowra, C.M., *A Book of Russian Verse*, Macmillan, London, 1943
Cooper, A., *Li Po and Tu Fu*, Penguin Books, 1973
Davis, A.R., *The Penguin Book of Chinese Verse*, Penguin Books, 1962
Heron-Allen, Edward, *Some Side-lights upon Edward Fitzgerald's Poem, The Rubáiyát of Omar Khayyám*, H.S. Nichols Ltd, London, 1898
Heron-Allen, Edward, *Edward Fitzgerald's Rubáiyát of Omar Khayyám*, Bernard Quaritch, London, 1899
Honda, H.H., *One Hundred Poems from One Hundred Poets*, The Hokuseido Press, 1956
Ingalls, D.H.H., *Sanskrit Poetry*, Harvard University Press, 1968
Kālidāsa, *The Loom of Time*, Penguin Classics, 1989

Maurer, H., *Tao, The Way of the Ways*, Wildwood House, 1982
Monier-Williams, M., *Shakoontala*, George Routledge & Sons, 1898
Nicholson R.A., *Selected Poems from the Divani Shamsi Tabriz*, University Press, Cambridge, 1898
Nippon Gakujutsu Shinkokai, *The Manyoshu*, Columbia University Press, 1965
Persia Society of London, *Selections from the Rubáiyát and Odes of Hāfiz*, John M. Watkins, London, 1920
Porter, W.N., *A Hundred Verses from Old Japan*, Tuttle, 1979
Ratushinskaya, I., *Grey is the Colour of Hope*, Sceptre, 1989
Ratushinskaya, I., *Pencil Letter*, Bloodaxe Books, 1986
Ratushinskaya, I., *No, I'm Not Afraid*, Bloodaxe Books, 1986
Shree Purohit Swami & Yeats, W.B., *The Ten Principal Upanishads*, Faber & Faber, 1937
Trevelyan, R.C., *From the Chinese*, Oxford University Press, 1945
Waley, A., *The Way and its Power*, George Allen & Unwin, London, 1934
Yevtushenko, *Selected Poems*, Penguin Books, 1962

12 – Substance and Form
Doolittle, H., *Sea Garden*, Constable, London, 1916
Holland, N.N., *The Shakespearean Imagination*, Indiana University Press, 1964

13 – Poetry's Figurative Element
Bradley, A.C., *Oxford Lectures on Poetry*, Macmillan, London, 1941
Clemen, W., *The Development of Shakespeare's Imagery* (2nd edn), Methuen, 1977
Conder, A., *Cassell's Anthology of French Poetry*, Cassell, 1950
Coward, Harold G. & Raja, K. Kunjunni, *The Philosophy of the Grammarians*, Princeton, New Jersey, 1990
De Masirevich, Constance, *On the Four Quartets of T.S. Eliot*, Vincent Stuart, 1953
Greimas, A.J., *On Meaning*, Selected Writings in Semiotic Theory, Frances Pinter, London, 1987
Hoffman, Y., *Japanese Death Poems*, Charles E. Tuttle, USA, 1986
Olsen, S.H., *The End of Literary Theory*, Cambridge University Press, 1987
Thornton, R.K.R. (ed), *All My Eyes See, The Visual World of Gerard Manley Hopkins*, Ceolfrith Press, 1975
Wagner, G.A., *Baudelaire, Selected Poems*, Falcon Press, 1946
Whalley, G., *Poetic Process*, Meridian Books, USA, 1967

14 – The Poet and His Faculties
Bowra, Maurice, *The Romantic Imagination*, Oxford Paperbacks, 1961
Herford, C.H., *Goethe*, T.C. & E.C. Jack, London, 1913
Hubler, E., *Shakespeare's Sonnets and the Commentators*, Routledge & Kegan Paul, London, 1962
Jamies, Jamie, *The Music of the Spheres*, Little, Brown & Co, 1993
Lloyd, Peter, *Perspective and Identities*, The Rubicon Press, London, 1989
Nicholson, R.A., *Rumi*, George Allen & Unwin, London, 1950
Ogden, C.K. & Richards, I.A., *The Meaning of Meaning*, Kegan Paul, Trench, Trubner, London, 1938
Pierce, David, *W.B. Yeats*, The Bristol Press, 1989

Sontag, Susan, *Against Interpretation*, Vintage, London, 1994
Wordsworth, Dorothy, *Illustrated Lakeland Journals*, Diamond Books, 1987

15 – Creativity

Culler, Jonathan, *Barthes*, Fontana Press, London, 1983
Sontag, Susan, *Against Interpretation*, Vintage, London, 1994
Sontag, Susan (ed, with introduction), *A Barthes Reader*, Jonathan Cape, London, 1982

16 – The Nature of Poetry

Brooke, Rupert, *Poems by*, Sidgwick & Jackson, 1916
Casey, J., *The Language of Criticism*, Methuen, 1966
Hough, Graham, *An Essay on Criticism*, Duckworth, 1966
Nowottny, W., *The Language Poets Use*, London University, 1962
Reeves, J., *The Critical Sense*, Heinemann, 1956
Schreiber, S.M, *An Introduction to Literary Criticism*, Pergamon Press, 1965
Wauchope, O.S, *Deviation into Sense*, Faber & Faber, 1948
Whalley, G., *Poetic Process*, Meridian Books, 1967

Index of Poets

Note: Although several critics, translators, and commentators who appear in the General Index are also poets, they are not included in the Index of Poets unless their poetry has been quoted in the text.

General Index